RENAISSANCE WOMAN:
A SOURCEBOOK

Renaissance Woman: A Sourcebook brings together extracts of significant accounts of women and femininity in early modern England. It provides representative and accessible readings of the discourses of gender construction during this period. The book encourages students to analyse the rhetorical strategies of literary texts as they operate within a broader historical context.

The volume is divided thematically into nine sections, each with an accessible introduction, notes on sources and an annotated bibliography. The sections are: theology; physiology; conduct; sexuality and motherhood; politics and law; education; work; writing and speaking; proto-feminisms.

Renaissance Woman: A Sourcebook contains sources ranging from medical documents and political pamphlets to sermons and the Bible, as well as literary texts. It will be an essential sourcebook for students and teachers of english, cultural history and women's studies.

Kate Aughterson teaches English at the University of Central England, specialising in feminism and the Renaissance.

RENAISSANCE WOMAN: A SOURCEBOOK

Constructions of Femininity in England

edited by

Kate Aughterson

London and New York

First published 1995
by Routledge
11 New Fetter Lane, London EC4P 4EE

Simultaneously published in the USA and Canada
by Routledge
29 West 35th Street, New York, NY 10001

© 1995 Kate Aughterson

Typeset in Garamond by
Solidus Bristol Limited
Printed and bound in Great Britain by
Biddles Ltd, Guildford and King's Lynn

British Library Cataloguing in Publication Data
A catalogue record for this book is available from the British Library

Library of Congress Cataloguing in Publication Data
A catalogue record for this book has been requested

ISBN 0-415-12045-4
0-415-12046-2 (pbk)

For my parents

CONTENTS

CONTENTS

CONTENTS

ILLUSTRATIONS

ACKNOWLEDGEMENTS

I would like to thank all my past students who asked the questions to which this book is a response, as well as all those students who read and commented on earlier versions of the texts in this book.

All the staff in the Bodleian Library, particularly those working in Duke Humphrey's, were unfailingly helpful, enthusiastic and efficient. I am extremely grateful to them.

It has been a pleasure to work with the editorial staff at Routledge, Talia Rodgers, Tricia Dever, Miranda Chaytor and Patricia Stankiewicz: their work has been rigorous, sympathetic and supportive.

I am grateful to the University of Central England for granting me writing time to help complete the book, in the form of a weekly research day.

Brendan Cook and Stephen O'Connor kindly helped with translations.

The book could not have been written without the advice and assistance of Elizabeth Maddison.

PERMISSIONS

The author and publishers gratefully acknowledge permission from the following to quote copyright material: material from the Loeb Classical Library, *Aristotle: The Generation of Animals* (vol. 366), translated by A.L. Peck, Cambridge, Mass.: Harvard University Press, 1943; Margaret Tallmadge May, *Galen: On the Usefulness of the Parts of the Body*, translated with an introduction by M. Tallmadge May, copyright 1968, Cornell University Press, used by permission of the publisher; E. Emmanuel Orchard, *Till God Will: Mary Ward Through her Writings*, London: Darton, Longman and Todd, 1985.

Every effort has been made to trace and acknowledge copyright holders, although this has not been possible in every case.

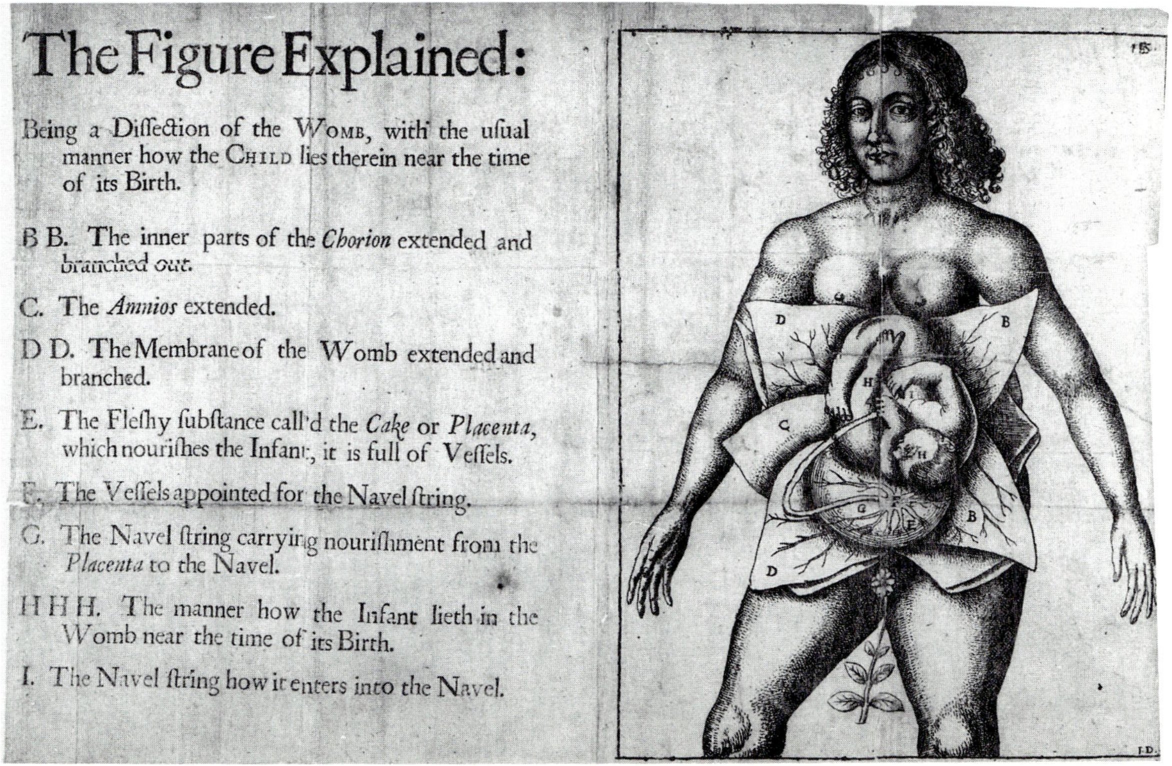

The Figure Explained:

Being a Dissection of the WOMB, with the usual manner how the CHILD lies therein near the time of its Birth.

B B. The inner parts of the *Chorion* extended and branched out.

C. The *Amnios* extended.

D D. The Membrane of the Womb extended and branched.

E. The Fleshy substance call'd the *Cake* or *Placenta*, which nourishes the Infant; it is full of Vessels.

F. The Vessels appointed for the Navel string.

G. The Navel string carrying nourishment from the *Placenta* to the Navel.

H H H. The manner how the Infant lieth in the Womb near the time of its Birth.

I. The Navel string how it enters into the Navel.

Figure 1 A dissection of the womb. *Source*: Jane Sharp, between ff. L3v and L4r of *The midwife's book*, 1671. By permission of The British Library.

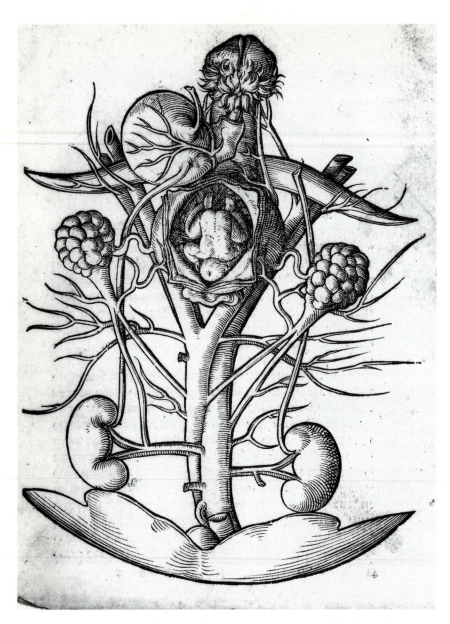

Figure 2 A dissection of the womb. *Source*: Eucharius Roesslin, Douce.R.146, engraving of a womb in *The birth of mankind*, 1545. By permission of the Bodleian Library, University of Oxford.

Figure 3 A cross-section of female sexual organs. *Source*: Eucharius Roesslin, Douce.R.146, engraving of a womb in *The birth of mankind*, 1545. By permission of the Bodleian Library, University of Oxford.

Figure 4 The English gentlewoman. *Source*: Richard Brathwait, 4°.B.25(3)Art. Frontispiece of *The English gentlewoman*, 1631. By permission of the Bodleian Library, University of Oxford.

The meaning of the *Frontispice*, wherein the *Effigies* it selfe; together with all the Emblemes, Deuices, Features, and Impre, zas thereto properly conducing, are to life described.

APPARELL.

APPARELL being by a Curtaine first discouered, where shee appeares sitting in a *Wardrobe* richly furnished, is expressed in a comely or seemely *Habit*; holding a *vaile* in her hand; poudred with teares, implying the *Necessity* of that *Liuery* to bee deriued from the losse of her *Originall* purity; as one therefore, neither impenitent for her *sinne*, nor ignorant of her *shame*, but constantly tender what may best suit or sort with her fame, shee deliuers her mind in this Mott. *Comely, not Gaudy.*

BEHAVIOVR.

BEHAVIOVR presents her selfe in a modest *attire*; with a cheerefull and gracefull *aspect*; by those *children* shee hath about her, she expresseth what she professeth; Breeding or Education of Youth; which she performes with that modest facility, and natiue liberty, as she admits of no *forraine fashion*, tasting of *affectation*, into her Company; which shee expresseth in this Mott. *Leuing Modesty is a Liuing Beauty.*

COMPLEMENT.

COMPLEMENT is accommodated like a *Courtier*; and at first Encounter seemes accosted by a *Phantasticke Gallant*, whose *sense* consists in *suit*; and whose *too much Congies* are his sole *Complement*; she makes knowne her neglect of him by sleighting or putting him aside by her hand; and presenting to his eye the obiect of an *Ape*, as a complete Embleme of his formality, and one vnworthy of her society, she molds her selfe in this Mot. *Ciuill Complement, my best Accomplishment.*

DECENCY.

DECENCY is portrayed in a louely but comely dresse; her *eye* modestly fixt on her glasse; Feathers with other like *Apish fauours*, are offered her, which she reiects; Chaplets of *Flowers* are presented her, which shee accepts; These she bestowes in her bosome, as Emblemes of those *flourishing vertues* which are lou'd by her, and only admitted to *iudge* with her: This she shadowes in her Mott. *Virgin-Decency is Vertues Liuery.*

ESTIMATION.

ESTIMATION is displayed, reposing her selfe in an Arbour; where shee is beleagred by two powerfull assailants; Price and Prayer, on her right hand, expressed by a *Purse* and a *Petition*; Feare and Fury on her left hand, discouered by a *Pistoll* and *Stiletto*; both which she sleights with a gracefull contempt: while eying the Bird *Porphyrio* houering aboue her head, who makes her desired bed her place of buriall; shee clozeth her resolues with this Mot. *My Price is her owne Praise.*

FANCY.

FANCY is featured with a louely and liuely presence; fixing her eye intentiuely on a *Tablet*, presenting the portraiture of her *Louer*: Drawing aside a Curtaine, she discouers an *amorous Picture*, and compares it with her *Tablet*, which enshrines her *best seature*. In the middle of the *Picture* is engrauen a *wounded heart*, implying loues intimacy; aboue it, a *burning Lampe*, importing loues purity; below it, a paire of *Turtles* mating, expressing loues constancy. All which expressiue Emblemes of her minde, she seconds with this Mot. *My Choyce admits no Change.*

GENTILITY.

GENTILITY is deblazoned by her proper *Crest* or *Cognizance*; A Pedigree furnished with variety of choyce and ancient Coats hanging by her; vnder these, a *Deaths head, houre-glasse*, and *spade*, memorials of her mortality; An aged Personage, seemingly deiected and in misery, presenting the person of *Hospitality*, shee embraceth, and offers her Precedency; A *Crowne* is presented to her by *Piety* with this Mott. *Desert Crownes Descent.*

HONOVR.

HONOVR is discouered vnder a Canopie; the *foure Corners* supported by foure *Cardinall vertues*; The *Three graces* goe before her; *Workes of Glory* after her; *Fame* standing on a Mount aboue her; Captiues inchained and led by her; Trophies of *honour* erected for her; which shee sleights, and tramples vnder foot, implying her noble contempt of *vaine-glory*; And standing vpon the *Globe of Earth*, shee passeth at it, as a thing vnworthy her *delight*; while viewing the *Globe of heauen*, she expresseth by her eye, the obiect of her *desire*; Retiring from the Theatre of *honour*, and reposing in a securer harbour: Where she is inclosed with a *flowry grene* of *Osiers*, implying *priuacy*; and impaled with a *Coronet of Sun-beames*, displaying her *felicity*; shee summes vp her content, and shewes her conceit in this Mott, *Honour is vertues harbour*.

In the middle, betwixt the *Vinnets*, is portrayed a modest comely personage, with a *Lily* in her bosome, implying the odor of purity; a *Mona-all* in her hand, importing the honour of piety; with this *Motto*, to conduct her to the Port of glory; *Grace my Guide, Glory my Goale*.

For other appropriates, attributes, or Compartments, whereby either the *Frontispice* might become better beautified, or the *deuices* fuller explained, they are onely shadowed, being by the weake hand of *Art* not to be otherwise expressed.

Each Subiect had distinguish'd beene by line,
And form'd their Modell to the first deuice,
But this choyce piece was hastened so by time,
It scarce got sight of that first Frontispice:
Yet from this shrine such natiue beames arise,
Impartiall eyes will iudge, right sure I am,
"Her grace improues the place from whence shee came:
"And well deserues an ENGLISH GENTLEMAN.

Figure 5 Explanatory table for the English gentlewoman. *Source*: Richard Brathwait, 4°.B.25(3)Art. Table from *The English gentlewoman*, 1631. By permission of the Bodleian Library, University of Oxford.

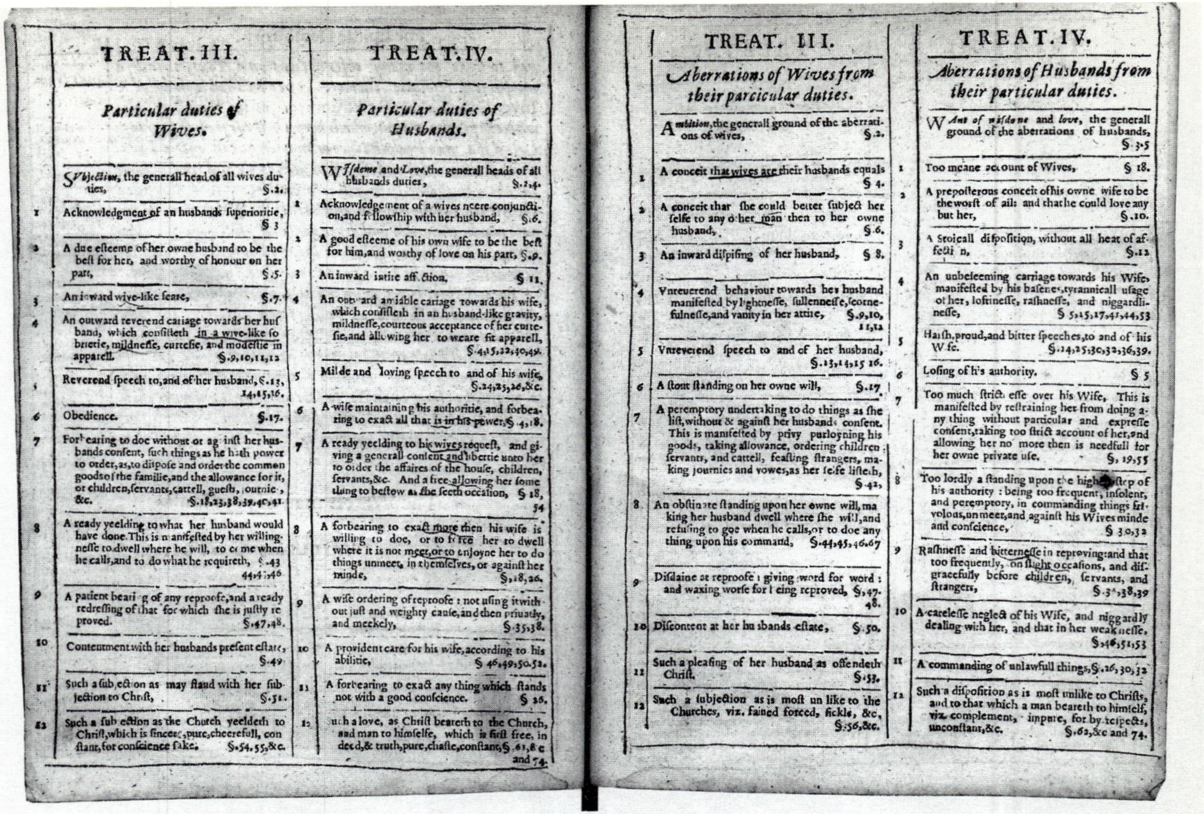

TREAT. III.

Particular duties of Wives.

Subjection, the generall head of all wives duties, §.2.
1 Acknowledgment of an husbands superioritie, § 3
2 A due esteeme of her owne husband to be the best for her, and worthy of honour on her part, §.5.
3 An inward wive-like feare, §.7.
4 An outward reverend cariage towards her husband, which consisteth in a wive-like sobrietie, mildnesse, curtesie, and modestie in apparell. §.9.10,11,12
5 Reverend speech to, and of her husband, §.13, 14,15,16.
6 Obedience. §.17.
7 Forbearing to doe without or against her husbands consent, such things as he hath power to order, as, to dispose and order the common goods of the familie, and the allowance for it, or children, servants, cattell, guests, journies, &c. §.18,23,38,39,40,41.
8 A ready yeelding to what her husband would have done. This is manifested by her willingnesse to dwell where he will, to come when he calls, and to do what he requireth, §.43 44,45,46
9 A patient bearing of any reproofe, and a ready redressing of that for which she is justly reproved. §.47,48.
10 Contentment with her husbands present estate, §.49
11 Such a subjection as may stand with her subjection to Christ, §.51.
12 Such a subjection as the Church yeeldeth to Christ, which is sincere, pure, cheerefull, constant, for conscience sake. §.54,55,&c.

TREAT. IV.

Particular duties of Husbands.

Wisdome and Love, the generall heads of all husbands duties, §.2,4.
1 Acknowledgement of a wives neere conjunction, and fellowship with her husband, §.6.
2 A good esteeme of his own wife to be the best for him, and worthy of love on his part, §.9.
3 An inward intire affection, § 11.
4 An outward amiable cariage towards his wife, which consisteth in an husband-like gravity, mildnesse, courteous acceptance of her curtesie, and allowing her to weare fit apparell, §.4,5,22,40,49.
5 Milde and loving speech to and of his wife, §.24,25,26,&c.
6 A wife maintaining his authoritie, and forbearing to exact all that is in his power, §.4,18.
7 A ready yeelding to his wives request, and giving a generall consent and libertie unto her to order the affaires of the house, children, servants, &c. And a free allowing her some thing to bestow as she seeth occasion, § 18, 54
8 A forbearing to exact more then his wife is willing to doe, or to force her to dwell where it is not meet, or to enjoyne her to do things unmeet, in themselves, or against her minde, §.18,26.
9 A wise ordering of reproofe: not using it without just and weighty cause, and then privatly, and meekely, §.35,38.
10 A provident care for his wife, according to his abilitie, § 46,49,50,52.
11 A forbearing to exact any thing which stands not with a good conscience. § 36.
12 Such a love, as Christ beareth to the Church, and man to himselfe, which is first free, in deed, & truth, pure, chaste, constant, § 61,&c and 74.

TREAT. III.

Aberrations of Wives from their particular duties.

Ambition, the generall ground of the aberrations of wives, §.2.
1 A conceit that wives are their husbands equals § 4.
2 A conceit that she could better subject her selfe to any other man then to her owne husband, §.6.
3 An inward dispising of her husband, § 8.
4 Unreverend behaviour towards her husband manifested by lightnesse, sullennesse, scornefulnesse, and vanity in her attire, §.9,10, 11,12
5 Unreverend speech to and of her husband, §.13,14,15 16.
6 A stout standing on her owne will, §.17
7 A peremptory undertaking to do things as she list, without & against her husbands consent. This is manifested by privy purloyning his goods, taking allowance, ordering children, servants, and cattell, feasting strangers, making journies and vowes, as her selfe listeth, §.42,
8 An obstinate standing upon her owne will, making her husband dwell where she will, and refusing to goe when he calls, or to doe any thing upon his command, §.44,45,46,67
9 Disdaine at reproofe: giving word for word: and waxing worse for being reproved, §.47, 48.
10 Discontent at her husbands estate, §.50.
11 Such a pleasing of her husband as offendeth Christ. §.53.
12 Such a subjection as is most unlike to the Churches, viz. fained forced, fickle, &c, §.56,&c.

TREAT. IV.

Aberrations of Husbands from their particular duties.

Want of wisdome and love, the generall ground of the aberrations of husbands, §.3.5
1 Too meane account of Wives, § 18.
2 A preposterous conceit of his owne wife to be the worst of all: and that he could love any but her, §.10.
3 A Stoicall disposition, without all heat of affection, §.12
4 An unbeseeming carriage towards his Wife, manifested by his basenes, tyrannicall usage of her, loftinesse, rashnesse, and niggardlinesse, § 5,15,17,41,44,53
5 Harsh, proud, and bitter speeches, to and of his Wife. §.24,25,30,32,36,39.
6 Losing of his authority. § 5
7 Too much strictnesse over his Wife, This is manifested by restraining her from doing any thing without particular and expresse consent, taking too strict account of her, and allowing her no more then is needfull for her owne private use. §, 19,55
8 Too lordly a standing upon the highest step of his authority: being too frequent, insolent, and peremptory, in commanding things frivolous, unmeet, and against his Wives minde and conscience, § 30,32
9 Rashnesse and bitternesse in reproving: and that too frequently, on slight occasions, and disgracefully before children, servants, and strangers, §.37,38,39
10 A carelesse neglect of his Wife, and niggardly dealing with her, and that in her weaknesse, §.46,51,53
11 A commanding of unlawfull things, §.26,30,32
12 Such a disposition as is most unlike to Christs, and to that which a man beareth to himself, viz. complement, impure, for by respects, unconstant, &c. §.62,&c and 74.

Figure 6 The particular duties of husbands and wives. *Source*: William Gouge, Antiq.e.E.1634.3, f.5v–6r in *Of domestical duties*, 1634. By permission of the Bodleian Library, University of Oxford.

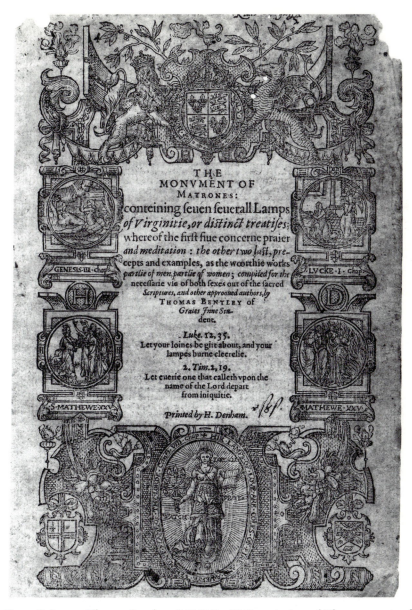

Figure 7 Source: Thomas Bentley, 4°.C.38.Jur(1). Frontispiece of *The monument of matrons*, 1582. By permission of the Bodleian Library, University of Oxford.

The several Gradations how the afore—

	January	Februar	March	April	May	June
	l. s. d.	l. s. d.	l. s. d.	l. s. d.	l. s. d.	l. s. d.
Flesh.						
Fish.						
Drink.						
Bread and Meal.						
Butter, Cheese, &c.						
Fruit, Herbs, Roots.						
Wages.						
Salteries, Pickles.						
Groceries.						
Fire and Candle.						
Laundry.						
Physick.						
Repairs.						
Brittle Ware.						
Houshold-stuff.						
Apparel.						
Rent and Taxes.						
Schooling & Books.						
Gifts and Charities.						
Inciden Charges.						

said Years Expences did arise.

	July	August	Septemb.	October	Novemb.	Decemb.	Total.
	l. s. d.	l. s. d.	l. s. d.	l. s. d.	l. s. d.	l. s. d.	l. s. d.
Flesh.							
Fish.							
Drink.							
Bread, &c.							
Butter, &c.							
Fruit, &c.							
Wages.							
Salteries.							
Groceries.							
Fire, &c.							
Laundry.							
Physick.							
Repairs.							
Brittle W.							
Houshol-st.							
Apparel.							
Rent & T.							
Schooling.							
Gifts.							
Incident.							

Figure 8 Annual housekeeping expenditure account. *Source:* 12.Theta.858, pp. 16–17, *Advice to the women and maidens of London*, 1678. By permission of the Bodleian Library, University of Oxford.

INTRODUCTION

In 1591 Philip Stubbes published the first edition of what was to become an extremely popular devotional biography, *A crystal glass for Christian women* (ch. 8). It opens thus:

> Calling to remembrance (most Christian reader) the final end of man's creation, which is to glorify God, and to edify one another in the way of true godliness: I thought it my duty, as well in respect of the one as in regard of the other, to publish this rare and wonderful example of the virtuous life and Christian death of Mistress Katherine Stubbes who, whilst she lived, was a mirror of womanhood and now, being dead, is a perfect pattern of true Christianity. She was descended of honest and wealthy parents. Her father had borne divers offices of worship in his company, amongst whom he lived in great account, credit and estimation all his days: he was zealous in the truth, and of a sound religion. Her mother was a Dutchwoman, both discreet and wise, of singular good grace and modesty and, which did most to adorn her, she was both religious and also zealous.... At fifteen years of age, her father being dead, her mother bestowed her in marriage to one Master Philip Stubbes with whom she lived four years and almost a half very honestly and godly, with rare commendation of all that knew her, as well for her singular wisdom, as also for her modesty, courtesy, gentleness, affability and good government; and above all for her fervent zeal which she bore to the truth, wherein she seemed to surpass many in so much as if she chanced at any time to be in place where either Papists or atheists were and heard them talk of religion, what countenance or credit soever they seemed to be of, she would not yield a jot, nor give place to them at all, but would most mightily justify the truth of God against their blasphemous untruths, and convince them, yea, and confound them by the testimonies of the word of God.

Stubbes transposes himself from husband to narrator from the beginning of this

1

text, thereby claiming a narrative objectivity in which we are asked to read the subsequent account as historical and spiritual truth. Katherine Stubbes is described as 'a mirror of womanhood' during her life and now the story of her death can become a 'pattern of true Christianity'. The elision of these two paradigms (one of womanhood, the other of ungendered salvation) promises us that each is a reflection of the other, one temporal and one spiritual. The whole text is structured to echo that relationship. Thus it begins with a conventional account of her parents, her marriage and her conduct as a daughter and then a wife; moves on to describe her dying farewells to friends and child, her confession of faith, her battle with Satan; and finally transcribes her dying greetings to Christ. Her whole life is delineated and artfully given meaning through this careful weaving of literary structure with a normative account of ideal Protestant womanhood merging apparently effortlessly into the ideal of a Christian salvation. Stubbes's final closure to the story of her death re-emphasises this construction:

> Thus thou hast heard gentle reader the discourse of the virtuous life and Christian death of this blessed and faithful servant of God, Mistress Katherine Stubbes, which is so much the more wonderful, in that she was but young and tender of years, not half a year above the number of twenty when she departed this life. The Lord give us grace to follow her example, that we may come to those unspeakable joys, wherein she now resteth, through Christ our Lord: to whom, with the Father and the Holy Ghost, be all honour, praise, dominion and thanksgiving, both now and evermore. Amen.

It is possible to read this account in two ways using a feminist critique: first as evidence of Katherine Stubbes's internalisation of the ideology of womanhood. This reading would focus on her acquiescence in 'modesty, courtesy, gentleness, affability and good government'; her reported delight in asking her husband questions at home; never leaving the house without his permission; or gossiping or arraying herself in finery, as a discovery of the perfect Renaissance wife. Her death, through what was probably puerperal fever, would then be read as a final physical submission to the actual and ideological hardships and oppression under which early modern woman is often seen to labour. The text is hence additionally conceived as a monologic structure and voice, through which only the masculine narrator is able to speak his construction of the world.

However, there is a second and more complex way of reading offered by this text, which is more rewarding to historians of early modern women's writing and representations. For this reading it is important to query that elision which Stubbes tries to make between ideal womanhood and Christian salvation, for if we examine his text closely, it is an elision made only by the narrator's voice, not by other voices in the text. For example, in the realm of theological dispute, Katherine Stubbes is described as an active and intelligent disputer against Catholics and atheists: 'she would not yield a jot, nor give place to them at all, but would most mightily justify the truth of God against their blasphemous untruths, and convince them.' Her ability and capacity to speak on theological matters is thus firmly placed in a public and earthly environment, despite Stubbes's later insistence both on her theological questioning only in private at home, and her acquiescence in the silent woman model, 'she obeyed the commandment of the apostle who biddeth women be silent, and to learn of their husbands at home.' Thus within the first pages of the text, a gap opens between Stubbes's ideally modelled woman and his actual description of her public actions. It is a gap in which discourse unevenly matches and accounts for feminine experience. Despite the fact that her life, actions and words are filtered through the male eyes, language and conceptions of Philip, the text and her life itself do not allow such monologism to work.

This gap widens as the text proceeds. For example, Katherine Stubbes's reported words form a large part of the main body of the text where the central drama of the account is her confession of faith and subsequent battle with Satan. In these accounts, although her words are filtered through the controlling narrator's voice, her words assert a speaking position which assumes a place of power. She says, for example:

beloved husband I bequeath this my child unto you: he is no longer mine, he is the Lord's and yours: I forsake him, you, and all the world, yea, and mine own self, and esteem all things but dung, that I may win Jesus Christ. And I pray you sweet husband, bring up this child in good letters, in learning and discipline: and above all things, see that he be brought up and instructed in the exercise of true religion.

Thus she makes specific provision for her child's education.

At the beginning of her confession of faith she describes her right to speak out publicly to her neighbours:

The first cause that moveth me thereto is, for that those (if there be any such here) that are not yet thoroughly resolved in the truth of God, may hear and learn what the spirit of God hath taught me out of his blessed and all-saving word. The second cause that moveth me is for that none of you shall judge that I died not a perfect Christian and a perfect member of the mystical body of Jesus Christ, and so by your rash judgement might incur the displeasure of God. The third and last cause is for that as you have been witness of part of my life, so you might be witnesses of part of my faith and belief also.

Through her own words, rather than through reported narrative, she places herself as speaker, prophet, pattern and community member: all roles which are active and public resistances to the dominant ideology of the silent, chaste and obedient woman.[1] Although these roles are all religious, they provide an autonomous space for women, and hence a crucial point of identity and potential resistance to dominant ideological discourses.

We can explore the extent of her resistance by looking at her account of a central event in religious history, frequently cited by her contemporaries to justify women's subordination: the Fall and Eve's transgressive role. In her reported words, she says:

> I believe and confess that the Lord our God ... created man after his own similitude and likeness: holy, pure, good, innocent and in every part perfect and absolute, giving him also wisdom, discretion, under-standing and knowledge above all other creatures (the holy angels only excepted) and which was more, he gave unto him a certain power, strength, faculty (which we call free will) by force whereof he might have continued and remained for ever in his integrity and holiness if he had would. But he had no sooner received the inestimable blessing of free will in innocency and integrity, but by hearkening to the poisoned suggestions of the wicked serpent, and by obeying of his persuasions, he lost his free will, his integrity and perfection, and we all his posterity to the end of the world, and of a Saint in heaven, he (and we in him) became fire brands in hell, vassals of Satan, miscreants and reprobates, abjects and cast-aways, before the face of God for ever.

This account of the Fall is notable for two distinctive points: it does not mention Eve as an agent of the temptation, and it includes all men and women in the generic (though gendered) 'man'. This double revisionary reading is atypical in the first omission, although conventional enough in the second (based subtextually on the phrase in Galatians, 'there is neither male nor female: ye are all one in Jesus Christ'). Nevertheless, the latter point is used more frequently by radical women writers and prophets than it is by men, and although in its promise of equality after death it can seem to modern feminists as a further means of justifying subordination on earth, it does have radical implications for women's power to speak and act in a religious field. This is even more powerfully true when the speaker is on her death-bed, occupying the literal space between a gendered and submissive present and an ungendered and equal future. The discovery of this space by Katherine Stubbes gives this account and her words a poignant power, and her rereading of the historical Fall in ungendered terms both a spiritual and a temporal significance.

A crystal glass for Christian women thus becomes a text which is a glass in which women can find not just a model of the ideal woman, but also ways of, and places for, articulating specific roles and powers which are not explicitly part of the dominant ideology. Despite the apparently monologic structure, the text is com-plexly dialogic: Katherine's voice interspersed with Philip's; Katherine's with Jesus' and God's; and then with Satan's; and finally her appropriation of other histories, and of Christ's own words as she dies ('into thy hands I commend my spirit'), show us a dialectical model of individualising Christian history and words for women.

The justification for this reading lies within the text, but it is also validated quite explicitly by Renaissance women writers, or by texts which use a female authorial voice. One example of this is *Jane Anger her protection for women* (ch. 9). Anger's language is very different from that of Katherine Stubbes, the genre within which she is given a voice is overtly polemical, thereby offering an overt space for oppositional language, unlike the biography where various voices co-exist. Nevertheless, Anger's conscious and self-confessed strategy is to use men's accounts and language and to invert it through appropriation to a new meaning, a methodology which recalls the oppositional strategies, whether physical or discursive, of some early modern women described in Natalie Davis's deservedly famed essay 'Women on top'.[2] Anger says:

> Wherefore if you listen, the surfeiter his pen with my hand shall forthwith show you.
> At the end of men's fair promises there is a labyrinth and therefore ever hereafter stop your ears when they protest friendship, lest they come to an end before you are aware whereby you fall without redemption. The path which leadeth thereunto is man's wit, and the mile's ends are marked with these trees: Folly, Vice, Mischief, Lust, Deceit and Pride. These to deceive you shall be clothed in the raiments of Fancy, Virtue, Modesty, Love, True-meaning and Handsomeness. Folly will bid you welcome on your way, and tell you his fancies concerning the profit which may come to you by this journey, and direct you to Vice, who is more crafty. He with a company of protestations will praise the virtues of women, showing how many ways men are beholden unto us, but our backs once turned he falls a railing.

Anger begins by telling us that the language and discourse she is going to use belong to that of the Petrarchan lover whose discourse she is attacking ('the surfeiter his pen'), but that it will undermine itself. She proceeds to exaggerate the allegorical figures of that discourse in order to ridicule it. Despite its wit, this appropriation is far clumsier than that of Katherine Stubbes: but each shares a consciousness of the genre within which they are speaking and performing, as well as an ability to negotiate an appropriative path through that genre and discourse. By such strategies Anger's voice enables women readers (to whom the work is addressed) to utilise her discursive strategies of inversion in order to resist dominant formulations of identity and behaviour.

How do these texts and this analysis relate to this anthology? The texts collected are drawn from a wide range of genres, discourses and modes, both popular and elite, in which women were described, inscribed, circumscribed and prescribed, as well as ones where women resisted, inverted and challenged such scripts. They include: sermons; translations of, and commentaries on, the Bible; conduct manuals; almanacs; pamphlets on the woman question; political treatises; educational tracts; medical books; prefaces to literary writings; prophecies; proverbs and autobiography. These texts construct women through language and through their place within particular institutional frameworks. The interrelation of such language with socio-economic, political or theological institutions is known in social and literary theory as a 'discourse'. This is a useful term with which to understand both the texts within this selection and their organisation into distinct areas. For example, the discourse of theology incorporates generic writings such as prayers and spiritual autobiography, sermons and commentaries, the Bible itself, as well as the institutional structure of the church, its intimate links with the state, and its control of sexuality through marriage rituals and practices.

The anthology is divided into nine chapters, many of which are identifiable as discursive fields during the early modern period because of their direct relation to specific institutions or institutionalised practices: such as theology, physiology, motherhood, politics, work and education. In addition to these, there are chapters on conduct, writing and speaking and proto-feminisms. The texts which are collected in the conduct chapter are commonly either educational or theological, but their focus upon the temporal conduct of women, their development of the emergent language about femininity and their relationship to the proliferation of conduct books for courtiers, gentry and a rising bourgeoisie suggests a discursive field which does not yet have a specific institutional place in this period, but relates to those of education, politics and theology. The chapters on speaking, writing and proto-feminisms are a convenient way of organising texts which partially seek to resist, escape and invert the discursive fields which represent, construct and exhort women. The issue of speaking, for example, is central to the dominant ideology of the Christian woman: when, how and to whom she can speak are all regulated and monitored through conduct books, theological exhortations, educational tracts and advice on motherhood. Yet, as we have seen in *A crystal glass*, such exhortations and representations often belie other voices, genres and silences within the texts. The two final chapters contain texts which make these voices and silences more available, and ask for them to be read in the light of the preceding discourses. The texts in the collection can therefore be read *in toto* as evidence of varying representations and ideologies of the feminine in the early modern period in England as well as of the contradictions and resistances within these. In addition, the texts may be read alongside other literary, theological, autobiographical, legal, political, geographical or private texts of the period to enable the reader to question a monolithic construction of the female and the feminine during this period, and to acknowledge the place which voices of women take in resisting, converting and inverting that monolith.

Compartmentalisation is always a problem with anthologies, and this one is no exception. The allocation of a text to a chapter is occasionally arbitrary: often a text crosses discursive boundaries and relates to texts apparently in other fields. I have tried to meet this problem in the introduction to each chapter by making cross-references to other related chapters, thus encouraging reading strategies which make connections both within and across individual chapters. Similarly, the title *Renaissance Woman: A Sourcebook. Constructions of Femininity in England* limits the contents and range in significant ways: particularly through the disputed term 'Renaissance'. Ever since Joan Kelly Gadol asked the question 'Did women have a Renaissance?,'[3] feminist historians and theorists have disputed both the use of traditional periodisation as applicable to the experience of women, and the connotations of certain cultural products implied in the term 'Renaissance'. It is clear from reading these texts that women did not experience the same self-fashioning as did men,[4] but that the proliferation of discourses, the discoveries, the economic, political and religious changes in which Renaissance man was involved, also embedded and constructed woman, albeit in different and differing ways. In addition, although the material represented here is commonly termed 'early modern' by scholars, it is a term which is not widely recognised outside the higher education academy. It is for these reasons that I have decided to use the title *Renaissance Woman*.

Over the past twenty years there has been a revolution in early modern historical and literary studies. The influence of feminist politics and scholarship on Renaissance studies is too large a topic to be covered here. The introduction to each chapter refers to the notes and a bibliography which provide some indicative reading on debates and scholarship in those specific areas. Nevertheless, it is useful to summarise the impact such studies have had, particularly in four areas. First, the gynocritical reclaiming of lost and forgotten women writers, speakers and preachers during this period has produced many new editions or first editions of texts. These enable us to read the experiences and discourses of women and to use these to challenge dominant masculine models of literary and political history.[5] Second, the work of social historians in focusing on marginal groups, whether women, criminals, witches, native Americans or peasants, enables us to see both common and divergent patterns of dominance and subordination amongst such marginal groups.[6] Third, feminism's focus on personal and private history has fuelled the further discovery of letters, diaries and other private forms, as well as encouraging an examination of all private histories, both male and female. This is an emergent area where much important work remains to be done. Fourth, the interest in gender as a category of constructed difference and play[7] has stimulated an awareness that Renaissance categories of gender, while hierarchical, are self-consciously constructed, and this promises to be a fruitful analytical tool in examining the writing and constructions of both men and women, masculinity and femininity, and of 'woman' as a category which varies across class, nation and racial differences. This anthology complements such debates and, by offering the texts to new readers, enables its future development.

INTRODUCTION

TEXTUAL AND EDITORIAL POLICY

The texts included in this anthology have been edited and chosen according to the following principles:

1   First English editions have been used wherever possible; the date provided with the title is the edition from which the extract is taken, unless the commentary says otherwise.
2   Selections are chosen for their relevance to the book's overall concerns: where authors' arguments or examples are too long for complete inclusion, I have omitted parts of the text, indicating this by ellipses where the omission is only of a sentence or two; where it is of several paragraphs, I have used three asterisks.
3   Spelling, punctuation, capitalisation and lay-out have been modernised, but the original emphasis has been retained.
4   Marginal references in the original text have been included within square brackets in the text.
5   Where authors use Latin or Greek and immediately translate the sense, I have omitted the Greek or Latin text; where they do not translate the original, I have placed a translation within square brackets.
6   Notes are placed at the end of the book.

1

THEOLOGY

INTRODUCTION

Religious belief, theological institutions and their help-meet, biblical exegesis, were central to both personal and public identities for early modern Europeans, whether Catholic, Anglican, Baptist, Brownist or Quaker, man or woman. Two crucial intellectual and political revolutions had a continuing impact throughout this period in England both on the ideology of womanhood and on women's actual lives: humanism and the Reformation. Each emphasised a radical restructuring of moral and public life, focusing, for example, on the re-evaluation of chaste marriage, rather than virginity, as central to salvation, and also on the family as a unit of ethical education for an individual's role in life. This had a dual impact on women: it placed them within the domestic and private sphere, but it also gave them a significant function as educator and moral counsellor within the home, and as partner to their husband within a Christian marriage. Another specific focus was the emphasis on the New Testament, particularly the Pauline epistles, which advocated a spiritual life and spiritual equality between men and women, both in the eyes of God and in terms of their eventual salvation (pp. 37–9). But depending on the exegesis of preachers or commentators, they also advocated womanly submission and bodily inferiority (pp. 11–18). For many women this was a source of hope and an opportunity for individualism: for others it meant postponing independence to the after-life.

The educational programme of the humanists and the Protestant insistence on a personal reading of the vernacular Bible meant that individual and private reading and interpretation became increasingly important during this period, for both women and men. Additionally, the growing popularity of public preaching and lecturing, particularly with the increased number of churches and sects during the seventeenth century, produced a kind of democratisation of listening and debating. Women attended such lectures in large numbers, and the growth in women's published and unpublished writing[1] suggests women participating in and responding to and even occasionally restructuring the terms and content of the debate: the examples of Ann Askew and Margaret Fell are pertinent here (pp. 18 ff., 37 ff.).[2] The demise of Catholicism as a national religion in England meant also the demise of the importance of various female saints (called upon in childbirth, for example) and the literal removal of the virgin Mary from churches as a figure who was worshipped alongside the male images of Christ and God. In addition, the Protestant emphasis on the male as head of household religion, replacing the wider constituency of the priest as head of his parishioners, gave symbolic religious power to the individual male householder within his own private sphere. Thus the institutionalisation of the Church of England meant that both the power of the male and the absence of virtuous public images of women helped construct an ideology of femininity which was confined to the domestic sphere, and defined in relation to the power of men.

In addition to these ideological shifts, the church and its theology were intimately linked to an increasingly centralised political state. There were increasing attempts to secure religious conformity through legislation: for example, a statute of 1543 under Henry VIII attempted to confine reading of the English Bible to men of the upper classes, thus women's access to vernacular debate was restricted through a masculine reader. A 1552 statute under Edward VI was renewed in 1559 by Elizabeth I as the Act of Uniformity, which empowered churchwardens to exact a fine of a shilling for failure to attend church.[3] The establishment of a national church under Elizabeth I, with its articles of government, catechism, prayers and practices makes the construction of woman within and through the Anglican church a crucial starting point for any examination of femininity in this period. Thus, for example, the 1604 canons, which homogenised those of Elizabeth's reign, dictated who was to learn the catechism and when (pp. 25ff.). They also continued the formal practice of churching rituals demanded by the church for women after giving birth, which have been interpreted as both purification rituals to cleanse the woman's material body after the filth of childbirth[4] and as rituals celebrated by women for women, thereby establishing an equation between childbirth, maternity and a women's subculture.[5]

The Act of Uniformity also required the published *Homilies* (pp. 20 ff.) to be read out regularly where the local priest was not licensed to preach on his own. The standardisation of preaching and public reading through these measures and through the appointment of young trained priests by Puritan bishops, meant that the circulation of interpretations of biblical stories, injunctions and images, which are represented here, was widespread even where men and women could not read the published texts. Finally, the existence of church courts, which had the power to enforce the Anglican canons and the Act of Uniformity, meant that local courts were actively involved in community policing,[6] on both theological and social issues. Sexual offences were considered by church courts before the Civil War. The elision between theological and social jurisdiction in the realm of sexual transgression is also found in the texts included in this section, which slide between spiritual, social and political issues. Thus the place of woman and the ideology of femininity are embedded in metaphysical accounts of creation, alongside physiological descriptions of her body, combined with political assertions of her subjection.

Some of the texts included in this chapter relate closely to the subjects of other chapters, for example, *A sermon of whoredom and uncleanness* (pp. 20 ff.) is equally relevant to chapter 4, and Whately's *A bride bush* (pp. 30 ff.) to chapter 3, and can valuably be read alongside them. They are included in this chapter because they were spoken or published within the national theological framework, the Church of England, and because they claim authority from biblical exegesis.

THE BIBLE

There are two versions of the creation myth present in the Bible. The texts which Renaissance writers refer to most frequently are included here. Text from: the Authorised translation, 1611.

Genesis

Chapter 1, verses 26–7

26. And God said, let us make man in our image, after our likeness: and let them have dominion over the fish of the sea and over the cattle and over all the earth, and over every creeping thing that creepeth upon the earth. 27. So God created man in his own image, in the image of God created he him; male and female created he them.

Chapter 2, verses 18–24

18. And the Lord God said, it is not good that the man shall be alone; I will make him an helpmeet for him. 19. And out of the ground the Lord God formed every beast of the field and every fowl of the air; and brought them unto Adam to see what he would call them: and whatsoever Adam called every living creature, that was the name thereof. 20. And Adam gave names to all cattle, and to the fowl of the air, and to the very beast of the field; but for Adam there was not found an help meet for him. 21. And the Lord God caused a deep sleep to fall upon Adam, and he slept; and he took one of his ribs, and closed up the flesh instead thereof; 22. And the rib, which the Lord God had taken from man, made he a woman, and brought her unto the man. 23. And Adam said, this is now bone of my bones, and flesh of my flesh: she shall be called woman, because she was taken out of man. 24. Therefore shall a man leave his father and his mother, and shall cleave unto his wife: and they shall be one flesh.

Chapter 3, verses 6–19

6. And when the woman saw that the tree was good for food, and that it was pleasant to the eyes, and a tree to be desired to make one wise, she took of the fruit thereof, and did eat, and gave also unto her husband with her; and he did eat. 7. And the eyes of them both were opened, and they knew that they were naked; and they sewed fig leaves together, and made themselves aprons. 8. And they heard the voice of the Lord God walking in the garden in the cool of the day: and Adam and his wife hid themselves from the presence of the Lord God amongst the trees of the garden. 9. And the Lord God called unto Adam, and said unto him, where art thou? 10. And he said, I hear thy voice in the garden, and I was afraid because I was naked; and I hid myself. 11. And he said, who told thee thou wast naked? Hast thou eaten of the tree, whereof I commanded thee that thou shouldest not eat? 12. And the man said, the woman whom thou gavest to be with me, she gave me of the tree and I did eat. 13. And the Lord God said unto the woman, what is it thou hast done? And the woman said, the serpent beguiled me, and I did eat. 14. And the Lord God said unto the serpent, because thou hast done this, thou art cursed above all cattle, and above every beast of the field; upon thy belly shalt thou go, and dust shalt thou eat all the days of thy life. 15. And I will put enmity between thee and the woman, and between thy seed and her seed; it shall bruise thy head and thou shalt bruise his heel. 16. Unto the woman he said, I will greatly multiply thy sorrow and thy conception; in sorrow thou shalt bring forth children; and thy desire shall be to thy husband, and he shall have rule over thee. 17. And unto Adam he said, because thou hast hearkened unto the voice of thy wife, and hast eaten of the tree, of which I commanded thee, saying, thou shalt not eat of it: cursed is the ground for thy sake; in sorrow shalt thou eat of it all the days of thy life; 18. Thorns also and thistles shall it bring forth to thee; and thou shalt eat the herb of the field; 19. In the sweat of thy face shalt thou eat bread, till thou return unto the ground; for out of it wast thou taken: for dust thou art, and unto dust shalt thou return.

Leviticus

Chapter 15, verses 19–24

19. And if a woman have an issue, and her issue in her flesh be blood, she shall be put apart seven days: and whosoever toucheth her shall be unclean until the even. 20. And everything that she lieth upon in her separation shall be unclean: everything that she sitteth upon shall be unclean. 21. And whosoever toucheth her bed shall wash his clothes, and bathe himself in

water, and be unclean until the even. 22. And whosoever toucheth anything that she sat upon shall wash his clothes and bathe himself in water, and be unclean until the even. 23. And if it be on her bed, or on anything whereon she sitteth, when he toucheth it he shall be unclean until the even. 24. And if any man lie with her at all, and her flowers[7] be upon him, he shall be unclean seven days; and all the bed whereon he lieth shall be unclean.

Proverbs

Chapter 31, verses 10–28

10. Who can find a virtuous woman? For her price is far above rubies. 11. The heart of her husband doth safely trust in her, so that he shall have no need of spoil. 12. She will do him good and not evil all the days of her life. 13. She seeketh wool and flax and worketh willingly with her hands. 14. She is like the merchants' ship; and bringeth her food from afar. 15. She riseth also whilst it is yet night, and giveth meat to her household and a portion to her maidens. 16. She considereth a field, and buyeth it: with the fruit of her hands she planteth a vineyard. 17. She girdeth her loins with strength, and strengtheneth her arms. 18. She perceiveth that her merchandise is good: her candle goeth not out by night. 19. She layeth her hands to the spindle, and her hands hold the distaff. 20. She stretcheth out her hand to the poor: yea, she reacheth forth her hands to the needy. 21. She is not afraid of the snow for her household: for all her household are clothed with scarlet. 22. She maketh herself coverings of tapestry; her clothing is silk and purple. 23. Her husband is known in the gates, when he sitteth among the elders of the land. 24. She maketh fine linen and selleth it; and delivereth girdles unto the merchant. 25. Strength and honour are her clothing; and she shall rejoice in time to come. 26. She openeth her mouth in wisdom; and in her tongue is the law of kindness. 27. She looketh well to the ways of her household, and eateth not the bread of idleness. 28. Her children arise up, and call her blessed; her husband also, and he praiseth her.

1 Corinthians

Chapter 11, verses 3–13

3. But I would have you know, that the head of every man is Christ; and the head of every woman is the man; and the head of Christ is God. 4. Every man praying or prophesying, having his head covered, dishonoureth his head. 5. But every woman that prayeth or prophesieth with her head uncovered dishonoureth her head: for that is even all one as if she were shaven. 6. For

if the woman be not covered, let her also be shorn: but if it be a shame for a woman to be shorn or shaven, let her be covered. 7. For a man indeed ought not to cover his head, forasmuch as he is the image and glory of God but the woman is the glory of the man. 8. For the man is not of the woman; but the woman of the man. 9. Neither was the man created for the woman; but the woman for the man. 10. For this cause ought the woman to have power on her head because of the angels. 11. Nevertheless, neither is the man without the woman, neither the woman without the man, in the Lord. 12. For as the woman is of the man, even so is the man also by the woman; but all things of God. 13. Judge in yourselves: is it comely that a woman pray unto God uncovered?

Chapter 14, verses 27–35

27. If any man speak in an unknown tongue, let it be by two, or at the most by three, and that by course; and let one interpret. 28. But if there be no interpreter, let him keep silence in the church; and let him speak to himself, and to God. 29. Let the prophets speak two or three, and let the other judge. 30. If any thing be revealed to another that sitteth by, let the first hold his peace. 31. For ye may all prophesy one by one, that all may learn, and all be comforted. 32. And the spirits of the prophets are subject to the prophets. 33. For God is not the author of confusion, but of peace, as in all the churches of the saints. 34. Let your women keep silence in the churches: for it is not permitted unto them to speak; but they are commanded to be under obedience, as also saith the law. 35. And if they will learn anything, let them ask their husbands at home: for it is a shame for women to speak in the church.

Galatians

Chapter 3, verses 25–8

25. But after the faith is come, we are no longer under a schoolmaster. 26. For ye are all the children of God by faith in Jesus Christ. 27. For as many of you as have been baptised into Christ have put on Christ. 28. There is neither Jew nor Greek, there is neither bond nor free, there is neither male nor female: for ye are all one in Christ Jesus.

JOHN CALVIN

Ephesians

Chapter 5, verses 21–25

21. Submitting yourselves one to another in the fear of God. 22. Wives, submit yourselves unto your own husbands, as unto the Lord. 23. For the husband is the head of the wife, even as Christ is the head of the church: and he is the saviour of the body. 24. Therefore as the church is subject unto Christ, so let wives be to their own husbands in everything. 25. Husbands, love your wives, even as Christ also loved the church, and gave himself to it.

1 Timothy

Chapter 2, verses 9–15

9. In like manner also, that women adorn themselves in modest apparel, with shamefacedness and sobriety; not with broided hair, or gold, or pearls, or costly array. 10. But (which becometh women professing godliness) with good works. 11. Let the woman learn in silence with all subjection. 12. But I suffer not a woman to teach, nor to usurp authority over the man, but to be in silence. 13. For Adam was first formed, then Eve. 14. And Adam was not deceived, but the woman being deceived was in the transgression. 15. Notwithstanding she shall be saved in childbearing, if they continue in faith and charity and holiness with sobriety.

John Calvin, *Sermons*

Calvin's exegetical commentary and sermons were widely used in churches. Text from: The Sermons of M. John Calvin upon the Epistle of S. Paul to the Ephesians, transl. Arthur Golding, 1577, fos 277ᵛ–283ᵛ; and Sermons of M. John Calvin upon the Epistle of Saint Paul to the Galatians, transl. Arthur Golding, 1574, fos 170ʳ–177ʳ.

Sermon on the Epistle of St Paul to the Ephesians

Whereas he saith, concerning wives, that they owe subjection to their husbands: we have to mark that this subjection is double. For man was already the head of woman even before the sin and fall of Eve and Adam [1 Tim. 2:13]. And St Paul alleging the same reason, to show that it is not meet that the wife should reign in equal degree with her husband, saith that the man came not of the woman, but the woman of the man, and that she is but a piece of his body. For God could have created Eve out of the earth as well as he did Adam, but he would not. Nay rather he matched the man and woman together with such condition that the man, knowing his wife to be

15

as his own substance and flesh, should be induced thereby to love her (as we shall see again hereafter), and that the wife knowing herself to have none other being but of the man, should bear her subjection patiently and with a willing mind. For if the hand being a member of the body should refuse to stand in his own place and would needs set itself upon the crown of the head, what a thing were it! So then if we look back to the creation of man and woman, the husband on his side ought to be induced to love and cherish his wife as himself: and the wife, seeing that she was taken out of the substance of the man, ought to submit herself quietly unto him, as to her head.

But there is also another bond which doubleth still the subjection of the wife: for we know that she was beguiled [Genesis 3:6; 1 Tim. 3:14]. Women therefore must remember that in being subject to their husbands, they receive the hire of Eve's sin: and they must consider that if marriage had continued sound and uncorrupt, there had been nothing but joy for man and wife. For know that things were blessed of God and there was not anything which should not have turned to gladness and felicity. But now although God's blessings shine forth everywhere both above and beneath, yet are there always tokens of cursing imprinted in them, so as we cannot behold neither heaven nor earth nor any other creature, but we may partly perceive that God is become a stranger unto us because our father Adam fell from that noble and excellent state, whereunto he was created afore. This is to be seen everywhere in all things, and specially in marriage. For women ought to feel the fruit of their sins: and men feel enough of it for their part. For surely if Adam and Eve had continued in the righteousness that God had given them, the whole state of this earthly life had been as a paradise, and marriage had been so beautified that man and woman being matched together should have lived in such accord as we see the angels in heaven do, among whom there is nothing but peace and brotherly love, and even so had it been with us. Therefore, as now when a man hath a curst and shrewd wife, whom he cannot wield by any means, he must consider with himself, *lo here the fruits of original sin, and of the corruption that is in myself.* And the wife also on her side must think, *good reason it is that I should receive the payment that cometh of my disobedience towards God, for that I held not myself in his awe.*

* * *

Now then let wives look well to their duties and understand that when they contend with their husbands, it is all one as if they would reject God because he hath not created them otherwise than with condition, and to the end they should be subject to their husbands. True it is that they will be so proud and stately as to say, should my husband have my head under his girdle? Yea but the wife that doth so showeth that she is loath that God should have any authority over her and would fain put God's law under her foot. Howbeit, forasmuch as there is no other shift but women must needs stoop and understand that the ruin and confusion of all mankind came in on their side, and that through them we be all forlorn and accursed and banished the kingdom of heaven: when women (say I) do understand that all this came of Eve and of the womankind (as St Paul telleth us in another place [1 Tim. 2:14]), there is none other way but for them to stoop and to bear patiently the subjection that God hath laid upon them, which is nothing else but a warning to them to keep themselves lowly and mild.

Sermon on the Epistle of St Paul to the Galatians

Now hereupon St Paul concludeth, *that there is neither Greek, nor Jew, bond nor free, male nor female, but that Jesus Christ is one in us all, and all we are one in him.* And by this sentence St Paul meant to express yet better that only faith ought to suffice us and that we must exclude all other means.... Therefore St Paul telleth us that we must be so united to our Lord Jesus Christ as none of us must advance himself as though he were better worth than his fellows: but acknowledge ourselves beholden to God's mere grace for all things. And both great and small must endeavour the same together and with one common consent confess that in our Lord Jesus Christ they have all that is to be wished for and therefore give over all the inventions and devices that can come in their own brain. Yet notwithstanding St Paul meant not to say that there be no diversity of degree as in respect of worldly policy, for we know there are masters and servants, magistrates and subjects: in a household there is the good man which is the head and the good wife which ought to be subject. We know then that this order is inviolable, and our Lord Jesus Christ is not come into the world to make such confusion as to abolish that which was stablished by God his father. But when St Paul saith that there is neither master nor servant, man nor woman, he meaneth that to be sure of their salvation men must not set up their tails like peacocks and stand gazing upon their own feathers, but look what worthiness so ever we ween to be in ourselves we must wipe it away and cast it underfoot, and acknowledge all to be but hindrances that turn us aside from coming to our Lord Jesus Christ. Therefore when both great and small acknowledge that they cannot bring ought of themselves, but must receive all things of God's only free goodness: then is our Lord Jesus Christ, himself alone, is all in all in us: that is to say we will not go about to add ought to the grace that he hath purchased for us and which he offereth us daily by his gospel, to the end we should be partakers of it and enjoy it to our salvation. Thus ye see in effect that on the one side we must keep the civil orders of this world. Let such as are great men and men of authority above others know that God intendeth to be served by them in that state. As, for example, let the magistrates consider that they be so much the more bound to do their duty seeing that God hath done them the honour to advance them after that fashion above others. Again they that are private persons and ought to obey the magistrates must look that they submit themselves, unless they purpose to strive with God and to make war against him. Yet see then that St Paul holdeth us in sobriety and modesty, and under a bridle which was not devised by men but dedicated of God to our use, because mankind could not continue without it. And truly we ought to honour and reverence the state of governance as a thing ordained of the Lord. And yet for all that, when we come to the heavenly life let us assure ourselves that all worldly things pass and vanish away, as the world and the fashion thereof passeth, saith St Paul: *but the kingdom of God endureth for ever* [1 Cor. 7:21].

The first examination of Ann Askew

Ann Askew was one of the first women to die for the Protestant faith in England, in 1546. John Bale published this text of her examination for heresy by Henry VIII's ministers, and annotated Askew's responses. His commentary is omitted here, apart from his summary at the end of the examination. Text from: Ann Askew, *The first examination of Ann Askew with the elucidation of John Bale*, 1546, fos A1ᵛ–B3ʳ.

Ann Askew. To satisfy your expectation, good people (saith she) this was my first examination in the year of our Lord MDXLV and in the month of March, first Christopher Dare examined me at Sadler's Hall, being one of the quest, and asked if I did not believe that the sacrament hanging over the altar was the very body of Christ really. Then I demanded this question of him, wherefore St Steven was stoned to death? And he said, he could not tell. Then I answered that no more would I assail his vain questioning.

*　*　*

Secondly, he said that there was a woman, which did testify that I should read how God was not in temples made with hands. Then I showed him the vii and xvii chapter of the Apostles' Acts, what Steven and Paul had said therein. Whereupon he asked me how I took those sentences? I answered that I would not throw pearls among swine, for acorns were good enough.

*　*　*

Thirdly, he asked me wherefore I said that I had rather read five lines in the Bible than hear five masses in the temple. I confessed that I said no less. Not for the dispraise of either the epistle or the gospel. But because the one did greatly edify me and the other nothing at all. As St Paul doth witness in the viii chapter of his first epistle to the Corinthians, where as he doth say, *if the trump giveth an uncertain sound, who will prepare himself to the battle?*

*   *   *

Fourthly, he laid unto my charge that I should say if an ill priest ministered it was the Devil and not God. My answer was that I never spake such thing. But this was my saying, that whatsoever he were, which ministered unto me, his ill conditions could not hurt my faith. But in spirit I received, nevertheless, the body and blood of Christ.

*   *   *

Fifthly, he asked me, what said I concerning confession? I answered him my meaning, which was as St James saith that every man ought to acknowledge his faults to other, and the one to pray for the other.

*   *   *

Sixthly, he asked me what I said to the king's book? And I answered him that I could say nothing to it, because I never saw it.

*   *   *

Seventhly, he asked me if I had the spirit of God in me? I answered if I had not, I was but a reprobate and cast away.

*   *   *

Then he said he had sent for a priest to examine me, which was there at hand. The priest asked me what I said to the sacrament of the altar? And requested much to know therein my meaning. But I desired him again to hold me excused concerning this matter. None other answer would I make him, because I perceived him a Papist.

*   *   *

Eighthly, he asked me if I did not think that private masses did help souls departed? And I said it was great idolatry to believe more in them than in the death which Christ died for us.

*   *   *

Then the bishop's chancellor rebuked me and said that I was much to blame for uttering the scriptures. For St Paul (he said) forbode women to speak or talk of the word of God. I answered him, that I knew Paul's meaning so well as he, which is *1 Corinthiorum xiiii*, that a woman ought not to speak in the congregation by the way of teaching. And then I asked him how many women he had seen go into the pulpit and preach? He said he never saw none.

Then I said he ought to find no fault in poor women, except they had offended the law.

John Bale. Plenteous enough is her answer here unto this quarrelling, and (as appeareth) unlearned chancellor. Many godly women both in the old law and the new were learned in the scriptures, and made utterance of them to the glory of God, as we read of Elizabeth, Mary, and Anna the widow (*Luke* 1 and 2), yet were they not rebuked for it. Yea, Mary, Christ's mother retained all that was afterward written of him (*Luke* 2), yet was it not imputed unto her an offence. Christ blamed not the woman that cried when he was preaching, *happy is the womb that bare thee* (*Luke* 11). The women which gave knowledge to his disciples that he was risen from death to life, discomforted not he, but solaced them with his most glorious appearance (*Matt.* 28. *John.* 20). In the primitive church, specially in St Jerome's time, was it a great praise unto women to be learned in the scriptures. Great commendations giveth our English chronicles to Helena, Ursula and Hilda, women of our nation, for being learned also in the scriptures. Such a woman was the said Hilda, as openly disputed in them against the superstition of certain bishops.

Certain sermons or homilies

Certain sermons or homilies (first edition, 1547, under Edward VI, second in 1562 under Elizabeth I) were required to be read in churches at appropriate points: only qualified MA scholars were licensed to preach their own words in churches, which meant that the official sermons were the texts most people heard. The first homily was often read out when a couple were required by the church to do public penance for fornication or adultery, and the second at marriage ceremonies. Text from: *Certain sermons or homilies appointed to be read in churches*, 1547, fos P2^v–P3^r, S1^r–^{v}; 1563, fos 255^v–6^r, 257^r–9^r, 263^v–4^v.

A sermon of whoredom and uncleanness: against adultery, 1547

Although there want not (good Christian people) great swarms of vices worthy to be rebuked (unto such decay is true godliness and virtuous living now come to): yet above other vices the outrageous seas of adultery, whoredom, fornication and uncleanness, have not only brast in but also overflowed almost the whole world, unto the great dishonour of God, the exceeding infamy of the name of Christ, the notable decay of true religion, and the utter destruction of the public wealth: and that so abundantly that through the customable use thereof, this vice is grown unto such an height that in a manner among many it is counted no sin at all, but rather a pastime, a dalliance, and but a touch of youth: not rebuked, but winked at: not punished, but laughed at. Wherefore it is necessary at this present to entreat of the sin of whoredom and fornication, declaring unto you the greatness of this sin, and how odious, hateful and abominable it is, and hath always been reputed before God and all good men, and how grievously it hath been punished, both by the law of God and the laws of divers princes. Again to show you certain remedies, whereby you may (through the grace of God) eschew this most detestable sin of whoredom and fornication, and lead your lives in all honesty and cleanness. And that ye may perceive that fornication and whoredom are (in the sight of God) most abominable sins, ye shall call to remembrance this commandment of God: *thou shalt not commit adultery.* By the which word adultery, although it be properly understood of the unlawful commixture or joining together of a married man with any woman beside his wife, or of a wife with any man beside her husband, yet thereby is signified also all unlawful use of those parts which be ordained for generation.

❊   ❊   ❊

To avoid fornication, adultery and all uncleanness, let us provide that above all things we may keep our hearts pure and clean from all evil thoughts and carnal lusts. For if that be once infected and corrupt we fall headlong into all kind of ungodliness. This shall we easily do if when we feel inwardly that Satan our old enemy tempteth us unto whoredom, we by no means consent to his crafty suggestions, but valiantly resist and withstand him by strong faith in the word of God, objecting against him always in our heart this commandment of God: it is written that thou shalt not commit whoredom. It shall be good also for us ever to live in the fear of God, and to set before our eyes the grievous threatenings of God against all ungodly sinners, and to consider in our mind how filthy, beastly and short that pleasure is, whereunto Satan moveth us. And again, how the pain appointed for that sin is intolerable and everlasting. Moreover, to use a temperance and sobriety in eating and drinking, to eschew unclean communication, to avoid all filthy company, to flee idleness, to delight in reading holy scripture, to watch in godly prayers and virtuous meditations, and at all times to exercise some godly travails, shall help greatly unto the eschewing of whoredom.

And here are all degrees to be monished, whether they be married or unmarried, to love, chastity and cleanness of life. For the married are bound by the law of God so purely to love one another, that neither of them seek any strange love. The man must only cleave to his wife, and the wife again only to her husband: they must so delight one in another's company, that none of them covet any other. And as they are bound thus to live together in all godliness and honesty, so likewise is their duty virtuously to bring up their children and to provide that they fall not into Satan's snare, nor into any uncleanness, but that they come pure and honest unto holy wedlock, when time requireth. So likewise ought all masters and rulers to provide that no whoredom, nor any point of uncleanness, be used among their servants. And again, they that are single and feel in themselves that they cannot live without the company of a woman, let them get wives of their own and so live godly together. For it is better to marry then to burn [1 Cor. 7]. And to avoid fornication saith the apostle, let every man have his own wife, and every woman her own husband. Finally, all such as feel in themselves a sufficiency and hability through the operation of God's spirit to lead a sole and continent life, let them praise God for his gift and seek all means possible to maintain the same, as by reading of holy scriptures, by godly meditations, by continual prayers, and such other virtuous exercises. If we all on this wise will endeavour ourselves to eschew fornication, adultery and all uncleanness, and lead our lives in all godliness and honesty, serving God with a pure and clean heart and glorifying him in our bodies by leading an innocent life, we may be sure to be in the number of those of whom our saviour Christ speaketh in the gospel in this manner: *blessed are the pure in heart for they shall see God, to whom alone be all glory, honour, rule and power, world without end* [Matt. 5].

An homily of the state of matrimony, 1562

The word of Almighty God doth testify and declare whence the original beginning of matrimony cometh and why it is ordained. It is instituted of God to the intent that man and woman should live lawfully in a perpetual friendly fellowship, to bring forth fruit, and to avoid fornication. By which means a good conscience might be preserved on both parties, in bridling the corrupt inclinations of the flesh within the limits of honesty. For God hath straightly forbidden all whoredom and uncleanness and hath from time to time taken grievous punishments of this inordinate lust, as all stories and ages hath declared. Furthermore it is also ordained that the church of God and his kingdom might by this kind of life be conserved and enlarged, not only in that God giveth children by his blessing, but also in that they be brought up by the parents godly in the knowledge of God's word, that this the knowledge of God and true religion might be delivered by the succession from one to another, that, finally, many might enjoy that everlasting immortality. Wherefore, forasmuch as matrimony serveth as well to avoid sin and offence as to increase the kingdom of God, you, as all other which enter that state, must acknowledge this benefit of God, with pure and thankful minds, for that he hath so ruled your hearts, that ye follow not the example of the wicked world who set their delight in filthiness of sin, where both of you stand in the fear of God and abhor all filthiness. For that is surely the singular gift of God, where the common example of the world declareth how the Devil hath their hearts bound and entangled in various snares, so that they in their wifeless state run into open abominations without any grudge of their conscience. Which sort of men that liveth so desperately and so filthily, what damnation tarieth for them, St Paul describeth it to them saying: *neither whoremongers nor adulterers shall inherit the kingdom of God* [1 Cor. 5]. This horrible judgement of God ye be escaped through his mercy, if so be that ye live inseparately, according to God's ordinance. And yet I would not have you careless without watching. For the Devil will assay to attempt all things, to interrupt and hinder your hearts and godly purpose, if ye will give him any entry. For he will either labour to break this godly knot, once begun betwixt you, or else at the least he will labour to encumber it with divers griefs and displeasures.

✻ ✻ ✻

Learn thou therefore, if thou desirest to be void of all these miseries, if thou desirest to live peaceably and comfortably in wedlock, how to make thy earnest prayer to God, that he would govern both your hearts by his Holy Spirit, to restrain the Devil's power, whereby your concord may remain perpetually. But to this prayer must be joined a singular diligence whereof St Peter giveth his precept saying: *you husbands deal with your wives according to knowledge, giving honour to the wife as unto the weaker vessel, and as unto them that are heirs also of the grace of life, that your prayers be not hindered* [1 Peter. 3]. This precept doth particularly pertain to the husband. For he ought to be the leader and auctor of love, in cherishing and increasing concord, which then shall take place if he will use measurableness and not tyranny and if he yield some things to the woman. For the woman is a weak creature, not endued with like strength and constancy of mind, therefore they be the sooner disquieted, and they be the more prone to all weak affections and dispositions of mind, more than men be, and lighter they be, and more vain in their fantasies and opinions. These things must be considered of the man: that he be not too stiff, so that he ought to wink at some things, and must gently expound all things, and to forbear. Howbeit, the common sort of men doth judge, that such moderation should not become a man. For they say, that it is a token of womanish cowardness and therefore they think that it is a man's part to fume in anger, to fight with fist and staff. Howbeit, howsoever they imagine, undoubtedly St Peter doth better judge what should be seeming to a man and what he should most reasonably perform. For he saith, reasoning should be used, and not fighting. Yea he saith more, that the woman ought to have a certain honour attributed to her, that is to say, she must be spared and born with, the rather for that she is the weaker vessel, of a frail heart, inconstant and, with a word, soon

23

stirred to wrath. And therefore considering these her frailties, she is to be the rather spared. By this means, thou shalt not only nourish concord, but shalt have her heart in thy power and will.

* * *

Now as concerning the wife's duty. What shall become her? Shall she abuse the gentleness and humanity of her husband, and at her pleasure turn all things upside down? No, surely. For that is far repugnant against God's commandment. For thus does St Peter preach to them: *ye wives be ye in subjection to obey your own husband*. To obey is another thing than to control or command, which they may do to their children and to their family. But as for their husbands, them must they obey, and cease from commanding, and perform subjection. For this surely doth nourish concord very much, when the wife is ready at hand at her husband's commandment, when she will apply herself to his will, when she endeavoureth herself to seek his contentation and to do him pleasure, when she will eschew all things that might offend him. . . . But on the contrary part, when the wives be stubborn, froward and malapert, their husbands are compelled thereby to abhor and flee from their own houses, even as they should have battle with their enemies. Howbeit, it can scantly be but that some offences shall sometime chance betwixt them, for no man doth live without fault, specially for that the woman is the more frail part. Therefore let them beware that they stand not in their faults and wilfulness: but rather let them acknowledge their follies, and say: *my husband, so it is, that by my anger I was compelled to do this or that, forgive me, and hereafter I will take better heed.* Thus ought women the more readily to do, the more they be ready to offend. And they shall not do this only to avoid strife and debate: but rather in the respect of the commandment of God.

* * *

For if we be bound to hold out our left cheek for strangers which will smite us on the right cheek: how much more ought we to suffer an extreme and unkind husband? But yet I mean not that a man should beat his wife, God forbid that: for that is the greatest shame that can be, not so much to her that is beaten, as to him that doth the deed. But if by such fortune thou chancest upon such an husband, take it not too heavily, but suppose thou that thereby is laid no small reward hereafter, and in this lifetime no small commendation to thee, if thou canst be quiet. But yet to you that be men, thus I speak. Let there be none so grievous fault to compel you to beat your wives. . . . For if she be poor, upbraid her not; if she be simple, taunt her not, but be the more courteous. For she is thy body and made one flesh with thee. But thou, peradventure, wilt say that she is a wrathful woman, a drunkard, and beastly,

24

without wit and reason. For this cause bewail her the more. Chase not in anger, but pray to almighty God. Let her be admonished and holpen with good counsel, and do thou thy best endeavour that she may be delivered of these affections. But if thou shouldst beat her, thou shalt increase her evil affections. For frowardness and sharpness is not amended with frowardness, but with softness and gentleness. Furthermore consider what reward thou shalt have at God's hand: for where thou mightest beat her, and yet for the respect of the fear of God thou wilt abstain and bear patiently her great offences, the rather in respect of that law which forbiddeth that a man should cast out his wife what fault soever she be cumbered with, thou shalt have a very great reward. And before the receipt of that reward, that shalt feel many commodities: for by this means, she shall be made the more obedient, and thou, for his sake, shalt be made the more meek.

Church of England, *Canons*

The Canons of 1604 set out the religious obligations of ministers and congregations. Text from: Church of England, *Constitutions and canons ecclesiastical*, 1604, fo. H1ʳ.

Ministers to catechise every Sunday

Every parson, vicar or curate upon every Sunday and holy day before evening prayer, shall for half an hour or more, examine and instruct the youth and ignorant persons of his parish in the ten commandments, the articles of belief, and in the Lord's Prayer: and shall diligently hear, instruct and teach them the catechism set forth in the Book of Common Prayer. And all fathers, mothers, masters and mistresses shall cause their children, servants and apprentices which have not learned the catechism, to come to the church at the time appointed, obediently to hear and to be ordered by the minister, until they have learned the same. And if any minister neglect his duty therein, let him be sharply reproved upon the first complaint, and true notice thereof given to the bishop or ordinary of the place. If after submitting himself, he shall wilfully offend therein again, let him be suspended. If so the third time, there being little hope that he will be therein reformed, then excommunicated, and so remain until he will be reformed. And likewise if any of the said fathers, mothers, masters or mistresses, children, servants or apprentices shall neglect their duties, as the one sort in not causing to come, and the other in refusing to learn, as aforesaid, let them be suspended by their ordinaries (if they be not children) and if they so persist in the space of a month, then let them be excommunicated.

Thomas Becon, *Catechism*

The catechism was an essential part of the theological education of adults and children (see p. 24). Becon's was particularly popular, and addressed to his children, Theodore, Basil and Rachel. Text from: first published in *Works*, 1564, fos 431ʳ–4ᵛ, 513ʳ–17ʳ.

Of the duty of maids and young unmarried women

Son. The maids, whether they be in their father's houses or abroad at service, must diligently take heed that they have continually before their eyes the fear of God, and above all things seek to please him and to frame their life according unto his holy word. And that they may the better this do, they ought many times to call upon God for his Holy Spirit and grace, that he may keep them safe and sound both in mind and body. For without his help and favour nothing can prosper or have good success: without his grace and without the comfort of his Holy Spirit, neither the bodies nor the minds of the maids can continue pure, chaste, continent and honest, but rather fall into all kinds of uncleanness. God therefore is at all times to be called upon with fervent prayers that he may preserve and keep them in all godliness, honesty and virtue . . .

Secondly, the duty of honest and godly maids is to be obedient to their masters and mistresses and diligently to do in the household affairs, whatsoever they are commanded and always to have an eye unto the godly doings of their mistresses and studiously learn to do the like, that when the time comes that they also shall be householders, they may the better know how to rule and govern their own house.

Thirdly, it appertaineth unto the office of virtuous maids never to be idle, but always to work some good thing. For idleness is a great occasion of many evils: as the wise man saith, idleness bringeth much evil. So soon as idleness occupieth the mind of any person, vain and evil thoughts brast in straightways, out of the which springeth all mischief, as pride, slothfulness, banqueting, drunkenship, whoredom, adultery, vain communication, betraying of secrets, cursed speaking, etc. To avoid these pestilences it shall become honest and virtuous maids to give themselves to honest and virtuous exercises: to spinning, to carding, to weaving, to sowing, to washing, to wringing, to sweeping, to scouring, to brewing, to baking and to all kind of labours without exception that become maids of their vocation, of whatsoever degree they be, rich or poor, noble or unnoble, fair or foul . . . all godly women from time to time have learned and practised some art or occupation, whereby they might get at the least some part of their living if necessity should require. And what is more brittle than brittle and flattering fortune, or more inconstant and flitting than the transitory possessions of the world? An occupation is a most certain patrimony.

Fourthly, not only idleness is to be excluded of those maidens which intend to be godly and virtuous, but also the running about unto vain spectacles, games, pastimes, plays, interludes etc, where rather vice than virtue, sin than soul health, wickedness than godliness is to be learned. Let them remember what chanced to Dinah, Jacob's daughter through going abroad to see vain sights [Gen. 34]. Was she not deflowered and lost her virginity? Virginity once lost, what remaineth safe and praiseworthy in a maid? The highest, best and greatest dowry that a maid can bring to her husband is honesty...

Fifthly, forasmuch as nothing doth so greatly hinder the good name and fame of maids as keeping company with naughty packs and persons of a dissolute and wanton life (for every man proveth such as he is with whom he is conversant), and contrariwise, nothing doth so much commend, avaunce and set forth their good name and fame as resorting unto such as are well reported and of an honest disposition: therefore shall it be requisite that all godly maids do refrain themselves from keeping company with light, vain and wanton persons, whose delight is in fleshly and filthy pastimes, as singing, dancing, leaping, skipping, playing, kissing, whoring, etc. All such must they avoid if they tender their good name, which once lost, they are of no more estimation, but condemned and despised of all good and godly persons...

Sixthly, this also must honest maids provide, that they be not full of tongue, and of much babbling, nor use many words, but as few as they may, yea and those wisely and discretely, soberly and modestly spoken, ever remembering this common proverb: *a maid should be seen and not heard.* Except the gravity of some matter do require that she should speak, or else an answer is to be made to such things as are demanded of her: let her keep silence. For there is nothing that doth so much commend, avaunce, set forth, adorn, deck, trim and garnish a maid, as silence. And this noble virtue may the virgins learn of that most holy, pure and glorious virgin Mary, which when she either heard or saw any worthy and notable thing, blabbed it not out straightways to her gossips, as the manner of women is at this present day, but being silent she kept all those sayings secret and pondered them in her heart, saith blessed Luke [Luke 2].

Seventhly, forasmuch as maids, no less than young men, after they come to fourteen years of age are so desirous to be married and to have the company of other to this end that they may be fruitful according to the work of God and nature: and notwithstanding such untimely marriages are not to be commended seeing that through them the bodies of the persons, so too soon married are greatly enfeebled and the fruit that cometh of them prove weaklings, of small stature, and almost of no strength, and so unprofitable for the commonwealth: it shall be convenient for all honest maids, if they tender

27

the health and conservation of their bodies and the prosperity of the fruit wherewith God shall bless them afterward and the continuance of the same, that they labour to the uttermost of their power to suppress that lust and desire in them by moderate eating and drinking, by using a temperate diet, and by avoiding all superfluity, and by keeping their bodies low either by fasting, or by receiving of such meat and drink as shall least of all enflame the body, or provoke it unto lust. It shall be necessary in this behalf that the maids use no fine and exquisite meats, but homely and usual, even such as may slay hunger and not kindle lust, satisfy nature and not pamper the body. The drink also that they shall use ought either to be pure water, or else thin ale, or small beer, that it may slake thirst and not kindle lust. For nothing doth so tame the raging lusts of the flesh, as slender and moderate diet: and contrariwise nothing doth so enflame and set on fire carnal concupiscence, as fine fare and hot wines.... By this means shall they keep their bodies in good temperature, conserve their health, quiet their minds, suppress carnal lusts, avoid unclean desires, eschew evil company, and set themselves in a goodly order against the time that God shall call them unto the holy state of honourable wedlock.

Eighthly, seeing that, as experience teacheth, maids desire nothing so greatly as gallant apparel and sumptuous raiment, and covet that so greatly that many times not a few of them labour to come by it, not only with the loss of their truth, but also of their honesty, it shall not be unfitting that all honest and godly disposed maids content themselves with comely and seemly apparel, even such as becometh their degree, state, vocation and calling, utterly rejecting and casting away all nice vanity and vain niceness of apparel, according to the doctrine of the gospel.... The lightness of apparel, is a plain demonstration of the lightness of the mind: so that whatsoever woman delight in gorgeous garments, she setteth forth herself to sale and declareth evidently her incontinency both of body and mind. Look how much the body is beautified with the gallantness of apparel, so much is the mind deformed with the corruption of arrogancy and vainglory. And the more humbly the body is outwardly clad, the more humble is the mind within and the better garnished with the riches of godly virtues. The decking and trimming of a Christian is inward, not outward: it consisteth in mind and not in body; in virtue and godliness, and not in gold and pearl.... The maid that desireth the garnishing of the bodily vesture, spoileth her soul of the beauty of virtues: neither hath she true chastity that goeth about with her gallant apparel to allure the eyes of other to behold her: neither keepeth her promise with Christ that seeketh rather to please the people than her husband.

And thus must it needs follow, that she which soweth lust to the eye of man, do reap wrath in the sight of God.

Of the duty of wives toward their husbands

Son. Divers things are remembered in the holy scripture which do belong unto the office and duty of a true, honest and godly wife, which I will recite in order. The first is that she submit herself to the will of her husband and be content to be admonished, ruled and governed by him, knowledging him to be her head and lord and giving him such reverence and honour as the wife oweth to the husband by the word of God ...

The second point of an honest and godly matron is that she truly, dearly, faithfully and unfeignedly love her husband. And this her love toward her husband shall not rise from any carnal pleasure, beauty, riches, strength, nobility, goodliness of personage, or of any outward thing, but only of obedience toward the commandment of God ...

The third point of a virtuous matron is to look unto her house: to provide that nothing perisheth, decay or be lost through her negligence: to see that whatsoever be brought into the house by the industry, labour and provision of her husband be safely kept and warily bestowed ...

The fourth point of an honest and godly matron is patiently and quietly to bear the incommodities of her husband: to dissemble, cloak, hide and cover the faults and vices of her husband: not to upbraid nor to cast in his teeth; not to exasperate or sharpen her husband's mind through her churlishness, but rather with her soft, gentle and sober behaviour to quiet him, to pacify his anger, to mitigate his fury.... But some women are more like the furies of hell.... For their whole delight and pleasure is to scold, to brawl, to chide, and to be out of quiet with their husbands: so far is it off that with their godly conversation and gentle behaviour they go about to maintain amity and concord in their houses. And when they are reproved for their misdemeanour towards their husbands, they shame not to answer: *a woman hath none other weapon than her tongue, which she must needs put in practice. They have been made dolts and fools long enough!*

SERMONS

Thomas Adams, *Meditations upon the creed*

Text from: first published in *Works*, 1629, p. 1133.

The woman hath many adversaries that disdain her competition with man. Some will not allow her a soul, but they be soulless men. God *in his image created them*: not *him* only, but him and her, *them, male and female* [Gen. 1:27]; therefore, she hath a soul. Some will not allow her to be saved; yet the scripture is plain: *she shall be saved by childbearing* [1 Tim. 2:15]. *Two shall be grinding at the mill* [Matt. 24:41]: *duae*, two women, so is it originally; *one of them shall be saved*. Though Christ honoured our sex in that he was a man, not a woman: yet he was born of a woman and was begot of a man. And howsoever wicked women prove the most wicked sinners: yet the worst and greatest sin that ever was done was committed by man, not by woman: the crucifying of our Lord Jesus, not a woman had a hand in it: even Pilate's wife was against it, charging her husband, *to have nothing to do with that just man*. Woman was the principal in killing the first Adam, himself being accessory. But in killing of the second Adam, man was the principal and woman had not a finger in it. In a word, God in his image created them both on earth and God in his mercy hath provided them both a place in heaven. Concerning the creation of woman I observe three things: man's necessity, God's bounty, and the woman's conveniency.

1. Man's necessity: a whole world to use and so many millions of creatures to command had not been a perfect content for him without a partner. *For Adam there was not a help meet found for him* [Gen. 2:20]. He saw all the creatures, he saw them fit to be his servants, none to be his companions. Not that the necessity was such as if the maker's wisdom could not have multiplied man without the woman.... Secondly, for the propagation of the world: she is a *fruitful vine*, which is one means of her salvation as one end of her creation. Thirdly, to increase the Church of God, and by replenishing the earth to supply and store the kingdom of heaven. Fourthly, that from her might come the *promised seed*, which alone doth save us all ...

2. God's bounty: when man was made we do not read that he found the want of a helper: he that enjoyed God could want no contentment.... So God *built the woman*, she is called a *building*. First, because man was an unperfect building without her. Secondly, because the building of the family is by her ...

3. The woman's conveniency and fitness for man. She was not made out of the earth, which was the matter of man, nor out of the inferior creatures, which were the servants of man: but out of himself that she might be dear in estimation and equal in condition to him. Therefore she took her denomination from him, as her being out of him: of *man, woman....* *This is bone of my bone, and flesh of my flesh* [Gen. 2:23], saith Adam: not so much for the contemplation of her likeness, or consideration of her fitness, or sensible alteration in himself, as for the knowledge of her matter and to show his authority over her, he gave a name unto her: *she shall be called woman*. If she had been made by the request or will of Adam, or with the pain and detriment of Adam, she might afterward have been upbraided with her dependency and obligation. Now she owes nothing but to her creator: Adam can no more challenge ought from her for his rib than the earth can challenge from him. From a rib to a helper was a happy change: who was ever a loser by God's alteration? Whatsoever we have is his: when he taketh from us his

own, which he had, he will give us better things which we shall keep. He that gave man a woman to his helper, gave him by that woman a man to be his saviour.

William Whately, *A bride bush*

First preached as a wedding sermon, and subsequently published. Whately claims that his book will be a great help for those in marriage 'which now find it to be a little hell'. Text from: the first edition, 1617, pp. 36ff.

Marriage is honourable amongst all men: but whoremongers and adulterers God will judge.

Heb. 13:4

27.   Now proceed we to the woman's duty, and giving the men leave to chew the cud awhile, request the women to listen with more diligence than before. The whole duty of the wife is referred to two heads. The first is to acknowledge her inferiority, the next to carry herself as inferior. First then, the wife's judgement must be convinced that she is not her husband's equal, yea that her husband is her better by far: else there can be no contentment, either in her heart or in her house. If she stand upon terms of equality, much more of being better than he is, the very root of good carriage is withered, and the fountain thereof is dried up. Out of place, out of peace. And woe to these miserable aspiring shoulders, that content not themselves to take their room next below the head. If ever thou purpose to be a good wife, and to live comfortably, set down this with thy self. *Mine husband is my superior, my better*: he hath authority and rule over me: nature hath given it him, having framed our bodies to tenderness, men's to more hardness. God hath given it to him, saying to our first mother Eve, *thy desire shall be subject to him, and he shall rule over thee*. His will is the tie and tedder even of my desires and wishes. I will not strive against GOD and nature. Though my sin hath made my place tedious, yet I will confess the truth, *mine husband is my superior, my better*. If the wife do not learn this lesson perfectly, if she have it not without book, even at her fingers' ends as we speak, if her very heart condescend not to it, there will be wrangling, repining, striving, vying to be equal with him, or above him. And thus their life will be but a battle, and a trying of masteries. A woeful living.

28.   Secondly, the wife being resolved that her place is the lower, must carry herself as an inferior. It little boots to carry his authority in word, if she frame not submission indeed. Now she shall testify her inferiority in a Christian manner by practising those two virtues of reverence and obedience, which are appropriate to the place of inferiors.

29.   And first for reverence, the wife owes as much of that to her husband as the children or servants do to her, yea, as they do to him: only it is allowed

that it be sweetened with more love and more familiarity. The wife should not think so erroneously of her place as if she were not bound equally with the children and servants to reverence her husband: all inferiors owe reverence alike. The difference is only this: she may be more familiar, not more rude than they, as being more dear, not less subject to him.

30.   Also this reverence of hers must be both inward and outward. First her heart must she keep inwardly in a dutiful respect of him, and she must regard him as God's deputy, not looking to his person but his place; nor thinking so much who and what an one he is, as whose officer. This the apostle doth very strictly enjoin, saying: *let the wife see that she fear the husband* [Eph. 5]. As if he had said: of all things let her most carefully labour not to fail in this duty: for if she do, her whole life besides will be rude and unbeseeming. And you must know that the apostle means here not a slavish but a loving fear, such as may stand with the nearest union of hearts as between Christ and his church. And this fear is when, in consideration of his place, she doth abhor it as the greatest evil, next to the breach of God's commandment, to displease and offend her husband. Men stand in right awe of God, when they loath it as the greatest of all evils to break his commandment and grieve his spirit: and the wife fears her husband in good manner when she doth shun it as the next evil, to displease, grieve and disobey her husband who is next to God above her in the family. Such regard her heart must have of her head, that it keep hand and tongue and all from disorder. I know this is not customable, nay it is scarce thought seemly amongst many women; nay they care as little for their husbands as they for them; yea they despise them; yea they have inverted this precept, and cause their husbands to fear them. This impudence, this unwomanhood tracks the way to the harlot's house, and gives all wise men to know that such have, or would, or soon will, cast off the care of honesty, as of loyalty...

31.   And as the heart principally, so next the outward behaviour must be regarded in three special things. First in speeches and gestures unto him. These must carry the stamp of fear upon them, and not be cutted,[8] sharp, sullen, passionate, tetchy; but meek, quiet, submissive, which may show that she consider who herself is, and to whom she speaks. The wife's tongue towards her husband must be neither keen, nor loose; her countenance neither swelling nor deriding; her behaviour not flinging, nor puffing, not discontented; but favouring of all lowliness and quietness of affection. Look what kinds of words or behaviour thou wouldst dislike from thy servant or child, those must thou not give to thine husband: for thou art equally commanded to be subject... how subject women are to disreverent behaviour, and withal how loathsome, how unwomanly they be. Yet for all these warnings we have some women that can chase and scold with their husbands, and rail upon them, and revile them, and shake them together with

32

such terms and carriage, as were unsufferable towards a servant. Stains of womankind, blemishes of their sex, monsters in nature, botches of human society, rude, graceless, impudent, next to harlots, if not the same with them. Let such words leave a blister behind them, and let the canker eat out these tongues ...

32.   Secondly, the wife must express reverence towards her husband in her speeches and gestures before him and in his presence to others. His company must make her more respective how she carries herself towards any else. Her words must not be loud and snappish to the children, to the servants in his sight. If she perceive a fault, yet she must consider that her better stands by and not speak without necessity; and then utter that in more still and mild manner, which in his absence she may set on with more roundness. No woman of government will allow her children and servants to be loud and brawling before her: and shall she before her husband be so herself? What is become of inferiority then? Yea her reverence doth enjoin her silence when she stands by. I mean not utter abstinence from speech, but using few words, and those low and mild, not eager, not loud ...

33.   Thirdly, the woman's speeches of the husband behind his back, must be dutiful and respective. She must not call him by light names, nor talk of him with any kind of carelessness and slightness of speech, much less with despiteful and reproachful terms. Herein the godly fact of *Sarah*, commended to our imitation, must be followed in practice. When she thought of her husband in the absence of all company she entitled him by the name of *my Lord*. If in her private conceit she gave him so good and honourable titles, what would she have done in company? What in his own presence? So the women must inure themselves to submissiveness of thoughts and speeches in their husband's absence, that they may the better practise the same in their presence: for custom in this thing hath great force. Who would brook a child speaking disgracefully and murmuringly of his father behind his back? And shall it be suffered in a wife? By how much here is more certain trail of her inward affection and disposition, by so much must she be more attentive to her words in such case. Very dread may make a woman give good words before her husband's face, because she dares do no other, and he will brook none other. But this shows a conscionable subjection, when she will not think nor speak of him, though he be far from hearing, without some note of good regard: that those which hear may perceive that she doth account of him as her governor and her better. He that allows not an evil thought of the prince, will not allow evil speeches of the husband in private talks between neighbours, for he is the household prince, the domestical king: though thy husband be from thee, let thy fear of him be with thee, that in mentioning him to others thou show not contempt ...

34.   Obedience follows: as concerning which duty a plain text avers it to

the full, saying: *let the wife be subject to her husband in all things, in the Lord.* What need we further proof? Why is she his wife if she will not obey? And how can she require obedience of the children and servants, if she will not yield to the husband? Doth not she exact it in his name, and as his deputy? But the thing will not be so much questioned, as the measure: not whether she must obey, but how far. Wherefore we must extend it as far as the apostle, to a generality of things, to all things, so it be in the Lord. In whatsoever thing obeying of him doth not disobey God, she must obey: and if not in all things, it were as good in nothing. It is a thankless service if not general. To yield alone in things that please herself, is not to obey him but her own affections. The trial of obedience is when it crosseth her desires. To do that which he bids when she would have done without his bidding, what praise is it? But this declares conscionable submission: when she chooseth to do what herself would not, because her husband wills it. And seeing she requireth the like largeness of duty in his name from the servants, herself shall be judge against herself, if she give not what she looks to receive. But it sufficeth not that her obedience reach to all things that are lawful, unless it be also willing, ready, without brawling, contending, thwarting, sourness. A good work may be marred in the manner of doing.... Then it is laudable, commendable, a note of a virtuous woman, a dutiful wife when she submits herself with quietness, cheerfully, even as a well-broken horse turns at the least turning, stands at the least check of the rider's bridle, readily going and standing as he wishes that sits upon his back: if you will have your obedience worth anything, make no tumult about it outwardly, allow none within.

35.   And for the less principal duties of husband and wife concerning their ordinary society, thus much. I come now to such as concern the marriage bed, which are as needful to be known as the former, because offences in that kind are more capital and dangerous, though not so public. Their matrimonial meetings must have three properties. First, it must be cheerful: they must lovingly, willingly, and familiarly communicate themselves unto themselves, which is the best means to continue and nourish their mutual natural love, and by which the true and proper ends of matrimony shall be attained in best manner: for the husband is not his own but the wife's, and the wife the husband's. Secondly, their meeting must be sanctified. *Paul* saith meat, drink and marriage are good and sanctified by prayer. Men and women must not come together as brute creatures and unreasonable beasts through the heat of desire; but must see their maker in that his ordinance, and crave his blessing solemnly as at meals (the apostle speaks of both alike), that marriage may indeed be blessed unto them. To sanctify the marriage bed and use it reverently with prayer and thanksgiving will make it moderate and keep them from growing weary of each other (as in many it falls out), and cause that lust shall be assuaged, which else shall be increased by these

meetings. Propagation and chastity, the two chief ends of marriage, are best attained by prayer and thanksgiving in the use thereof, without which they will hardly come, or not with comfort. Neither is it more than needs, to see God in that which so nearly toucheth ourselves, as the hope of posterity; him, as the increase of his kingdom. Let Christians therefore know the fruit of prayer, even in all things. Thirdly, their nuptial meetings must be seasonable, and at lawful times. There is a season when God and Nature sejoins[9] man and wife in this respect. The woman is made to be fruitful; and therefore also moist and cold of constitution. Hence it is that their natural heat serves not to turn all their sustenance into their own nourishment; but a quantity redounding is set apart in a convenient place to cherish and nourish the conception, when they shall conceive. Now this redundant humour (called their flowers or terms) hath (if no conception be) its monthly issue or evacuation (and in some oftener) unless there be extraordinary stoppings and obstructions, lasting for six or seven days in the most. Sometimes also this issue, through weakness and infirmity of nature, doth continue many more days. Always after childbirth there is a larger and longer emptying because of the former retention, which continueth commonly for four, five or six weeks, and some longer. Now in all these three times and occasions, it is simply unlawful for a man to company with his own wife. The Lord tells us so. *Leviticus* 15 vers 19–25; also ch. 18 ver. 19; also ch. 20 ver. 18. Of which places it is needful that married persons should take note: to which I send them. Neither let women think themselves disgraced, because I have laid this matter open in plain but modest speeches. Where God threatens death to the offender, can the minister be faithful if he do not plainly declare the offence? This fault is by GOD condemned to the punishment of death, *Leviticus* 20:18.

WOMEN PREACHING

Thomas Edwards, *Gangraena*

Edwards's work was one of the major attacks against: 'the blasphemies and pernicious practices of the sectaries of this time, vented and acted in England in these last four years' (frontispiece). Text from: the first edition, 1646, pp. 116–18.

Among all the confusion and disorder in church matters, both of opinions and practices, and particularly of all sorts of mechanics taking upon them to preach and baptise, as smiths, taylors, pedlars, weavers, etc., there are also some women preachers in our times who keep constant lectures, preaching weekly to many men and women. In ... London are women who for some time together have preached weekly on every Tuesday about four of the clock, unto whose preachings many have resorted. I shall particularly give the reader an account of the preaching of two women (one a lace woman that sells lace in Cheapside, and dwells in Bell Alley in Coleman Street, the other a major's wife living in the Old Bailey).... These women came with their Bibles in their hands and went to a table, the lace woman took her place at the upper end; the gentlewoman, the major's wife, sat on one side by her; the third woman stood on the other side of the table; the lace woman at the upper end of the table turned herself first to this gentlewoman (who was in her hoods, necklace of pearl, watch by her side, and other apparel suitable) and entreated her to begin, extolling her for her gifts and great abilities. This gentlewoman refused to begin, pleading her weakness; and extolling this lace woman who spake to her; then the lace woman replied again to the gentlewoman, this was nothing but her humility and modesty, for her gifts were well known; but the gentlewoman refused it again, falling into a commendation of the gifts of the lace woman; whereupon this lace woman turned herself to the company and spake to some of them to exercise, excusing herself that she was somewhat indisposed in body and unfit for this work, and said if anyone there had a word of exhortation let them speak; but all the company kept silent, none speaking. Then the lace woman began with making a speech to this purpose, that now those days were come and that was fulfilled which was spoken of in the scriptures, that God would pour out of his spirit upon the handmaidens and they should prophesy, and after this speech she made a prayer for almost half an hour, and after her prayer took that text, *if ye love me keep my commandments*. When she had read the text she laboured to analyse the chapter as well she could, and then spake upon the text, drawing her doctrines, opening them, and making two uses, for the space of some three-quarters of an hour; when she had done she spake to the company and said, if any had anything to object against any of the matter delivered they might speak, for that was their custom to give liberty in that kind (but though there was a great company both of men and women) yet no man objected, but all held their peace. Then the gentlewoman that sat at the side of the table began to speak, making some apology that she was not so fit at this time in regard of some bodily indispositions and she told the company she would speak upon that matter her sister had handled and would proceed to a use of examination whether we love Christ or no; and in the handling of it she propounded to open what love was, and what were the grounds of our love, and how we should know it and as she was preaching one in the company cried *speak out*: whereupon she lifted up her voice; but some spake the second time, *speak out*, so that upon this the gentlewoman was disturbed and confounded in her discourse, and went off from that of love to speak upon 1 John 4, *of trying the spirits*, but she could make nothing of it, speaking nonsense all along; whereupon some of the company spake again and the gentlewoman went on speaking, jumbling together some things against those who despised the ordinances of God and the ministry of the word; and upon that some present spake yet once more, so that she was amazed and confounded, that she knew not what she said, and was forced to give over and sit down. The lace woman who preached first, seeing all this, looked upon those who had interrupted her sister with an angry bold countenance, setting her face against them and she fell upon concluding all with prayer, and in her prayer she prayed to God about them who despised his ambassadors and ministers that he had sent into the world to reconcile the world; whereupon some fell a-speaking in her prayer, *ambassadors, ministers, you ambassadors!*, with words to that purpose; and upon those words she prayed expressly that God would send some visible judgement from heaven upon them: and upon those words some of the company spake aloud, praying God to stop her mouth and so she was forced to give over. In brief there was such laughing, confusion, and disorder at that meeting, that the minister professed he never saw the like: he told me the confusions, horror and disorder which he saw and heard there was unexpressible and so he left them fearing least the candles might have gone out and they have fallen to kill or mischief one another.[10]

Margaret Fell Fox, *Women's preaching justified*

Fell Fox preached and consulted with all the figures in the Quaker movement, and was regarded as a prophet by many of them. Text from: the first edition, 1666, pp. 3ff.

And it shall come to pass, in the last days, saith the Lord, I will pour out of my spirit upon all flesh; your sons and daughters shall prophesy.

(Acts 2:27. Joel 2:28)

It is written in the prophets, they shall be all taught of God, saith Christ.

(John 6:45)

And all thy children shall be taught of the Lord, and great shall be the peace of thy children.

(Isa. 54:13)

And they shall teach no more every man his neighbour, and every man his brother, saying, know the Lord; for they shall all know me from the least to the greatest of them, saith the Lord.

(Jer. 31:34)

Whereas it hath been an objection in the minds of many, and several times hath been objected by the clergy and ministers and others, against women's speaking in the church; and so consequently may be taken that they are condemned for meddling in the things of God; the ground of which objection is taken from the apostle's words, which he writ in his first epistle to the *Corinthians* [14:34,35]. And also what he writ to *Timothy* in the first epistle, 2:11,12. But how far they wrong the apostle's intentions in these scriptures, we shall show clearly when we come to them in their course and order. But first let me lay down how God himself manifested his will and mind concerning women and unto women.

And first, when *God created man in his own image; in the image of God he created them, male and female; and God blessed them and said unto them, be fruitful and multiply, and God said, behold I have given you every herb &c.* Here God joins them together in his own image and makes no such distinctions and differences as men do; for though they be weak, he is strong; and as he said to the apostle, *his grace is sufficient, and his strength is made manifest in weakness,* 2 Cor. 12:9. And such the Lord hath chosen, even *the weak things of the world, to confound the things that are mighty; and things which are despised, hath God chosen to bring to nought things that are,* 1 Cor. 1. And God hath put no such difference between the male and the female as men would make ...

Let this word of the Lord, which was from the beginning, stop the mouths of all that oppose women's speaking in the power of the Lord: for he hath put enmity between the woman and the serpent; and if the seed of the woman speak not, the seed of the serpent speaks: for God hath put enmity between the two seeds, and it is manifest that those who speak against the woman and her seed's speaking, speak out of the enmity of the old serpent's seed: and God hath fulfilled his word and his promise, *when the fullness of time was come, he hath sent forth his son, made of a woman, made under the Law, that we might receive the adoption of sons,* Gal. 4:4,5.

Moreover, the Lord is pleased, when he mentions the church, to call her by the name of *woman* by his prophets, saying: *I have called thee as a woman forsaken, and grieved in spirit, and as a wife in youth,* Isa. 54 ...

Thus much may prove that the Church of Christ is a woman, and those that speak against woman's speaking, speak against the Church of Christ, and the seed of woman, which seed is Christ: that is to say, those that speak against the power of the Lord, and the spirit of the Lord speaking in a woman, simply by reason of her sex or because she is a woman, not regarding the seed and spirit and power that speaks in her, such speak against Christ and his church and are of the seed of the serpent, wherein lodgeth the enmity. And as God the father made no such difference in the first creation, nor never since between the male and the female, but always out of his loving mercy and kindness had regard unto the weak, so also his son Jesus Christ confirms the same thing when the Pharisees came to him and asked him whether it were lawful for a man to put away his wife? He answered and said unto them, *have you not read that he that made them in the beginning, made them male and female, and said: for this cause shall a man leave his father and mother and cleave unto his wife, and they twain shall be one flesh, wherefore they are no more twain but one flesh. What therefore God hath joined together let no man put asunder, Matt. 19.*

✢ ✢ ✢

Mark this, you that despise and oppose the message of the Lord God that he sends by women: what had become of the redemption of the whole body of mankind if they had not believed the message that Lord Jesus sent by these women of and concerning his Resurrection? And if these women had not thus, out of their tenderness and bowels of love, who had received mercy and grace, and forgiveness of sins, and virtue and healing from him; which many men also had received the like, if their hearts had not been so united and knit unto him in love, that they could not depart as the men did, but sat watching and waiting, and weeping about the sepulchre until the time of his Resurrection, and so were ready to carry his message, as is manifested; else how should his disciples have known, who were not there?

✢ ✢ ✢

And now to the apostle's words, which is the ground of the great objection against women's speaking. And first 1 Cor. 14, let the reader seriously read that chapter, and see the end and drift of the apostle in speaking these words: for the apostle is there exhorting the *Corinthians* unto charity, and to desire spiritual gifts, and not to speak in an unknown tongue; and not to be children in understanding, but to be children in malice, but in understanding to be men; and that the spirits of the prophets should be subject to the prophets, for God is not the author of confusion, but of peace: and then he saith: *let your women keep silence in the church &c.*

Where it doth plainly appear that the women, as well as others that were among them, were in confusion: for he saith: *how is it brethren? When we come together every one of you had a psalm, hath a doctrine, hath a tongue, hath a revelation, hath an interpretation? Let all things be done to edifying.* Here was no edifying, but all was in confusion speaking together; therefore he saith: *if any man speak in an unknown tongue, let it be by two, or at most three, and that by course, and let one interpret; but if there be no interpreter, let him keep silence in the church.* Here the man is commanded to keep silence as well as the woman, when they are in confusion and out of order.

But the apostle saith further: *they are commanded to be in obedience, as also saith the Law; and if they will learn anything, let them ask their husbands at home; for it is a shame for a woman to speak in the church.*

Here the apostle clearly manifests his intent, for he speaks of women that were under the Law, and in that transgression as Eve was, and such as were to learn, and not to speak publicly, but they must first ask their husbands at

39

home, and it was a shame for such to speak in the church: and it appears clearly that such women were speaking among the *Corinthians*, by the apostle's exhorting them from malice and strife and confusion, and he preacheth the law unto them, and he saith in the Law it is written: *with men of other tongues and other lips will I speak unto this people*, ver. 2.

And what is all this to women's speaking? That have the everlasting gospel to preach, and upon whom the promise of the Lord is fulfilled, and his spirit poured upon them according to his word, *Acts* 2:16,17,18. And if the apostle would have stopped such as had the spirit of the Lord poured upon them, why did he say just before, *if any thing be revealed to another that sitteth by, let the first hold his peace?* And: *you may all prophesy one by one.* Here he did not say that such women should not prophesy as had the revelation and spirit of God poured upon them; but their women that were under the law and in the transgression and were in strife, confusion and malice in their speaking . . .

2

PHYSIOLOGY

INTRODUCTION

In 1617 Jacques Olivier wrote a popular misogynist tract which was republished seventeen times in the subsequent hundred years, and translated into English in 1662 by an anonymous author (T.M.). Several rather worn editions of the original French versions are available in British libraries, suggesting an eager English readership. Part of the preface reads:

> [woman] you live here on earth as the world's most imperfect creature: the scum of nature, the cause of misfortune, the source of quarrels, the toy of the foolish, the plague of the wise, the stirrer of hell, the tinder of vice, the guardian of excrement, a monster in nature, an evil necessity, a multiple chimera, a sorry pleasure, Devil's bait, the enemy of angels.
>
> (*An Alphabet of Women's Imperfections*, p. 1)[1]

This extreme assertion of misogyny is striking to a modern reader because it combines and interweaves an essentialist account of woman's function ('the most imperfect creature ... an evil necessity') with assertions about woman's character, and consequently her theological, social and political inferiority.

The construction of womanhood in the early modern period was based upon two essentialist ideologies: the Hebraic-Christian tradition of equating Eve with the Fall (represented in chapter 1) and the Galenic-Aristotelian account of her 'nature' – that is, her physiology and biological function. The essential explanations about women's identity are continually used in most writings about women and form the base upon which her place and function in society was described. In this sense, little has changed in 400 years: women are still described and circumscribed by biology as the basis of all identity, whilst men are characterised as beyond or above biology in every area except ageing.[2]

Despite the increase in scientific and empirical knowledge in the sixteenth century about the skeleton and the body, discoveries about woman's physiology were remarkably slow. Thus, for example, the microscopic sperm was discovered in

41

the late seventeenth century, a few years after the first use of the microscope, but the ovum was not discovered until 1827. Beliefs about woman's physiology continued to be based upon Aristotle and Galen (pp. 43 ff. and pp. 47 ff.). Aristotle provided the philosophical underpinning of understanding about gender through his distinction between form (masculine) and matter (feminine) whilst Galen provided the physiological framework in which woman's health and identity were discussed. The issues upon which medical, scientific and advice books focused were: what do the sexual organs look like and how do they work (pp. 57, 64)? What are sperm, and do both sexes produce them (pp. 44–50)? What determines sex (pp. 64–5)? Why do women menstruate (p. 47)? How can women's illnesses be explained and cured (pp. 48–9, 60–4)? What function does woman have in the generative process (pp. 43–7)? With the exception of the last question, the answers to these remained fairly constantly based upon humoral theory throughout the early modern period.

Galenic humoral theory stated that all humans were constructed of a mixture of the four humours (hot, dry, moist and cold), and that men were hot and dry, whilst women were moist and cold. Good health was maintained by recognising a perfect balance between the humours, and letting blood where necessary to obtain that balance and in order to rid the body of excess and poisonous humours. Sperm and woman's 'seed' were concocted from the humours and reflected respectively the nature of the man (hot and dry) or the woman (cold and moist). Menstruation was explained as the need for women to expel poisonous humours which could not be absorbed and burned into her body because her humour was too cold.[3] Women's illnesses were nearly all ascribed to disturbances in her menstrual and humoral cycle, and the balance of her humours also explained the structure of her internal sexual organs, which in turn determined women's diseases (pp. 48, 59).[4]

In addition to the humoral account of physiology, the role of the woman in reproduction was discussed in terms of anatomy. Until the late sixteenth century in scientific circles, and long after in popular accounts, men and women's sexual organs were described and explained using the same terms, wherein women's organs had simply been left inside the body because there was not sufficient heat to push them out. Thus both men and women had testes and gonads; they both produced 'seed', although woman's was not capable of generation. In anatomical drawings of this period the labia, vagina and womb are rendered as an inverted penis and testicles (see the drawing from Raynald's translation of *The birth of mankind*, figure 3).

After the development of anatomy studies inspired by Vesalius, Fallopius published his *Anatomical Observations* in 1562, which described the sexual organs of both men and women as distinct to each sex. This discovery subsequently informed both descriptive accounts of women's bodies and theoretical explanations of her function in generation (pp. 51–2). Thus, for example, Crooke's *Microcosmographia* (1631, p. 56) suggests that by this time popular medical writing had acknowledged the uniqueness of woman's place in this process, and saw the sexes as different. Nevertheless, accounts of generation still gave priority, in the older Aristotelian way, to the man's seed: his was active and the woman's 'seed' was the passive receptacle or bed in which his seed might grow. Such accounts continued to uphold the Galenic theory of the humours which, despite the anatomical observations, effectively continued to assign woman an inferior physiological state to that of man. Thus even Harvey's publication in 1651 of his *De generatione animalium*, in which he posited the existence of a female egg, analogous to that in chickens, continued to describe the sperm as the formative generative force.[5] In other words, even in the most advanced scientific texts of the day the old essentialist notions of woman as cold, moist and passive dominated the way in which scientists interpreted their evidence. These accounts privilege gender (that is, the characteristics associated culturally and socially with a biological sex), over biological sex. The humours are descriptions of socialised characteristics, which were sexualised.[6] In humoral theory sexual identity can thus exist on a continuum: there can be manly women and womanly men, because there can be dry cold women or moist hot men. Gender identity is thus more fluid in this period, before anatomical sex becomes the defining feature of sexual identity.

Finally, although sexual pleasure is not central to any of these accounts (sex was for procreation or, in extremes, humoral excretion), Galenic theory claimed that women needed to achieve an orgasm in order to conceive, because that was the only means by which her seed could be released (pp. 57–8). In addition, some writers either advise women suffering from womb hysteria to marry, or encourage midwives to manipulate their clitorises to expel the evil humours (p. 62). In theory, then, sexual pleasure for Renaissance women was thus intimately linked to the fundamental purpose of sexual intercourse: hence advice on how to achieve 'healthy' orgasms is part and parcel of the physiological literature.

ARISTOTLE

Aristotle's works were still the dominant scientific textbooks for laymen as well as trainee physicians and surgeons during the seventeenth century. They were printed in Latin. Text from: *The history of animals*, transl. T. Taylor, 1812, vol. 6, p. 342 (bk 9, ch. 1); and *The generation of animals*, ed. and transl. A.L. Peck, Loeb Library, vol. 366, Cambridge, Mass., 1943, pp. 95–7.

The history of animals

In all those genera of animals, however, in which there is the male and the female nature has nearly similarly distinguished the manners of the females from those of the males; but this is particularly evident in the human species, in the larger animals and in the viviparous quadrupeds. For the manners of the females are more soft, they more rapidly become mild, and are more tractable and docile.... Vestiges, indeed, of these manners are, as I may say, in all animals; but they are more apparent in those whose manners are more characteristic, and most of all man. For man has the most perfect nature of all animals so that all these habits are in him more apparent. Hence woman is more compassionate than man, and has a greater propensity to tears. She is also more envious, more querulous, more slanderous, and more contentious. Further still, the female is more dispirited, more despondent, more impudent, and more given to falsehood, than the male. She is, likewise, more easily deceived, and more apt to remember; and again the female is more vigilant, less active, and, in short, less disposed to motion, and receptive of less nutrient than the male. But the male, as we have observed, is more disposed to give assistance in danger, and is more courageous than the female.

The generation of animals

Thus much then is evident: the menstrual fluid is a residue, and it is the analogous thing in females to the semen in males. Its behaviour shows that this statement is correct. At the same time of life that semen begins to appear in males and is emitted, the menstrual discharge begins to flow in females, their voice changes and their breasts begin to become conspicuous; and similarly in the decline of life the power to generate ceases in males, and the menstrual discharge ceases in females. Here are still further indications that this secretion which females produce is a residue. Speaking generally, unless the menstrual discharge is suspended, women are not troubled by haemorrhoids or bleeding from the nose or any other such discharge, and if it happens that they are, then the evacuations fall off in quantity, which suggests that the substance secreted is being drawn off to the other discharges. Again, their blood vessels are not so prominent as those of males; and females are more neatly made and smoother than males, because the residue which goes to produce those characteristics in males is in females discharged together with the menstrual fluid. We are bound to hold, in addition, that for the same cause the bulk of the body in female Vivipara is smaller than that of the males, as of course it is only in Vivipara that the menstrual discharge flows externally and most conspicuously of all in women who discharge a greater amount than any other female animals. On this account it is always very noticeable that the female is pale and the blood vessels are not prominent and there is an obvious deficiency in physique as compared with the males.

Now it is impossible that any creature should produce two seminal secretions at once, and as the secretion in females which answers to semen in males is the menstrual fluid, it obviously follows that the female does not contribute any semen in generation; for if there were semen there would be no menstrual fluid; but as the menstrual fluid is in fact formed, therefore there is no semen.

We have said why it is that the menstrual fluid as well as semen is a residue. In support of this, there are a number of facts concerning animals which may be adduced. (1) fat animals produce less semen than lean ones, as we said before, and the reason is that fat is a residue just as semen is, i.e., it is blood that has been concocted, only not in the same way as semen. Hence it is not surprising that when the residue has been consumed to make fat, the semen is deficient.... (2) Here is an indication that the female does not discharge semen of the same kind as the male, and that the offspring is not formed from a mixture of two semens, as some allege. Very often the female conceives although she has derived no pleasure from the act of coitus; and on the contrary side, when the female derives as much pleasure as the male, and they both keep the same pace, the female does not bear, unless there is a proper amount of menstrual liquid (as it is called) present.

☆ ☆ ☆

By now it is plain that the contribution which the female makes to generation is the *matter* used therein, that this is to be found in the substance constituting the menstrual fluid, and finally that the menstrual fluid is a residue.

There are some who think that the female contributes semen during coition because women sometimes derive pleasure from it comparable to that of the male and also produce a fluid secretion. This fluid, however, is not seminal; it is peculiar to the part from which it comes in each several individual; there is a discharge from the uterus, which though it happens in some women does not in others. Speaking generally, this happens in fair-skinned women who are typically feminine, and not in dark women of a masculine appearance. Where it occurs, this discharge is sometimes on quite a different scale from the semen discharged by the male, and greatly exceeds it in bulk. Furthermore, differences of food cause a great difference in the amount of discharge produced: e.g. some pungent foods cause a noticeable increase in the amount.

The pleasure which accompanies copulation is due to the fact that not only semen but also *pneuma* is emitted: it is from this *pneuma* as it collects together that the emission of semen really results. This is plain in the case of boys who cannot yet emit semen, though they are not far from the age for it, and in infertile men, because all of them derive pleasure from attrition. Indeed, men whose generative organs have been destroyed sometimes suffer from looseness of the bowels caused by residue which cannot be concocted and converted into semen being secreted into the intestine.

Further a boy actually resembles a woman in physique, and a woman is as it were an infertile male; the female, in fact, is female on account of inability of a sort, viz. it lacks the power to concoct semen out of the final state of the nourishment (this is either blood, or its counterpart in bloodless animals) because of the coldness of its nature. Thus, just as lack of concoction produces in the bowels diarrhoea, so in the blood vessels it produces discharges of blood of various sorts, and especially the menstrual discharge (which has to be classed as a discharge of blood, though it is a natural discharge, and the rest are morbid ones).

Hence, plainly, it is reasonable to hold that generation takes place from this process; for, as we see, the menstrual fluid is semen, not indeed semen in a pure condition, but needing still to be acted upon. It is the same with fruit when it is forming. The nourishment is present right enough even before it has been strained off, but it stands in need of being acted upon in order to purify it. That is why when the former is mixed with the semen, and when the latter is mixed with pure nourishment, the one effects generation, and the other effects nutrition.

An indication that the female emits no semen is actually afforded by the fact that in intercourse the pleasure is produced in the same place as in the male by contact, yet this is not the place from which the liquid is emitted ... Here is an indication that semen resides in the menstrual discharge. As I said before, this residue is formed in males at the same time of life as the menstrual discharge becomes noticeable in females; which suggests that the places which are the receptacles of these residues also become differentiated at the same time in each sex; and as the neighbouring places in each sex become less firm in their consistency, the pubic hair grows up too. Just before these places receive their differentiation, they are swelled up by *pneuma*: in males this is clearer in regard to the testes, but it is also to be noticed in the breasts; whereas in females it is clearer in the breasts; it is when the breasts have risen a couple of fingers' breadth that the menstrual discharge begins in most women.

* * *

The male provides the 'form' and the 'principle of the movement', the female provides the body, in other words, the material. Compare the coagulation of milk. Here the milk is the body, and the fig-juice or the rennet contains the principle which causes it to set. The semen of the male acts in the same way as it gets divided up into portions within the female.

* * *

Consider now the physical part of the semen. (That is which, when it is emitted by the male, is accompanied by a part of the soul-principle and acts as its vehicle. Partly this soul principle is separable from physical matter – this applies to those animals where some sort of divine element is included, and what we call reason is of this character – partly it is inseparable.) This physical part of the semen, being fluid and watery, dissolves and evaporates; and on that account we should not always be trying to detect it leaving the female externally, or to find it as an ingredient of the fetation when that has set and taken shape, any more than we should expect to trace the fig-juice which sets and curdles milk. The fig-juice undergoes a change; it does not remain as a part of the bulk which is set and curdled; and the same applies to the semen.

We have now determined in what sense fetations and semen have soul and in what sense they have not, they have soul *in potentiality*, but not in *actuality*.

As semen is a residue, and as it is endowed with the same movement as that in virtue of which the body grows through the distribution of the ultimate nourishment, when the semen enters the uterus it sets the residue produced by the female and imparts to it the same movement with which it is itself endowed. The female's contribution, of course, is a residue too, just as the male's is, and contains all the parts of the body *potentially*, though none in *actuality*; and all includes those parts which distinguish the two sexes. Just as it sometimes happens that deformed offspring are produced by deformed parents, and sometimes not, so the offspring produced by a female are sometimes female, sometimes not, but male. The reason is that the female is as it were a deformed male; and the menstrual discharge is semen, though in an impure condition: i.e. it lacks one constituent, and one only, the principle of soul.

2 Galen, *On the usefulness of the parts of the body*

Galen's writings were the physiological base for all medical knowledge and practice until the eighteenth century. Text from: Galen, *On the usefulness of the parts of the body*, transl. Margaret Tallmadge May, Cornell University Press, 1968, vol. II, pp. 630–2.

1. Now just as mankind is the most perfect of all animals, so within mankind the man is more perfect than the woman, and the primary instrument. Hence in those animals that have less of it, her workmanship is necessarily more imperfect, and so it is no wonder that the female is less perfect than the male by as much as she is colder than he. In fact, just as the mole has imperfect eyes, though certainly not as imperfect as they are in those animals that do not have any trace of them at all, so too the woman is less perfect than the man in respect to the generative parts. For the parts were formed within her when she was still a foetus, but could not because of the

47

defect in the heat emerge and project on the outside, and this, though making the animal itself that was being formed less perfect than one that is complete in all respects, provided no small advantage for the race: for there needs must be a female. Indeed you ought not to think that our creator would purposely make half the whole race imperfect and, as it were, mutilated, unless there was to be some great advantage in such a mutilation.

2.   Let me tell what this is. The foetus needs abundant material both when it is first constituted, and for the entire period of growth that follows.... Accordingly it was better for the female to be made enough colder so that she cannot disperse all the nutriment which she concocts and elaborates.... This is the reason the female was made cold, and the immediate consequence of this is the imperfection of the parts, which cannot emerge on the outside on account of the defect in the heat, another very great advantage for the continuance of the race. For, remaining within, that which would have become the scrotum if it had emerged on the outside, was made into the substance of the uteri, an instrument fitted to receive and retain the semen and to nourish and perfect the foetus.

3.   Forthwith, of course, the female must have smaller, less perfect testes, and the semen generated in them must be scantier, colder and wetter (for these things too follow of necessity from the deficient heat). Certainly such semen would be incapable of generating an animal.... The testes of the male are as much larger as he is the warmer animal. The semen generated in them, having received the peak of concoction, becomes the efficient principle of the animal. Thus from one principle, devised by the creator in his wisdom, that principle in accordance with which the female has been made less perfect than the male, have stemmed all these things useful for the generation of the animal: that the parts of the female cannot escape to the outside; that she accumulates an excess of useful nutriment and has imperfect semen and a hollow instrument to receive the perfect semen; that since everything in the male is the opposite (of what it is in the female), the male member has been elongated to be most suitable for coitus and the excretion of semen; and that his semen itself has been made thick, abundant, and warm.

GYNACEA

Gynacea collected up-to-date medical texts and published them for physicians and surgeons during the sixteenth and early seventeenth centuries. This particular edition by Spachius combined all the earlier works. Text from: Johann Spachius, ed., Gynacea, 1597, transl. Stephen O'Connor, 1994, pp. 774–7, 803–6.

Martin Akakia, *On women's illnesses*

On the procreation of humankind and the nature of woman

Since of the two originators of generation, one corresponds to form, the other to matter, the female seeks the male in the same way as matter seeks form, and the more perfect the species to which the female belongs, as in the human race, the more the female desires the male, because the more efficient is sought by the woman, since she has greater knowledge than the female in other animals. And as the female seeks males, so the male seeks females. But also in the human race, nature, because of the nobility of the species, does not distort this attraction: the males seeks so that they may be emptied, the females so that they may be filled. This goes back, as we understand, to the Peripatetics: that the female only gives place and matter to future generations, but does not provide seed for generation. So ch. 20, book 1 of *De generatione animalium* says that a woman is like a man without seed, and has a certain impotence, which is established partly by probable reasons and partly by necessity. The probable are, that a woman in copulation excretes a certain fluid (of the kind which lubricates the genitals) yet it does not carry seed, but belongs to the womb since its large quantity exceeds the amount of semen. Secondly, that in conception the same thing happens as in the curdling of milk: for the body or matter is the milk, the sap is the curdling agent or cause of the reaction. So in conception the female supplies matter only, namely the blood, the male provides the form, that is to say the semen ... but there is one form of one thing, not many: therefore if male and female were to make semen for generation, since semen contains the principle of form, it should follow that there is a double form of the one that is generated, seeing that there are two seeds. Therefore as there can only be one form for one thing, so there can only be one originator containing that form, therefore one semen.

* * *

When I say man and woman I am putting them in the prime of life, neither growing up nor growing old, but that perfect age in which both can be said to be perfect: although the prime of life does not always produce semen that generates, because as Aristotle says, ch. 18, book 1, *De gen. animal.*: some have too little semen, others do not ejaculate anything, not through imbecility but because they carry less in the body and they become fleshier and fatter: for fattening goats have less semen, or none. Besides it is established in book I, *De semine* ch. 9 and *De gen. animal.* ch. 4, book II, in certain species even at the perfect age semen which is ejected at the first copulation is less generative, but is more so at the second and the third, although reason would seem to hold the opposite. But it happens accordingly because at the first copulation certain discharges, moist and full of phlegm are mixed with it, and it is shown from ch. 1, book vii, *De historia animalium*.... And Aristotle has written this in ch. 18, book 11, *De generatione animalium*, that menstrual fluid in virgins and semen in the effeminate, and in those not yet in puberty and in the infertile is lacking altogether or at least there is very little. Although, it is true, vigorous old age and puberty carry semen, it is either infertile or at least of the kind that from it only women are born. Aristotle defines vigorous old age (ch. 6, book vii, *De historia animalium*) in males at 60 or at most 70, which is the latest point at which young can be generated: in women up to their fiftieth year is very rare. Generally speaking 56 is the end of procreation for males and 45 for females. Puberty he defines at 14, since the voice in the males begins to deepen and the testes to swell and the genitals to be covered with hair. So in woman at 12, for by that time, the menstrual cycle has begun and the breasts swell. In both, the semen is not fruitful, according to Aristotle ch. 1, book vii, *De hist. anim.*.... For the first emission of semen in the young is either infertile or if it is fertile, procreates imbeciles only or smaller offspring. This being the case, Plato in the *Republic* recommends that men should not marry before they are 30 and women not before 20, and he requests that a man refrain from this activity at 55 and a woman at 40, because between these ages animal vigour is whole, but either side of them it is not. Aristotle is not very different from his master: in ch. 6, book vii of the *Politics* he says that the end of fertility for men is 70, for women 50, and that they should so marry that they reach this limit in age at the same time. For he says that the union of adolescents lacks the skill for procreating children, because births are imperfect and a woman is born more frequently than males, and they are of short stature, from which arises the conjecture that in those states in which it is the custom for adolescent males to marry young girls, there are maimed and weak bodied men. For self-control it is also useful to marry later: for those who grow accustomed too soon to making love become wanton. They also stunt the growth of their bodies if they have sex before they are fully-grown. For this reason girls ought to marry at 18, men at 36: for at this time their bodies are large and at the same time by their advancing age they mark themselves out to procreate suitably. And children should not be too distant in age from their father, so that they may show gratitude to their fathers and for their part their parents have the ability to help their sons. But equally they should not approach too closely their father's age, for when this happens children do not show sufficient respect towards their parents, seeing as they are almost equals. Be that as it may, however, it is not wise to wait to this limit in time when it is possible to achieve procreation before turning one's attention to having children: for as of too young men, so of too old: the offspring are imperfect in body and mind [*Politics*, ch. 17, book vii], so that time should be most approved when firstly the intelligence is flourishing and the body is strong: that is mostly around the age of 50. Therefore those who have gone 4 or 5 years beyond this age should abandon all thought of procreation and henceforth practise sex for reasons of health or some other cause: such as for instance to relieve themselves of a build-up of seminal fluid. For men if they are wise will only copulate to have children or to release redundant semen, since its retention might be harmful, but not for pure pleasure, as ignorant men do.

* * *

Males are born more in northern winds than southern and there are some shepherds who say that it is of great importance to the breeding of male or female sheep not only if copulation occurs in northern or southern winds, but also whether, when the sheep copulates, it is facing north or south. Winter time, as approved by Aristotle ch. 6, book vii, *Politics*, is the proper time for love-making, in which Aristotle agrees with Hesiod who said that males were more suited to sexual activity in the winter, and women in the summer. Hippocrates, *De superf.* said that spring was the most suitable season for both sexes, on account of the inequality of all qualities, although it is ridiculous to want to define a time of copulation for women, because, as Hippocrates said, *De genit. mulier*, the more a woman indulges in sex the healthier she is: the less she does so, the less healthy she is.

Ludovic Mercatus, *On the common conditions of women*

The difference between the sexes

For the principle of the generation of an animal is that there is male and female (the male to provide the motion and origin of the generation, the female to provide the matter) and it is proved by Aristotle by many more reasons: for to give effect to what is generated it was necessary for the man's seed to be received in some part where it might fall to the task, for which, as it were most suitable place, nature has created the womb. There was without doubt among all philosophers, astronomers, and other most scholarly men such evident and proven reason for the distinction of sex that no one is in any doubt that the most powerful cause of the fecundity of all things lies in the distinction of sex.... For I think it is clear to them that if male adheres to the male sex, or female to the female sex, or happens to contemplate the same, production will cease and congress be made sterile. But if opposites pursue each other, male combines with female or female with male, everything springs up out of the influx and is fertile and full in that time. And for not dissimilar reasons philosophers think that the first principles and elements of all things in the making of combinations display the strongest alternation of male and female, believing that fire is the father and author of every combination, whereas earth is the mother. Thus Plato in the *Timaeus* affirmed that the world is evidently established of these two elements, as though of parents. Fire is without doubt the author and 'man' of all actions: earth, as it were, the nurturer and refuge like a mother, by the best of rights and rejoicing in that name, by the judgement of all philosophers.

✼　✼　✼

So I think that it has been proved that the female sex stands side-by-side with men in association, not in union. Now it remains to prove that there should be mutual mingling. This the blessed Thomas assuredly proves in an elegant argument when he says: it was necessary for woman to be created to help man, for woman assists in generation. This is seen as a proof against those who assert that a woman was necessary to perform other functions together with man. But woman was given to man for the sole function of generation, by which he proves that man alone was not sufficient to perform the task of generation and consequently, although he is fit for generation, he requires assistance. Such was woman, and, therefore, necessary. From this it proves that woman is necessary for the function of generation. For it is necessary that animals which exist in nature exist as a result of genital semen and menstrual blood. These must be provided by male and female, and these origins were necessary both in animals and humans, in whom it was impossible that all the suitable power of generation should emanate from one sex alone. And so it was necessary not only to be different in power but also in parts of the body, in which male and female certainly differ. The male receives parts marked by shape and position for the purpose of generation, the female receives others.... Therefore some parts suitable for procreation are required and they are in themselves various and different for male and female. For although (as Aristotle rightly observes) the whole animal may be called male or female, no part or function of it is male or female except in a certain fixed virtue and part. So those parts which are separate and distinct, since they are unable alone to fulfil the function of generating, should be brought together. A necessary joining of male and female is therefore required for procreation. From which it is clear (as Aristotle reports) that Empedocles spoke truly when he said that it was a symbol of male and female that the whole is performed by neither, and that the same things do not come out from both: therefore the one desires the copulation and bonding of the other, in which the female provides matter, the male the principle of motion.... And since generation proceeds from joining and copulation (which cannot in any way be performed without the joining of male and female) it is evidently necessary that certain matter is emitted from both, in which the power and capacity in them generates a third. We have set down all the causes why male and female are necessary for copulation and cannot fulfil the function of generation without the other; that although the male has power to beget, he does not have the place in which what has been conceived might be shaped and formed: while the female has places suitable for containing and shaping the conception, but lacks the principle: so it is that neither can produce a perfect foetus without the other. By which it can be demonstrated that in all things, and especially in animals and with even stronger cause in humans, it was necessary to have distinction of sex for the reasons I have adduced ...

On the irritation and hysteria of the womb

Womb hysteria, whose nature belongs partly to the natural appetite of the womb which has been damaged by upsetting its equilibrium, and in part to the brain, which the womb draws also into partnership. Womb hysteria (as I shall call it from the beginning: for in calling it thus the other conditions which are similar to it will easily be noted) is therefore an immoderate and unbridled desire to copulate, so strong and unquenchable that the woman appears mad and delirious as a result of this excessive and insatiable appetite. Concerning such a condition one should consider first the kind of disease that has taken hold, what its symptoms are and by what causes they are produced.

Aetius[7] supposes quite rightly that the disease is a hot distemper of the womb, which I do not think is the case with any form of distemper, but only that which is excessive and virtually habitual, and is therefore malignant, which you can readily infer from the words of the same author. We are to conclude that this distemper lies in that part of the womb where the appetite is strongest, rather like priapism in men. For although the whole substance of the womb has the natural appetite of taking in semen ... the whole neck of the uterus and most strongly its mouth, have the power to copulate and to derive pleasure from this: and these parts require intense heat to become active, which occurs in this condition. From such an imbalance taking place in the aforesaid parts an immoderate appetite is produced, just as thirst is said to proceed from heat and hunger from cold, in the mouth of the belly. For since natural appetite arises when there is moderate heat, so also the same appetite grows as the heat increases, but not of every one, but only of that which extends beyond the natural mean and has also become congenital and produces an appetite in the manner of a natural one. Just as surely as bulimia or unquenchable thirst occur in the mouth of the belly, an implacable desire to copulate occurs and arises in parts of the womb as a result of the aforesaid cause, which is not satisfied by any copulation, and does not rest, a certain kind of moisture assisting this action as well as the aforesaid heat. . . . Add to this (so that the whole nature of the condition might be set out) the error of the guiding powers of the brain emanating from the vapours issuing forth from the heated semen and menstrual blood, which when they reach the head arouse a frenzy in the mind and this irrational appetite: it is for this reason that doctors call such a condition womb hysteria.

Helkiah Crooke, *Microcosmographia*

Crooke's work combines and comments on both popular and medical learning about the human body. Text from: the first edition, 1618, pp. 270–2, 276.

Where the history of the infant is accurately described, as also the principles of generation, the conception, the conformation, the nourishment, the life, the motion and the birth of the infant, as near as may be according to the opinion of Hippocrates

Question 1: *Of the difference of the sexes* Aristotle in his books of the history and generation of creatures doth often inculcate that the difference of sexes is most necessary unto perfect generation, which is also sufficiently proved by the final cause the most noble of all the rest, moving the other causes itself remaining immoveable. For as in the seed of a plant, the power of the whole tree is potentially included and contained, which notwithstanding never breaketh into act unless that act is stirred up by the heat of the earth, right so the seeds of the parents containing in them the idea or form of the singular parts of the body are never actuated, never exhibit their power and efficacy unless they be sown and, as it were, buried in the fruitful field or garden of nature, the womb of the woman.

It was therefore necessary that there should be a double creature, one which should beget another, and another that should generate in itself: the first we call a male, the second a female. The male is originally the hotter and therefore the first principle of the work, and besides affordeth the greater part of the formative power or faculty. The female is the colder, and affordeth the place wherein the seed is conceived and the matter whereby the conception is nourished and sustained, which matter is made of the crude and raw remainders of her own aliment.[8] The place is the womb, which by a natural disposition looseneth the bonds wherein the spirit of the seed is fettered, and withal helpeth to add vigour and efficacy thereunto. For if the seed should be poured into any other part of the body it would not be as we use to say, conceived, but putrefied, not preserved but corrupted. The matter whereby the seed is nourished is the mother's blood. The excrement or surplusage rather the last aliment of the fleshy parts.

This difference of the sexes does not make the essential distinction of the creature, the reasons are: first because (as Aristotle saith in his second book *De generatione animalium* and the 4. chapter and in his 4. book *De historia animalium* and the 17. chapter) in all creatures there is not this distinction or diversity of sexes. Secondly, because essential differences do make a distinction of kinds, now we know that the male and female are both one kind, and only differ in certain accidents. But what these accidental differences are is not agreed upon as yet.

The peripatetics think that nature ever intendeth the generation of a male, and that the female is procreated by accident out of a weaker seed which is not able to attain the perfection of the male. Wherefore Aristotle thinketh that the woman or female is nothing else but an error or aberration of nature, which he calleth by a metaphor taken from travellers which miss of their way, and yet at length attain their journey's end; yea he proceedeth further and saith that the female is a *by-work* or prevarication, yea the first monster in nature.

Galen in the 6. and 7. chapters of his 14. book *De usu partium* following Aristotle something too near, writeth that the formative power which is the seed of man being but one, doth not always intend the generation of one, that is male; but if she err from her scope and cannot generate a male, then bringeth she forth the female which is the first and most simple imperfection of a male, which therefore he calleth a creature lame, occasional and accessory, as if she were not of the main, but made by the by.

Now herein he putteth the difference betwixt her and the male, that in males the parts of generation are without the body, in females they lie within because of the weakness of the heat which is not able to thrust them forth. And therefore he saith that the neck of the womb is nothing else but the virile member turned inward and the bottom of the womb nothing but the scrotum or cod inverted.

But this opinion of Galen and Aristotle we cannot approve. For we think that nature as well intended the generation of a female as of a male: and therefore it is unworthily said that she is an error or a monster in nature. For the perfection of all natural things is to be esteemed and measured by the end: now it was necessary that woman would be so formed or else nature must have missed of her scope because she intended a perfect generation, which without a woman cannot be accomplished.

Those things which Galen urgeth concerning the similitude of the parts of generation or their differing only in site and position, many men do esteem very absurd. Sure we are that they savour very little of the truth of anatomy, as we have already proved in the book going before, wherein we have showed how little likeness there is betwixt the neck of the womb and the yard, the bottom of it and the cod. Neither is the structure, figure, or magnitude of the testicles one and the same, nor the distribution and insertion of the spermatic vessels alike; wherefore we must not think that the female is an imperfect male differing only in the position of the genitals.

Neither yet must we think that the sexes do differ in essential form and perfection, but in the structure and temperature of the parts of generation.

The woman hath a womb ordained by nature as a field or seed-plot to receive and cherish the seed, the temper of her whole body is colder than that of a man because she was to suggest and minister matter for the nourishment of the infant. And this way Aristotle in the second chapter of his first book *De generatione animalium* seemeth to incline where he saith *that the male and female do differ as well in respect as in sense*: in respect because the manner of their generation is diverse: for the female generateth in herself, the male not in himself, but in the female: in sense, because the parts appear other and otherwise in the sexes. The parts of the female are the womb, and the rest which by a general name are called *matrices*, the parts of a man are the virile member and the testicles. And so much shall be sufficient to have been concerning the difference of the sexes. But because there is more difference of the tempers in men and women, we will insist somewhat more upon the point.

* * *

That females are more wanton and petulant than males, we think happeneth because of the impotency of their minds: for the imaginations of lustful women are like the imaginations of brute beasts which have no repugnancy or contradiction of reason to restrain them. So brutish and beastly men are more lascivious, not because they are hotter than other men, but because they are brutish. Beasts do couple not to engender but to satisfy the sting of lust: wise men couple that they might not couple.

That women's testicles are hidden within their bodies is also an argument of the coldness of their temper, because they want heat to thrust them forth. Yet for all this we do not say that women do generate more than men, for they want the matter and the spirit. Indeed they have more blood, as we said even now, and that is by reason of their cold temperament which cannot discuss the reliques of aliment: add hereto that the blood of women is colder and rawer than the blood of men. We conclude therefore that universally men are hotter than women, males than females, as well in regard of their natural temper as that which is acquired by diet and the course of life.

But now I had need here to apologise for myself in speaking so much of women's weakness: but they must attribute something to the heat of disputation, most to the current stream of our authors, least of all to me who will be as ready in another place to flourish forth their commendations as I am here to huddle over their natural imperfections.

Nicolas Culpeper, *A directory for midwives; or a guide for women in their conception, bearing and suckling their children*

Culpeper's work aimed at a popular audience, rather than just midwives. It was reprinted many times. It aimed to cover all areas of women's health and illness, although the focus is inevitably on sexual health and the experience of maternity. Text from: the first edition, 1651, pp. 21–8, 29–31, 40–3.

The anatomy of the vessels of generation

Of the genitals in women   Having served my own sex, I shall see now if I can please the women who have no more cause than men (that I know of) to be ashamed of what they have, and would be grieved (as they had cause, for they could not live), if they were without: but have cause, if they rightly consider of it, to thank me for telling them something they knew not before. I shall divide it into these chapters: 1. Of the privy passage. 2. Of the womb. 3. Of the stones. 4. Of the spermatic vessels. (All these are far more exactly described in Vesalingius, *Anatomy in English*.[9] And also in Riolan's *Anatomy* they are most clearly described with the diseases incident to those parts. And for the cure of diseases, see Riverius *Practice of Physic*[10] in English.)

Of the privy passage   In this I shall consider but these seven following parts.
  1.   The lips which are visible to the eye at the first sight, they are framed of the common coverings of the body, and have pretty store of spongy fat: this ruse is to keep the internal parts from cold and dust.
  2.   The *nyphae*[11] or wings which appear when the lips are severed, they are framed of soft and spongy flesh and the doubling of the skin placed at the sides of the neck: they compass the *clitoris*, and in form and colour resemble the comb of a cock.
  3.   The *clitoris* is a sinewy and hard body, full of spongy and black matter within, as the side ligaments of the yard[12] are, in form it resembles the yard of a man and suffers erection and falling as that doth: this is that which causeth lust in women, and gives delight in copulation, for without this a

woman neither desires copulation or hath pleasure in it, or conceives by it. Some are of opinion, and I could almost afford to side with them, that such kind of creatures they call *hermaphrodites*, which they say bear the genitals both of men and women, are nothing else but such women in whom the *clitoris* hangs out externally, and so resembles the form of the yard, leave the truth or falsehood of it to be judged by such who have seen them anatomised: however, this is agreeable both to reason and authority, that the bigger the *clitoris* is in women, the more lustful they are.

4. Under the *clitoris* and above the neck is the passage of the women's urine, so that the urine of the woman comes not through the neck of the womb, neither is the passage of the urine common as in men, but particular and by itself: therefore in injections for suppressing of urine in women or the like, you may, if you have not a care, easily err by putting the syringe into the neck of the womb instead of the passage of urine.

5. Near this are four caruncles, or fleshy knobs, which because they resemble the form of myrtle berries the Latins call them *myrtiforms*: these are round in virgins, but hang flagging when virginity is lost; the uppermost of them is largest and forked, that so it may receive the neck of the passage of urine, the other are below this on the sides, they all keep back both air and other things from entering the neck of the womb.

6. In virgins these caruncles or knobs are joined together with a thin and sinewy skin or membrane, interlaced with many small veins which hath a hole in the midst, through which the menstrual blood passeth, about the bigness of one's little finger in such as are grown up, this is that noted skin which is called *hymen* and is a certain note of virginity wherever it is found, for the first act of copulation breaks it. I confess much controversy hath been amongst anatomists concerning this: some holding there is no such thing at all; others that it is, but it is very rare; the truth is most virgins have it, some hold all; I must suspend my judgement till more years bring me more experience: yet this is certain, it may be broken without copulation, as it may be gnawn asunder by defluxion of strong humours, especially in young virgins because it is thinnest in them; as also by unkind applying of pessaries to provoke the terms; and how many ways else, God knows . . .

Of the womb   Hippocrates in his first book of the diseases of women affirms, that the often use of the act of copulation makes the womb slippery and hinders conception. As also that though authors say it is the inversion, or hardness, or ulcers, or scars of the womb hinders conception by such means as I recited, it is not probable to me: for nature, being set in the world by the eternal God for the increase and multiplication of things in the elementary world, hath placed a magnetic virtue in the womb that it draws the seed to it, as the loadstone draws the iron, or the fire the light of a candle.

I rather think therefore that the reason these hinder conception is this: because the womb is so bruised in succouring itself that it cannot perfect any conception: you know that a man that is sick and wounded cannot work, though his work lie beside him ...

Of the stones[13]   The stones of women (for they have such kinds of toys as well as men) differ from the stones of men:

1   In place: for they are within the belly in women, but without in men.
2   In magnitude: for they are less in women than in men.
3   In form: for they are uneven in women, but smooth in men.
4   They are not stayed in women by muscles, but by ligaments.
5   They have no prostates.
6   They differ in figure, for they are depressed in, or flattish, in women, but oval in men.
7   They have but one skin whereas men have four; and the reason is because men are exposed to the cold as being without the belly: so are not women's.
8   Their substance is more soft than in men.
9   In temperature they are colder than men's are.

The use of stones in women are the same that they are in men viz. to concoct seed; and of this judgement was Hippocrates in ancient days, and yet Aristotle had the face to deny that women had any seed at all, though against both reason and experience. Also Jovian Pontanus in his *Celestial Observations* goes about to prove the very same thing in the moon, which Aristotle quotes in women: he affirms that the moon only provides matter for the sun to work upon in the generation of things here below, even as the female doth to the male in the generation of man; and that he learneth of Aristotle, and so he confesses; but those that have studied Hermetical philosophy know well enough that the moisture which the moon bestows upon the earth hath an active principle in it, yea such an active principle that the world cannot stand without it, nor philosophers operate without it.

✻   ✻   ✻

The formation of the child in the womb   Having spoken of the proper parts of the child, we come next to speak of its formation. But before I begin this, give me leave to premise that this is the difficultest piece of work in the whole book, nay in the whole study of anatomy because such anatomies are hard to be gotten, most women that lie on their death-beds, when they are with child, miscarry before they die, if not all; besides Galen never saw a woman anatomised in his lifetime, as I shall prove by and by (and yet our anatomies

59

follow him as a little god a-mighty and his *ipse dixit* [*he himself has said it*] serves the turn; and so the blind leading the blind, you know what will come of them both). *Columbus*[14] is the most rational in this point that I know; the rest, some follow Galen, some Vesalius, some their fancies, and some quibble about it. Myself saw one woman opened that died in child-bed not delivered, and that is more by one than most of our dons have seen, yet they are as confident as Aesop's crow was that he was an eagle, but he was made a mocking stock to the boys for his labour; and so will they be shortly for their foolish model of physic, that I may give it no worse name.

And then secondly, I hope you will give me leave to be a little critical: for there is need enough if you knew but so much as I, if I commit any failings they are unknown to me, let the honesty of my intentions deface them with a *deleatur* [*let it be deleted*]. Now to the business.

1. The testicles or stones of a woman are for generation of seed, where many times (if the doctors and surgeons were not high base and denied your admittance) you might see it in an anatomy, white, thick, and well concocted.

2. In the act of copulation, the woman spends her seed as well as the man, and both are united to make the conception.

3. The reason why sometimes a male is conceived, sometimes a female, is the strength of the seed: for if the man's seed be strongest, a male is conceived; if the woman's a female. The greater light obscures the lesser by the same rule, and that's the reason weakly men get mostly girls, if they get any children at all.

Nicholas Fontanus, *The woman's doctor*

This textbook was aimed at English physicians and lay readers. Text from: the first edition, 1652, pp. 1ff, 51–60.

Women's diseases

Of the consent between the diseases of the matrix, and those of the other parts
Women were made to stay at home and to look after household employments, and because such business is accompanied with much ease, without any vehement stirrings of the body, therefore hath provident nature assigned them their monthly courses, that by the benefit of those evacuations, the feculent and corrupt blood might be purified which otherwise as being the purest party of the blood, would liable to take poison should it remain in the body and putrefy, like the seed ejaculated out of its proper vessels. Hippocrates had a perfect understanding of these things, as may appear by

those words, in his book, *De locis in homine*, where he saith that the matrix is the cause of all those diseases that happen to women; and it is no strange thing, which he speaketh, for the matrix hath a sympathy with all parts of the body; as with the brain by nerves and membranes of the parts about the spine, from whence sometimes ariseth the pains in the fore part, and then hinder part of the head; with heart also, both by the spermatic and the epigastric arteries, or those that lie about the abdomen at the bottom of the belly, from hence cometh the pain of the heart, fainting and swounding fits, the passion of the heart, anxiety of mind, dissolution of the spirit, insomuch as you cannot discern whether a woman breathes or not, or that she hath any pulse; it hath likewise a consent with the breasts, and from hence proceed those swellings, that hardness, and those terrible cancers that afflict those tender parts, that a humour doth flow upwards from the matrix to the breasts, and downwards again, from the breasts to the matrix, is the unanimous assertion of Galen, Hippocrates ... and others; moreover it hath a sympathic with the liver, and thus the sanguification is perverted, and the body inclines to a dropsy; and with the stomach and kidneys also, as those pains which great-bellied women do feel, and the torments which some virgins undergo, when they have their courses, sufficiently witness. And lastly, Hippocrates hath taught us, that this consent holdeth with the bladder and the straight gut, for, saith he, when that part is enflamed, then the urine cometh away by drops; and the patient hath frequent desires and solicitations to go to stool, but without any performance.

Women's diseases are divided into four classes, whereof the first containeth the diseases that are common to all women: the second comprehendeth such as are peculiar to widows and virgins; the third part specifieth those affects that concern barren women, and such as are fruitful; and the fourth treateth of such diseases as befall women with child, and nurses; of all which we shall now speak, one after another in their order.

Those diseases that are common both to widows and wives, both to barren women and women that are fruitful, as also to young maids and virgins, proceed from the retention or stoppage of their courses, as the most universal and most usual cause; when these come upon them in a due and regular manner, their bodies are preserved from most terrible diseases; but otherwise they are immediately subject to the falling sickness, the palsy, the consumption, the whites,[15] the mother, the melancholy, burning fevers, the dropsy, inward inflammations of all principal parts, the suppression of the urine, nauseating, vomiting, loathing of meat, yexing,[16] and a continual pain in the head, arising from ill vapours communicated from the matrix to the brain.

Wives are more healthful than widows or virgins, because they are refreshed with the man's seed, and ejaculate their own, which being excluded, the cause of the evil is taken away. This is evident from the words of

Hippocrates, who adviseth young maids to marry, when they are thus troubled. That women have stones and seed, no true anatomist will deny. The woman's seed, I confess, in regard of the small quantity of heat, is more imperfect than the seed of the man, yet it is most absolute in itself, and fit for generation. Another cause also may be added, besides that which is alleged from Hippocrates, namely that married women by lying with their husbands, do loosen the passages of the seed, and so the courses come down more easily thorough them. Now in virgins it falls out otherwise, because the blood is stopped by the constipation and obstruction of the veins and, being stopped, putrefies, from which putrefaction gross vapours do arise, and from thence the heaviness of mind and dullness of spirit; a benumbedness of the parts; timorousness, and an aptness to be frighted, with a sudden propensity to fall into fits of the mother, by reason of much blood oppressing and burthening the heart; also continual anxiety, sadness, and want of sleep, with idle talking, and an alienation of the mind. But that which most commonly afflicts them is a difficulty and pain to fetch their breath, for the chest by a continual dilatation and compression, draweth the blood from the matrix to itself in a large proportion, and sometimes produceth asthmatical effects. But what shall we say concerning widows, who lie fallow and live sequestered from these venerous conjunctions? We must conclude that if they be young, of a black complexion and hairy, and are likewise somewhat discoloured in their cheeks, that they have a spirit of salacity, and feel within themselves a frequent titillation, their seed being hot and prurient, doth irritate and inflame them to venery, neither is this concupiscence allayed and qualified but by provoking the ejaculation of the seed: as Galen propounds the advice in the example of a widow who was afflicted with intolerable symptoms, till the abundance of the spermatic humour was diminished by the hand of a skilful midwife, and a convenient ointment. Which passage also furnishes us with this argument that the use of venery is exceeding wholesome if the woman will confine herself to the laws of moderation, so that she feel no wearisomeness, nor weakness in her body, after those pleasing conflicts.

Most certain it is, that barren women are more tormented with sickness, than those who are fruitful, because they who have children live in a more healthful condition, by reason of opening of the veins, and the coming away of the superfluous blood, which being of an earthy and feculent substance, must needs introduce prodigious symptoms in the bodies of other women, who have no seasonable means to vent and purge it out, and daily experience doth witness it to the private consideration of such women, that very many obstructions breed in their livers, mesenteries[17] and matrices. That women in childbed also, and such as nurse their own children, are subject to most bitter and vehement affects, Galen doth daily teach us, by an undeniable reason; for whereas the child in the womb is nourished by the sweetest, fattest, and most elaborate part of the menstruous blood, in its own nature filthy and dreggish, when the woman is delivered that blood is forcibly evacuated by a critical kind of motion and violent ebullition, whereupon the spirits are exhausted and the feeble creature is precipitated into mortal infirmities, as fainting fits, incredible torments and frequent soundings . . .

Of the mother   That disease which we commonly call the mother, the physicians term the strangulation or suffocation of the matrix, and some-times the ascent of the matrix. Galen took it to be a drawing back of the matrix to the upper parts. Hereupon some of the ancients conceived the matrix to be some straggling creature, wandering to and fro thorough several parts, to which fantastical conceit, Fernelius[18] . . . contributed a credulous assent; for though a woman be dead, yet can you not with an ordinary strength remove the matrix from the natural place; neither is that reason, which Fernelius allegeth, of any moment, who saith that in these diseases he hath touched it upwards, seeing that this is not the true matrix, but a gross windy swelling of a roundish figure, and somewhat resembling the matrix; you will say the matrix doth remove, and slip from its proper place; I grant it, for by reason of the moisture, wherewith these parts abound, the matrix is loosened and exceedingly stretched: and this is the truth of the whole matter.

The cause of this disease is twofold: the retention of the seed and the menstruum, which are the material cause: and a cold and moist distemper of the matrix, breeding phlegmatic and thick juices, which is the efficient cause. For when the seed is retained and the menstruum hath not the customary and usual vent, they burthen the matrix and choke and extinguish the heat thereof. Then upon the diminishment of the natural heat, windy humours are bred, especially in the matrix, which by nature is a cold, nervous and bloodless part; after the same manner, if the seed be kept too long, it disturbeth the function of the spiritous parts and the midriff, it oppresseth the heart, causeth fainting and sounding fits, bindeth as it were and girdeth about the parts, and seems in such a manner to stop the breath that the sick woman is in danger to be strangled. Her pulse is sometimes weak, various and obscure. She hath inward discontents and anxieties, and is most commonly invaded by, at least very subject unto, convulsion fits. She lies as if she were astonished and void of sense and from her belly you may hear rumbling and murmuring noises. She breatheth so weakly that it is scarce discernible, and indeed she is so sad an object that the bystanders may easily mistake her to be dead. The drowsy and sleepy disease called carus differs from this, because those who are affected with it, have the use of their breath free, without any molestation: and it differs from catalepsy, another drowsy disease casting the sick into a profound and dead sleep, because they who are taken with that lie without any motion, but they who have the mother are tormented with convulsion fits, their legs and their hands are stretched and writhed into unusual figures, and strange postures; and by this it is indistinguishable from an apoplexy, unto which it is exceedingly like.

Galen wondereth how these women can live, who are troubled with these cruel fits of the mother, without any pulse, or breathing, inasmuch as it is impossible for one that liveth not to breathe, or for one that breatheth not, to live; for as long as we live, so long we breathe. To this I answer that, although these women live without respiration, yet do they not live without transpiration: for this being performed thorough the pores of the skin, by the motion of the arteries conserves the symmetry of the vital heat; for then that small heat retiring to the heart, as to a castle, may be preserved by this benefit of transpiration alone.

Now to procure an assurance whether the woman be living or dead, hold a feather or a looking glass to her mouth, if the former stir, or the latter be spotted, it is an undoubted sign that she liveth.

This is a most acute disease and soon dispatcheth the sick woman, especially if it took beginning from some very contagious and poisonous vapours; lecherous women and lusty widows that are prone and apt to venery are most subject to it: but married women that enjoy the company of their husbands, and such as with are child, are seldom invaded by it.

The complete midwife's practice enlarged

Although published anonymously, four doctors initialise the title page of this work, one of whom was probably Thomas Chamberlain. The preface claims that this is the first such book since *The birth of mankind* (see chapter 4 of this volume), and attacks Culpeper's book (see pp. 57 ff.) as false, probably because the College of Physicians objected to Culpeper's mission to provide textbooks in the vernacular. This text claims authority from Louise Bourgeois (1563–1636), the midwife of Marie de Medici, who published *Observations diverse sur la sterilité* in 1609. Text from: the first edition, 1656, pp. 10–11, 35–6, 41–2, 46–7.

Concerning the utility of the testicles and their parts

The structure of the testicles being thus known, it remains that we show you their use. This is first discovered from their situation. For of those creatures that have stones, some have them in their bodies, as fowl, others have them without, though not pendent; others have them hanging downwards, as men. Men therefore have their testicles without their bodies for two causes; first, because it is required that the testicles of the male should be bigger and hotter than those of the female, so that it were impossible for them to be contained with the body, because of their quantity. Besides, the seed of the male being the effective original of the creature, and therefore hottest, it is also required that the seed should be more abundant than could be contained in the testicles, were they placed within the body; for the seminal passages must have been less, and the veins themselves would not have afforded such plenty of matter as they now do.... The clitoris is a certain substance in the upper part of the great cleft, where the two wings concur, this in women is the seat of venereal pleasure: it is like the yard in situation, composition and erection, and hath something correspondent both to the prepuce[19] and glans in man. Sometimes it grows out to the bigness of the yard, so that it hath been observed to grow out of the body the breadth of four fingers.

This clitoris consists of two spongy and sinewy bodies, having a distinct original, from the bones of the pubes. The head of this is covered with a most tender skin, and hath a hole like the glans, though not quite through, in which, and in the bigness, it differs from the yard...

Of the stones in women   The stones of women although they do perform the same actions and are for the same use as men's, yet they differ from them in situation, substance, temperament, figure, magnitude and covering.

They are seated in the hollowness of the abdomen; neither do they hang out as in men, but they rest upon the muscles of the loins, and this for that cause that they might be more hot and fruitful; being to elaborate that matter which with the seed of men engenders men.

In this place arises a question not trivial; whether the seed of woman be the efficient or the material cause of generation? To which it is answered that though it have a power of acting, yet that it receives the perfection of that power from the seed of man.

The stones of women differ from men's also as to their figure, because they are not so round and oval as those of men, being in their fore and hinder part more depressed and broad; the external superficies being more unequal, as if a great many knots and kernels were mixed together. There is also another difference as to the subject, because they are softer and moister than those of men, being loose and ill compacted.

Their magnitude and temperament do also make a difference, for the stones of women are much colder and lesser than men's; which is the reason that they beget a more thin and watery seed.

Their coverings also do make a difference, for men's are wrapped up in divers tunicles, because being pendent outward, they were otherwise more subject to external injuries; but the stones of women have but one tunicle, which though it stick very close to them, yet are they also half clothed over with peritoneum...

Of the actions of the womb   The first use of the womb is to attract the seed by a familiar sympathy, just as the load stone draws iron.

The second use is to retain it, which is properly called conception.

The third is to cherish the seed thus attracted, to alter it, and change it into the birth, by raising up that power which before lay sleeping in the seed, and to reduce it from power into act. The fourth action of the womb is to send forth the birth at the time prefixed; the apt time of expulsion is when the expulsive faculty begins to be affected with some sense of trouble, that is when the birth afflicts and oppresses the womb with its own weight.

Besides these uses, it hath these moreover: to nourish the birth and to dilate itself, which it doth by the help of veins and arteries, which do fill more and more with matter, as nature requires.

The chiefest action of the womb and most proper to it, is the retention of the seed; without which nothing of other action could be performed for the generation of man ...

Whether she have conceived a male   If she have conceived a male child, the right eye will move swifter, and look clearer than the left. The right pap will also rise and swell beyond the left, and grow harder, and the colour of the teats will change more suddenly. The milk will increase more suddenly, and if it be milked out and be set in the sun it will harden into a clear mass, not unlike pearl. If you cast the milk of the woman upon her urine, it will presently sink to the bottom. Her right cheek is more muddy, and the whole colour of her face is more cheerful; she feels less numbness, the first motion of the child is felt more lively in the right side for the most part of the sixtieth day. If her flowers flow the fortieth day after conception. The belly is more acute towards the navel. As the woman goes she always puts her right leg forward, and in rising she eases all she can her right side sooner than her left.

Whether she have conceived a female   If she have conceived a female the signs are for the most part contrary to those aforesaid.

The first motion is made most commonly the ninetieth day after conception, which motion is made in the left side; females are carried with greater pain, her thighs and genital members swell; her colour is paler, she hath a more vehement longing. Her flowers flow the thirtieth day after conception. Girls are begot of parents who are by nature more cold and moist, their seed being more moist, cold and liquid.

3

CONDUCT

INTRODUCTION

A popular proverb published in John Ray's *A Collection of English Proverbs* in 1678 succinctly summarises the central ideology of womanhood in this period:

> A little house well-filled, a little land well-tilled and a little wife well-willed.

(p. 62)

The ideology of woman's behaviour is thus defined in relation to the power of the man ('well-willed') and linked explicitly with a well-stocked house and an efficient agricultural smallholding. In other words, a submissive, careful wife complements and aids the productive abilities and output of the smallest economic unit in a larger mercantile enterprise.

Conduct literature, which ranges from homilies, prayers and sermons, through educational and how-to tracts to satires and defences, had a booming market share in early modern England.[1] Most of the texts were not actually addressed to women, but to men who had responsibility for women, whether as fathers, husbands or brothers. Only three books[2] written by women and published posthumously can be said to relate to conduct through their focus on their children's education into a world where conduct is gendered.[3]

The genre of conduct literature is a fluid one and, as with the theological texts in chapter 1 of this book, encompasses other genres and other purposes. For example, sermons and homilies need to be read as both theological descriptions and as ideological constructions of necessary behaviour. Nevertheless, the texts grouped here have a common purpose and are characterised by several distinctive features.

First, conduct literature is addressed ultimately to women, even if filtered through the reading of men. Secondly, it is exhortative, claiming certain rules for the public and private behaviour of women (pp. 69 ff., 85 ff.). Thirdly, the content of the exhortation is structured around certain characteristics, described as ideal feminine virtues: chastity, obedience, humility and silence (pp. 69–85). These form the basis of a woman's character and are to be taught by fathers and husbands. It is thus possible to argue that this discourse, unlike those of theology and physiology, suggests that gender is something constructed[4] and hence more fluid and developmental than theological and physiological texts encourage us to believe. Fourthly, the specific areas of women's lives and their duties within each sphere are delineated for the reader: the young girl; the affianced woman; the wife; the widow (p. 69 ff.). Finally, woman's ideal behaviour in dress, manners and speech is set forth (pp. 69–79).[5] Thus the function, content and form of these works play out for us images of a dominant culture's view of woman: it is safe to argue that conduct literature shows us how and what women were asked to be. It does not, of course, tell us what they were: although the extract by Dorothy Leigh (pp. 98–101) suggests that many women did internalise the dominant conduct ideology.

Conduct literature is thereby amongst the most overtly ideological in this period. It exhorts women, whether aristocratic or bourgeois, to behave according to certain gendered preconceptions of feminine or masculine behaviour, and asks them to internalise that knowledge in terms of both internal and external compliance. It often does so by constructing and reasserting the old dichotomy of women as virgin or whore, and in asserting a particular space for good women (the home) and bad women (the streets). Many of the extracts here demonstrate this precisely (pp. 69–72, 79–80). Occasionally, however, these texts can surprise: Smith (pp. 82–3) when describing the typical nurturing role a woman must learn as an ideal wife, suggests she needs to be 'a woman physician'. This area of conduct, it is suggested, is one where women's skills have some equality with a male professional. It has been suggested that this ideology of containment belongs to and came from the middle classes:[6] nevertheless it is a message that widens its appeal with the decline in old aristocratic values,[7] the increasing emphasis on the home and what Laurence Stone calls the development of the 'restricted patriarchal family' in early mercantile capitalism. This association is one we have already seen in the proverb recorded by Ray.

Women themselves did more than merely internalise this ideology. The writing of Leigh is typical: although she exhorts her children to develop according to the (literally) prescribed roles for boys and describes and continually asserts her own role within the conventional model for femininity, she still argues that her writing needs some kind of public forum. In this sense she has side-stepped two exhortations: to be silent and to keep out of the public arena. Thus Leigh shares with many women a consciousness of her function which goes beyond the prescriptions, although it is not a consciousness that extends to denying her role. Nevertheless, it does demonstrate that the simple oppositional debate of the *querelle des femmes* tradition, which informs the content of the debate about conduct, is far too simple.[8] The women who did get involved in political and theological debates, or managed estates, or fought their husbands did not internalise the ideological message either.

On the one hand, we are presented with a picture of women in need of counselling, instructing and leading, being socialised into a condition of submission. On the other, we have accounts of active and successful women struggling with both this ideology and other economic, social and political troubles.

Thus, as with any ideological discourse, some women are intelligently conscious of its contradictions. They use the discourse, as does Leigh, to assert a specific voice and function for her role as mother, incorporating all the male values she has been asked to, but at the same time elegantly transgressing those boundaries by finding for herself a space and a language with a new public. Whilst the majority of texts in this chapter maintain that the natural inferiority of women's bodies and minds dictates certain social roles, they also evince tremendous anxieties about women's transgression of those roles. This suggests in turn that the supposed norms of gender roles are either ones which are being flouted, or that other social anxieties, such as those of class and status, are being displaced on to anxieties about proper gender behaviour.

Juan Luis Vives, *The instruction of a Christian woman*

Vives was a Spanish humanist, a friend and correspondent of More and Erasmus, and patronised by Catherine of Aragon, for whose daughter Mary, later the first queen regnant of England, he wrote this text. It was first published in Latin in 1523, and translated into French, German, Italian and English (first in 1529). Text from: the 1540 edition, transl. Richard Hyrde, book 1, chs 8, 11, 12, book 3, ch. 7, fos 18^r–22, 32^{v}ff, 38^r–44^v, 138^v.

Of the ordering of the body in a virgin

Though it were not for this purpose to speak of the body, notwithstanding for as much as some things that be in the mind come of the reason and complexion of the body. Therefore must we speak something of the ordering of the body of a virgin. First of all, methinks, that it is to be told their father and mother, as Aristotle doth bid in his history of beasts, that is, that they keep their daughters, specially when they begin to grow from child's state, and hold them from men's company. For that time they be given unto most lust of the body. Also the maidens should keep themself, both at all other and at that time specially, from either hearing or saying or yet thinking any foul thing, which thing she shall labour to do. Nevertheless, at other times too and unto the time that they be married, much fasting shall be good, which doth not feeble the body, but bridle it and press it down and quench the heat of youth. For these be only the very and holy fasts. Let their meat be mean and easy to get, neither hot of itself, nor spiced with spices, nor delicate. And they ought to remember that our first mother for meat was cast out of paradise ...

Physicians and such as write the natures of men's bodies, and specially Galen in the book of health, saith that the bodies of children and young men and those that be in a lusty age, both men and women, be very hot of a natural heat, and that all meats that increase heat be very noisome for them, and that it is good for them to use all cold things in meats and drinks: as in contrariwise unto old men, and such as be full of phlegm and cold, hot meats and old wine be best . . .

Of the virtues of a woman and examples that she should follow

A woman shall learn the virtues of her kind altogether out of books, which she shall either read herself, or else hear read. And it becometh every woman to be involved with all kind of virtue, but some be necessary for her: as all vice is shameful, and some abominable and cursed: and some virtues be for wives, some for widows, some for religious women, but I will speak of such as belong unto the whole kind of women.

First let her understand that *chastity* is the principal virtue of a woman, and counterpoiseth with all the rest: if she have that, no man will look for any other, and if she lack that no man will regard other. And as the Stoic philosophers reckon that all goodness standeth in wisdom, and all ill in folly, insomuch that they said only the wise man to be rich, free, a king, a citizen, fair, bold, and blessed: and a fool, poor, a thrall, an outlaw, a stranger, foul, a cowherd, and wretched; likewise it is to be judged of chastity in women, that she that is chaste is fair, well favoured, rich, fruitful, noble, and all best things that can be named: and contrary, she that is unchaste is a see and treasure of all illness. Now shamefastness and sobriety be the inseparable companions of chastity, insomuch as she cannot be chaste that is not ashamed: for that is as a cover and veil of her face. For when nature had ordained that our faces should be open and bare of clothes, she gave it the veil of shamefastness, wherewith it should be covered and that for a great commendation that whoso did look upon it should understand some great virtue to be under that cover. Nor no man should see it covered with that veil, but he should love it: nor none see it naked of that, but he should hate it. Our Lord curseth an unchaste woman, saying, *thou hast the face of an harlot, thou art past shame*. Of shamefastness cometh demureness and measurableness: that whether she think ought, or say, or do; nothing shall be outrageous, neither in passions of mind, nor words nor deeds, nor presumptuous, nor nice, wanton, pert, nor boasting, nor ambitious. And as for honours, she will neither think herself worthy, nor desire them, but rather flee them: and if they chance unto her, she will be ashamed of them, as of a thing not deserved, nor be for nothing high-minded, neither for beauty, nor properness, nor kindred, nor riches, being sure that they will soon perish, and that pride shall have everlasting pain.

Now *soberness* keepeth countenance, like as drunkenness and excess drive it out. Every man wotteth what follow surfeit. And unto soberness is jointed measurable and slender diet, which things be in householding the woman's party, as Plato and Aristotle say full well. The man getteth, the woman saveth and keepeth. Therefore he hath stomach given him to gather lustily, and she hath it taken from her that she may warily keep. And of this soberness of body cometh soberness of mind: nor the fantasies of the mind shall, as they were drunken, trouble and disease the quietness of virtue, but that she may both think well and do well.

Let her apply herself to virtue, and be content with a little, and take in worth that she hath, nor seek for other that she hath not, nor for other folks, whereof riseth envy, hate or curiosity of other folks' matters. The devotion of holy things most agreeth for women. Therefore it is a far worse sight of a woman that abhoreth devotion. She must have much strife with envy, which is both a foolish vice and shameful in women, and yet I wot not how it assaulteth them the most sore. But she that is of good behaviour, and hath enough to serve her with, shall have no cause to envy other, nor to be curious in other body's house: and she that is shamefast, sober and reasonable of mind, shall neither be ragious angry, nor fall to railing, cruelty or beastliness. For when it is natural for women to be kind and gentle because they be feeble and need the aid of other, who can be content with outrageous ire and cruelty in a woman? ...

How the maid shall behave herself forth abroad

Forth she must needs go sometimes, but I would it should be as selde[9] as maybe, for many causes. Principally because as oft as a maid goeth forth among people, so often she cometh in judgement and extreme peril of her beauty, honesty, demureness, wit, shamefastness and virtue. For nothing is more tender than is the fame and estimation of women, nor nothing more in danger of wrong: insomuch that it hath been said, and not without a cause, to hang by a cobweb, because those things that I have rehearsed be required perfect in a woman: and folks' judgements be dangerous to please, and suspicious ... if a slander once take hold in a maid's name by folks' opinion it is in a manner everlasting, nor cannot be washed away without great tokens and shows of chastity and wisdom. If thou talk little in company folks think thou canst but little good: if thou speak much, they reckon thee light: if thou speak uncunningly, they count thee dull-witted; if thou speak cunningly thou shalt be called a shrew; if thou answer not quickly thou shalt be called proud or ill brought up; if thou answer they shall say thou wilt be soon over comen;

if thou sit with demure countenance, thou art called a dissembler; if thou make much moving, they will call thee foolish: if thou look on any side, then will they say thy mind is there; if thou laugh when any man laugheth, though thou do it not a purpose, straight they will say thou hast a fantasy unto the man and his saying, and that it were no great mastery to win thee. Whereto should I tell how much occasion of vice and naughtiness is abroad?... A woman should be kept close, nor be known of many, for it is a token of no great chastity or good name, to be known of many, or be sung about in the city in songs, or to be marked or named by any notable mark, as white, lame, goggle-eyed, little, great, fat, maimed or stutting,[10] these ought not to be known abroad in a good woman.

Why then say some: *should we never walk out of our own doors, should we ever lie at home? That were as though we should lie in prison.* So too doth some proud souls take this saying, that desire to see and to be seen. Nay verily, they shall go forth sometime, if need require, and if their father command or their mother: but afore she go forth at door, let her prepare her mind and stomach none otherwise than if she went to fight. Let her remember what she shall hear, what she shall see, and what herself shall say. Let her consider with herself that some thing shall chance on every side that shall move her chastity and her good mind. Against these darts of the Devil flying on every side, let her take the buckler of stomach defended with good examples and precepts and a firm purpose of chastity, and a mind ever bent towards Christ. And let her know that she goeth but to vanity which, least she be taken with it, she had need to provide wisely; and that that she shall see forth abroad is to be counted none other thing but a show of the life of the world, by whose vices, set before her eyes, she may learn not only to keep herself out of the contagiousness, but moreover to amend her own faults. And that whatever hour so ever she turneth herself from God unto men, whether she like them or be liked of them, she forsaketh Christ and, of Christ's spouse, suddenly becometh an adulterer...

Now when she is appointed with these thoughts and such other let her go forth with her mother, if she have any, and have leave to go, if she have no mother, let her go with some sad woman, that is a widow or a wife, or some good maid of virtuous living, sober of speech, and holy shamefastness.... When she goeth forth abroad, let her not bear her breasts and her neck bare, but hide her face and with scarcely an eye open to see her way withal. Neither let her desire to see, nor to be seen, not cast her eyes unstable hither and thither; nor be busy to know who dwelleth in this place, or in that, which ought scantly to know her own neighbours. He would have all hid, save the eyes to lead her the way. Nor I cannot see what honesty or goodness can be in showing the neck bare; howbeit that may be suffered, but to bare the breast and the paps and between the shoulders on the back, and almost the shoulders: how foul a thing is that, as the common saying is, a blind man may espy! When those that see it, some abhor the abominableness, and some wanton men seeing the part of the body not used to be seen, are set on fire therewith. Whereto were gloves ordained, but to hide the hands, that they should not appear, except it were in work? ...

In going, let the woman neither walk over fast, nor over slowly.

Now when she is in company of people, let her show great soberness, both in countenance and all the gesture of her body, which thing let her not do of any pride, or to make herself the more comely, but of sober and very Christian mind; nor let her not behold men much; nor think that they behold her ...

And forasmuch as we be in hand with laughing, which is a sign of a very light and dissolute mind, let her see that she laugh not unmeasurably. For this I need not to bid her, that she shall not laugh again unto young men that laugh toward her, which none will do but she that is nought, or else a fool. Let her not suffer to be plucked at, or to be touched wantonly: let her change her place, or go away and need be, let her give nothing to no man, nor take ought of any man. The wise man saith: he that taketh a benefit, selleth his liberty. And there is in France and Spain a good saying: *a woman that giveth a gift, giveth herself: a woman that taketh a gift, selleth herself.* Therefore an honest woman shall neither give nor take.

Full of talk I would not have her, no not among maids. For as for among men to be full of babble, I marvel that some regard shame so little that they do not dispraise it. That custom was confirmed, as I trow, by the decree of the Devil that women should be praised for talking eloquently and promptly with men, and that by many hours together. What, I pray you, should an ignorant maid talk with a young man ignorant of goodness, and cunning enough in naughtiness? What should fire and tow[11] do together? What should they talk of so long? I am sure of Christ and Our Lady! Nay, but rather by their communication they shall be incensed and kindled, and whether they will or no, shall be compelled to talk of their heat: and such they call *women of court*, and I trow well, of such courts as be nowadays that be even the fathers of outrageous vice and the seats of satans!

Of second marriages

For to condemn and reprove utterly second marriages, it were a point of heresy. Howbeit that better it is to abstain than marry again, is not only counselled by Christian pureness, that is to say, by divine wisdom, but also by pagans, that is to say, by worldly wisdom. Cornelius Tacitus, as I have rehearsed, saith: the women of Allmayne were not wont to marry but of maids, and though they were widows in their youth, yet would they not marry again, and specially noble women . . .

Notwithstanding, widows lay many causes wherefore they say they must marry again, of whom St Jerome speaketh in this manner writing unto the holy woman Furia: *young widows, of whom there hath many gone backward after the Devil, after that they have had their pleasure by marrying in Christ, be wont to say: my goods spill daily, the heritage of my ancestry perisheth, my servants speak stubbornly and presumptuously, my maid will not do my commandment, who shall go before me forth? Who shall answer for my house rent? Who shall teach my young sons? Who shall bring up my young daughters?* And so they lay that for a cause to marry for, which should rather let them from it. For she bringeth upon her children an enemy, and not a nourisher, not a father, but a tyrant. And she, enflamed with vicious lust, forgetteth her own womb: and she that late afore sat mourning among her children, that perceive not their own loss and harms, now is picked up a new wife. Where to layest thou the cause in thine inheritance and pride of thy servants? Confess thine own viciousness. For none of you taketh a husband but to the intent that she will lie with him, nor except her lust prick her. What a ragiousness[12] is it, to set thy chastity common like a harlot, that thou maist gather riches! And for a vile, and a thing that shall soon pass away, to file thy chastity that is a thing most precious and everlasting. If thou have children all ready, what needest thou to marry? If thou have none, why dost thou not fear the barrenness, that thou hast proved before, and adventurest up on an uncertain thing, and forgotest thine honesty and chastity that thou wast sure of? Now thou hast writing of spousage made thee, that within short while after, thou maist be compelled to write a testament. The husband shall feign himself sick and shall do, on live and in good health, that he would have to do when thou shalt die. And if it chance that thou have children by the second husband, then riseth strife and debate at home within thy house. Thou shalt not be at liberty to love thine own children equally neither to look indifferently upon them that thou hast born: thou shalt reach them meat secretly, he will envy him that is dead, and except that thou hate thine own children thou shalt seem to love their father yet.

THE DEBATE ON DRESS

Philip Stubbes, *The anatomy of abuses*

Stubbes's puritan attack on social abuses partially masks itself by its dialogic form, and by its fictionalising the place as 'an island called AILGNA'. The two interlocutors are Spudeus and Philoponus. Text from: the first edition, fos E7^{v}ff.

A particular description of the abuses of women's apparel in
AILGNA

Ph. The women of AILGNA use to colour their faces with certain oils, liquors, unguents and waters made to that end whereby they think their beauty is greatly decored [sic]: but who seeth not that their souls are thereby deformed and they brought deeper into the displeasure and indignation of the Almighty, at whose voice the earth doth tremble and at whose presence the heavens shall liquify and melt away? Do they think thus to adulterate the Lord his workmanship and to be without offence? Do they not know that he is *Zelotipus*, a jealous God, and cannot abide any alterations of his works, otherwise than he hath commanded?

    If an artificer or craftsman should make anything belonging to his art or science and a cobbler should presume to correct the same: would not the other think himself abused, and judge him worthy of reprehension?

    And think thou (oh, woman) to escape the judgement of God, who hath fashioned thee to his glory, when thy great and more than presumptuous audacity dareth to alter and change his workmanship in thee?

    Thinkest thou can make thyself fairer than God who made us all?

*   *   *

Sp. St Cyprian amongst all the rest, saith a woman through painting and dyeing of her face, showeth herself to be more than whorish. For (saith he) she hath corrupted and defaced (like a filthy strumpet or brothel) the workmanship of God in her, what is this else but to turn truth into falsehood?

*   *   *

Ph. Then followeth the trimming and tricking of their heads in laying out their hair to the show, which of force must be curled, frisled and crisped, laid out (a world to see) on wreaths and borders from one ear to another. And least it should fall down, it is under-propped with forks, wires, and I cannot tell what, rather like grim stern monsters than chaste Christian matrons...

Sp. The apostle Paul (as I remember) commandeth women to cherish their hair, saying that it is an ornament to them and therefore methink, this abuse of curling and laying it out (if either were lawful) is much more tolerable than dyeing their faces.

Ph. If curling and laying out their natural hair were all (which is impious and at no hand lawful notwithstanding, for it is the ensign of pride and the stern of wantonness to all that behold it) it were the less matter, but they are not simply content with their own hair, but buy other hair, dyeing it of what colour they list themselves.

*　*　*

Sp. As in a *chameleon* are said to be in all colours, save white, so I think, in these people are all things else, save virtue and Christian sobriety. *Proteus* that monster could never change himself into so many forms as these women do, belike they have made an obligation with hell and are at agreement with the Devil, else they would never outrage thus, without either fear of God or respect to their weak brethren whom herein they offend.

Ph. The women also there have doublets and jerkins as man have here, buttoned up the breast and made with wings, welts, and pinions on the shoulder points, as man's apparel is for all the world and though this be a kind of attire appropriate only to man, yet they blush not to wear it, and if they could as well change their sex and put on the kind of man, as they can wear apparel assigned only to man, I think they would as verily become men indeed as now they degenerate from godly sober women in wearing this wanton, lewd kind of attire proper only to man. It is written in the 22. of *Deuteronomy* that what man soever weareth women's apparel is accursed, and what woman weareth man's apparel is accursed also. Now, whether they be within the bands and limits of that curse, let them see to it themselves. Our apparel was given us as a sign distinctive to discern betwixt sex and sex, and therefore one to wear the apparel of another sex is to participate with the same, and to adulterate the verity of his own kind. Wherefore these women may not improperly be called *hermaphroditi*, that is monsters of both kinds, half women, half men.... So that when they have all these goodly robes upon them, women seem to be the smallest part of themselves, not natural women, but artificial women, not women of flesh and blood, but rather puppets or mamets[13] of rags and clowts compact together. So far hath this canker of pride eaten into the body of the commonwealth that every poor yeoman his daughter, every husbandman his daughter, and every cottager his daughter will not spare to flaunt it out, in such gowns, petticoats and kirtles, as these. And notwithstanding that their parents owe a brace of hundred pounds more than they are worth, yet will they have it either by hook or by crook, by right or wrong as they say, whereby it cometh to pass that one can scarcely know who is a noble woman, who is an honourable, or worshipful woman, from them of meaner sort.

Sp. This over great lenity and remiss liberty in the education of youth, in respect of the event and success in the end may rather be counted an extreme cruelty than a fatherly pity towards their children: for what maketh them so soon whores, strumpets and bawds, as that cockering[14] of them both? What maketh them apt and prone to all kinds of naughtiness, but this? Nothing in the world so much. For give a wild horse the liberty of the head never so little, and he will run headlong to thine and his destruction also.

John Rainoldes, *The overthrow of stage plays*

Rainoldes's attack on plays takes as its main predicate the Deuteronomy prohibition against cross-dressing. Text from: the first edition, 1599, pp. 10–11.

It is a commandment therefore of the moral law that women shall not attire themselves like men, neither men like women. And hereof it followeth that if a man might save his life or benefit many by putting on women's raiment, yet ought he not to do it because it is evil. Nay (which addeth greater weight unto the reason) it is a notorious and detestable evil: as the spirit showeth by the words ensuing, *for all that do so are abomination to the Lord thy God* [Deut. 22:5]. And seeing that himself hath given this censure, God forbid but we should think it most true and just: although our weak eyesight could discern no cause why so small a matter, as flesh and blood might count it, should be controlled so sharply. Howbeit, if we mark with judgement and wisdom, first, how this precept is referred by learned divines to the commandment, *thou shalt not commit adultery,* some expressly making it a point annexed thereto, some impliedly in that either they knit it to modesty, a part of temperance, or note the breach of it as joined with wantonness and impurity... thirdly what sparkles of lust to that vice the putting on of woman's attire on men may kindle in unclean affections... if we consider these things, I say, we shall perceive that he who condemneth the female whore and male, and detesting specially the male by terming him a dog, rejecteth both their offerings with these words, that *they both are abomination to the Lord thy God* [Deut. 24:17;18] might well control likewise the means and occasions whereby men are transformed into dogs, the sooner to cut off all incitements to that beastly filthiness, or rather more than beastly.

John Williams, *A sermon of apparell*

This sermon was preached before the king on 22 February 1619 and published by James's special commandment. It echoes the account given of James I's attack on women dressing in masculine dress in John Chamberlain's letter to Sir Dudley Carlton of 25 January 1619, where he writes: 'yesterday the Bishop of London called together all his clergy about this town, and told him he had express commandment from the king to will them to inveigh vehemently and bitterly in their sermons against the insolency of our women, and their wearing of broad brimmed hats, pointed doublets, their hair cut short or shorn... adding withal that if pulpit admonitions will not reform them he would proceed by another course'. Text from: the first edition, 1620, pp. 6–7, 19–21.

This world is a school, men are the scholars, the creatures are the characters by which we spell and put together the greatness of the creator, whom thus to our happiness we learn to see. But such is our waywardness and present corruption, that these things which God did see to be good (Gen. 1:31), we do not now think so good to see. For the Devil, an imitating and an apish thing as Damascen[15] calls him, instead of that old, hath brought forth unto us to a new world of creatures: and human kind, forsaking (as Tertullian speaks[16]) his true maker, from a clean contrary artificer, God had made us whole ears (saith St Cyprian)[17] but the Devil hath bored them; he hath made us bare necks, but the Devil hath chained them; he had given us white sheep, but the Devil hath dyed them; he had created free bodies, but the Devil hath bound them; he had made natural faces, but the Devil hath changed them. In a word he had divided male and female, but the Devil had joined them, that *mulier formosa* [*beautiful woman*] is now become, *mulier monstrosa superne* [*a monstrous woman*], half man half woman, all (outwardly) of her new maker, and these are the creatures we are gone out to see.

* * *

When thou comest thus rigged to the house of God (for that's nowadays the theatre of all this vanity), saith St Cyprian: *thou art no better than poison in the veins, and a sword in the heart for all thy brethren.* Thy colours glitter in their rolling eyes, when they should be reading. Thy silks do rattle in their itching ears, when they should be hearing. Thy fashions swim in their idle brains, when they should be thinking. And thou takest up all the power of their souls, when they should be praying. And thus (instead of worshipping God) they worship (with Jeroboam) a golden calf [1 Kings 12:28], as though their coming hither was only to see thyself clothed in soft raiments. Lastly suppose the people were so attentive as not to regard this vanity of men, what flesh and blood hath his thoughts so staunch, but must be distracted in his church devotions at the prodigious apparition of our women? ...

For a woman therefore to come into a church *chimera*-like, half male and half female; or as the priests of the Indian Venus, half black, half white as it were, and there ... first to profess repentance and remorse for sin. But how? By holding up unto God a pair of painted hands, and by lifting up to his throne two plastered eyes and a polled head. Secondly to humble herself. But how? In satin (I warrant you) instead of sackcloth, and covered with pearls instead of ashes. Thirdly to move God to be gracious. But how? With a face and a countenance he never saw before, composed for smiling more than for sorrowing, and purled with onions, instead of tears. Lastly to protest amendment and newness of life. But how? As standing most manly upon her points, by wagging a feather to defy the world, and carrying a dagger, to kill (no doubt) the flesh and the Devil.

MARITAL CONDUCT BOOKS

Robert Dod and John Cleaver,
A godly form of household government

Both Puritan clergymen wrote and preached extensively on marital conduct from the 1590s onwards. This book went through nine, extended, editions. It was first published in 1598. Text from: the 1614 edition (first edition 1598), pp. 93–5, 217ff.

But what need such as can live by their lands, to labour with their hands? What need had the woman that Solomon speaketh of? The conscience of doing good in the world should draw them to do that which no need drive them unto. Remember that the virtuous woman *stretcheth out her hand to the poor and needy* (Prov. 21:20). She giveth not of her husband's, she giveth of her own: she found a way to do good without the hurt of her husband. St Paul requireth that women should array themselves with good works [1. Tim. 2:10], the comeliest ornament in the world, if women had spiritual eyes to discern it. Dorcas, in the *Acts* 9:36, teacheth wives how to get this array, for she made garments to clothe the naked and the poor. Thus might women find how to set themselves a work, though they could live of their own. But for such as have but a mean allowance, God thereby showeth that he will have them occupy themselves in some honest labour to keep them from idleness, and the evils that issue therefrom. They therefore must labour, if not to sell cloth as *Solomon's* woman did, not to clothe the poor as Dorcas did; yet to clothe her family, that they may not care for the cold. Let her avoid such occasions as may draw her from her calling. She must shake off sloth and love of ease. She must avoid gossiping further than the law of good neighbourhood doth require. St Paul would have a woman a good *home-keeper*. The virtuous woman is never so well, as when she is in the middest of her affairs. She that much frequenteth meetings of gossips seldom cometh better home. Some count it a disgrace to come much abroad, lest they should be counted gossips, which name is become odious: but they must have tattlers come home to them to bring them news and to hold them in a tale, least they should be thought to be idle without a cause. They perceive not how time runneth, nor how untowardly their business goeth forward while they sit idle. They know not that great tale bearers be as great carriers, and that such make their game of carrying and recarrying. The wise woman will be wary whom she admitteth into her house to sit long there, knowing that their occupation is but to mark and carry. Towards her neighbours she is not sour, but courteous, not disdainful to the basest, but affable with modesty; no scorner nor giber, but bearing with infirmities, and making the best of things; not ready to stomach them for every light matter, and so to look big, but passing by offences for unity's sake; not angry, but mild; not bold but bashful; not full of words, pouring out all in her mind and babbling of her household matters, that were more fitter to be concealed, but speaking upon good occasion, and that with discretion. Let her hear and see and say the best, and yet let her soon break off talk with such in whom she perceiveth no wisdom, nor favour of grace. Let her not be light to believe reports nor ready to tell them again to fill the time with talk; for *silence* is far better then such unsavoury talk. Let her not be churlish, but helpful in all things to prevent breaches; or else to make them up again, if by the waywardness of others there be any made. Let her not be envious but glad of the good of others, nor fond of everything that she seeth her neighbours have, but wisely considering what is meet for herself and what her state will bear. Let her not be gawish[18] in apparel, but sober and modest: not nice nor coy, but handsome and housewifelike: no talker of other men's matters, nor given to speak ill of any for fear of the like measure ...

What the duty of a wife is towards her husband

The duty is comprehended in these points; First that she reverence her husband. Secondly, that she submit herself and be obedient unto him. And lastly that she do not wear gorgeous apparel, beyond her degree and place, but that her attire be comely and sober, according to her calling.... The second point is that wives submit themselves and be obedient unto their husbands, as to the Lord, because the husband is by God's ordinance the wife's head, that is her defender [Eph. 5:22; 1 Cor. 11; 14:4], teacher, and comforter: and therefore she oweth her subjection to him, like as the church doth to Christ, and because the examples of Sarah, the mother of the faithful which obeyed Abraham [Gen. 18:12] and called him Lord, moveth them thereunto. This point is partly handled before in the first point, as also in the duty of the husband to the wife. As the church should depend upon the wisdom and discretion and will of Christ and not follow what itself listeth: so must the wife also submit and apply herself to the discretion and will of her husband, even as the government and conduct of everything resteth in the head, not in the body. Moses writeth that the serpent was wise above all beasts in the field [Gen. 3:1], and that he did declare in assaulting the woman, that when he had seduced her, she might also seduce and deceive her husband. St Paul noting this among other the causes of the woman's subjection, doth sufficiently show that for the avoiding of the like inconveniences, it is God's will that she should subject herself to her husband, so that she shall have no other discretion or will, but what may depend upon her head. The Lord also by Moses saith the same: *thy desire shall be subject to thy husband and he shall rule over thee.* This dominion over the wife's will doth manifestly appear in this, that God in old time ordained that if the woman had vowed anything unto God [Num. 30:7], it should notwithstanding rest in her husband to disavow it: so much is the wife's will subject to her husband. Yet it is not meant that the wife should not employ her knowledge and discretion which God hath given her in the help and for the good of her husband: but always as it must be with condition to submit herself unto him, accordingly acknowledging him to be her head, that finally they may agree in one, as the conjunction of marriage doth require ...

Further there is a certain discretion and desire required of women to please the nature, inclinations and manners of their husbands, so long as the same importeth no wickedness. For as the looking-glass, howsoever fair and beautifully adorned, is nothing worth if it show that countenance sad which is pleasant; or the same pleasant that is sad: so the woman deserveth no commendation that, (as it were) contrarying her husband when he is merry, showeth herself sad, or in sadness uttereth her mirth. For as men should obey the laws of their cities, so women the manners of their husbands. To some women a beck of her husband's is sufficient to declare that there is somewhat amiss that displeaseth him, and specially if she bear her husband any reverence. For an honest matron hath no need of any greater staff, but of one word, or sour countenance. Moreover a modest and chaste woman that loveth her husband, must also love her house, as remembering that the husband that loveth his wife, cannot so well like the sight of any tapestry, as to see his wife in his house. For the woman that gaddeth from house to house to prate confoundeth herself, her husband and her family: *Titus* 2:5. But there are four reasons why the woman is to go abroad. First, to come to holy meetings according to the duty of godliness. Second, to visit such as stand in need, as the duty of love and charity doth require. The third for employment and provision in household affairs committed to her charge. And lastly, with her husband, when he shall require her, *Gen.* 20:1. The evil and unquiet life that some women have, and pass with their husbands, is not so much for that they commit with and in their persons, as it is for that they speak with their tongues. If the wife would keep silence when her husband beginneth to chide, he should not have so unquiet dinners, neither she the worse supper. Which surely is not so: for at the same time that the husband beginneth to utter his grief, the wife beginneth to scold and chafe: wherefof doth follow that, now and then, most unnaturally, they come to handy-gripes,[19] more beast-like than Christian-like, which their so doing is both a great shame, and foul discredit to them both. The best means therefore that a wife can use to obtain, and maintain the love and good liking of her husband, is to be silent, obedient, peaceable, patient, studious to appease his choler if he be angry, painful and diligent in looking to her business, to be solitary and honest. The chief and special cause why most women do fall (in not performing this duty to their husbands) is because they be ignorant of the word of God, which teacheth the same.

Henry Smith, *A preparative to marriage*

Smith was a well-known and popular Puritan preacher in London. This marriage sermon was published shortly after he delivered it. Text from: the first edition, 1591, pp. 69ff.

So he must not look to find a wife without a fault, but think that she is committed to him to reclaim her from her faults, for all are defectives: and if he find the *Proverbs* true, that in space cometh grace, he must rejoice as much at his wife when she mendeth as the husbandman rejoiceth when his vineyard beginneth to fructify ...

Likewise the woman may learn her duty out of her names. They are called goodwives, as goodwife A and goodwife B. Every wife is called goodwife; therefore if they be not goodwives, their names do belie them and they are not worth their titles, but answer to the wrong name as players do upon a stage. This name pleaseth them well: but besides this a wife is called a *yoke-fellow* to show that she should help her husband to bear his yoke, that is, his grief must be her grief; and whether it be the yoke of poverty, or the yoke of envy, or the yoke of sickness, or the yoke of imprisonment, she must submit her neck to bear it patiently with him, or else she is not his yoke-fellow but his yoke, as though she were inflicted upon him for a penalty, like *Job*'s wife whom the Devil sent to torment him [Job. 9], when he took away all beside. The apostle biddeth to rejoice with them that rejoice, and mourn with them that mourn. With whom should the wife rejoice rather than with her husband? Or with whom should she mourn willingier than with her own flesh? ... Besides a yoke-fellow she is called a *helper*, to help him in his business, to help him in his labours, to help him in his troubles, to help him in his sickness, like a woman physician, sometime with her strength, sometime with her counsel: for sometimes as God confoundeth the wise by the foolish, and the strong by the weak, so he teacheth the wise by the foolish and helpeth the strong by the weak. Therefore Peter saith *Husbands are won by the conversation of their wives* [1 Pet. 3:1]. As if he should say, sometimes the weaker vessel is the stronger vessel, and Abraham may take counsel of

Sarah as Naaman was advised by his servant [Gen. 15:2] . . .

Besides a helper she is called a *comforter* too, and therefore the man [Prov. 5:18] is bid to rejoice in his wife, which is as much as to say that wives must be the rejoicing of their husbands, even like David's harp to comfort Saul [1 Sam. 16]. Therefore it is said of *Rebecca* [Gen. 27:9] that she prepared meat for her husband such as he loved: so a good wife is known when her words and deeds and countenances are such as her husband loveth, she must not examine whether he be wise or simple, but that she is his wife, and therefore they which are bound must obey, as Abigail [1 Sam. 25:3] loved her husband though he was a fool: for the wife is as much despised for taking rule over her husband as he for yielding unto her. It becomes not the mistress to be master, but both to sail with their own wind.

Lastly we call the wife *housewife*, that is housewife, not a street wife like Thamar [Gen. 38:14], nor a field wife like Dinah [Gen. 34:1], but a housewife, to show that a good wife keeps her house: and therefore Paul biddeth Titus [Tit. 2:5] to exhort women that they be chaste and keeping at home: presently after *chaste*, he saith, *keeping at home*, as though home were chastity's keeper. And therefore Solomon depainting the whore setteth her at the door [Prov. 7:12], now sitting upon her stalls, now walking about the streets, now looking out of the windows like curled Jezebels [2 Kings 9:30], as if she held forth the glass of temptation for vanity to gaze upon. But chastity careth to please but one, and therefore she keeps her closet, as though she were still at prayer . . .

As it becometh her to keep home, so it becometh her to keep silence, and alway speak the best of her head. Others seek their honour in triumph, but she must seek her honour in reverence, for it becometh not any woman to set light by her husband nor to publish his infirmities. For they say it is an evil bird that defileth his own nest: and if a wife use the husband so, how may the husband use the wife? Because that is the quality of that sex to overthwart and upbraid and sue the pre-eminence of their husbands, therefore the philosophers could not tell how to define a wife, but called her *the contrary to a husband*, as though nothing were so cross and contrary to a man as a wife. This is not scripture, but no slander to many. . . . We say not all are alike, but this sect hath many disciples. Doth the rib that is in a man's side fret him or gall him? No more should she which is made of the rib. Though a woman be wise and painful and have many good parts yet if she be a shrew her troublesome jarring in the end will make her honest behaviour unpleasant, as her over-pinching at last causeth her good housewifery to be evil spoken of. Therefore though she be a wife, yet sometimes she must observe the servant's lesson, *not answering again* [Tit. 2:9] and hold her peace to keep the peace. Therefore they which keep silence, are well said to hold their peace, because silence oftentimes doth keep the peace, when words would break it.

Richard Brathwait, *The English gentlewoman*

The title page of this work bears the motto: *modestia non forma*, modesty rather than beauty (see figure 4). The companion work, *The English gentleman*, was published with this text in its second edition in 1641. Text from: the first edition, 1631, pp. 88–91.

Truth is, their tongues are held their defensive armour: but in no particular detract they more from their honour than by giving too free scope to that glibbery member. . . . What restraint is required in respect of the tongue, may appear by that ivory guard or garrison with which it is impaled. See how it is double-warded, that it may with more reservancy and better security be restrained! To give liberty to the tongue to utter what it list, is the argument of an indiscreet person. In much speech there can never want sin, it either leaves some tincture of vainglory which discovers the proud heart from whence it proceeded: or some taste of scurrility which displays the wanton heart from whence it streamed; or some violent and dispassionate heat which proclaims a rancorous heart from whence it issued. Whereas a well-disposed mind will not speak before it conceive; nor deliver ought by way of expression, till it be prepared by a well-reasoned deliberation. . . . Volubility of tongue in these argues either rudeness of breeding or boldness of expression. The former may be reclaimed by a discreet tutor, but the latter, being grounded on arrogancy of conceit, seldom or never. It will beseem you, gentlewomen, whose generous education has estranged you from the first, and whose modest disposition hath weaned you from the last, in public consorts to observe rather than discourse. It suits not with her honour for a young woman to be prolocutor. But especially when either men are in presence, or ancient matrons to whom she owes a civil reverence, it will become her to tip her tongue with silence. Touching the subject of your discourse, when opportunity shall exact it of you and without touch of immodesty expect it from you, make choice of such arguments as may best improve your knowledge in household affairs and other private employments. To discourse of state matters will not become your auditory, nor to dispute of high points of divinity, will it sort well with women of your quality. These she-clerks many times broach strange opinions, which, as they understand them not themselves, so they labour to entangle others of equal understanding to themselves. That divine sentence being made an individuate comfort to their memory, would reclaim them from this error and free them from this opinionate censure: God forbid that we should not be readier to learn than to teach. Women, as they are to be no speakers in the church, so neither are they to be disputers of controversies of the church. . . . In one word, as modesty gives the best grace to your behaviour, so moderation of speech to your discourse. Silence in woman is a moving rhetoric, winning most, when in words it wooeth least. Now to give speech and silence their distinct attributes or personal characters: we may gather their several tempers by the several effects derived from them. More shall we fall into sin by speech than by silence: yea whosoever intendeth himself to speak much, seldom observes the course of doing what is just.

In the whole course of your discourse, let no light subject have any course with you; this, as it proceeds from a corrupt and indisposed heart, so it corrupts the hearer. Likewise beware of self-praise, it argues you have slow neighbours or few defects. Let not calumny run descant on your tongue, it discovers your passion too much; in the mean time, venting of your spleen affords no cure to your grief, no salve to your sore. If opportunity give your sex argument of discourse: let it neither taste of affectation, for that were servile; nor touch upon any wanton relation, for that were uncivil; nor any state political action, for the height of such a subject, compared with your weakness, were unequal. If you affect rhetoric, let it be with that familiarity expressed, as your plainness may witness for you, that you do not affect it. This will make your speech seem gracious to the hearer, confer a native modesty on the speaker, and free you of all prejudicate censure.

BRIDES' DUTIES

Samuel Rowlands, *The bride*

Text from: the first edition, 1617, fos A4ᵛff.

Mistress Susan

Good mistress bride, now we have heard your speech,
In commendation of your nuptial choice,
Give me a little favour, I beseech,
To speak unto you with a virgin's voice:
    Though divers elder maids in place there be,
    Yet I'll begin, trusting they'll second me.

We are your fellows but to church you say,
As custom is that maids should bring the bride,
And for no longer than the wedding day,
You hold with us, but turn to t'other side:
    Boasting of honour you ascend unto,
    And so go forward making much ado.

But this unto you I justly object,
In the defence of each beloved maid,
Virginity is life of chaste respect,

85

No worldly burden thereupon is laid,
   Our single life all peace and quiet brings,
   And we are free from careful earthly things.

We may do what we please, go where we list,
Without *pray husband will you give me leave?*
Our resolutions no man can resist,
Our own's our own, to give or to receive,
   We live not under this same word: *obey,*
   Till death depart us at our dying day.

*   *   *

Bride

You that intend the honourable life,
And would with joy live happily in the same,
Must note eight duties do concern a wife,
To which with all endeavour she must frame:
   And so in peace possess her husband's love,
   And all distaste from both their hearts remove.

The first is that she have domestic cares,
Of private business for the house within,
Leaving her husband unto his affairs,
Of things abroad that out of doors have been
   By him performed, as his charge to do,
   Not busy-body like inclined thereto.

Nor intermeddling as a number will,
Of foolish gossips such as do neglect,
The things which do concern them, and too ill,
Presume in matters unto no effect:
   Beyond their element when they should look,
   To what is done in kitchen by the cook.

Or unto children's virtuous education,
Or to their maids, that they good housewifes be,
And carefully contain a decent fashion,
That nothing pass the limits of degree:
   Knowing her husband's business from her own,
   And diligent do that, let his alone.

The second duty of the wife is this,
(Which she in mind ought very careful bear),

To entertain in house such friends of his,
As she doth know have husband's welcome there:
>   Not her acquaintance without his consent,
>   For that way jealousy breeds discontent . . . .

Third duty is, that of no proud pretence,
She move her husband to consume his means,
With urging him to needless vain expense,
Which toward the counter or to Ludgate leans,
>   For many idle housewives (London knows)
>   Have by their pride been husband's overthrows.

A modest woman will in compass keep,
And decently unto her calling go,
Not diving in the frugal purse too deep,
By making to the world a peacock show:
>   Though they seem fools, so yield unto their wives,
>   Some poor men do it to have quiet lives.

Fourth duty is, to love her own house best,
And be no gadding gossip up and down,
To hear and carry tales amongst the rest,
That are the news reporters of the town:
>   A modest woman's home is her delight,
>   Of business there, to have the oversight.

At public plays she never will be known,
And to be tavern guest she ever hates,
She scorns to be a street wife (idle one)
Or field wife ranging with her walking mates:
>   She knows how wise men censure of such dames,
>   And how with blots they blemish their good names. . . .

Fifth duty of a wife unto her head,
Is her obedience to reform his will,
And never with a self-conceit be led
That her advice proves good, his counsel ill:
>   In judgement being singular alone,
>   As having all the wit, her husband none. . . .

When as the husband bargains hath to make,
In things that are depending on his trade,
Let not wife's boldness power unto her take,
As though no match were good but what she made:
>   For she that thus hath oar in husband's boat,

Let her take breech, and give him petticoat.
Sixth duty is to pacify his ire,
Although she find that he impatient be,
For hasty words, like fuel add to fire,
And more, and more infenceth wrath's degree:
    When she perceives his choler in a fit,
    Let her forbear, and that's a sign of wit.

Many occasions unto men do fall,
Of adverse crosses, women not conceive,
To find us honey, they do meet with gall,
Their toil for us do their own joys bereave:
    Great shame it were, that we should add their woe,
    That do maintain, and keep, and love us so.

If that a hasty word sometime be spoke,
Let us not censure therefore they are foes,
Say 'tis infirmity that doth provoke,
Their hearts are sorry for their tongues, God knows:
    Since we by proof each day and hour find,
    For one harsh word, they give ten thousand kind.

The seventh duty that she must endeavour,
Is to observe her husband's disposition,
And thereunto conform herself for ever,
In all obedient sort, with meek submission:
    Resolving that, as his conditions are,
    Her rules of life she must according square.

His virtues and good parts which she doth find,
She must endeavour for to imitate,
The vices whereunto he is enclin'd,
She must in patience bear in mild estate:
    So that the meekness of her loving carriage,
    May be peace-maker of all strife in marriage.

She must not do as foolish women use,
When they are met about the gossip's chat,
Their absent husbands with their tongues abuse,
But utterly abhor to offer that:
    Resolving that a husband's least disgrace,
    Should cause the wife to have a blushing face.

The eighth last duty she must take upon her,
To bind all t'other seven to be done,

Is love and chief regard to husband's honour,
Which if at true affection it begun,
   Then be he poor or sick, or in distress,
   She still remains most firm in faithfulness.

William Gouge, *Of domestical duties*

One of the most comprehensive of Renaissance marriage guides, and first published in 1622, this text treats all aspects of conduct and education within the family. Text from: the third, revised, edition, 1634, the third treatise, SS4, 9, 14, 18, 42, 43, 51, 52, pp. 273–4, 279–80, 285, 289–91, 314–18, 328–33.

Of wives' particular duties

Wives submit yourselves unto your own husbands, as unto the Lord. For the husband is the head of the wife, even as Christ is the head of the church: and he is saviour of the body. Therefore as the church is subject to Christ, so let wives be subject to their husbands in everything. . . .

(Ephesians 5:22–24)

Of a fond conceit that husband and wife are equal   Contrary to the forenamed subjection is the opinion of many wives who think themselves every way as good as their husbands and no way inferior to them.

The reason whereof seemeth to be that small inequality which is betwixt the husband and the wife, for of all degrees where there is any difference betwixt person and person, there is the least disparity betwixt man and wife. Though the man be as the head, yet is the woman as the heart, which is the most excellent part of the body next the head, and almost equal to the head in many respects and as necessary as the head. As an evidence that the wife is to man as the heart to the head, she was at her first creation taken out of the side of man where his heart lieth; and though the woman was at first *of the man* created out of his side, yet *is the man also of the woman* [Gen. 2:21; 1 Cor. 11:12]. Ever since the first creation man hath been born and brought forth out of the woman's womb, *so as neither the man is without the woman, nor the woman without the man: yea as the wife hath not power of her own body but the husband, so the husband hath not power of his own body but the wife* [1 Cor. 7:4]. They are also heirs together of the grace of life [1 Pet. 3:7]. Besides wives are mothers of the same children whereof their husbands are fathers (for God said to both, multiply and increase) and mistresses of the same servants whereof they are masters (for Sarah is called a mistress) [Gen. 16:4], and in many other respects there is a common equity betwixt husbands and wives; whence many wives gather that in all things there ought to be a mutual equality.

But from some particulars to infer a general is a very weak argument.

1. Doth it follow that because in many things there is a common equity betwixt Judges of Assize, Justices of the Peace, and Constables of Towns that therefore there is in all things an equality between them?

2. In many things there is not a common equity: for the husband may command his wife, but not she him.

3. Even in those things where there is a common equity, there is not an equality, for the husband hath verily even in all things a superiority: as if there be any difference even in the aforenamed instances, the husband must have the stroke: as in giving the name of Rachel's youngest child, where the wife would have one name, the husband another, that name which the husband gave stood, *Gen.* 35:18.

Though there seem to be never so little disparity, yet God having so expressly appointed subjection, it ought to be acknowledged: and though husband and wife may mutually serve one another through love, yet the apostle suffereth not a woman to rule over the man. ...

Of wife-like sobriety A wife's outward reverence towards her husband is a manifestation of her inward due respect of him. Now then seeing the intent of the heart and inward disposition cannot be discerned by man simply in itself, that the husband may know his wife's good affection towards him, it is behoveful that she manifest the same by her outward reverence.

A wife's outward reverence consisteth in her reverend ⎱ gesture
⎰ speech.

For the first, that a reverend gesture and carriage of herself to her husband, and in her husband's presence, beseemeth a wife, was of old implied of the veil which the woman used to put on when she was brought unto her husband.... This reverend conversation consisteth in a wife-like sobriety, mildness, courtesy, and modesty.

By sobriety I mean such a comely, grave, and gracious carriage as giveth evidence to the husband that his wife respecteth his place, and the authority which God hath given him. Sobriety in general is required of all women by reason of their sex, and surely it doth well become them all: but much more doth it become wives, most of all in their husband's presence ...

Contrary to this sobriety is lightness and wantonness: which vices in a wife, especially before her husband, argueth little respect, if not a plain contempt of him. ...

Of the titles which wives give their husbands As their words must be few, so those few words must be reverend and meek: both which are also implied under the forenamed word, silence: which in the original signifieth also quietness.

Reverence hath respect to the titles whereby a wife nameth her husb
meekness to the manner of framing her speech to him.

For the titles which a wife, in speaking to her husband or naming him, giveth unto him they must be such as signify superiority and so savour of reverence. Such are the titles wherewith husbands are named in the scripture, they are the titles of honour.... Contrary are those compellations which argue equality or inferiority, rather than superiority: as, *brethren, cousin, friend, man, &c.* If a stranger be in presence, how can he tell by this manner of compellation that he whom thou speakest unto is thy husband? If he espy any matrimonial familiarity betwixt you, what can he judge of it otherwise to be but lightness and wantonness? Remember the fearful issue that had like to have fallen out by reason of such compellations given by Sarah and Rebecca to their husbands [Gen. 12:19; 20:2]. Not unlike to those that are such as these: *sweet, sweeting, heart, sweet-heart, love, joy, dear, &c.*; and such as these: *duck, chick, pigsnie, etc.*; and husbands' Christian names, as: *John, Thomas, William, Henry, &c.*, which if they be contracted (as many use to contract them thus: *Jack, Tom, Will, Hal*), they are much more unseemly: servants are usually so called.

But what may we say of those titles given to an husband by his wife, not seldom in passion but usually in ordinary speech, which are not fit to be given to the basest men that be, as *grub, rogue* and the like, which I am even ashamed to name, but that the sins of women are to be cast as dirt on their faces that they may be more ashamed?

Objection. Many of the forenamed titles are titles of amity and familiarity.

Answer. Subjection is that mark which wives are directed to aim at in their thoughts, words, deeds and whole conversation towards their husband. Such tokens of familiarity as are not withal tokens of subjection and reverence, are unbeseeming a wife because they swerve from that mark ...

Of the cases wherein a wife hath power to order things of the house without her husband's consent   A wife's obedience requireth } submission / contentment.

Submission in yielding to her husband's mind and will: contentment in resting satisfied and content with his estate and ability.

That submission consisteth in two things: first in abstaining from doing things against her husband's mind; secondly in doing what her husband requireth. The former of these requireth that a wife hath her husband's consent for the things which she doth. For the better clearing whereof we are to consider,

1   What kinds of husbands they must be whose consent is required.
2   How many ways his consent may be given.

nings whereabout his consent is to be expected.

on the one side it oft falleth out that a wise, provident and
married to a foolish woman, a very idiot that hath no
f whom there can be no question but that such a wife is to
erself and of her own head, but altogether to be ordered by
on the other side it oft falleth out that a wise, virtuous and
graw.... n is married to an husband destitute of understanding, to a
very natural (as we say) or a frenzy man, or to one made very blockish and
stupid, unfit to manage his affairs through some distemper, wound or
sickness. In such a case, the whole government lieth upon the wife, so as her
husband's consent is not to be expected.

*Question. What if the husband be a wicked and profane man, and so
blinded and stupefied in his soul, doth not his spiritual blindness and
blockishness give a religious wife as great liberty as natural stupidity?*

Answer. No verily: for St Paul exhorteth faithful wives that were married
to infidel husbands *to be subject* to them, and that *in fear* [1 Pet. 3:1,2].

The reason is clear, for spiritual blindness disableth not from civil
government; indeed nothing that such a man doth is acceptable to God or
available to his own salvation, but yet it may be profitable to man: a wicked
man may be provident enough for wife, children, and whole family, in
outward temporal things.

Again it oft falleth out that an husband is a long time far off absent from
the house; sometimes by reason of his calling, as an ambassador, soldier, or
mariner; sometimes also carelessly or wilfully neglecting house, goods, wife,
children and all; and in his absence hath left no order for the ordering of
things at home. In this case also there is no question but the wife hath power
to dispose matters without her husband's consent, provided that she observe
those rules of God's word concerning justice, equity, truth and mercy, which
an husband in his disposing of them ought to observe.

The first of these cases declareth an *impotency* in the husband, the other
an *impossibility* for him to order matters: wherefore the wife being next to
the husband, the power of ordering things is devolved on her: she is not
bound to have his consent ...

***Of aberrations contrary to a wife's subjection in doing things without or
against their husband's consent*** Now consider we the usual vices and
aberrations contrary to those duties: the general sum of all is for a wife to take
on her to do what she list, whether her husband will or no, either not willing
that he should know what she doth, or not caring though it be against his
mind and will. Of this sort are:

1. Such as privily take money out of their husbands' closets, or other like

places where he laith it, never telling him of it, nor willing that he should know it: likewise such as after the like manner, take ware out of the shop, corn out of the garner, sheep out of the flock, or any other goods to sell and make money of, or to give away, or otherwise to use so as their husbands shall never know if they can hinder it. Such wives herein sin heinously, and that in many respects.... So as what with wives purloining one way, and the children and servants another way, a man's estate may be wasted as dew before the sun and he not know which way.

2. Such as will have what allowance they think best for themselves and family, and scornfully say, *they will not be at their husband's finding: they know best what allowance is fittest for the family, and that it shall have.* Many will make their husband's ear tingle again, yea, and make the whole house (if not the street also) ring of it, if they think their allowance be not answerable to the uttermost extent of their husband's estate. This impatiency and insolency, as it crosseth God's ordinance, so it maketh both their lives uncomfortable.

3. Such as cocker,[20] attire, or any way bring up their children otherwise than their husbands would, even to the grief and dishonour of their husbands: keeping them at home, when their husband for their better education would have them abroad. As these sin in hindering the good of their children, so also in not yielding to their husbands.

4. Such as will have their own will about servants, taking them in and putting out whom they please and when they please; using some servants whom they find for their turn to the prejudice of their husband, and carrying themselves so sharply and shrewishly to others that are for their husbands turn, as a good, trusty, faithful servant cannot long stay in the house.

5. Such as secretly lend out their husband's horses, or other like cattle, more respecting to pleasure a vain friend than to please a good husband. The fault is so much the greater, when it is done to the damage and prejudice of the husband.

6. Such as are then most frolic and jolly when their husbands are furthest off and cannot know it. *Solomon* sets it down as the mark of a strumpet [Prov. 7:19] then to trick up her house and seek for guests when her husband is gone of a journey far off. Then ought she to be most solitary, and by abstaining from merry meetings to show there can be no greater damp to her mirth than the absence of her husband.

7. Such as think their houses a prison unto them that cannot long tarry at home: they think they have power to go when and whither they will, and to tarry out as long as they list, think their husbands of it what they will ...

8. Such as care not what or how they bind themselves unto without their husband's consent or knowledge: herein especially offend such as, being seduced by Jesuits, Priests or Friars, take the sacrament and thereupon by

solemn vow and oath bind themselves never to read the English Bible, nor any Protestant books; no, nor to go to any of their churches or to hear any of their sermons: and such most of all as enter into some popish nunnery, and vow never to return to their husbands again . . .

Of a wife's active obedience It is a good proof and trial of a wife's obedience to abstain from doing such things as otherwise she should do if her husband's contrary will did not restrain her, but yet that is not sufficient; there must be an active as well as a passive obedience yielded. That old law before mentioned (*thy desire shall be subject to thine husband and he shall rule over thee*) implieth so much also. If she refuse to do what he would have her do, her desire is not subject to him, but to herself . . .

Of cases wherein a wife ought not to forbear what her husband forbiddeth *Subjection must be yielded to the husband as to Christ*, whence will follow two conclusions, one negative, which is this: *the wife must yield no other subjection to her husband than what may stand with her subjection to Christ.*

The other affirmative, which is this, *the wife must be subject herself to her husband in that manner which she would or should subject herself to Christ.*

The former is a necessary condition required of all inferiors in their subjection and obedience (as I showed before), much more in a wife's subjection to her husband because there is, of all unequals, the least disparity betwixt husbands and wives.

Hence for our present purpose, I gather two more particular conclusions: the first whereof is this:

1. *If God expressly command the wife any duty, and her husband will not by any means give consent that she shall do it, but forbid her: she may and ought to do it without, or against, his consent.*

Two cautions are warily to be observed about this conclusion:

1. That the wife be sure that God hath commanded her that which she doth without or against her husband's consent. If she doubt, then she must stay and forbear till she gain his consent. When two opposite cases meet together, and the one be doubtful, the other plain and express: the doubtful case must give place to the more evident. Now the law of subjection is indefinite, *thy desire shall be subject to thine husband*; the extent of it is general *in everything*; the only reservation and exception is *in the Lord*: wherefore if the wife be not sure that that which her husband forbiddeth her is *against the Lord*, she must forbear to do it.

The second caution is that she use all good means she can to gain her husband's consent before she do, even that which is commanded against his consent. Thus she shall testify her subjection both to God and her husband. To God in that nothing can keep her from doing his express commandment:

she will rather offend her husband than God when one of them must needs be offended. To her husband, in that she putteth it to the utmost push, and useth all the means she can to avoid his offence, insomuch as he himself might see (if the God of this world blinded not his eyes) that the offence is in no way given on her part, but merely taken on his.

For proof of this, it is without all contradiction true, that the wife is not bound to greater subjection to her husband than the subject is unto the magistrate: but a subject ought not to forbear a bounded duty commanded of God because his governor forbids him. Instance the example of Daniel who daily made his prayers to God, though the king had made a solemn decree that none should ask any petitions of God or man within thirty days but of the king [Dan. 6:7]. Instance also the apostles who preached the gospel, though they were expressly forbidden [Acts 4:18].

Though the scripture be plentiful in affording examples of wives' subjection, yet it is very sparing in recording examples of those who in such warrantable cases refused to be subject, least wives from thence should take too great liberty.

Some are recorded, but such as are either extraordinary, or not every way justifiable. *Abigail's* example [1 Sam. 25:18] was extraordinary and therefore not imitable, but in such like extraordinary cases ...

Of cases where a wife ought to forbear what her husband requireth
The other particular conclusion is this, that: *If an husband require his wife to do that which God hath forbidden, she ought not do it.* Two cautions, like the former, are likewise to be observed about this point.

First, that she be sure (being truly informed by God's word) that that which she refuseth to do at her husband's command, is forbidden by God.

Secondly, that she first labour, with all meekness and by all good means that she can, to dissuade her husband from urging and pressing that upon her which with a good conscience she cannot do.

Banabe Rich, *My lady's looking glass*

Like many other conduct books, Rich tries to distinguish good women from bad by outward signs. Text from: the first edition, 1616, pp. 11ff.

My promise was to give rules how to distinguish between a good woman and a bad and promise is debt; but I must be well advised how I take the matter in hand, for we were better to charge a woman with a thousand defects in her soul than with that one abuse of her body; and we must have two witnesses, besides our own eyes, to testify, or we shall not be believed: but I have bethought myself of a couple that I hope will carry credit.

The first is the *Prophet of Esau*, that in his days challenged the daughters of *Sion* for their stretched out necks, their wandering eyes, at their mincing and wanton demeanour as they passed through the streets: these signs and shows have been ever thought to be the especial marks whereby to know a *harlot*. But *Solomon* in a more particular manner doth better furnish us with more assured notes, and to the end that we might the better distinguish the good woman from the bad, he delivereth their several qualities and wherein they are opposite. And speaking of a good woman he saith, *she seeketh out wool and flax and laboureth cheerfully with her hands: she overseeth the ways of her household and eateth not the bread of idleness* [Prov. 31].

Solomon thinketh that a good woman should be a home housewife, he pointeth her out her housework. *She overseeth the ways of her household*, she must look to her children, her servants and family: but *the paths of an harlot* (he saith) *are moveable, for now she is in the house, now in the streets, now she lieth in wait in every corner*, she is still gadding about from place to place, from person to person, from company to company, from custom to custom; she is ever more wandering: her feet are wandering, her eyes are wandering, her wits are wandering. *Her ways are like the ways of a serpent*: hard to be found out.

A good woman (again) *openeth her mouth with wisdom, the law of Grace is in her tongue: but an harlot is full of words, she is loud and babbling*, saith Solomon.

She is bold, she is impudent, she is shameless, she cannot blush: and she that hath lost all these virtues, hath lost her evidence of honesty; for the ornaments of a good woman is temperance in her mind, silence in her tongue, and bashfulness in her countenance.

It is not she that can lift up her heels highest in the dancing of a galliard, that is lavish of her lips or loose of her tongue.

Now if Solomon's testimony be good, the woman that is impudent, immodest, shameless, insolent, audacious, a nightwalker, a company-keeper, a gadder from place to place, a reveller, a ramper, a roister, a rioter: she that hath these properties hath the certain signs and marks of an harlot, as Solomon hath avowed. Now what credit his words will carry in the commissaries' court I leave to those that be advocates and proctors in women's causes.

William Vaughan, *The golden grove*

Inspired by the translations of the pseudo-Aristotelian *Economics* and Xenophon's *Economicus*, this work is part of the popular revival of economic writing at the beginning of the seventeenth century. Text from: the first edition, 1608, fos N7ᵛ–N8ᵛ.

The duties of a husband towards his wife

The duties of a husband toward his wife are 7 [*sic*] [1 Pet. 3]. The first that he give honour to his wife as the weaker vessel, for she is partaker of the grace of life. The second, he must patiently brook the hastiness of his wife, for there is nothing in the world more spiteful than a woman if she be hardly dealt withal or egged to indignation. Hence is the proverb, *anger thy dog, and he will bite thee*. The third duty, the husband in any case must not have carnal copulation with any other but his own wife for that is very unjust by reason it dissolveth the girdle of faith and chastity, and is the next way to cause her to hate him: a woman is jealous and naturally suspicious, and sith her husband breaketh with her she will not stick to break with him and privily borrow a night's lodging with her neighbour. The fourth duty, the husband must not injure his wife by word or deed, for a woman is a feeble creature and not endued with such a noble courage as the man, she is sooner pricked to the heart or moved to passions than man; and again, he that injureth his wife doth as if he should spit into the air and the same spittle return back upon his own self. The fifth, the husband in disputations with his wife, must sometimes confess himself vanquished by her. The sixth, the husband must provide for his wife and for her housekeeping, according to his ability. The seventh, the husband must suffer his wife to be merrily disposed before him otherwise (a woman's nature is such) she will by stealth find out some secret place or other to tattle in and to disport herself. The eighth and chiefest duty is that the husband have a special regard not to make two beds, for so he may take away all causes of displeasure: also if either of them chance to jar, by this means they may be soon pacified.

The duties of the wife towards her husband

But what shall the woman do? Shall she do what seemeth good in her eyes? No. For St Peter speaketh unto wives in this wise: *let wives be subject to their husbands*, which is as much to say as they must not contradict them in any point, but rather endeavour to please them by all means. The second duty, the wife must not forsake her husband in adversity, or deride him as Job's wife did when she bad him, *curse God and die* [Job . 2], but she ought to comfort and cherish him as a part of her own body. The third, she must esteem the manners of her husband to be the legal rules of her life. The fourth, she must not be too sumptuous and superfluous in her attire, as: decked with frizzled hair, embroidery, precious stones, gaudy raiments and gold put about, for they are the forerunners of adultery. *But let her have the inward man in her heart, which consisteth in the incorruption of a meek and quiet spirit, that is before God a thing much set by. For even after this manner in time past did the holy women, which trusted in God, attire themselves, and were subject to their husbands* [1 Pet. 3]. The fifth, she must not be jealous, or mistrust her husband's absence. The sixth duty of a wife is carefully to observe her household and to bring up her children and servants in the fear of God. The seventh, she must not discover her husband's imperfections and faults to any, for by disclosing them either she makes herself a jesting stock, or else she ministereth occasion for knaves to tempt her to villainy. The eighth duty of a wife is that she gibe not, nor flout her husband, but bear with him as long as she may.

Dorothy Leigh, *The mother's blessing*

Leigh's work was published posthumously, like those of Grymestone (ch. 4) and Joceline (ch. 6), by male friends or relatives after their death. The title page reads that the work was: 'left behind her for her children, containing many good exhortations and godly admonitions, profitable for all parents to leave as a legacy to their children, but especially for those, who by reason of their young years, stand most in need of instruction'. Text from: the first edition, 1616, sigs A6–A8, pp. 1–6, 14–18, 47–8.

To my beloved sons, George, John and William Leigh, all things pertaining to life and godliness

My children, God having taken your father out of this vale of tears, to his everlasting mercy in Christ, myself, not only knowing what a care he had in his lifetime that you should be brought up godlily, but also at his death being charged in his will by the love and duty which I bare him, to see you well instructed and brought up in knowledge, I could not choose but seek (according as I was duty bound) to fulfil his will in all things, desiring no greater comfort in the world than to see you grow in godliness, that so you might meet your father in heaven where I am sure he is, myself being a witness of his faith in Christ. And seeing myself going out of the world and you but coming in, I know not how to perform his duty so well as to leave you these few lines, which will show you as well the great desire your father had both of your spiritual and temporal good, as the care I had to fulfil his will in this, knowing it was the last duty I should perform unto him. But when I had written these things unto you, and had (as I thought) something fulfilled your father's request, yet I could not see to what purpose it should tend unless it were sent abroad to you: for should it be left with the eldest, it is likely the youngest should have but little part in it. Wherefore setting aside all fear, I have adventured to show my imperfections to the view of the world, not regarding what censure shall for this be laid upon me, so that herein I may show myself a loving mother, and a dutiful wife: and thus I leave you to the protection of him that made you, and rest till death,

Your fearful, faithful and careful mother.

98

The occasion of writing the book was the consideration of the care of parents for their children

My children, when I did truly weigh, rightly consider, and perfectly see the great care, labour, travail, and continual study which parents take to enrich their children, some wearying their bodies with labour, some breaking their sleeps with care, some sparing from their own bellies, and many hazarding their souls, some by bribery, some by simony, others by perjury, and a multitude by usury, some stealing on the sea, others begging by land portions from every poor man, not caring if the whole commonwealth be impoverished, so their children be enriched: for themselves they can be content with meat, drink and cloth, so that their children by their means may be made rich, always abusing this portion of scripture: *he that provideth not for his own family, is worse than an infidel* [1 Tim. 5:8]: ever seeking for the temporal things of this world and forgetting those things which be eternal: when I considered these things, I say, I thought good (being not desirous to enrich you with transitory goods) to exhort and desire you to follow the counsel of Christ: *first seek the kingdom of God and his righteousness, and then all these things shall be administered unto you* [Matt. 6:33].

The first cause of writing is a motherly affection

But least you should marvel, my children, why I do not, according to the usual custom of women, exhort you by word and admonitions, rather than by writing, a thing so unusual among us, and especially in such a time when there be so many godly books in the world that they mould in some men's studies, while their masters are marred because they will not meditate upon them, as many men's garments moth-eat in their chests, while their Christian brethren quake with cold in the street for want of covering: know therefore that it was the motherly affection that I bare unto you all, which made me now (as it often hath done heretofore) forget myself in regard of you: neither care I what you or any shall think of me if among many words I may write but one sentence which may make you labour for the spiritual food of the soul, which must be gathered every day out of the word, as the children of Israel gathered manna in the wilderness. By the which you may see it is a labour: but what labour? A pleasant labour, a profitable labour: a labour without the which the soul cannot live ...

The second cause is to stir them up to write

The second cause, my sons, why I write unto you (for you may think that had I but one cause, I would not have changed the usual order of women) is needful to be known and may do much good. For where I saw the great mercy of God towards you in making you men and placing you amongst the wise, where you may learn the true written word of God, which is the pathway to all happiness and will bring you to the chief city, the New Jerusalem, and the seven liberal sciences, whereby you shall have at least a superficial sight in all things: I thought it fit to give you good example and by writing to entreat you that when it shall please God to give both virtue and grace with your learning, he having made you men, that you may write and speak the word of God without offending any, that then you would remember to write a book unto your children of the right and true way to happiness, which may remain with them and theirs for ever.

The third cause is to move women to be careful of their children

The third is to encourage women (who, I fear, will blush at my boldness) not to be ashamed to show their infirmities, but to give men the first and chief place: yet let us labour to come in the second; and because we must needs confess that sin entered by us into our posterity, let us show how careful we are to seek to Christ to cast it out of us and our posterity, and how fearful we are that our sin should sink any of them to the lowest part of the earth; wherefore let us call upon them to follow Christ, who will carry them to the height of heaven ...

Choice of wives

Now for your wives, the Lord direct you, for I cannot tell you what is best to be done. Our Lord saith: *first seek the kingdom of God, and his righteousness, and all things else shall be ministered unto you.* First, you must seek a godly wife, that she may be a help to you in godliness; for God said *it is not good for man to be alone, let him have a helpmeet for him*; and she cannot be meet for him, except she be truly godly, for God counteth that the man is alone still if his wife be not godly. If I should write unto you how many the scripture maketh mention of that have been drawn to sin because they married ungodly wives, it would be tedious for you to read.

The world was drowned because men married ungodly wives. Solomon, who was not only the wisest man that ever was, but was also mightily endued with the spirit of God, by marrying idolatrous women fell for the time to idolatry [1 Kings 11:4]. Never think to stand where Solomon fell. I pray God that neither you, nor any of yours, may at any time marry with any of those which hold such superstitions as they did, or as some do now, as namely: to pray to saints, to pray in Latin, to pray to go to purgatory, &c. Let no riches or money bring your posterity to this kind of tradition . . .

Be not unequally yoked [2 Cor. 6:14] (saith the Holy Ghost). It is indeed very unequal for the godly and the ungodly to be united together, that their hearts must be both as one, which can never be joined in the fear of God and faith of Christ. Love not the ungodly; marry with none except you love her, and be not changeable in your love; let nothing, after you have made your choice, remove your love from her, for it is an ungodly and very foolish thing of a man to mislike his own choice.

4

SEXUALITY AND
MOTHERHOOD

INTRODUCTION

Popular proverbs from John Ray's 1678 collection are often cited in accounts of women's experiences in early modern England, but his subsequent exegetical comments on them are more often not cited:

England is the paradise of women. And well it may be called so, as might easily be demonstrated in many particulars, were not all the world already therein satisfied. Hence it hath been said that if a bridge were made over the narrow seas all the women in Europe would come over hither. Yet it is worth noting that though in no country of the world the men are so fond of, so much governed by, so much wedded to their wives, yet hath no language so many proverbial invectives against women.

(p. 64)

Ray alerts the reader to the partial nature of proverbs at the same time as he claims universality for them ('were not all the world already therein satisfied'): this double strategy allows us to focus on the contradictions of meaning here. There are two discourses about women, he suggests: the paradisal and the invective. The duality of this discourse is particularly evident in contemporary accounts of female sexuality.

These accounts are framed within the two dominant discourses of chapters 1 and 2: theology and physiology. The account of sexuality differs slightly within each, since the former emphasises more strongly the function of female sexuality within a social and moral order, that is, within marriage as understood by theological and patriarchal norms. According to the theologians, in their addresses to men, there were three main aims of marriage: procreation, avoidance of concupiscence and mutual love. Marriage is thus overtly described as a means of controlling human sexuality. Woman's place within that system was defined by her sexual status:

virgin, wife, widow or whore; and her function within it as motherhood. Thus (hetero)sexual behaviour and its concomitant relationship to a particular man (or men) defined womanhood, legally and politically. Supposedly aberrant sexual behaviour was tried and controlled in the church courts, or in the consistory courts, which heard defamation cases.

In the physiological realm women are framed as creatures weaker than men, but also as sexually active, both in their own needs and in their equal production of 'seed', despite the controversy over whether their seed was active or passive. Writers of medical textbooks and popular medical advice books are careful to describe sexual experience and practice within the dominant theological moral framework, but are likely to suggest, even if only subtextually, other less norm-referenced ways in which women behaved. There are two good examples of this. First, in the writings about menstruation and conception. Theological texts place sexual behaviour within legal marriage (pp. 106–8). Sexual pleasure is thus mean-ingful only within the concept of generation and reproduction (pp. 126–7). As many recent historians have noted, the herbals, popular medical books and commonplace books all include sections on 'provoking the terms', as well as ones on 'causes of abortion' (pp. 109, 127, 128): it does not take much imagination to read these as oblique advice for post-conception control of fertility and hence of an underground history of sexual behaviour which is not controlled by the ideological assertions of the theologians.[1] When combined with population studies on fertility rates, examination of the cases before the church courts, as well as diaries and letters, social historians have been able to construct a picture of early modern England where sexuality was managed, but not in quite the way the church represents. Thus fertility was to some extent controlled: by age of marriage; through herbal means; religious taboos on the timing of sexual intercourse; through lactation; through coitus interruptus; and in the last resort by physical abortions. The second example of non-standardised habits of behaviour is in the buried references to sexual pleasure obtained through non-penetrative sex, references which can also be interpreted as acknowledgements of tribadic (or lesbian) sexuality (pp. 62, 129–30).

The link between sexual pleasure, conception and legal marriage is maintained through the dominant ideological modes and laws of the time: unmarried mothers had their children removed from them and were forced to undergo a church penance and to live in a house of correction. Pregnant women were hurried into marriages in order to avoid this shame and to maintain some economic freedom.[2] Midwives were asked to swear not to dispose of foetuses 'in the jakes' (chapter 7, pp. 212–14), and to disclose the name of a father if the mother was concealing it. The sermons, conduct books and mother's advice books all placed sexuality within the framework of motherhood (pp. 107–8, 114–15, 122–3): controlled by economic and political subordination to the husband and circumscribed by the end for which woman's sexuality had been ordained: the bearing of children (pp. 105–6, 123–4).

This selection deliberately echoes that ideological organisation of women's sexuality. This enables us to read that organisation of sexuality within motherhood for ourselves. Secondly, it enables us to see that such texts are self-consciously ideological: exhorting ideal behaviour, from which we might infer that such ideals were far from the norm. Thirdly, it also allows us to read such texts 'against the grain' (for example reading recipes 'to provoke the terms' as potential abortifacients) and to hypothesise early modern reading strategies in the same way. Finally, it helps us to see that a uniquely female experience (motherhood) had its own resonances, myths and spaces for women and a women's community, which, whilst dominated by male discourses, continued with a vitality and organisation of its own (pp. 114–15, 116–20).[3]

Once again, we may observe the double standard which male writers apply to women and which many women then internalise, or in seventeenth-century terms, make *conscionable*.[4] Nevertheless, there are two authentically female spaces, one of which is central to the ideology I have been delineating, and the other of which is marginal. The first is women's own writings about motherhood and maternity, represented by Grymestone, Clinton and Bentley's collection of prayers on childbirth and for children by various women (pp. 114–15, 116 ff., 120 ff.). Each of these shows that, circumscribed as they are by the masculine discourse, women find a language for celebrating fecundity and maternal love, as well as their fears of childbirth. The second is the language of romantic love between women, here represented by Aphra Behn. Whether such texts are lesbian or not,[5] their significance at the very least lies in their delineation of a space and experience which is not part of the dominant and patriarchal masculine world.

Desiderius Erasmus, *The woman in childbed*

Eutrapelus arrives at Fabulla's home where she has just given birth to a son. He proceeds to advise her about childcare, and specifically breast-feeding. Text from: *The Colloquies*, transl. H.M., 1671 (first edition, in Latin, 1519), pp. 301–2.

Eu. Suppose that there were no matter at all what milk the young infant sucks, or what spittle it swallows down with the meat chewed before for it; suppose there shall fall out to be such a nurse, as I know not whether any can be found out, dost thou think that there is anyone which can away with all the irksomeness of nursing a child like as the mother, the excrements, attendances, the cryings, diseases, and the never sufficiently diligent care to look to it? If there be any who can love it so well as the mother doth, there will be some that may take as much care of it. Moreover, this besides will fall out, that thy son may love thee the less, when the natural love is divided as it were between two mothers. Neither wilt thou be carried with the like natural affection towards thy son, because being afterward grown bigger, he will less willingly obey thy commands, and thou wilt take the less care of him, in whose behaviour it may be thou wilt see his nurse. And the chief furtherance of learning is a mutual love betwixt the teacher and the scholar. Therefore if he shall lose nothing of the fragrancy of his natural affection, thou wilt more easily instil into him precepts how to live well. For herein the mother hath no small power, even for this reason, because she hath to deal with very yielding matter, and pliable to all things.

Fa. As far as I perceive, it's not such an easy thing to bear children, as the common people think it.

Eu. If thou givest little credit to me, lo, Paul speaking plainly of the woman: *she shall be saved*, quoth he, *by bearing children.*

Fa. Is she safe then which hath born children?

Eu. No such matter: but he adds, *if the children shall abide in the faith.* Thou hast not fully performed the duty of a mother, unless thou shalt first fashion the tender little body of thy son, and afterwards his no less tender mind with good education.

Fa. Why, but that is not in the mother's power, that her children should persevere in godliness.

Eu. It may be so, but careful instruction is of so great moment, as that Paul thinks that it is to be charged upon the mothers if the children take evil courses. To conclude, if thou wilt do what lieth in thee, God will give his assistance to thy diligence.

Fa. Truly, Eutrapelus, thy words have persuaded me, if thou canst in like manner persuade my parents and my husband.

Henry Bullinger, *The Christian state of matrimony*

Bullinger's writing was extremely popular amongst continental and English reforming Protestants. This translation went through eight editions in the hundred years after its first publication. Text from: the 1541 edition, transl. Miles Coverdale, chs 13, 23, fos 31ʳff, 75ʳ.

How shameful, vicious, and abominable the sin of whoredom is

In the fifth of the proverbs doth Solomon say after this manner: *the lips of an harlot are as a sweet dropping honey-comb, and her throat is softer than oil: but her end is bitterer than death, and as sharp as a two-edged sword. Her feet lead unto death, and her path draweth unto hell. Therefore see that thou go not in unto her, neither draw nigh to the doors of her house, lest strangers have thy substance and least the cruel get thine increase.* With few words doth Solomon decipher the short and sweet deceitfulness of whoredom, which yet leaveth behind it a perpetual bitterness and briefly he showeth how that whoredom destroyeth in soul, in honour, in body and in good. As for examples, we need not to set forth any, there are too many before our eyes, the more pity. The stories do testify that the french pox came of an harlot into the world through whoredom. How many a man hath consumed all his substance and goods with harlots, and at the last hath been hanged, drawn or headed?

Yet go the shameless harlots forth still in to their own perdition, vice and abomination, yea and undertake to blaspheme wedlock and somewhat to excuse their own mischief. Therefore talk they of much trouble that is in wedlock. And as for their whorish life it is nothing else but open vice and abomination before God and all honest people. Filthy is filthiness still, although the filthy swine delight therein. They speak much of evil wives which, when some men had taken, they could not be rid of them with any fair means. And yet they cannot leave their vain, crafty and unfaithful harlots of whom they themselves are mocked and scorned to the uttermost, yea and are fain to suffer more of such vicious and filthy bodies than any man doth of his honest wife. They speak much likewise of bringing up of children which are born in wedlock. And yet they themselves in whoredom are fain to bring up the bastards which they have gotten, like as aforetime they were wont to build mawmet[6] houses and field chapels with collections and gatherings of every man.

They speak of much travail and carelessness, how the household must be brought up and provided for in wedlock. And yet the doting fools themselves are fain to nourish those shameful harlots with much greater care and yet be afraid that when they have done their best, the greedy sack will not be filled and that the filthy strumpet will yet bring forth a greater reckoning upon the trencher,[7] and all to get the bag of money into her own hands. Moreover among whores is wasting and expenses most regarded: neither art thou welcome but thy money. *No more money, no more love. I must have the money and purse,* saith the harlot, *take thou thy cloak and thy baggage. Let another come that hath more money, for he hath been in the bath and is dispatched.* Thus may he bite his lip and scratch his pate, and take that for his farewell that he getteth of his harlot.

They complain moreover of the crying of children in the nights and how the married folks cannot sleep, but must watch by the means thereof. And yet the doting fools themselves go all night long up and down through the streets and keep the Devil's watch with painfulness, frost and unrest. Let no reasonable man therefore be snared still in whoredom by such harlots, to the slander and dishonour of holy wedlock. Whoredom (no doubt) hath much more disquietness, anguish and trouble than hath the state of holy marriage. The pain also that is in marriage is godly and honest. God giveth such patience, strength and good will unto the faithful that can easily away with all manner of conjugal cares. As for harlots they are the Devil's martyrs and have always dishonour and shame ...

How daughters and maidens must be kept

As for this thing every discreet parent shall know by the foresaid rules how to order them to avoid all wantonness and niceness in words, gestures, and deed, to eschew all unhonest games and pastimes, to avoid all unhonest loves and occasions of the same, as unhonest dancing, wanton communication, company with ribalds[8] and filthy speeches: teach them to avert their sight and senses from all such inconveniences, let them avoid idleness, be occupied either doing some profitable thing for your family, or else reading some goodly book. Let them not read fables of fond and light love, but call upon God to have pure hearts and chaste, that they might cleave only to their spouse Christ, unto him married by faith which is the most purest wedlock of us all, pure virgins being both the married and the unmarried. Evil words, saith Paul, corrupt good manners, uncleanness and covetousness let them not once be named among you, nor no foolish ribaldry talking, nor light jesting, which are not comely, but be occupied in prayers and thanksgiving. Books of Robin Hood, Bevis of Hampton, Troilus and such like fables do but kindle in liars like lies and wanton love, which ought not in youth with their first spettle to be drunken in, least they ever remain in them. If ye delight to sing songs ye have the psalms and many goodly songs and books in English right fruitful and sweet. Take the New Testament in your hands and study it diligently and learn your profession in baptism to mortify your flesh and to be received in the spirit; learn the use of the Lord's supper to remember his death, and to give him perpetual thanks for thy redemption. Mothers must also teach their daughters to work to love their husbands and children. And let them lay their hands to spin, sew, weave, &c.

3 Eucharius Roesslin,
The birth of mankind, otherwise named the woman's book

Raynald's translation of Roesslin's texts was the first midwife's book published in English, first in 1540 and republished thirteen times in the next hundred years. It was also distinguished by its illustrations, mostly appropriated from continental editions of Vesalius. It aimed at a popular audience, rather than a learned one, and hence was read by mothers as well as midwives, rather than surgeons. Text from: the 1545 edition, transl. Thomas Raynald, fos B2ʳff.

A prologue to the women readers

And think not the utility and profit of this first book, and knowledge thereof, to be of little or small value, but take it as the foundation and ground by the perseverance whereof your wits and understanding shall be illuminate and lightened, the better to understand how everything cometh to pass within your bodies in time of conception, bearing and of birth. And further, by the perfect knowledge of this book ye shall clearly perceive the reason of many diseases which happen peculiarly to women and the causes thereof, by which perseverance again ye shall have the readier understanding how to withstand and remedy the said infirmities and diseases. For note ye well that as there is no man, whatsoever he be, that shall become an absolute and perfect physician unless he have an absolute and perfect knowledge of all the inwards and outwards of man's and woman's body: even so ye shall never groundly understand the matters contained in the second book or any other communication or writing touching the same intent, except ye first have true and just cognisance in the first book. Again when that a woman come to a physician for counsel concerning something that may be amiss in the part, the answer of the physician and reasonable allegations of causes to the same infirmity is many times obscure, dark, and strange to be comprehended by the woman for lack of due knowledge of the situation, manner and fashions of the inwards. And truly when a person is sick or diseased in any part, it is half a comfort, yea half his health, to understand in what part the disease is, and how that part lieth in his body. This knowledge also ministereth yet a further engine and policy to invent infinitely the better how the medicine should be applied and after the most profitable sort ministered and set to the diseased plot. To be short, all the witnesses and artificial crafty invention, and divers manners of ministrations in the noble science of physic proceedeth and springeth of the profound knowledge of anatomy.

* * *

Wherefore considering that there is nothing in this world so necessary, nor so good, holy or virtuous, but that it may by wickedness be abused, it shall be no great wonder though this little book also be made, written and set forth for a good purpose, yet by light and lewd persons be used contrary to goodness, honesty or the intent of the writer thereof. The abusion of this book (in my simple judgement) consisteth only in these two points: the one is, least that some ill-disposed person would wickedly abuse such medicines as be here declared for a good purpose, to some devilish and lewd use. What

I mean by lewd use of them, they that have understanding right soon will perceive. The second point is lest that this book happening into any light merchant's hands should minister matters unto such to devise of these things at unset and unseemly times, to the derision or ashaming of such women as should be in presence. To these reasons can I make no better answer than hath been alleged before. Notwithstanding, yet I say that I trust, yea, and do not doubt, but that this book shall be so discreetly divided abroad that none of them shall fall in such persons' handling.

* * *

For truly as for my part considering the manifold and imminent dangers and perils the which all manner of women of what estate or degree so ever they be, in their labours do sustain and abide, yea many times with peril of their life (of the which there be so many examples needless here to be rehearsed), I thought it should be a very charitable and laudable deed and right thankfully to be accepted of all honourable and other honest matrons, if by my pains this little treatise were made to speak English. . . . So that to them which diligently will advert and give heed to the instructions of this little book, it may supply the tool and place of a good midwife and advise them many times of sundry cases, chances, and remedies wherein peradventure right wise women and good midwives shall be full ignorant. And truly (as I have been credibly informed by divers persons worthy to be believed) there be sith the first setting forth of this book, right many honourable ladies and other worshipful gentlewomen, which have not disdained the oftener by the occasion of this book to frequent and haunt women in their labours, carrying with them this book in their hands and causing such part of it as doth chiefly concern the same purpose, to be read before the midwife and the rest of the women then being present, whereby oft times then all have been put in remembrance of that wherewith labouring women have been greatly comforted and alleviated of her throngs and travail.

Thomas Becon, *The book of matrimony*

Becon was one of the licensed preachers at Canterbury cathedral under Edward VI and Elizabeth I, his works and sermons expressing Protestant beliefs in a straightforward fashion. Included here are short extracts from Book Two, and a longer piece from Book Four, referring specifically to women. Text from: *Works*, 1564 (the first edition of *The book of matrimony*), fos 627, 652ᵛ, 673ʳ–8ᵛ.

For they [Christians] may by no means put away their wives for any displeasure, for any fault either of body or of mind (whoredom only excepted), although the civil laws give liberty to the man to put away his wife if she be such one as would poison him (as is a murderer, a thief), haunteth the company of strange men, liveth abroad in the nights without her husband's consent, &c. Deformities of body with the sickness and diseases thereof, again the unperfection of the mind with the infirmities thereof, are no sufficient causes why a Christian man may lawfully put away his wife from him: so that neither diseases, although never so grievous, painful, and long; neither old age, although never so crooked and tedious; neither barrenness, although never so ingrate and unpleasant; neither poverty, although never so great and intolerable; neither the frowardness of the tongue nor yet the unruliness and impatiency of the mind, although never so unsufferable; nor any other human case (whoredom only excepted) can dissolve matrimony between man and wife.

* * *

Bastard children be not lawful and therefore by the ancient canons he is not to be admitted unto the ecclesiastical ministry, whose mother is not knit to his father by lawful copulation in this most worthy order of matrimony for a bondage of perpetual fellowship. Again, a bastard is straightly prohibited both by human laws and constitutions of wise men to be the heir of temporal lands and goods. For they have no lawful heir which by neglecting and despising matrimony for the wanton and enticing lust of the flesh, unlawfully company together. And it is the common sentence and judgement of lawyers that he hath an uncertain father and a naughty mother which is not born in matrimony. For he is base-born and is the son of the people, yea rather the son of no man, which is the child of a woman not lawfully married. But he is the true heir and true son whose mother, without the infamy of sin, without the blame of kinfolk, without the offence of God, is married to a certain, well-known father, and without slander abideth by him continually. Therefore only matrimony maketh children to be certain and giveth true and undoubtful heirs; it maketh the company of man and wife together honest and lawful; it bringeth glory, honour and worship; it maintaineth a good conscience; it increaseth the stock and family; it gathereth alliance; it contenteth all good men.

How married folk ought to live in the holy state of honourable wedlock

The duty of a married woman toward her husband First it belongeth to a godly married woman to understand, that as God in his holy ordinance hath appointed the husband to be head ruler and governor of his wife: so likewise hath he ordained even from the beginning, that the wife should be in subjection and obedience to her own husband, as it is written: *thy lust shall*

111

pertain to thy husband and he shall have the rule of thee . . .

Secondly, as the woman's duty is to be in subjection to her husband: so likewise is she bound by the commandment of God to be chaste, pure and honest in deed, in word, in gesture, in apparel and in all her behaviour, that no point of lightness appear in her, but all modesty, sobriety, gravity, chastity, honesty, womanliness, &c., that whosoever beholdeth her, may justly seem to look upon a perfect pearl of precious purity. For nothing doth so dishonest an honest woman as lightness, wantonness and dishonesty. In her deeds let her provide that no uncomeliness appear. Let her refrain herself from all wicked company. Let her not accustom herself to strange flesh [Prov. 6], but content herself only with the love of her husband. For if shipwreck of a woman's honesty be once made, there remaineth nothing in her praiseworthy. For as the wise man saith [Eccles. 23], first she hath been unfaithful unto the law of the highest; secondly she hath forsaken her own husband; thirdly, she hath played the whore in adultery and gotten her children by another man. She shall be brought out of the congregation and her children shall be looked upon. Her children shall not take root and, as for fruit, her branches shall bring forth none. A shameful report shall she leave behind her and her dishonour shall not be put out . . .

And as it is the duty of an honest wife in all her acts and deeds to be chaste and pure: so likewise must she provide that her words be utterly estranged from all wantonness, jesting, filth speaking, and whatsoever may offend chaste cares, according to this commandment of the apostle: *let no filthy communication proceed out of your mouth but that which is good to edify withal as oft as need is, that it may minister grace to the hearers* [Eph. 4]. Again, as *for fornication and all uncleanness or covetousness, let it not once be named among you, as it becometh saints: or filthiness or foolish talking or jesting, which are not comely, but rather giving of thanks* [Eph. 5]. It is unseemly for a man to use unclean talk: but for a woman to use it, it is more than twice unseemly, seeing that there is nothing that so garnisheth a woman as silence. Few words in a woman is ever most commendable: even as nothing doth more discommend a woman then the multitude of words, according to the common proverb: a woman should be seen and not heard. It is good for every honest woman to remember this saying of our saviour Christ, *that at the day of judgement we shall render an accompt of every idle word that we have spoken* [Matt. 12].

Not only from unseemly and unhonest deeds and words shall a godly wife abstain, but also from all light gestures, whether it be with the head, eyes, tongue, lips, hands, feet, or with any other parts of the body, with this remembrance: that her body is the temple of the Holy Ghost and that it is not lawful to take the members of Christ and to make them the members of a whoremonger [1 Cor. 3:6]. Unchaste gestures are evident signs of an unchaste mind. The eye showeth the disposition of the heart. It is truly said of the wise man: the whoredom of a woman may be known by the pride of her eyes and eye lids. If thy daughter be not shamefast hold her straightly, lest she abuse herself thorough overmuch liberty. Beware of all the dishonesty of her eyes, and marvel not if she do against thee [Eccles. 16] ...

Thirdly, it is the duty of an honest and godly wife diligently to look unto those things which are within her house and by no means to suffer anything to perish, or to be unfruitfully and wastefully spent. For as the man is bound to make provision for his family and to bring it home, so is it the part of an honest and wise woman to provide that all things be safely kept and spent in due order, as we be taught by the very fowls of the air.... And that she may give the more diligence in this behalf, it is fitting and convenient that she be no idle and vain gadder abroad, nor haunter of other men's houses (much less taverns and alehouses or brothel's houses), which thing St Paul grievously rebuketh in the widows of his time [1 Tim. 5], but that she continually keep at home, except some urgent, grave, weighty and necessary cause constrain her to go forth: yea and that she being at home, be not idle or spend her time playing at the dice or cards, and in such like vain and unfruitful pastimes, but that she rather spend her time in fruitful and necessary occupations, profitable to her husband, to herself, to her family and to the commonweal. For there is not a more evident token of a light woman or harlot then seldom to tarry at home, and many times causeless to gad abroad ...

Fourthly, whatsoever woman will do the office of a true married wife, she may not only train her life after such sort as I have heretofore described, but she must also have a diligent eye to the virtuous education and bringing up of her children, but specially her daughters, which principally appertain unto her cure, and to the godly and honest governance of her woman servants. But first of all as touching her daughters, she shall at all times with all diligence labour to train them up in the knowledge of God and of his holy word, in the faith, fear and love of God, and teach them often to pray and to call on the name of our Lord God, and to give him most humble thanks for his benefits, and also hear them read the holy scriptures themselves, or else cause them to hear others read the word of God unto them, that even from their cradles (as they use to say) they may drink in godliness and grow daily more and more in the knowledge of God and of his most blessed will and so at the last wax ancient in Christ. Again she shall continually, with most sweet motherly exhortations, move them unto virtue, and stay them from vice; declaring unto them what a precious jewel virtue is in the sight of God, and contrariwise what a horrible monster sin is before the eyes of God's majesty: the one worthy of praise and glory, the other to be rewarded with plagues in this world and in the world to come, with pains everlasting.

Elizabeth Grymestone, *Miscelanea, meditations, memoratives*

Grymestone's work was written for her only surviving child, and published after her death. Text from: the first edition, 1604, fos A3ʳff.

To her loving son, Bernie Grymestone

My dearest son, there is nothing so strong as the force of love; there is no love so forcible as the love of an affectionate mother to her natural child; there is no mother can either more affectionately show her nature, or more naturally manifest her affection, than in advising her children out of her own experience to eschew evil and incline them to do that which is good.... I leave thee this portable *veni mecum* for thy counsellor in which thou maist see the true portraiture of thy mother's mind, and find something either to resolve thee in thy doubts, or comfort thee in thy distress; hoping that, being my last speeches, they will be kept in the conservance of thy memories, which I desire thou will make a register of heavenly meditations ...

I have prayed for thee that thou mightest be fortunate in two hours of thy life time: in the hour of thy marriage, and at the hour of thy death. Marry in thine own rank, and seek especially in it thy contentment and preferment: let her neither be so beautiful as that every liking eye shall level at her; nor yet so brown as to bring thee to a loathed bed. Defer not thy marriage till thou comest to be saluted with a *God speed you sir*, as a man going out of the world after forty; neither yet to the time of *God keep you sir*, whilst thou art in thy best strength after thirty; but marry in the time of *you are welcome sir*, when thou art coming into the world. For seldom shalt thou see a woman out of her own love to pull a rose that is full blown, deeming them always sweetest at the first opening of the bud.... Let thy life be formal, that thy death may be fortunate: for he seldom dies well that liveth ill. To this purpose as thou hast within thee reason as thy counsellor to persuade or dissuade thee, and thy will as an absolute prince with a *fiat vel evetetur*, with a *let it be done or neglected*; yet make thy conscience thy *censor morum* [*censor of behaviour*], and chief commander in thy little world: let it call reason to account whether she have subjected herself against reason to sensual appetites. Let thy will be censured, whether her desires have been chaste or as a harlot she hath lusted after her own delights. Let thy thoughts be examined. If they be good, they are of the spirit (quench not the spirit), if bad, forbid them entrance: for once admitted, they straightways fortify and are expelled with more difficulty, than not admitted.

* * *

114

My desire is that thou mightest be seasoned in these precepts in thy youth that the practice of thy age may have a taste of them. And because that is incident to quick spirits to commit rash attempts, as ever the love of a mother may challenge the performance of her demand for a dutiful child, be a bridle to thyself to restrain thee from doing that which indeed thou maist do: that thou maist the better forbear that which in truth thou oughtest not to do; for *he seldom commits deadly sins, that makes a conscience of a venial scandal.*

Thou seest my love hath carried me beyond the list I resolved on, and my aching head and trembling hand have rather a will to offer, than ability to afford, further discourse. Wherefore with as many good wishes to thee, as good will can measure, I abruptly end, desiring God to bless thee with sorrow for thy sins, thankfulness for his benefits, fear of his judgement, love of his mercies, mindfulness of his presence: that living in his fear, thou maist die in his favour, rest in his peace, rise in his power, remain in his glory for ever and ever.

Thine assured loving mother,
Elizabeth Grymestone

Christopher Newstead, *An apology for women: or women's defence*

Although this work participates in the Jacobean debate on the virtues or otherwise of women, Newstead historicises this debate by arguing that gender roles have changed over time, and that motherhood gives woman a significant and central role in any society. Text from: the first edition, 1620, pp. 2ff, 48–53.

It is true, at first, when there was but two actors upon this theatre of the world, woman was the siren that allured man unto evil: but now each man with *Tiresias*, is metamorphosed into a woman: pleasures and delights are the engendering serpents that have womanised their affections: men were the more perfect by nature, but women now than they by industry (and it is more difficult to reobtain virtue than to keep it). Eve then tempted Adam, but now Adam tempts Eve, and it is better to be conquered by nature than by art. It is Catullus his saying that he could, in those things which nature gave to man, suffer patiently himself to be subdued but not in those that might be assequated[9] and got by our endeavours. For to be delinquent or faulty by nature, that is not ours but nature's fault; but to be ill by corruption, that is not nature's but our fault. What if she were an instrumental cause of our fall, was she not as much the cause of our rising? But we all sooner forget benefits than injuries: we are eagle-eyed in espying their faults, but dark-sighted owls in perceiving their virtues.

SEXUALITY AND MOTHERHOOD

That children are most obliged to their mothers

Educing, education and affection are the threefold cords that should tie each child to the love of its mother: first by educing or inducing to this world, wherein every mother is as a good landlord to her child, giving it both house-room and nutriment when it, like an unruly tenant, doth grieve and vex her, and, which is against the lease of equity, many times cuts and crops the flourishing trees of their beauty, and grown too great for their places, as many men's minds are for their estates, they seek for a more ample habitation ... and yet women show themselves the truest lovers, they love them that hurt them; and that it is better not to begin a good action at all than to desist, having begun, they persevere in their benefits giving them that other nature, education: nourishing our bodies as the pelican, though not with the blood, yet with the substance of their breasts, and when they are able instruments to exercise the faculties of the soul they (and that is, the greatest benefit which perfects the soul) suckle our minds with the milk of good manners, training us up as *Tanaquil*[10] did her son, in religion and learning. The two *Gracchi*[11] reaped all the flowers of their oratory, from the garden of their mother's virtues. Caesar obtained his eloquence by conversing with his mother. And Socrates, that Athenian eagle, exhausted all his wisdom from the well-spring of *Diclinna's*[12] instructions ... Two reasons may be given why they do most affect their children. First because they are certain they are theirs. Wherefore Telemachus being asked, if it were true that Ulysses was his father? Answered, *my mother saith he was.* Secondly for that they have most sorrow by them: for, *we love that most dearly that costs us dearest.* There is one honour (saith Aristotle) due to the father, another to the mother: we owe most honour to our father in a geometrical proportion in respect of dignity, but most to our mother in an arithmetical proportion, in respect of desert. For we have of them principally our essence; secondly our nourishment; thirdly our education: and: *love is the loadstone of love, and he is the most obdure, that doth not repay it.* There is no ingratitude comparable to that which is committed against the mother.

Elizabeth Clinton, *The Countess of Lincoln's nursery*

Unlike the other writings on motherhood by women, this was published during the Countess's lifetime. It is addressed to her daughter-in-law. Text from: the first edition, 1622, pp. 12ff.

Epistle to the right honourable and approved virtuous Lady Bridget, Countess of Lincoln:
For the better expressing and keeping in memory my love and your worthiness, I do offer unto your ladyship the first work of mine that ever

116

came in print, because your rare example hath given an excellent approbation to the matter contained in this book: for you have passed by all excuses and have ventured upon, and do go on with, that loving act of a loving mother, in giving the sweet milk of your own breasts to your own child; wherein you have gone before the greatest number of honourable ladies of your place in these latter times.

The Countess of Lincoln's nursery

Because it hath pleased God to bless me with many children and so caused me to observe many things falling out to mothers and to their children, I thought it good to open my mind concerning a special matter belonging to all childbearing women seriously to consider of, and, to manifest my mind the better, even to write of this matter so far as God shall please to direct me: in sum the matter I mean is the duty of nursing due by mothers to their own children.

In setting down whereof I will first show that every woman ought to nurse her own child; and secondly I will endeavour to answer such objections as are used to be cast out against this duty to disgrace the same.

The first point is easily performed. For it is the express ordinance of God that mothers should nurse their own children, and, being his ordinance, they are bound to it in conscience. This should stop the mouths of all repliers, for God is most wise [Isa. 31:2], and therefore must needs know what is fittest and best for us to do: and to prevent all foolish fears or shifts, we are given to understand [Gen. 17:1] that he is also all sufficient, and therefore infinitely able to bless his own ordinance and to afford us means in ourselves (as continual experience confirmeth) toward the observance thereof.

If this (as it ought) be granted, then how venturous are those women that dare venture to do otherwise, and so to refuse and, by refusing, to despise that order which the most wise and almighty God hath appointed and instead thereof to choose their own pleasures? Oh, what peace can there be to these women's consciences, unless through the darkness of their understanding they judge it no disobedience?

And then they will drive me to prove that this nursing and nourishing of their own children in their own bosoms is God's ordinance; they are very wilful or very ignorant if they make a question of it, for it is proved sufficiently to be their duty, both by God's word and also by his works.

* * *

And so I come to the last part of my promise; which is to answer objections made by divers against this duty of mothers to their children.

First it is objected that Rebecca had a nurse and that therefore her mother did not give her suck of her own breasts, and so good women in the first ages did not hold them to this office of nursing their own children. To this I answer, that if her mother had milk and health, and yet did put this duty from her to another, it was her fault, and so proveth nothing against me. But it is manifest that she that Rebecca calleth her nurse was called so either for that she most tended her while her mother suckled her; or for that she weaned her; or for that during her nonage and childhood she did minister to her continually such good things as delighted and nourished her up . . .

Secondly, it is objected that it is troublesome, that it is noisome to one's clothes; that it makes one look old, &c. All such reasons are uncomely and unchristian to be objected and therefore unworthy to be answered: they argue unmotherly affection, idleness, desire to have liberty to gad from home, pride, foolish fineness, lust, wantonness and the like evils. Ask Sarah, Hannah, the blessed virgin, and any modest loving mother, what trouble they counted it to give their little ones suck? Behold most nursing mothers and they be as clean and sweet in their clothes, and carry their age and hold their beauty as well as those that suckle not; and most likely are they so to do, because keeping God's ordinance they are sure of God's blessing; and it hath been observed in some women that they grow more beautiful and better favoured by very nursing their own children.

But there are some women that object fear, saying that they are so weak and so tender that they are afraid to venture to give their children suck, lest they endanger their health thereby. Of these I demand, why then they did venture to marry and so to bear children; and if they say they could not choose and that they thought not that marriage would impair their health, I answer that for the same reasons they should set for themselves to nurse their own children, because they should not choose but do what God would have them do; and they should believe that this work will be for their health also, seeing it is ordinary with the Lord to give good stomach, health and strength to almost all mothers that take these pains with their children . . .

Now if any reading these few lines return against me, that it may be I myself have given my own children suck and therefore am bolder, and more busy to meddle in urging this point, to the end to insult over, and to make them to be blamed that have not done it. I answer, that whether I have or have not performed this my bounden duty, I will not deny to tell my own practice. I know and acknowledge that I should have done it, and having not done it was not for want of will in myself, but partly I was overruled by another's authority, and partly deceived by some ill counsel, and partly I had not so well considered of my own duty in this motherly office, as since I did when it was too late for me to put it in execution. Wherefore being pricked in heart for my undutifulness, this way I study to redeem my peace, first by repentance towards God, humbly and often craving his pardon for this my offence; secondly, by studying how to show double love to my children to make them amends for neglect of this part of love to them, when they should have hung on my breasts and have been nourished in mine own bosom; thirdly by doing my endeavour to prevent many Christian mothers from sinning in the same kind, against our most loving and gracious God.

And for this cause I add unto my performed promise this short exhortation: namely I beseech all godly women to remember how we elder ones are commanded to instruct the younger to love their children: now, therefore, love them so as to do this office to them when they are born, more gladly for love's sake than a stranger, who bore them not, shall do for lucre's sake. Also I pray you set no more so light by God's blessing in your own breasts, which the Holy Spirit ranketh with other excellent blessings; if it be unlawful to trample underfoot a cluster of grapes, in which a little wine is found; then how unlawful is it to destroy and dry up those breasts, in which your own child (and perhaps one of God's very elect, to whom to be a nursing father is a king's honour; and to whom to be a nursing mother is a queen's honour) might find food of sincere milk even from God's immediate providence, until it were fitter for stronger meat? I do know that the Lord may deny some women, either to have any milk in their breasts at all, or to have any health, or to have a right mind: and so they may be letted from this duty by want, by weakness, by lunacy, &c. But I speak not to these: I speak to you, whose consciences witness against you that you cannot justly allege any of those impediments.

Do you submit yourselves to the pain and trouble of this ordinance of God? Trust not other women, whom wages hire, to do it better than yourselves, whom God and nature ties to do it. I have found by grievous experience such dissembling in nurses, pretending sufficiency of milk, when indeed they had too much scarcity; pretending willingness, towardness, wakefulness, when indeed they have been most wilful, most forward and most slothful, as I fear the death of one or two of my little babes came by the default of these nurses. Of all those which I had for eighteen children, I had but two which were thoroughly willing and careful. Divers have had their children miscarry in the nurse's hands, and are such mothers (if it were by the nurse's carelessness) guiltless? I know not how they should, since they will shut them out of the arms of nature and leave them to the will of a stranger; yea to one that will seem to estrange herself from her own child, to give suck to the nurse-child. This she may fain to do upon a courteous composition, but she frets at it in her mind, if she have any natural affection.

Therefore be no longer at the trouble and at the care to hire others to do your own work; be not so unnatural to thrust away your own children; be not so hardy as to venture a tender babe to a less tender heart; be not accessory to that disorder of causing a poorer woman to banish her own infant for the entertaining of a richer woman's child, as it were bidding her unlove her own to love yours. We have followed Eve in transgression, let us follow her in obedience. When God lay the sorrows of conception, of breeding, of bringing forth and bringing up her children upon her, and so upon us in her loins, did she reply any word against? Not a word; so I pray you all mine own daughters, and others that are still childbearing, reply not against the duty of suckling them when God hath sent you them.

Think always that, having the child at your breast and having it in your arms, you have God's blessing there. For children are God's blessings. Think again how your babe crying for your breast, sucking heartily the milk out of it, and growing by it, is the Lord's own instruction: every hour, and every day that you are suckling it, instructing you to show that you are his new born babes, by your earnest desire after his word and the sincere doctrine thereof, and by your daily growing in grace and goodness thereby, so shall you reap pleasure and profit. Again you may consider that when your child is at your breast, it is a fit occasion to move your heart to pray for a blessing upon that work and to give thanks for your child and for ability and freedom unto that which many a mother would have done and could not, who have tried and ventured their health and taken much pains and yet have not obtained their desire. But they that are fitted every way for this commendable act have certainly great cause to be thankful: and I much desire that God may have glory and praise for every good work, and you much comfort that do seek to honour God in all things. Amen.

DEVOTIONAL ADVICE ON CHILDBIRTH

Thomas Bentley, *The monument of matrons*

Bentley uses and transcribes the words of women martyrs, noblewomen and the Bible to construct a kind of commonplace prayer book for women. Bentley's own words are in the headings and the parentheses. Text from: the first edition, 1582, p. 6.

The prayer or vow of Hannah for a son

1 Samuel 1:11
O Lord of hosts if thou wilt look on the trouble of thine handmaid, and remember me and not forget thine handmaid, but give unto thine handmaid a manchild: then I will give him unto the Lord all the days of his life, and there shall no razor come upon his head.

*The song and thanksgiving of Hannah, after she by prayer
had obtained a son called Samuel*

1 Samuel 2

Mine heart rejoiceth in the Lord, and mine horn is exalted in the Lord (for
I have recovered strength and glory by his benefit) mine mouth is enlarged
or wide open over mine enemies: (so that I can now answer them that reprove
my barrenness) for I rejoice in thy salvation.

There is none holy as the Lord, yea there is none besides thee, and there
is no God like our God.

Speak no more presumptuously (against God in condemning my barrenness) let not arrogancy come out of your mouth: for the Lord is a God of
knowledge, and his purposes come to pass, and by him enterprises are
established.

The bow with the mighty men are broken, and they that were weak, have
girded themselves with strength.

They that were full are hired forth for bread (and sell their labours for
necessary food) and the hungry are no more hired (but cease to have need)
so that the barren hath born seven (even many) and she that hath many
children is waxen feeble.

The Lord killeth and maketh alive: bringeth down to the grave and raiseth
up again.

The Lord maketh poor and maketh rich: bringeth low and exalteth up on
high.

He raiseth up the poor out of the dust, and (according to his own will)
lifteth up the beggar from the dunghill, to set them among princes, and to
make them inherit the seat of glory: for the pillars of the earth are the Lord's,
and he hath set the world upon them: (therefore he may dispose all things at
his pleasure, and prefer whom he will to honour).

For a sick child

*The song of the blessed Virgin Mary, the mother of our Saviour Christ, which
she made at the time that she felt herself conceived of our Saviour Jesus in her
womb.*

Luke 1:46

My soul magnifieth the Lord: and my spirit rejoiceth in God my saviour.

For he hath looked on the poor degree and lowliness of his handmaiden
and servant: for behold from henceforth, now shall all generations call me
blessed. Because he that is mighty hath done for me great things: and holy
is his name. And his mercy is on them that fear him, from generation to
generation. He hath showed strength with his arm: he hath scattered the

proud in the imagination of their hearts. He hath put down the mighty from their seats and exalted them of low degree. He hath filled the hungry with good things: and hath sent away the rich empty. He hath upholden and helped his servant Israel, being mindful of his mercy. Even as he spake to our fathers Abraham, and to his seed for ever.

Christopher Hooke, *The childbirth*

Hooke advertises this sermon on the title page with the following words: 'very necessary to be read and known of all young married and teeming women, and not unprofitable for men of all sorts'. The book is dedicated to two women whose childbirths he attended. It is the kind of sermon which may have been delivered at a churching ceremony. Text from: the first edition, 1590, fos D1ᵛff.

Before she travailed, she brought forth; and before her pain came, she was delivered of a man child.

What this great mercy was which the Lord had showed upon Elizabeth may be understood by that which hath been said, to wit, that whereas she had been a long time barren, and thereby a reproach among women, now the Lord had given her to conceive, to accomplish her full time, to be delivered and to bring forth a son. Every one of these is a great mercy, as severally it hath been showed, how much more then, when they come all together in their full perfection, as a reek[13] of corn cometh in due season into the barn. This teacheth women especially, and so all other generally, what account they have to make of the conception and bearing of their children, and from whence it doth proceed: namely that they have to account of it as of a great mercy and as proceeding from the great mercy of God. Wretched therefore are they that account it as an ordinary thing, proceeding from the mutual conjunction of man and woman: for who hath so bewitched them, that they see not many to want this blessing: to die without an heir and to leave their possessions to strangers, if not to enemies, though a long time, beginning in the flower of their ages, they have lived a married life?

This opinion it seemeth Rachel had conceived when she said to Jacob, give me children or else I die; but Jacob corrected her fondness saying, *am I in God's stead that I should give thee children* [Gen. 30:1,2]? Children therefore, again we see, come from God, without whose blessing a woman remaineth barren, not able to conceive; or, conceiving, without strength to bring forth her fruit. Look therefore and account how many children you have born, and reckon that so many mercies, yea great mercies (whereof every one containeth a number of mercies) ye have received from the Lord.

That whereas others have remained as dry chips, you have been as fruitful Dives in your husband's houses. And this, as you must account a mercy, so you must acknowledge it to proceed from the free mercy of God; without any desert or merit of yours. It is from his mercy that you conceive, that you fulfil your time, that you are delivered of children, not of monsters. Were it not for his mercy, your sins (even the best of the whole sex) deserve that in some of these, if not in all of these, you should miscarry. The multiplying of your pains in the conception [Gen. 3:16] and bringing forth, it proceeded of the curse of God; the deliverance from those pains, that therein you perish not, is of the great mercy of God. This Elizabeth and her cousins here confess, and this, no doubt, all such women as fear God do with thanksgiving acknowledge.

And this cannot be but a great comfort unto you, to consider when, as in other things, so in your children especially, you have such notable pledges of the Lord his mercy towards you; for thus may you say, if the Lord in this and this child, and so in all the rest, had not showed me, contrary to my defects, great mercy, the curse of sorrows (which justly I deserve) had overwhelmed me, that I should never have lived to praise the Lord in the land of the living. As therefore (to conclude) you have the greatest tokens of God his mercy towards you, so you must labour that in you may appear the greatest signs of all dutiful obedience unto the Lord. Otherwise the Lord for your unthankfulness will cut off his mercies from you, whereby you shall die, not only in your sorrows, to the loss of your lives, but in your sins, to the loss of your souls. But if according to the example of all holy matrons, and especially this our Elizabeth, you render thanks unfeignedly, and cause thanks by many to be rendered unto the Lord for his great mercies upon you, then be you assured that his mercies shall never cease from following you in this life, till you have received the sum of all mercies in life everlasting.

Alexander Niccholes, *A discourse of marriage and wiving*

This work is one of a number during the first few decades of the seventeenth century which participates in the debate about women's nature. It is addressed to men. Text from: the first edition, 1615, pp. 8ff, 33–5.

The best way to continue a woman chaste is not the magician's ring, nor the Italian's lock, nor a continual jealousy, ever watching over her, nor to humour her will in idle fancies, adorn her with new fangles (as the well-appayed[14] folly of the world in this kind can witness): but for him that would not be basely mad with the multitude, would not bespeak folly to crown him, would not set that to sale that he would not have sold (for who sets out his ware to be cheapened and not bought?); that would not for his shop have his wife for a relative sign, is to adorn her decently, not dotingly; thriftily, not lasciviously; to love her seriously, not ceremoniously; to walk before her in good example (for otherwise how canst thou require that of thy wife that thou art not, wilt not be thyself? Wouldst thou expect thy wife a conqueror when thou thyself liest soiled at the same weapon?) To acquaint her with, and place about her, good and chaste society, to busy and apply her mind and body in some domestic, convenient and profitable exercises, according to her education and calling, for example to the frailty of that whole sex hath a powerful hand, as it shall induce either to good or evil.

*　　*　　*

Therefore whoever thou art that wouldst not wink at such a shame [having a wife who is unchaste] that, so profit doth succeed, wouldst not regard whether hand brought it in, use a good endeavour, such foresight and wariness as may provide for competency, prevent indigence and want, two great allayers of affection, and a main inciter of unpatient bearers to this folly and abuse, and above all seek to plant in her religion, for so she cannot love God but withal she must honour thee; increase her knowledge in good things, and give her certain assurance and testimony of thy love, that she may with hers again the more reciprocally equal thy affection. For true love hath no power to think much less act amiss: and these discreetly put in practice shall more preserve at all times and temptations, than spies or eyes, jealousy, or any restraint, for these sometimes may be deluded, or over-watched, or prevented by opportunity, but this never.

Nicolas Culpeper, *A directory for midwives*

Text from: the first edition, 1651, pp. 68ff, 96ff, 113ff.

Of what hinders conception together with its remedies

It is most certain that all men and women desire children partly because they are blessings of God, and so saints desire them: *Psal. 127:3 Lo children are an heritage of the Lord, and the womb is his reward*; as also *Psal. 128.* from the beginning to the later end prove it. Or else because they are pretty things to play withal, every like desiring to play with his like. Or lastly, and most probably, lust is the cause of begetting more children than the desire of the blessings of God; for where the desire of children moves one to the act of copulation, the pleasure in the act moves an hundred, and such corrupt principles prove usually baseness in the middle and bitterness in the latter end, to those that use them. It being apparent by the curse of God upon Eve, *I will exceedingly multiply thy conception*, that many children come into the world as a curse. But I am not now to act the part of a divine, but of a physician: and therefore to the purpose in hand.

124

Of natural barrenness Natural barrenness, I call that which causeth barrenness in women: the instruments of generation being perfect in both herself and her husband, no preposterous or diabolical course used to cause it, yet the woman remains naturally barren: neither age nor natural defect, and disease impeding, yet she conceives not.

To find out all the reason of this requires a stronger headpiece than I have, yet what the Lord hath imparted unto me, I shall freely impart to you.

1. The man and the wife that are both of one complexion seldom have children: and the reason is clear from the universal course of nature, which being formed by an all-wise God of a composition of contraries, cannot be composed by a composition of likes; and although to find two people just in every particular of a complexion be a system too rare to find, or very seldom found, yet if they be very near of complexion, my reason will hold good, and I know no remedy for it, unless they should part: for if the main cause of marriage be the procreation of children, I know not but that marriage which denies this may be unlawful. The truth is that marriage is the greatest natural action of man's life, and he that waits upon God for his direction in it shall not do amiss.

2. Want of love between man and wife is another cause of barrenness. That there is an essential, vital spirit in the seed of both sexes, is without all question. And that made up the basis of Onan's sin mentioned in scripture, in spilling his seed (the other as circumstances did but aggravate it), for this God slew him: I believe God hath been more merciful to many in England in the same case, yet he is as just now he was in Onan's days ...[15]

3. A third cause of natural barrenness is, the letting of virgins' blood in the arm before their courses come down: these come down in virgins usually in the 14th year of their age, seldom before the 13th, never before the 12th. And because usually all young virgins are out of frame before they first break down, the mother takes the daughter's piss and away to Doctor Dunce runs she who, knowing something by her water, as much as he could if he looked in a crow's nest, and gathering by the mother's talk and by seeing the party, that fullness of blood offended, straight prescribes bloodletting in the arm (bleeding and purging and vomiting being all the medicines that many country physicians to my knowledge have skill in, or commonly use they to whip diseases out of the body, as sextons whip dogs out of the church) this is done, and then she is well for a time, the superstitious blood being taken away, the next year (if she stay so long) she falls in the same case, then the other bout of bleeding, and in three or four times so serving, especially if the maid use much exercise, the blood comes not down to the womb as it doth in other women, but the womb dries up and becomes for ever barren.

For preventing this for the time to come, let no virgins be let blood in the arm before their menstruis come well down (cases of necessity excepted) but rather in the foot, for this provokes the blood downwards and by that means it provokes the terms.

4. A fourth cause of natural barrenness is loss of carnal copulation, men and women come to the school of Venus, either not at all, or so frigidly, that as good never a whit as never the better.

Medicines for a woman that would have children
By way of caution:

1. Use not the act of copulation too often: some say it makes the womb slippery, I rather think it makes the womb more willing to open than shut. Satiety gluts the womb and makes it unfit to do its office, and that's the reason whores so seldom have children; and also the reason why women after long absence of their husbands, when they come again usually soon conceive.

2. Let the time be convenient, for fear of surprise hinders conception.

3. Let it be after perfect digestion; let neither hunger nor drunkenness be upon the man or woman.

4. Let the desire of copulation come naturally, and not by provocation. The greater the woman's desire for copulation is, the more subject is she to conceive.

5. Women are most subject to conceive a day or two after their monthly terms are stayed.

6. Avoid eating or bearing about you all such things as cause barrenness: such be the bone of a stag's heart, emeralds, sapphires, ivy berries, jet, burnet,[16] leaves and roots, hart's tongue, steel-dust, mints, &c.

7. Apish ways and manners of copulation hinder conception.
By way of precept:

1. The runner of an hare mixed in a little cotton and put up into the womb as a pessary and remaining there a day, is an excellent remedy. But let it be done presently upon the stopping of the menstruis, and tied up in a linen cloth and a string tied to it, that so you may draw it out again, else you will make mad work.

2. If the woman's body be too hot, letting blood in the vein *saphaena*[17] profits much. 1 Because it cools. 2. Because it cleanseth the womb.

3. A load-stone carried about the woman causeth not only conception, but concord between man and wife.

4. The heart of a male quail, carried about the man, and of the female about the woman, furthers conception exceedingly and causeth mutual love.

5. The roots of eryngo, peony and satyrion,[18] being eaten cause conception.

6. Exercise your body before you take counsel of the undersheet: go to

the school of Mars before you go to the school of Venus.

7. A plaster of laudanum spread upon leather and applied to the region of the womb, mightily disposeth it to conception.

Of miscarriage in women

Of the causes of abortion   The ordinary causes of abortion are these:

1. A weakness or corruption of the womb when it is weakened or offended by vicious, slimy or slippery, phlegmatic or watery humours, that so it cannot retain the fruit received.

2. Aposthumes or inflammations of the womb hinder it through pain, that it cannot perform its office.

3. Being extremely bound in body in forcing to stool, forceth the child down which was before much oppressed by the right gut, being filled with hard dung ...

4. The haemorrhoids or piles many times cause miscarriage.

5. Fat women are subject to miscarry by reason of the slipperiness of their wombs, and very lean women for want of nourishment for the child in it.

6. Bleeding in the time she goes with child.

7. Strong purges are very bad, but vomits worse.

8. Great cold and heats, a bath and a hot house favour not the child in the womb: for they heat it so, that it labours to come out where 'tis cooler.

9. Hunger starves the child in the womb, surfeiting by much meat or drink strangles it.

10. Outwardly it may be done many ways, as by falls, blows, anger, fear, sorrow, running, leapings, liftings, immoderate exercise, &c.

Sarah Jinner, *An Almanac*

Jinner's almanac is the only one extant written by a woman in this period. In her 1659 edition she describes herself as a 'student in physic', and gives recipes for gynaecological medicines. Text from: the first edition, 1658, fos B4ʳ–B8ᵛ.

Physical observations

Things by nature cool, which move the terms[19]   The seeds of small endive, of melons, of gourds, of pumpkins, cucumbers and lettuce, of which pessaries may be made to use in the womb; but have a care you put a string to them, to get them out again when you please.

A syrup to take away the obstructions in the body which hinder the terms
Take madder, two ounces of the roots of lovage, sporage, capers and grass, each an ounce and a half; penny mountain and balm, of each two ounces; spica indie, half a dram: licorice, currants, rosemary flowers ... of each an ounce: six ounces of honey and nine ounces of sugar, boil it in a syrup and take thereof two ounces at a time.

A powder to be used in the nature of a pessary, against the suffocation of the matrix, or fits of the mother   Take red storax, lignum aloes, cloves, of each a dram; make them together into a powder, and then bind it up in a cloth in the form of a pessary, and put it up into the matrix.

If the patient be a maid, a husband is the best medicine, if she can get one: but in case that cannot be, then let her abstain from strong wines and flesh meat, and all such things as increase natural spirits.

A potion to further conception in a woman   Take wormwood, mugwort, of each a handful: boil them together in a quart of goat's milk till almost half be wasted, and let the woman drink thereof first and last, every morning and evening, a good draught.

A most excellent plaster to strengthen women with child, to wear all the time they be with child   Take oil olive, two pound and four ounces: red lead, one pound; spanish soap, twelve ounces: incorporate them together in an earthen pot, and when the soap cometh upwards, put it upon a small fire of coals: and continue it an hour and a half, stirring it with an iron or stick, then drop a drop of it upon a trencher, if it cleave not, it is enough: spread it on cloths, or lay it on a board till it cools, then make it up into rolls: it will last twenty years, the older the better; and when you have occasion to use it for this purpose, spread a plaster of it, and apply it to the back: and when you have tried it you will give me thanks for it. It is likewise good for the bloody flux, running of the reins, or any weakness in the back. For any bruise, to draw out a thorn out of the flesh, and easeth corns, and is good for a strain, and for the headache, being applied to the temples.

But to proceed when the woman with child begins to draw near her time; then let her use such meats and drinks as nourish well, but use no excess of either; but special let her take care to keep her body soluble.

Of the superfluity of milk, and other accidents happening after birth
Excessive abounding of the milk, after a woman is delivered, if it flow more than the child can grow, there oftentimes ensues impostumes and other

inflammations and distempers, in the breasts; for remedies whereof, use these prescriptions following.

The patient must eat and drink but moderately, and avoid all such things as engender much blood, and use means to dry and take away the superfluous blood, as rue and wild rue, with the seeds basil, and stamped together; if one take every day a quarter of an ounce, the same is very good to dry up the milk.

Jane Sharp, *The midwife's book*

Sharp's book is the only seventeenth-century textbook written by a woman midwife. It combines populist beliefs with those of more academic physicians of the time, although its main focus is the education of women and women midwives (see ch. 8). Text from: the first edition, 1671, pp. 43–7.

Of the secrets of the female sex and first of the privy passage

The clitoris is a sinewy hard body, full of spongy and black matter within it, as it is in the side ligaments of a man's yard, and this clitoris will stand and fall as the yard doth, and makes women lustful and take delight in copulation, and were it not for this they would have no desire nor delight, nor would they ever conceive. Some think that hermaphrodites are only women that have their clitorises greater, and hanging out more than others have, and so show like a man's yard. And it is so called, for is a small exuberance in the upper, forward and middle part of the share,[20] in the top of the greater slit where the wings end. It differs from the yard in length, the common pipe and the want of one pair of muscles, which the yard hath, but it is the same in place and substance: for it hath two sinewy bodies round, without thick and hard, but inwardly spongy and full of holes, or pores, that, when the spirits come into it, it may stretch, and when the spirits are dissipated, it grows loose again: these sinews as in a man's yard are full of gross, black, vital blood.... The head of this counterfeit yard is called *tertigo*, and the wings joining it cover it with a fine skin like the foreskin; it hath a hole, but it does not go through, and vessels run along the back of it as upon a man's yard; commonly it is but a small sprout, lying close hid under the wings, and not easily felt, yet sometimes it grows so long that it hangs forth at the slit like a yard, and will swell and stand stiff if it be provoked, and some lewd women have endeavoured to use it as men do theirs. In the Indies and Egypt they are frequent, but I never heard but of one in this country: if there be any, they will do what they can for shame to keep it close.

The clitoris in women, as it is very small in most, serves for the same purposes as the bridle of the yard doth, for the woman's stones lying far distant from the man's yard, the imagination passeth to the spermatical vessels by the clitoris moving and the lower ligatures of the womb, which are joined to the carrying vessels of the seed that lieth deep in the body; so, by the stirring of the clitoris, the imagination causeth the vessels to cast out that seed that lieth deep in the body; for in this, and the ligaments that are fastened in it, lies the chief pleasure of love's delight in copulation; and indeed were not the pleasure transcendently ravishing in us, a man or woman would hardly ever die for love.

I told you the clitoris is so long in some women that it is seen to hang forth at their privities, and not only the clitoris that lieth behind the wings, but the wings also, for the wings being two skinny caruncles, in each side one, join almost at first, arising from a welt or guard of the skin, or a ligamental substance in the back part of the slit of the neck, and they lie hid betwixt the two lips of the lap: they always almost touch one the other, and they go up to the end where the share bone meets, and when they join they make a fleshy rising and cover the clitoris with a foreskin, and so they rise to the top of the great cleft.

Francesco Barbaro, *Directions for love and marriage*

Text from: the first edition, 1677, translated anonymously, pp. 97–8.

Concerning the regulation of congress

So truly the matter is that what rules of meat and drink, such a proportion of congress should in a manner be observed: for truly, congress itself followeth the rules of life as a young chick her dam; and this may be understood by many reasons and examples. We cannot in this place begin more wisely and aptly to the purpose of our discourse than from nature itself, that we may briefly declare whatsoever we think. First, indeed, because the union of man and wife (as we have above said) was chiefly ordained and ought to be esteemed for the sake of children, they must use conjugal embraces chiefly with the hope of propagating issue: we sufficiently understand and perceive what manner of nature there is in most beasts, which for this reason hath appointed them certain laws of congress, that the mortal kinds of living creatures might in a manner be rendered immortal by a perpetual succession wherein they may be examples to us (to whom a more free and noble desire is given), that we should not mutually embrace for the sake of pleasure, but of generating issue. Wherefore we admonish (that I may use the words of Julia, the daughter of Augustus) that when the ship is full, they admit no other passengers; neither therefore should they think beasts are chiefly upon that account beasts because never when great with young,

130

but always for the sake of generation, they inhabit their venereal appetites; but if women shall pass these limits, even at least let them govern themselves so that they may be, and be accounted, modest in this part of moderation, from which modesty is nominated. To which matter we think it may chiefly conduce if, at the first, husbands shall accustom them to seem to be helpers not of lust, but of necessity: but they should so evidence their nuptial honour and modesty that in their congress decency may accompany their embraces, lest by their avidity and immodesty they be both defective in their honour, and also less acceptable to their tacit husbands. Herodotus writes that women lay aside their modesty with their inner garments if they embrace adulterers, we plainly confess it, but if their husbands, they will always observe a decency. When a certain woman was drawn by force from the presence of Philip because of her lust and fury, she said, every woman, if thou takest away the light, is like and the same with others: this may truly be said to adulterers, but wives, although the light be far removed should not make themselves like to vile women.

Aphra Behn, *To the fair Clorinda*

Text from: *A miscellany of poems by several hands*, published with *Lycidus, or the lover in fashion*, transl. from the French by Aphra Behn, 1688, pp. 175–6.

> Fair lovely maid, or if that title be
> Too weak, too feminine for nobler thee,
> Permit a name that more approaches truth,
> And let me call thee, lovely charming youth.
> This last will justify my soft complaint,
> While that may serve to lessen my constraint;
> And without blushes I the youth pursue,
> When so much beauteous woman is in view.
> Against thy charms we struggle but in vain
> With thy deluding form thou giv'st us pain,
> While the bright nymph betrays us to the swain.
> In pity to our sex sure thou wert sent,
> That we might love, and yet be innocent:
> For sure no crime with thee we can commit;
> Or if we should – thy form excuses it.
> For who, that gathers fairest flowers believes
> A snake lies hid beneath the fragrant leaves.
>
> Thou beauteous wonder of a different kind,
> Soft Cloris with dear Alexis joined;
> When e'er the manly part of thee would plead

Thou tempts us with the image of the maid,
While we the noblest passions do extend
The love to Hermes, Aphrodite the friend.

5

POLITICS AND LAW

INTRODUCTION

The most public political debate about women during the Renaissance was the legal and constitutional debate about women monarchs. At the beginning of Elizabeth's reign, John Aylmer published one of the major defences of woman's ability to rule *An harborow for faithful and true subjects* (1559) (pp. 140–2), defending a woman's equal right to inherit, and therefore, in certain cases, to inherit the rule of a kingdom. Although he immediately qualified this right by arguing that such cases are exceptional elections by God, he initiates a public political discourse in which women (or one woman) are seen to have political and legal rights. Nevertheless, he does so by reinstating and reasserting the dichotomy of the ordinary weak woman ('feeble in body' and politically subject to a husband) and the extraordinary woman, fit for magistracy through the word of God. The legal precedent for the authority of a woman monarch was the parliamentary statute enacted at the beginning of Mary's reign, which states: 'that what and whensoever statute or law doth limit and appoint that the king of this realm may or shall ... do anything as king ... the same the queen ... may by the same authority and power likewise ... do.'[1] This statute effectively rendered a queen masculine for the purposes of her public and princely function. The indirect precedent for this usage and interpretation was the well-established concept of the monarch's 'two bodies', the individual mortal one and the political immortal one.[2] The concept of a woman's weak physical nature is particularly effective for such a theory: it can acknowledge both her weakness and the hidden purpose of God's will for the continuity of the public, political body.

However, there is another important way in which Aylmer uses the concept of nature which has consequences for subsequent arguments about patriarchy and women's rights. He argues, in refutation of Knox's assertion in *First blast of the trumpet against the monstrous regiment of women* (1558) (pp. 138–9) that it is absolutely unnatural for women to rule:

you take this word nature too largely, you deceive yourself wittingly,

133

thinking that because it is not so convenient, so profitable, or meet, therefore it is unnatural.... If you take it as it is in the order of nature, for the most part ... and then reason it is against nature for an old man to have black hairs, or against nature for a woman to bring forth two children or three at a burden, no man would allow your reasoning. For though the one be according to nature as it is for the most part: yet is not the other, that happeneth sometime, utterly against nature. In like manner, though it be for the most part seen that men and not women do rule commonwealths, yet when it happeneth sometime by the ordinance of God and course of inheritance that they bear rule, it is not to be concluded that it repugneth against nature: no more than the old man's black hairs, or the woman's two twins. So that you see that in this acception of nature, their rule cannot be against nature.

(An harborow)

Woman, then, is the theoretical equal to man in natural law, because natural law, rather than being a hierarchy of absolutes as Knox argues, exists on a continuum. Here is an implicit rejection of the Aristotelian hierarchical version of nature in which woman, on the basis of physiological inferiority, is denied rights and placed under male subjection. Once James I inherited the throne, most such arguments were set aside in the reassertion of the natural law of patriarchal monarchy, but they are the basis of later claims for equality by both men and women excluded from public life and the political process.

However, despite these public defences of women's rights (to inherit and rule), these ideas are uniquely applied to women monarchs: there is no public attempt to extend them on the basis of revised versions of natural law, to other women. Both theological versions of woman's creation (*from* the man) and of the Fall (*Eve's* fault) and physiological accounts of her bodily weakness are used to justify her political impotence. Thus the theory of patriarchy, in its implicit form throughout the early period, and in its explicit form in the writings of the Stuart monarchs and their supporters, most notably Filmer (p. 161), structures writings on theology, conduct, and marriage, as well as politics (pp. 137, 144–5, 147–9, 150, 157–9).

According to the anonymous legal clerk's formulation in *The law's resolution of women's rights* (pp. 152–7), women had no public access to political power as well as no rights:

women have no voice in parliament. They make no laws, consent to none, they abrogate none. All of them are understood either married or to be married, and their desires are subject to their husband: I know no remedy, though some women can shift it well enough. The common law here shaketh hand with divinity.

Some women actually lost legal and inheritance rights during the sixteenth

134

century, as the common law increasingly asserted the primacy of the law of masculine inheritance over that of an ungendered primogeniture: Anne Clifford's unsuccessful fight for her inheritance of her father's estates and titles as an only surviving child with the courts, her male relatives and James I is one such example,[3] but it was not atypical. There is also evidence that women were increasingly denied the right to belong to guilds and to run their husband's business after their death (see chapter 7).

Nevertheless, it is also evident that some women did have considerable, if circumscribed, power: particularly where they ran and managed large estates (where they had power over male servants and labourers); ran a business; or acted as educators to their children.[4] Some women used the Court of Chancery in order to sue for goods or land which was owed them by male executors or heirs as their dower when their husband died, or as an inheritance which had been appropriated by guardians. Chancery gave judgements on the basis of equity, and often found in the woman's favour, thus enforcing her legal rights to dower or to the terms of a will or a jointure (p. 156).[5] Thus a minimal level of property rights was sustained, but in an extraordinary court, run by the Lord Chancellor, rather than local courts of common law.

The period of the Civil War and Interregnum provided an opportunity for female activity in the public arena in a number of ways, some more publicised than others. There were several petitions made to parliament by women, and although some were mock petitions, these provided a public voice and public action, albeit at the margins of the great political events of the day. Although none of these petitions actually demands an extension of the franchise to women, even those supporting the Diggers and Levellers,[6] it is clear that the articulation of the right to petition as women is at once both a reiteration of submissive status and a claim to a public forum (this chapter, pp. 159–60 and chapter 9, pp. 280–2).

The double bind of patriarchal theory, encompassing public political submission to rulers and magistrates and private political, economic and physical submission to fathers and husbands (pp. 137, 149–50, 157–9) reads as a catalogue of a totalitarian system. But the voices of women, directly through the petitions, and indirectly in the account Gouge (p. 149) gives of female parishioners speaking out in church against the absolutism of the message, give a picture of some resistance to the ideology of patriarchy. The strength and number of each assertion of the subjection of woman to man in the private and public spheres tends also to suggest that the preachers and politicians are trying to regulate behaviour and practices which they regard as antipathetic to good order. Thus, whilst the public face of Renaissance political and legal theory is patriarchal, private truths may be both better and worse than benevolent absolutism.

135

Aristotle, *Politics*

This edition is translated from that of Louis le Roy, the noted French Aristotelian. It is dedicated to Robert Sidney. Text from: *Aristotle's politiques*, 1598 edition, pp. 55–8.

Of the other parts of house government which belong to the husband and the father: also of such virtues as are respectively requisite for governors and obeyers

As concerning these villeins and bondmen, it may be doubted whether, besides they serve for instruments and ministers, there be any other virtues in them honourabler than these: as modesty, manhood, justice and other such habits; or whether they be destitute of all other virtues saving those that pertain to the body and slavery. For it may be a doubt on both sides: as if they have, how much they differ from free men? And it were altogether absurd to say they have them not, sith they be men and partakers of reason. In a manner the same doubt may be moved touching the woman and the child, whether there be any virtues in them: and whether the woman should be temperate, womanly, and just; and the child intemperate, or temperate, or not.... Therefore it appeareth that it is necessary for each of them to participate of virtue, in such difference nevertheless as is found in those things that are in subjection by nature: this is straightaway perceived in the soul where the one part commandeth by nature and the other obeyeth: the virtue of which part we affirm to differ, as the virtue of that part which is endowed with reason and the unreasonable part. It is certain that the like is observed in other things, insomuch that by nature there be divers sorts of rulers and obeyers: for the free man governeth the bondman one way, the male the female another way, and the man the child in another sort: and in all them are the parts of the soul, howbeit with difference: the bondman is altogether deprived of that part which belongeth to deliberation; the wife hath it, howbeit weak; the child hath it also, but imperfect. The like is to be deemed of the moral virtues. And we must suppose that they ought to have them, howbeit not after the same manner and measure, but in such measure as is convenient for the office and exercise of everyone. Therefore it is expedient for a governor to have perfect moral virtue: for his office is simply and absolutely to command and give order for the execution of affairs, and reason beareth the sway in commanding and appointing: but it sufficeth every of the other persons to have such portions of the same as is needful for their own exercise. Let us conclude therefore that all the persons afore-mentioned have moral virtue: and that the modesty of the husband and wife are not the selfsame, nor their fortitude, nor justice, as Socrates held opinion: but the one hath fortitude apt to govern, the other to serve: and likewise in other virtues, as more plainly may appear by the particular consideration of the same. For they that speak universally, do deceive themselves who affirm that having of the soul well disposed, or well-doing, or any other like thing, is virtue.... But as concerning the husband and the wife, the father and the children, and every of their virtues and mutual conservation, and by what matters they follow good and fly evil, we shall necessarily treat thereof in our discourse of the forms of government. For sith every house is parcel of the city, and all the matters above spoken of are parts of the house, and the virtue of the part is to be imputed to the whole, it is necessary to refer the instructing and ordering of women and children to such magistrates as have the oversight of the states of cities, if it be convenient for the making of a virtuous city to have virtuous women and children; which is most requisite, for that women are the moiety of free men, and of children do come the partakers and fellows of the commonwealth and of the government of the city.

Juan Luis Vives, *Instruction of a Christian woman*

This work is addressed to Queen Catherine of England and her daughter Mary, later queen regnant. Text from: the 1540 edition, transl. Richard Hyrde, fos 71^r–71^v. The first edition was published in 1529.

How she shall behave herself unto her husband

Now then, what woman will be so presumptuous and so haughty to disobey her husband's bidding, if she consider, that he is unto her instead of father and mother and all her kin, and that she oweth unto him all the love and charity that were due to them all? A ragious[7] and a foolish woman doth not consider this, the which is disobedient unto her husband. Except peradventure she would say, she oweth none obedience, neither to father, nor to mother, nor to none of her kin. For if she obey them, she must needs obey her husband: in whom by all rights, by all customs, by all statutes and laws, by all precepts and commandments, both natural, worldly and heavenly she ought to account allthing to be.

The woman is not reckoned the more worshipful among men, that presumeth to have mastery above her husband: but the more foolish and the more worthy to be mocked: yea and moreover than that, cursed and unhappy: the which turneth backward the laws of nature, like as though a soldier would rule his captain, or the moon would stand above the sun, or the arm above the head. For in wedlock the man resembleth the reason, and the woman the body. Now reason ought to rule, and the body to obey if man will live. Also St Paul saith: *the head of the woman is the man* [1 Cor. 11].

John Knox, *The first blast of the trumpet against the monstrous regiment of women*

Knox was a renowned Calvinist divine in Scotland, who fought publicly against Mary Queen of Scots ascending the throne, meanwhile attacking Queen Mary of England. This text was written as part of the Scottish debate, and coincidently was published just before Elizabeth was crowned in England. Text from: the first edition, 1558, pp. 2ff, 9'ff.

Veritas temporis filia
[Truth is the daughter of time]

The first blast of the trumpet to awake women degenerate

To promote a woman to bear rule, superiority, dominion or empire above any realm, nation, or city is repugnant to nature, contumely to God, a thing most contrarious to his revealed will and approved ordinance, and finally it is the subversion of good order, and all equity and justice.

In the probation[8] of this proposition, I will not be so curious as to gather whatsoever may amplify, set forth, or decore[9] the same, but I am purposed, even as I have spoken my conscience in most plain and few words, so to stand content with a simple proof of every member, bringing in for my witness God's ordinance in nature, his plain will revealed in his word, and the minds of such as be most ancient amongst godly writers.

And first, where I affirm the empire of a woman to be a thing repugnant to nature, I mean not only that God by the order of his creation hath spoiled women of authority and dominion, but also that man hath seen, proved and pronounced just causes why that it so should be. Man, I say, in many other cases blind, doth in this behalf see very clearly. For the causes be so manifest that they cannot be hid. For who can deny that it repugneth to nature, that the blind shall be appointed to lead and conduct such as do see? That the weak, the sick and the impotent persons shall nourish and keep the whole and strong, and finally, that the foolish, mad and frenetic shall govern the discreet, and give counsel to such as be sober of mind? And such be all women compared unto man, in bearing of authority. For their sight in civil regiment is but a blindness: their strength weakness: their counsel foolishness: and judgement frenzy, if it be rightly considered.

I except such as God by singular privilege and for certain causes known only to himself hath exempted from the common rank of women, and speak of women as nature and experience do this day declare them. Nature, I say, doth paint them forth to be weak, frail, impatient, feeble and foolish: and experience hath declared them to be unconstant, variable, cruel, and lacking the spirit of counsel and regiment. And these notable faults have men in all ages espied in that kind, for the which not only they have removed women from rule and authority, but also some have thought that men subject to the counsel or empire of their wives were unworthy of all public office. For thus writeth Aristotle in the second of his *Politics: what difference shall we put, saith he, whether that women bear authority, or the husbands that obey the empire of their wives be appointed to be magistrates? For what ensueth the one, must needs follow the other, to wit: injustice, confusion, disorder.* The same author further reasoneth, that the policy or regiment of the Lace-domians (who other ways amongst the Grecians were most excellent) was not worthy or reputed to be accompted amongst the number of com-monwealths that were well governed, because the magistrates and rulers of the same were so much given to please and obey their wives. What would this writer (I pray you) have said to that realm or nation where a woman sitteth crowned in parliament amongst the midst of men? Oh, fearful and terrible are thy judgements (oh, Lord) which thus hast abased man from his iniquity! I am assuredly persuaded that if any of those men, which illuminated only by the light of nature, did see and pronounce causes sufficient why women ought not to bear rule nor authority, should this day live and see a woman sitting in judgement, or riding from parliament in the midst of men, having the royal crown upon her head, the sword and sceptre born before her, in sign that the administration of justice was in her power: I am assuredly persuaded that such a sight should so astonish them that they should judge the whole world to be transformed into Amazons, and that such a metamorphosis and change was made of all the men of that country as poets do feign was made of the companions of Ulysses, or at least, that albeit the outward form of man remained, yet should they judge that their hearts were changed from the wisdom, understanding, and courage of men, to the foolish fondness and cowardice of women. Yea, they should further pronounce that where women reign or be in authority, that there must needs vanity be preferred to virtue, ambition and pride to temperancy and modesty, and finally that avarice the mother of all mischief must needs devour equity and justice.... They neither may be judges, neither may they occupy the place of the magistrate, neither yet may they be speakers for others. The same is repeated in the third and the sixteenth books of the digests: where certain persons are forbidden, that *they be no speakers nor advocates for others.* And among the rest are women forbidden, and this cause is added, that they do not against their shamefast-ness intermeddle themselves with the causes of others, neither yet that women presume to use the offices due to men. The law in the same place doth further declare that a natural shamefastness ought to be in womankind, which most certainly she loseth whensoever she taketh upon her the office and estate of man.

John Aylmer, *An harborow for faithful and true subjects*

Aylmer instructed Lady Jane Grey, spent Mary's reign in exile and returned on the accession of Elizabeth. He later became Bishop of London. His argument refutes that of Knox, in defence of woman's rule. Text from: the first edition, 1559, fos B1ʳff, C4ʳ.

Many daughters there be, that gather riches together: but thou goest above them all. As for favour it is deceitful, and beauty is a vain thing, but a woman that feareth the Lord: she is worthy to be praised. Give her of the fruit of her hands, and let her own works praise her in the gate.

Proverbs

Happening... not long ago to read a little book strangely written by a stranger, to prove that the rule of women is out of rule, and not in a commonwealth tolerable: and weighing at the first what harm might come of it, and feeling at the last that it hath not a little wounded the conscience of some simple, and almost cracked the duty of true obedience: I thought it more than necessary to lay before men's eyes the untruth of the argument, the weakness of the proofs and the absurdity of the whole. In the sifting whereof I mind to use such modesty that it shall appear to all indifferent men that I seek to defend the cause and not to deface the man, seeing this error arose not of malice but of zeal.... Only in this was he not to be excused (unless he alleged ignorance) that he swerved from the particular question to the general, as though all the government of the whole sex were against reason, right and law; because that the present state then through the fault of the person and not of the sex, was unnatural, unreasonable, unjust and unlawful. If he had kept him in that particular person, he could have said nothing too much, nor in such wise as could have offended any indifferent man. And this again would have been considered; that if the question were to be handled, yet was it not meet to bring it into doubt at that time, when it could not, nor yet can be, redressed (were it never so evil), without manifest and violent wrong of them that be in place. For if it were unlawful (as he will have it) that the sex should govern, yet is it not unlawful that they should inherit, as hereafter we shall prove. And in this point their inheritance is so linked with the empire, that you cannot pluck from them the one, without robbing them of the other. This doubt might better have been moved when the sceptre was or shall be in the hand of the male. And so if it were found evil (as I am persuaded it shall never be), it might without the wronging of any be reformed. But now being stablished by law, confirmed by custom and ratified by common consent of all the orders in the realm: it can be no equity to take it from them, nor any colour of honesty or godliness to move any plea against them. If nature hath given it them by birth: how dare we pull it from them by violence? If God hath called them to it either to save or to spill, why should we repine at that which is God's will and order? Are we wiser than

140

he in bestowing it: or so bold to alter that he purpose should come of it? If he able women, shall we unable them? If he meant not they should minister, he could have provided other.... Placeth he a woman weak in nature, feeble in body, soft in courage, unskilful in practice, not terrible to the enemy, no shield to the friend, well (saith he): *my strength is most perfect when you be most weak* [2 Cor. 12], if he join to his strength: she cannot be weak. If he put to his hand she cannot be feeble, if he be with her, who can stand against her? ... It is as easy for him to save by few than as by many, by weak as by strong, by a woman as by a man. Yea his most wonderful works are always wrought in our most weakness [Jude 5], as infinite examples and testimonies do show. Yet mean I not to bar policy, when without breach of God's ordinance it may have place, for policy is God's gift either given man immediately of God, or gotten by study, experience and practice, or won by quickness of wit. But when God chooseth himself by sending to a king, whose succession is ruled by inheritance and lineal descent, no heirs male: it is a plain argument that for some secret purpose he mindeth the female should reign and govern.

* * *

If it were unnatural for a woman to rule because she lacketh a man's strength, then old kings which be most meet to rule for wit and experience, because they lack strength, should be unmeet for the feebleness of the body. Yea, say you, God hath appointed her to be subject to her husband... therefore she may not be the head. I grant that so far as pertaineth to the bands of marriage and the office of a wife, she must be a subject, but as a magistrate she may be her husband's head. For the scripture saith not *thine eye must be to the man*, but *to thy husband*. Neither oweth every woman obedience to every man, but to her own husband. Well, if she be her husband's subject, she can be no ruler. That followeth not, for the child is the father's subject and the father the child's ruler, and as Aristotle saith (whom you so much urge) his rule is kinglike over his child. But the husband's is civil, then if the child by nature a subject may be by law a head, yea the head of his father, and his father his subject, why may the woman not be the husband's inferior in matters of wedlock, and his head in the guiding of the commonwealth? ... If then they may govern men in the house by St Paul's commission, and an household is a little commonwealth, as Socrates in Xenophon saith, then I cannot see how you can debar them of all rule, or conclude that to be heads of men is against nature. Which if you grant, is enough to disprove of your minor. If you put to and say, in a commonwealth yet it will not serve, for the proof of that is because (say you) she is the man's subject. I have showed how, in that she is his wife, not in that she is a woman. For as you see, she may be some man's head, as in her household. But while you take this word nature too largely, you deceive yourself wittingly, thinking that because it is not so convenient, so profitable, or meet, therefore it is unnatural. But that is too large a scope. Wherefore that we may understand how far you stretch this word nature, I will ask you whether you take it as it is for the most part; or all together, that is universal. If you take it as it is in the order of nature, for the most part (as it is natural for an old man to have white hairs in his age, or for a woman to bring forth one child at a burden) and then reason it is against nature for an old man to have black hairs, or against nature for a woman to bring forth two children or three at a burden: no man would allow your reasoning. For though the one be according to nature as it is for the most part, yet is not the other, that happeneth sometime, utterly against nature. In like manner, though it be for the most part seen that men and not women do rule commonwealths, yet when it happeneth sometime by the ordinance of God and course of inheritance that they bear rule, it is not to be concluded that it repugneth against nature: no more than the old man's black hairs, or the woman's two twins. So that you see that in this acception of nature, their rule cannot be against nature. On the other side, if you take it in a generality, as whensoever the stone moveth upward, it is violent and against nature: or whensoever the fire consumeth not the matter that is put to it: then you are further wide. For it chanceth not seldom but oft not in one country, but in many, not among the barbarous, but in the chiefest empires and monarchies, and not only in them, but in the commonwealth of the Jews, more than once or twice, that women being inheritors, have ruled over their parents, wives after their husbands: and sisters after their brethren, as I shall at large declare. But before I come to that point I must wade a little further with him in his argument of nature. Wherefore I reason against him thus: whatsoever preserveth commonwealths and destroyeth them not is not against nature, but the rule of women hath preserved commonwealths, ergo it is not against nature.

John Leslie, *A defence of the honour of the right high, mighty and noble princess Marie Queen of Scotland*

Leslie was a Scottish Catholic bishop, who defended Mary against Knox's party. Text from: the first edition, 1569, fos 135^v–8.

*Wherein it is declared that the regiment of women is
conformable to the laws of God and nature*

Ye say the Jews were commanded to take no king but *ex fratribus*, a brother,
ergo, we can have no sister to our queen.... *Frater* is the masculine gender
(ye say) and therefore women are to be removed. Then by this rule women
also must be excluded from their salvation, because scripture saith: *he that
shall believe and be baptised shall be saved.* Holy scripture aboundeth of like
places, as *blessed is the man that walketh not in the counsel of the ungodly*
[Ps. 1,40; Matt. 5]. And by this rule women are excluded from the eight
beatitudes! But we will not shift your own words, brother. We say, therefore,
that this word must not be taken so straightly and narrowly as ye take it: for
first not only in scripture, but in old, ancient, profane authors, it comprehendeth the brother's child: yea and sometime in civil law cousin germans,
coming of two brethren ...

Again as in the civil law the masculine gender comprehendeth the
feminine, so doth it in your word brother.... Scevola[10] saith the bequests
made by the testator to his brethren, shall be beneficial to his sisters also,
unless it may be proved that the testator meant otherwise. Now, when the
holy scripture saith, *thou shalt not hate thy brother; thou shalt not lend upon
usury to thy brother; let every man use his brother mercifully; if thy brother
trespass against thee forgive him; withdraw yourselves from every brother
walking disorderly; he that hateth his brother is in darkness,* with a number
of like suit; shall we infer thereupon that we may hate our sister, that we may
oppress our sister with usury, that we may use our sister as unmercifully as
we will, without any remorse of conscience, and are not bound to forgive her,
nor to eschew her company being excommunicated, or a notorious offender?
Wherefore neither this word brother excludeth a sister, nor this word *king*
in scripture excludeth a queen: in the Greek tongue one word representeth
both brother and sister saving that there is a difference of gender; after the
same rate the words king and queen are knit up in both one, as well in the
Greek ... and in the French, *roy* and *royne* and from this the Latin tongue
rex and *regina*, doth not far disagree. Seeing then by interpretation this word,
brother, containeth the word sister also in scripture, and the word king, by
property of one and the same voice and signification, expresseth the queen
both in scripture and in other tongues: why should we not as well
communicate to women the dignity appertaining to the name, and resembled
by the same, as the name itself? For even in this our own country, albeit the
names of the king and of the queen do utterly vary one from the other, and
also the ancient statutes of the realm do not only attribute and refer all
prerogative and preeminence, power and jurisdiction, unto the name of a
king, but do give also, assign and appoint the correction and punishment of

all offenders against the realm and dignity of the crown and the laws of the realm, unto the king: yet are all manner of the foresaid jurisdictions and other prerogatives, and ought to be, as fully and wholly and as absolutely in the prince female, as in the male, and so was it ever deemed, judged and accepted before the statute made for the further declaration in that point [An. Marie. 1, ca. 2].

Thomas Smith, *The commonwealth of England, and manner of government thereof*

Smith's career as a prominent lawyer, scholar and diplomat qualified him to write this major work of political theory on England during the early period. Text from: the first edition, 1589, pp. 12–14, 27–9.

The first sort, or beginning of an house, or family

Then if this be a society and consisteth only of free men, the least part thereof must be of two. The naturalest and first conjunction of two, toward the making of a further society of continuance, is of the husband and of the wife, after a divers sort each having care of the family: the man to get, to travail abroad, to defend; the wife to save that which is gotten, to tarry at home, to distribute that which cometh of the husband's labour for the nutriture of the children and family of them both, and to keep them all at home neat and clean. So nature hath forged each part to his office: the man stern, strong, bold, adventurous, negligent of his beauty and spending; the woman weak, fearful, fair, curious of her beauty and saving. Either of them excelling other in wit and wisdom, to conduct those things which appertain to their office, and therefore where their wisdom doth excel, therein it is reason that each should govern. And without this society of man and woman, the kind of man could not long endure.... So in the house and family is the first and most natural (but private) appearance of one of the best kinds of a commonwealth, that is called *Aristocratia*, where a few, and the best, do govern; and where not one always, but sometime and in something, one, and sometime and in something, another doth bear the rule. Which, to maintain for his part, God hath given to the man great wit, bigger strength, and more courage to compel the woman to obey by reason, or force: and to the woman, beauty, fair countenance, and sweet words to make the man to obey her again for love. Thus each obeyeth and commandeth other, and they two rule together the house. The house I call here: the man, the woman, the children, their servants bond and free, their cattle, their household stuff and all other things which are reckoned in their possession, so long as all these remain together in one, yet this cannot be called

Aristocratia but *metaphorice* [*by a metaphor*]: for it is but an house, and a little spark, resembling as it were that government.

The division of the parts and persons of the commonwealth

To make all things yet clear before as we shall go, there ariseth another division of the parts of the commonwealth. For it is not enough to say that it consisteth of a multitude of houses and families, which make streets and villages, and the multitude of the streets and villages make towns, and the multitude of towns, the realm, and that freemen be considered only in this behalf as subjects and citizens of the commonwealth, and not bondsmen who can bear no rule nor jurisdiction over freemen, as they who be taken but as instruments and the goods and possessions of others. In which consideration also we do reject women, as those whom nature hath made to keep home and to nourish their families and children, and not to meddle with matters abroad, nor to bear office in a city or commonwealth, no more than children and infants: except it be in such cases as the authority is annexed to the blood and progeny, as the crown, a duchy or an earldom; for there the blood is respected, not the age nor the sex. Whereby an absolute queen, an absolute duchess or countess (those I call absolute which have the name, not by being married to a king, duke or earl, but by being the true, right, and next successors in the dignity, and upon whom by right of the blood that title is descended); these, I say, have the same authority, although they be women or children in that kingdom, duchy or earldom, as they should have if they had been men of full age. For the right and honour of the blood, and the quietness and surety of the realm, is more to be considered than either the tender age, as yet impotent to rule, or the sex not accustomed (otherwise) to intermeddle with public affairs, being by common intendment understood that such persons never do lack the counsel of such grave and discreet men as be able to supply all other defects.

James I, *The true law of free monarchies*

This publication was a reissue in England of the first, 1598, edition on James's ascent to the English throne. Text from: the 1603 edition, fos B3ᵛ–C1ʳ.

By the law of nature the king becomes a natural father to all his lieges at his coronation. And the father, of his fatherly duty, is bound to care for the nourishing, education and virtuous government of his children: even so is the king bound to care for all his subjects. As all the toil and pain that the father can take for his children, will be thought light and well bestowed by him, so that the effect thereof redound to their profit and weal: so ought the prince to do towards his people. As the kindly father ought to see all inconvenients and dangers that may arise towards his children and, though with the hazard of his own person, press to prevent the same: so ought the king towards his people. As the father's wrath and correction upon any of his children that offendeth ought to be by a fatherly chastisement seasoned with pity as long as there is any hope of amendment in them: so ought the king towards any of his lieges that offends in that measure.

And shortly, as the father's chief joy ought to be in procuring his children's welfare, rejoicing at their weal, sorrowing and pitying at their evil, to hazard for their safety, to avail for their rest, wake for their sleep, and, in a word, to think that his earthly felicity and life standeth and liveth more in them, nor in himself: so ought a good prince think of his people.

* * *

For, as fathers, the good princes and magistrates of the people of God acknowledged themselves to their subjects. And for all other well ruled commonwealths, the rule of *pater patriae* [*father of the people*] was ever, and is, commonly used to kings. And the proper office of a king towards his subjects agrees very well with the office of the head towards the body, and all members thereof. For from the head, being the seat of judgement, proceedeth the care and foresight of guiding and preventing all evil that may come to the body, or any part thereof. The head cares for the body, so doth the king for his people. As the discourse and direction flows from the head, and the execution according thereunto belongs to the rest of the members, every one according to his office: so is it betwixt a wise prince and his people. As the judgement coming from the head may not only employ the members, every one in their own office, as long as they are able for it; but likewise in case any of them be affected with any infirmity, must care and provide for their remedy, in case it be curable, and if otherwise, cut them off for fear of infecting the rest: even so is it betwixt the prince and his people. And as there is ever hope of curing any diseased member by the direction of the head, as long as it is whole, but by the contrary, if it be troubled all the members are partakers of that pain: so is it betwixt the prince and his people.

And now first for the father's part (whose natural love to his children I described in the first part of this my discourse, speaking of the duty that kings owe to their subjects) consider I pray you, what duty his children owe to him, and whether, upon any pretext whatsoever, it will not be thought monstrous and unnatural to his sons to rise up against him, to control him at their appetite, and when they think good, to slay him or cut him off, and adopt to themselves any other they please in his room. Or can any pretence of wickedness or rigour on his part be a just excuse for his children to put hand into him? And although we see by the course of nature, that love ever useth to descend more than to ascend, in case it were true that the father hated and wronged the children never so much, will any man, indued with the least spark of reason, think it lawful for them to meet him with the like? Yea suppose the father were furiously following his sons with a drawn sword: is it lawful for them to turn and strike again, or make any resistance but by flight? I think surely, if there were no more but the example of brute beasts and vulnerable creatures, it may serve well enough to qualify and prove this my argument. We read often the piety that the storks have to their old and decayed parents. And generally we know that there be many sorts of beasts and fowls that with violence and many bloody strokes will beat and banish their young ones from them, how soon they perceive them able to fend themselves. But we never read or heard of any resistance on their part, except among the vipers: which proves that such persons as ought to be reasonable creatures and yet unnaturally follow this example, to be indued with their viperous nature.

Robert Pricke, *The doctrine of superiority, and of subjection*

The title page advertises the contents as the sermons Pricke gave to his parishioners. The doctrine is presented as a catechism. Text from: the first edition, 1609, fos B1ᵣff.

Q. *What are the words?*
A. *Honour thy father and mother*, that they may prolong thy days in the land which the Lord God hath given thee ...
Q. *By what reasons may we further be persuaded of this?*
A. First of all it doth in certain inferior persons train men up, as it were, in a certain inferior school, to rise up to the knowledge of the sovereign Lord, and to give unto him the reverence and honour due to his divine majesty. Secondly it upholdeth and continueth all those estates, degrees, and orders whereby the society or fellowship of man is, as it were, by certain joints and sinews, joined and knit together, and without which it would by a certain pernicious confusion be clean dissolved and utterly perish. Thirdly, if the duties of this commandment be not performed, the general duties of the other commandments must needs fail: for he that will not perform a duty toward him to whom he is bound by a certain straight and peculiar band, much less will he perform duties to them that are further removed ...
Q. *Why are these two joined together in regard of honour and duty?*
A. First because they meet together in the work of procreation. Secondly to prevent and meet with the corruption and partiality of children, who otherwise would either condemn the mother and yield all honour and

147

duty to the father, by reason of his principality; or else, because the mother doth bear them and is most tenderly affected toward them, would be wholly addicted unto her, excluding and making no account of the father.

Q. *How may it appear that this is the reason?*

A. By many clear places of the word, as *Levit.* 19:3; *Prov.* 13:12; and ch. 10, ver. 1; *Ephes.* 6:11,2; *Col.* 3:10.

Q. *Are no other persons contained under these?*

A. Yes, all such as are instead of parents, not only in regard of superiority, but also for that they are to provide for the good and benefit of their inferiors, both in soul and body. For so wise and merciful is the Lord, as he hath appointed natural parents to beget and bring forth children, and thereby to give them simply a being in this life: so hath he ordained other persons (as it were parents) to tender and give them a well and happy being.

Q. *Who are those persons whom you mean?*

A. Kings, princes, and magistrates, ministers of the word of God, householders, schoolmasters and teachers. Those that are endued with any excellent grace and gift above others. Lastly the aged and grey-headed.

Q. *How can you prove that these are contained under the title of parents?*

A. First, for that as in all the rest of the commandments under one general are contained all special things of the same nature, so it is in this commandment. Secondly, if these persons be not here understood they are contained properly in no commandment: which were a great defect and disgrace to the perfection of the law. Thirdly, these persons are termed by the name of father and mother in divers places of the holy scripture: as kings, queens, and magistrates are called by the name of nursing fathers, and nurses. *Isai.* ch. 49, ver. 23. In regard hereof, some of the heathen called kings *Abimelch*, which signifieth, my father the king. Ministers of the word of God are called by the name of fathers, 2 *Cor.* ch. 4, ver. 15:3; 2 *King.* ch. 13, ver. 14; masters are so called, 2 *King.* 5:15, and ch. 2, ver. 12.

Q. *Why is the name of father and mother given to superiors?*

A. To draw and allure men to the willing obedience and practice of this commandment, and that not without cause. For first, as we are untoward by nature to the practice of any commandment, so especially of this: because it so greatly importeth the glory of God, and the benefit of man. Again the crooked heart of man will hardly stoop unto superiority. First by reason of a certain natural pride, whereby all men do desire to be aloft and under none other. Secondly for that superiors in this corrupt and miserable world do oftentimes abuse their authority to the hurt of others: therefore to subdue men to the ordinance of God,

148

he hath set upon all superiors the sweet and amiable name of father and mother.

William Gouge, *Of domestical duties*

Text from: the third, revised, edition, 1634 (first published in 1622), pp. 1ff.

The epistle dedicatory

To the right honourable, right worshipful, and other my beloved parishioners, inhabitants of the precinct of Blackfriars London, such sufficiency of grace as may bring them to fullness of glory.

Oh, if the head and several members of a family would be persuaded every one of them to be conscionable in performing their own particular duties, what a sweet society and happy harmony would there be in houses! What excellent seminaries would families be to church and commonwealth! Necessary it is that good order be first set in families: for as they were before other polities, so they are somewhat the more necessary: and good members of a family are like to make good members of church and commonwealth.

*   *   *

I remember when these *Domestical duties* were first uttered out of the pulpit, much exception was taken against the application of a wife's subjection to the restraining her from disposing the common goods of the family without, or against, her husband's consent. But surely they that made those exceptions did not well think of the *Cautions and Limitations* which were then delivered, and are now again expressly noted, which are: that the aforesaid restraint be not extended to the *proper goods of a wife*, no nor over-strictly to such *goods as are set apart for the use of the family*, nor to *extraordinary cases*, nor always to an *express consent*, not to the *consent of the husbands as are impotent, or far and long absent*. If any other warrantable caution shall be showed me, I will be as willing to admit it, as any of these. Now that my meaning may not still be perverted, I pray you in reading the restraint of wives' power in disposing the goods of the family, ever bear in mind these cautions. Other exceptions were made against some other particular duties of wives. For, many that can patiently enough hear their duties declared in general terms cannot endure to hear those general exemplified in their particular branches. This cometh too near the quick and pierceth too deep. But (to interpret all according to the rule of love, in better part) I take the main reason of the many exceptions which were taken to be this: that wives' duties (according to the apostle's method) being in the first place handled, there was taught (as must have been taught, except the truth should have been betrayed) what a wife in the uttermost extent of that subjection under which God hath put her is bound unto, in case her husband will stand upon the uttermost of his authority: which was so taken as if I had taught that an husband might and ought to exact the uttermost, and that a wife was bound in that uttermost extent to do all that was delivered as duty, whether her husband exact it or no. But when I came to deliver husbands' duties, I showed that he ought not to exact whatsoever his wife was bound unto (in case it were exacted by him) but he ought to make her a joint governor of the family with himself and refer the ordering of many things to her discretion, and with all honourable and·kind respect to carry himself towards her. In a word, I so set down an husband's duties as, if he be wise and conscionable in observing them, his wife can have no just cause to complain of her subjection. That which maketh a wife's yoke heavy and hard is an husband's abuse of his authority and more pressing his wife's duty than performing his own, which is directly contrary to the apostle's rule. This just apology I have been forced to make, that I might not ever be judged (as some have censured me) an hater of women. Now, that in all those places where a wife's yoke may seem most to pinch, I might give some ease, I have to every head of wives' duties made a reference, in the margin over against it, to the duties of husbands answerable thereunto, and noted the reference with this mark *, that it might be the more readily turned unto.[11]

William Perkins, *Christian economy*

Perkins was a well-known and learned preacher, publishing many texts which were popular amongst the devout middle classes. This text models itself on Xenophon, in a Christian context. Text from: the first edition, 1609, transl. Thomas Pickering, pp. 1–2, 9–11.

Of Christian economy, and of the family

Christian economy is a doctrine of the right ordering of a family.

The only rule of ordering the family is the written word of God. By it Daniel resolved to govern his house when he saith, *I will walk in the uprightness of my heart in the midst of my house*, Psalm 101:2. And Solomon affirmeth that, *through wisdom an house is builded, and with understanding it is established*, Prov. 24:3.

A family is a natural and simple society of certain persons, having mutual relation to one another under the private government of one. These persons must be at least three; because two cannot make a society. And above three under the same head, there may be a thousand in one family, as it is in the households of princes and men of state in the world...

Of married folks

Marriage is the lawful conjunction of the two married persons, that is, of one man, and one woman into one flesh. So was the first institution of marriage, *Gen.* 2:21. which is expounded by our saviour Christ, *Matt.* 19:6. *Therefore they are no more two, but one flesh.* And also by Paul, *Ephes.* 5:31. *For this cause shall a man leave father and mother, and shall cleave unto his wife* (as two boards are joined together with glue) *and they which were two, shall be one flesh.* Wherefore this is an eternal law of marriage, that two, and not three or four, shall be one flesh. And for this cause, the fathers, who had many wives and concubines, it may be that through custom they sinned of ignorance, yet they are not in any wise to be excused.

Marriage of itself is a thing indifferent, and the kingdom of God stands no more in it than in meats and drinks; and yet it is a state in itself, far more excellent than the condition of single life. For first, it was ordained by God in paradise, above and before all other states of life, in Adam's innocency before the fall. Again it was instituted upon a most serious and solemn consultation among the three persons of the Holy Trinity, Gen. 1:26, *let us make man in our image, according to our likeness, and let them rule over &c.* Gen. 2:18 Jehovah Elohim said *it is not good that man should be himself alone, I will make him an helpmeet for him.* Thirdly, the manner of this conjunction was excellent, for God joined our first parents Adam and Eve together immediately. Fourthly, God gave a large blessing unto the estate of marriage saying, *increase and multiply and fill the earth.* Lastly, marriage was made and appointed by God himself to be the fountain and seminary of all other sorts and kinds of life, in the commonwealth and in the church.

William Heale, *An apology for women*

This text was written in opposition to Gager's infamous oration at Oxford in 1608 that 'it was lawful for husbands to beat their wives'. Text from: the first edition, 1609, pp. 3–10.

That it is not lawful for a husband to beat his wife, as proved by reasons drawn from nature

Man the great creator's greatest creature, endued with remembrance, a register to recount former events; with wisdom, a glass to behold the present estate of things; with providence, an oracle to conjecture of future accidents; above all with reason, a balance to weigh out all his actions, must now become cruel and tyrannous, nay more savage and barbarous than very beasts, who neither have remembrance of things past, wisdom in things present, providence of all things to come, nor reason in any thing at all. The doves are observed to be most exquisite in their love, and at the fatal departure of one the other pines to death with sorrow. The nightingale makes pleasant melody in his love's welfare, but in her distress he mourns in sadder tunes. The swan is of a nature suitable to his feather, white and fair, and all his fear is to keep his mate from fear. Go therefore into the fields, and the doves will read thee a lecture of love; return into the woods and the nightingales will sing thee madrigals of love; walk by the river and the swans will school thee the art of love; everywhere such loving couples in brutish beasts will shame the disagreeing matches in reasonable creatures. For shall the bare instinct of a sensible nature work so powerfully in this case with beasts, as none are so beastly as to infringe it, and shall the help of a purer essence take none effect in man and he not adjudged worse than a beast? The lion that spareth no creature, is said to tremble at a woman, and hardly prefereth her that violence which usually he doth to man: as though nature had taught him a more gentle behaviour towards so fair a personage ...

It may well be the world's motto, all things have nature for their guide. And of this all, especially man the world's commander: which we may observe, as in the common course of life, in ordering his diet, in wearing his apparel, in taking his rest: so likewise in the perfect habit of sciences, in his smoothing rhetoric, in his solid disputation, in his profound philosophy: in all which the greatest pre-eminence art can challenge is to add perfection where nature hath laid a foundation.[12] The law then being an artificial collection of natural precepts, how can it dispense with so unnatural an action as for a husband to beat his wife, the one part of himself, nay his other self, or his better half? No man did ever willingly hurt himself: or if any man hath, certainly he may justly of all men be held a mad man: and therefore what mutual blows can lawfully pass between man and wife, who are one and the selfsame?

T.E., *The law's resolution of women's rights*

The editor (T.E.) of this text claims that the collection was made 'long since'. The title page indicates the purpose and projected readership of the book in its subtitle: 'Law's provision for women, a methodical collection of such statutes and customs, with the cases, opinions, arguments and points of learning in the law, as do properly concern women'. Text from: the first edition, 1632, pp. 1–9, 68–70, 128–9, 129–30, 144, 147–8, 182–3, 390–3.

Though I be unworthy to have the marshalling of the titles of law to bring all matter cohering under them, yet I will make a little assay what I am able to do if I were put to it in a popular kind of instruction, following a frame by distinction of persons, chasing the primary distribution of them made before the world was seven days old, *masculum & foeminam fecit eos* [*male*

152

and female he made them], of which division because the part that we say hath least judgement and discretion to be a law unto itself (women, only women), they have nothing to do in constituting laws or consenting to them, in interpreting of laws or in hearing them interpreted at lectures, leets[13] or charges, and yet they stand strictly tied to men's establishments, little or nothing excused by ignorance, methinks it were pity and impiety any longer to hold from them such customs, laws and statutes as are in a manner proper or principally belonging unto them. Laying aside therefore these titles which include only the masculine, as bishop, abbot, prior, monk, dean and chapter, viscount, coroner, together with those which be common to both kinds, as heretic, traitor, homicide, felon, laron,[14] parricide, cutpurse, rogue, with feoffor,[15] feoffee, donor, donee, tendor, tendee, recognisor, recognisee, etc. I will in this treaty with as little tediousness as I can, handle that part of the English law which containeth the immunities, advantages, interests, and duties of women, not regarding so much to satisfy the deep learned or searchers for subtility, as womenkind, to whom I am a thankful debtor by nature.

The punishment of Adam's sin

Return a little to Genesis, in the 3. chapter whereof is declared our first parents' transgression in eating the forbidden fruit: for which Adam, Eve, the serpent first, and lastly the earth itself is cursed: and besides the participation of Adam's punishment, which was subjection to mortality, exiled from the garden of Eden, enjoined to labour; Eve, because she had helped to seduce her husband, hath inflicted on her an especial bane: *in sorrow shalt thou bring forth thy children, thy desires shall be subject to thy husband, and he shall rule over thee.*

See here the reason of that which I touched before, that women have no voice in parliament. They make no laws, consent to none, they abrogate none. All of them are understood either married or to be married, and their desires are subject to their husband: I know no remedy, though some women can shift it well enough. The common law here shaketh hand with divinity, but because I am come too soon to the title of baron and feme, and Adam and Eve were the first and last that were married so young, it is best that I run back again to consider of the things (which I might seem to have lost by the way) that are fit to be known concerning women before they be fit for marriage.

The ages of a woman

The learning is 35 Hen. 6, fol. 40, that a woman hath divers special ages: at the 7th year of her age her father shall have aid of his tenants to marry her. At 9 years' age, she is able to deserve and have dowry. At 12 years to consent to marriage. At 14 to be *hors du guard*:[16] at 16 to be past the lord's tender of a husband. At 21, to be able to make a feoffment: and *per Ingleton*[17] there in the end of the case, a woman married at 12 cannot disagree afterward, but if she be married younger, she may dissent till she be 14 ...

Statutes concerning marriage

Yet it is very needful here that I show you here what the laws of England have needfully concerning marriage established. 32 H8, ca. 38 declareth all persons lawfully to marry, which are not prohibited by God's law. And it was ordained that all marriages contracted and solemnised in face of the church and consummate with bodily knowledge, should remain indefeasible,[18] notwithstanding any pre-contract, &c. Further, that neither dispensation, prescription, law, reservation, prohibition, or anything (God's law excepted) shall trouble or impeach any marriage made without the Levitical degrees,[19] nor any man be received in spiritual court to process, plea or obligation contrary to this act. This statute, though it seemed to be made upon good and great considerations (because pre-contracts too slenderly proved, and sometime but only surmised, helped the Romish oppression and separated those which were at quiet in an honest conjunction); yet men did after the making of it very dissolutely come from their first vows and, as it were in spite of conscience and ecclesiastical censure, coupled themselves bodily with such as they newly fancied, slipperily leaving their former contracts ...

The baron may beat his wife

If a man beat an outlaw, a traitor, a pagan, his villein, or his wife, it is dispunishable, because by the law common these persons can have no action: God send gentlewomen better sport or better company.

But it seemeth to be very true that there is some sort of castigation which law permits a husband to use; for if a woman be threatened by her husband to be beaten, mischiefed or slain, Fitzherbert sets down a writ which she may sue out of Chancery to compel him to find surety of honest behaviour towards her, and that he shall neither do nor procure to be done to her (mark I pray you) any bodily damage otherwise than appertains to the office of husband for lawful and reasonable correction.

How far that extendeth I cannot tell, but herein the sex feminine is at no very great disadvantage. For first for the lawfulness: if it be in none other regard lawful to beat a man's wife, then because the poor wench can sue no other action for it, I pray why may not the wife beat the husband again, what action can he have if she do?... The actionless woman beaten by her husband, hath retaliation left to beat him again, if she dare. If he come to the Chancery or justices in the country of the peace against her, because her recognizance alone will hardly be taken, he were best be bound for her, and then if he be beaten again the second time, let him know the price of it on God's name.

That which the husband hath is his own

But the prerogative of the husband is best discerned in his dominion over all external things, in which the wife by combination divesteth herself of propriety in some sort, and casteth it upon her governor: for here practice everywhere agrees with the theoric of law, and forcing necessity submits women to the affection thereof, whatsoever the husband had before coverture, either in goods or land, it is absolutely his own, the wife hath therein no seisin at all. If anything when he is married be given him, he taketh it by himself distinctly to himself...

The very goods which a man giveth to his wife, are still his own: her chain, her bracelets, her apparel, are all the goodman's goods.

That which the wife hath is the husband's

For thus it is, if before marriage the woman were possessed of horses, neat, sheep, corn, wool, money, plate, and jewels, all manner of moveable substance is presently by conjunction the husband's to sell, keep, or bequeath if he die. And though he bequeath them not, yet are they the husband's executor's, and not the wife's which brought them to her husband.

Of elopement

It is commonly holden (saith Parkins) that a woman shall lose her dower by voluntary elopement, though her abiding be involuntary, and though she make none abode with her adulterer. But if she be ravished, and demur with the ravisher against her will, she loseth no dower. If when the husband is commorant[20] at one manor, his wife depart to another of his manors and there live in adultery, this is none elopement, for it cannot but be intended, she cannot abide there without gree and goodwill of her baron...

The husband's power in lands which the wife holdeth in dower or otherwise for life

The husband's sovereignty over his wife, her goods, and chattels personal or real, is no less than hath been declared. The dominion likewise over all manner of frank tenements, his own or his wife's, is supereminent in him during coverture, but so that he standeth well bridled from doing anything *a per luy* [*of his own will*], whereby either the dower which his wife had by a former marriage, or expecteth by the present, or any other estate for life or in fee, can be taken from her when he is gone. If a widow tenant in dower marry, and her new husband surrendereth[21] etc., this is good during coverture, but if the feme survive, or if there be a divorce, *causa precontractus* [*because of a pre-contract*], the feme may enter and defeat the surrender, though he to whom it was made be dead, and his heir in by descent.

Of jointures

All husbands are not so unkind or untrusty as to endanger their wives by alienation of their lands: but contrariwise the greatest part of honest, wise and sober men, are of themselves careful to purchase somewhat for their wives, if they be not, yet they stand sometimes bound by the woman's parents to make their wives some jointure.

If husband, father, mother, and all would be unmindful of provision in this point, yet very many of our Englishwomen have, with their singular virtue, so much wisdom of their own, as to foresee for themselves and discern the difference between that which we call dower and jointure: jointures ... are made for the most part to baron and feme jointly, or to the feme only, this also is comprehended under the term jointure before marriage or after for sustenation of the charge and necessities of espousals; and they are made *causa matrimonii et gratis* [*freely given on the occasion of marriage*] without the consideration of money, bargain, or anything saving love and affection of the baron or his ancestors, and these jointures are a present possession. But dower must be tarried for, till the husband be dead. It must be demanded, sometimes sued for, sometime neither with suit or demand obtained. Again, dower was subject to forfeiture in times past, by felony done and proved in the baron by the baron's treason, by the wife's elopement, and every question in the validity of marriage maketh a scruple of dower, all which inconveniences being wisely foreseen, women did learn to become joint purchasers with their husbands of such estates, as would avoid all weathers, and a good while they did enjoy jointures and dowers after their husbands were dead.

Appeal of rape

Now let us consider a little how these laws ought to be put in practice, if any virgin, widow, or single woman be ravished, she herself may sue an appeal of rape, prosecute the felon to death, and the king's pardon (it seemeth) cannot help him. If a feme covert be ravished, she cannot have an appeal without her husband, as appears 8 Hen. 4, fol. 21. But if a feme covert be ravished and consent to the ravisher, the husband alone may have an appeal, and this by statute 6 Rich. 2, cap. 6. The husband that this statute speaketh of, which may sue the appeal, must be a lawful husband in right and possession, for *ne unques accouple* [*failure to consummate*] in loyal matrimony is a good plea against him.

Matthew Griffith, *Bethel, or a form for families*

Griffith was made royal chaplain in 1643. This text adheres to a model of the familial and political world which is strictly hierarchical. Text from: the first edition, 1634, pp. 322ff, 330.

What is the particular duty of the wife?

Wives must be in subjection to their husbands. The duties of wives may be learned out of the duties of husbands; for, first, if the husband must edify, and instruct, then the wife must learn; secondly, if the husband must make her his companion, then she must not affect to rule as lord, and so by usurped dominion to make his house his hell. Thirdly, if the husband must honour her as the weaker vessel, then she must require his forbearance with reverence. Fourthly, if the husband must sometimes suffer himself to be advised, then she must take care that she give wholesome and reasonable counsel. Fifthly, if the husband must forsake father and mother, and cleave unto his wife, then she must embrace him as the ivy doth the oak, she must spread upon him as the vine doth upon the wall, or house that supports it ...

Indeed there is a law of man which makes the daughter to be in the power of her father and not of her husband; but it is contrary to the law of God and of nature, &c.

Now this duty of subjection, the apostle urgeth (as I told you) from a twofold order, viz.

1. Of creation, because Adam was first formed. And if upon this ground it should be objected that beasts should then be preferred before both, because they were created before either? The solution is, that the apostle proves not man's superiority merely for his priority; but from such a priority as makes Adam the end, and Eve serving to that end as an helper; and

therefore, in reason, that which serves is less than the end to which it serves ...

2. Of corruption; because Eve was first deformed; and so brought that into the world, which brought the whole world into bondage. *The creature* etc. [Rom. 8:20: *For the creature was made subject to vanity.*]

These two are the apostle's reasons; and to them we may add two more, viz.

1. From that union which is betwixt man and wife: *for the husband is the head of his wife, as Christ of his church*; and therefore as the members are subject to the head without reasoning so should the wife be unto the husband: he (under God) provides all, defends all, and answers for all; and is it not reason that he should rule all?

2. From the light of nature which taught heathenish Ahasuerus to set down this decree, that women should give their husbands honour both great and small, and that every man should bear rule in his own house [Est. 1:20]. ... And if such baseness creep into any family that man will prostitute his crown and dignity as a pander unto his lust; and for a little effeminate dalliance, become a slave to her whom he ought to rule; let the rumination of this check his folly, that wives must be subject by the laws of God and men etc ...

Thou maist and must consider before marriage whether he be, and likely to be, a wise man or a fool: but after, know that he is thy husband and thou must be subject. Whatsoever his unworthiness be, yet God thinks him not unworthy to rule over thee; and whatsoever his unfitness be, yet he cannot be so unfit to govern thee, as thou art unfit to govern him. Thou wert taken to be his help, not his head; and how monstrous a thing were it in nature for any member, yea though it were the heart (and more thou canst not be) to direct the head ...

What, must they be in such slavery? This is harsh and who can endure it?

This subjection (which I have spoken of) is far from slavery; for there be two sorts of servants, the one bond, the other free. And though wives must obey and serve, yet it is not in the nature of bond-servants that serve for trades, wages, meat and drink, &c, but they are free as their fellows; for they are free of their husbands and all that they have, and are freely to receive from them such familiarity, maintenance and comforts as no servant whatsoever can expect.

Though one be a nobleman and have lordships and tenants under him, yet he is also a subject and lives under the laws of his prince; yet is he not in the nature of a servant that taketh wages, but as a free subject, and doth enjoy his goods and lands under the prince's protection, and is called by him with gracious words as, our loving subject, our truly and well-beloved cousin, &c.

A true copy of the petition of the gentlewomen and tradesmen's wives

The title page advertises the contents thus: 'delivered to the honourable, the knights, citizens and burgesses of the house of commons in parliament, the 4th of February, 1641. Together with the reasons why their sex ought thus to petition as well as the men; and the manner how both their petition and reasons was delivered'. Text from: the first edition, 1641, pp. 1–6.

To the honourable knights, citizens and burgesses of the house of commons assembled in parliament, the most humble petition of the gentlewomen, tradesmen's wives, and many other of the female sex, all inhabitants of the city of London and the suburbs thereof. With lowest submission showing:

... And whereas we, whose hearts have joined cheerfully with all those petitions which have been exhibited unto you in the behalf of the purity of religion, and the liberty of our husbands' persons and estates, recounting ourselves to have an interest in the common privileges with them, do with the same confidence assure ourselves to find the same gracious acceptance with you for easing those grievances, which in regard of our frail condition, do more nearly concern us and do deeply terrify our souls; our domestical dangers with which this kingdom is so much distracted especially growing on us from those treacherous and wicked attempts already are such as we find ourselves to have as deep a share as any other.... We thought it misery enough (although nothing to that we have just cause to fear) but few years since for some of our sex, by unjust divisions from their bosom comforts, to be rendered in a manner widows, and the children fatherless, husbands were imprisoned from the society of their wives, even against the laws of God and nature, and little infants suffered in their father's banishments: thousands of our dearest friends have been compelled to fly from episcopal persecutions into desert places amongst wild beasts, there finding more favour than in their native soil, and in the midst of all their sorrows, such hath the pity of the prelates been, that our cries could never enter into their ears or hearts, nor yet through multitudes of obstructions could never have access or come nigh to those royal mercies of our most gracious sovereign, which we confidently hope would have relieved us: but after all these pressures ended we humbly signify that our present fears are, that unless the blood-thirsty faction of the

Papists and prelates be hindered in their designs, ourselves here in England as well as they in Ireland shall be exposed to that misery which is more intolerable than that which is already past, as namely to the rage not of men alone, but of Devils incarnate (as we may so say) besides the thraldom of our souls and consciences in matters concerning God, which of all things are most dear unto us . . .

The reasons follow:

It may be thought strange, and unbeseeming our sex to show ourselves by way of petition to this honourable assembly: but the matter being rightly considered, of the right and interest we have in the common and public cause of the church, it will, as we conceive (under correction) be found a duty commanded and required.

First, because Christ hath purchased us at as dear a rate as he hath done men, and therefore requireth the like obedience for the same mercy as of men.

Secondly, because in the free enjoying of Christ in his own laws, and a flourishing estate of the church and commonwealth, consisteth the happiness of women as well as men.

Thirdly, because women are sharers in the common calamities that accompany both church and commonwealth, when oppression is exercised over the church or kingdom wherein they live; and an unlimited power have been given to prelates to exercise authority over the consciences of women, as well as men; witness Newgate, Smithfield, and other places of persecution, wherein women as well as men have felt the smart of their fury.

Neither are we left without example in scripture for when the state of the church, in the time of King Ahasuerus was by the bloody enemies thereof sought to be utterly destroyed, we find that Esther the queen and her maids fasted and prayed and that Esther petitioned to the king in the behalf of the church: and though she enterprised this duty with the hazard of her own life, being contrary to the law to appear before the king before she were sent for, yet her love to the church carried her through all difficulties, to the performance of that duty.

On which grounds we are emboldened to present our humble petition unto this honourable assembly, not weighing the reproaches which may and are by many cast upon us, who (not well weighing the premises) scoff and deride our good intent. We do it not out of any self conceit, or pride of heart, as seeking to equal ourselves with men, either in authority or wisdom; but according to our places to discharge that duty we owe to God, and the cause of the church, as far as lieth in us, following herein the example of the men, which have gone in this duty before us.

160

* * *

A relation of the manner how it was delivered, with their answer sent by Mr Pym.

This petition with their reasons was delivered the 4th of Feb. 1641, by Mrs Anne Stagg, a gentlewoman and a brewer's wife, and many others with her of like rank and quality, which when they had delivered it, after some time spent in reading of it, the honourable Assembly sent them answer by Mr Pym, which was performed in this manner.

Mr Pym came to the commons door and called for the women and spake unto them in these words: good women, your petitions and the reasons have been read in the house; and is very thankfully accepted of, and is come in seasonable time: you shall (God willing) receive from us all the satisfaction which we can possibly give to your just and lawful desires. We entreat you to repair to your houses, and turn your petition which you have delivered here, into prayers at home ready for us; for we have been, are, and shall be (to our utmost power) ready to relieve you, your husbands, and children, to perform the trust committed unto us, towards God, our King and Country, as becometh faithful Christians and loyal subjects.

Robert Filmer, *Patriarcha, or the natural power of kings*

Filmer wrote this during the political debates of the Civil War but he refused to publish it, despite requests from his friends. It was, however, widely circulated, particularly in royalist circles. Text from: the first edition, pp. 1–24.

That the first kings were fathers of families

I come now to that argument which is used by Bellarmine,[22] and is the one and only argument I can find produced by my author for the proof of the natural liberty of the people. It is thus framed: *that God hath given or ordained power is evident by scripture; but God hath given it to no particular person, because by nature all men are equal; therefore he hath given power to the people or multitude.*

To answer this reason, drawn from the equality of mankind in nature, I will first use the help of Bellarmine himself, whose very words are these: *if many men had been together created out of the earth, they all ought to have been princes over their posterity.* In these words we have an evident confession, that creation made man prince of his posterity. And indeed not only Adam, but the succeeding patriarchs had, by right of fatherhood, royal authority over their children. Nor dares Bellarmine deny this also. That the patriarchs (saith he) were endowed with kingly power their deeds do testify: for as Adam was lord of his children, so his children, under him, had a command and power over their own children, but still with subordination to the first parent, who is lord paramount over his children's children to all generations, as being the grandfather of his people.

I see not then how the children of Adam, or any man else can be free from subjection to their parents: and this subjection of children being the fountain of royal authority, by the ordination of God himself; it follows that civil power, not only in general, is by divine institution, but even the assignments of it specially to the eldest parents, which quite takes away that new and common distinction which refers only power universal and absolute to God, but power respective in regard of the special form of government to the choice of the people.

* * *

By manifest footsteps we may trace this paternal government unto the Israelites coming into Egypt, where the exercise of supreme patriarchal jurisdiction was intermitted, because they were in subjection to a stronger prince. After the return of these Israelites out of bondage, God, out of a special care of them, chose Moses and Joshua successively to govern as princes in the place and stead of the supreme fathers: and after them likewise for a time, he raised up judges, to defend his people in time of peril. But when God gave the Israelites kings, he re-established the ancient and prime right of lineal succession to paternal government. And whensoever he made choice of any special person to be king, he intended that the issue should also have benefit thereof, as being comprehended sufficiently in the person of that father, although the father only was named in the grant.

It may seem absurd to maintain that kings now are the fathers of their people, since experience shows that contrary. It is true all kings be not the natural parents of their subjects yet they all either are, or are to be reputed, the next heirs to those first progenitors, who were at first the natural parents of the whole people, and, in their right, succeed to the exercise of supreme jurisdiction: and such heirs are not only lords of their own children, but also of their brethren and all others that were subject to their fathers ...

As long as the first fathers of families lived, the name of patriarchs did aptly belong unto them; but after a few descents, when the true fatherhood itself was extinct and only the right of the father descends to the true heir, then the title of prince or king was more significant, to express the power of him who succeeds only to the right of that fatherhood which his ancestors did naturally enjoy; by this means it comes to pass that many a child, by succeeding a king, hath the right of a father over many a grey-headed multitude and hath the title of *pater patriae*.

* * *

In all kingdoms or commonwealths in the world, whether the prince be the supreme father of the people, or but the true heir of such a father, or whether he come to the crown by usurpation, or by election of the nobles, or of the people, or by any other way whatsoever, or whether some few or a multitude govern the commonwealth: yet still the authority that is in any one, or in many, or in all these, is the only right and natural authority of a supreme father. There is, and always shall be continued to the end of the world, a natural right of a supreme father over every multitude, although by the secret will of God, many at first do most unjustly obtain the exercise of it.

To confirm this natural right of regal power, we find in the Decalogue[23] that law which enjoins obedience to kings, is delivered in the terms of *honour thy father*, as if all power were originally in the father. If obedience to parents be immediately due by a natural law, and subjection to princes but by the mediation of an human ordinance: what reason is there that the laws of nature should give place to the laws of men? As we see the power of the father over his child gives place and is subordinate to the power of the magistrate.

If we compare the natural rights of a father with those of a king, we find them all one, without any difference at all but only in the latitude or extent of them: as the father over one family, so the king, as father over many families, extends his care to preserve, feed, clothe, instruct, and defend the whole commonwealth. His war, his peace, his courts of justice, and all his acts of sovereignty tend only to preserve and distribute to every subordinate and inferior father, and to their children, their rights and privileges; so that all the duties of a king are summed up in an universal fatherly care of his people.

6

EDUCATION

INTRODUCTION

Batty's *The Christian man's closet* (pp. 182–3) was translated into English in 1581, with a dedication to the translator's patrons, Thomas and Brian D'Arcy, which argued that one of the purposes of the translation was the circulation of training and instruction through the agency of fathers:

> And for that your worships are fathers of many children (which I am persuaded are daily beloved unto you), and masters of great families, whereof I know you have care to be virtuously instructed, guided, governed and trained up in the fear of God.

It is notable that a humanist educational treatise, with the expressed aim of furthering 'the godly training up of children' should be addressed solely to the male householder as responsible for the welfare and education of the children. The book is set out as a dialogue between Theophilus, Theodidactus and Mattina, the mother, although in the small part of the text devoted to girls' education, the mother is not given a part in the discussion. Education, its theory and practice, is a battle-ground in any society: humanism made education central to a social revolution where a centralised state, overseen by a powerful, if enlightened, magistrate, was served by highly educated and functional civil servants and diplomats. Grammar schools were instituted to educate boys for this life of public service. During the sixteenth century many of these schools developed specific bans on girls either attending at all, or attending once they reached the age of nine.[1]

In this radical redefinition of its content and function, education was no longer simply a clerical affair. Women actually had fewer educational opportunities than under Catholicism and feudalism where women might receive vocational education for life as a nun or, for aristocratic women, be sent to another large household to learn the skills necessary to help manage a landed estate with a future husband. One of the eventual consequences of the humanist educational revolution was to intensify the developing split between men's public function and place and women's private function and place. The Christian educational curriculum and aim remained

165

the model for educating girls. Thus Vives' *Instruction of a Christian woman* (pp. 168–71), often hailed as a liberal treatise advocating a careful and structured educational programme for girls and women, still bases both his educational philosophy and curriculum on the texts of the Christian Fathers, such as Jerome's letters to Eustochium and Furia, Tertullian's *De cultu feminarum* or St Cyprian's *De habitu virginum*. These advocate education in the virtues of modesty and obedience, with reading as a subsidiary private pastime, in contradistinction to the humanist programme of classical and pagan reading and learning recommended for boys (see pp. 183–6 also).[2]

Nevertheless, one of the modern myths about humanism,[3] which has been difficult to dispel, is that Renaissance English women during the sixteenth century benefited from humanist educational theories and revolutions. The career of learned women of sixteenth-century England is illustrative. There were some exceptionally well-educated women in the public eye: Margaret More (later Margaret Roper) as the daughter of Thomas More; Mary and Elizabeth Tudor; Lady Jane Grey; and the three Cooke sisters, who all married prominent public men (Elizabeth, Anne, and Mildred to Thomas Hoby, Nicholas Bacon and William Cecil respectively). These women were extensively educated in humanist texts and methods and most of them produced their own translations of theological works, yet few of them voluntarily published that writing. Anne and Elizabeth Cooke's were published in their names and dedicated to their mother and daughter respectively, thus maintaining the fiction of a closed female readership. All other work was published anonymously and by the men in their lives. Where the women did express a private view about the function of their humanist education, it was firmly placed within a framework of marital subjection and the acquisition of chaste, wifely virtues. Richard Hyrde's preface to Margaret Roper's translation of Erasmus's *A devout treatise upon the paternoster* (pp. 173–5) is a case in point. Roper does not speak overtly in her own voice at any point in the translation or the publication: instead Hyrde's preface uses her translation as a platform for reinforcing norms for feminine behaviour through education. He argues, for example, that women's education is crucially important, but only so that marriage can be more perfect. Thus the potentially radical agenda of educational humanism is appropriated to the conventional model of femininity. This is a mode of argumentation which is used over one hundred years later by Bathshua Makin in her plea for women's education (pp. 186–91). Thus even where the content of women's own work shows a desire for equal access to educational opportunities, those opportunities are only defined in exact reference to woman's conventional social function. There is perhaps less contrast than many have thought between the assertions of Salter and others (pp. 177–8) who argue that woman's physiology unfits her for intellectual knowledge, and those who argue she is man's intellectual equal (or near enough), but that her education must be channelled into the single purpose for which she was created: namely, the work of marriage.

Not only were there very few articulate, educated women during the sixteenth century,[4] but there was no great shift of educational policy for women.[5] Indeed, it is possible to say that medieval Catholicism provided more opportunities for female education through nunneries and the valuation of the scholarly life of a nun, than did early modern Protestantism. The most radical plea for female education represented here, is that by the Catholic Mary Ward (chapter 7, pp. 206–7): she asks the pope for permission to establish an educational nunnery, with the aim of providing educated Catholic women in order to further the conversion of England. The one specific plea for structured female Protestant education in sixteenth-century England, made by Becon in his *Catechism* (pp. 176–7), is framed within the ideological structure and discourses which construct femininity and was ignored by all his contemporaries.

Protestant writing on education for girls focused on two specific aims: the cultivation of virtue and the development of the skills of housewifery. The former was principally defined as the avoidance of the sin of pride and cultivation of the virtue of chastity, which are also specifically angled towards the girl's one function in life: to become a wife and mother (pp. 168–71, 177–8, 186–91). The curriculum for girls reflects this in its emphasis on biblical and theological readings, alongside practical skills such as weaving, sewing, basic medical knowledge, singing and dancing, and in the frequent dire warnings against girls being allowed to read medieval romances or classical love poetry (pp. 169–71, 178). The texts in chapters 3, 4 and 7 on conduct, motherhood and work in this collection are all aimed also at educating girls in their true purpose. Unlike the realm of motherhood or theology, educational writing does not, however, give women a discrete space in which specific women's interest and identity can be developed: educational aims and curriculum are part of the gendered hierarchy of explicit political patriarchal practice and theory. It is this fact which makes education a key area for early feminism: it is both the means whereby and the place where equality is sought.

Literacy levels are a good measure of the indifference of the intellectual revolutions of humanism and Protestantism to women's education: despite the humanist aim of literacy for women, their curricula made it clear such education was only for the high-born, and for use only within the private domain. Reading and writing was taught at dame schools, but only for those who had the money and leisure to afford it. Literacy levels remained much lower for women than for men during this period, as they were far lower for those of lower social status. Female illiteracy has been estimated at 90 per cent in the 1640s, with male rates at 70 per cent, dropping to 70 per cent and 55 per cent, respectively, in the early eighteenth century, although the measures used have been much debated: women who could not sign their name, for example, may well have been able to read, or to understand accounts.[6] Similarly, although there were, increasingly, both day and boarding schools for young women during the seventeenth century, for example the one which Makin herself advertises at the end of her *Essay to revive the ancient learning* (pp. 186–91), their curriculum and clientele were limited by the aims for which girls' education was circumscribed and by social status, respectively. More so than for boys, where the grammar schools at least theoretically provided scholarships for bright boys from poor families, education for girls was limited to the aristocracy, gentry and middle ranks.

Girls and women, therefore, were imprisoned within an ideology which promised freedom for men at the expense of circumscribing women's access to knowledge and learning. It is nevertheless noticeable, that whilst the ideological message of humanism and Protestantism places women within the constraining model of chaste and silent wife, women themselves begin to articulate an analysis of this constraint: Makin argues that it is the lack of education which disinherits women from the public sphere and which keeps them foolish. When Mary Astell published her *A serious proposal to the ladies* in 1697, a text included in Vivien Jones's *Women in the Eighteenth Century* (1990), her plea was for a fair and comprehensive educational system to better the status of women: such a plea looks both to the future of feminist struggle and to the previous century and a half's debate on education.

Juan Luis Vives, *Instruction of a Christian woman*

Text from: the 1540 edition, transl. Richard Hyrde, fos 5ᵛ–12ᵛ.

Of the learning of maids

Of maids some be but little meet for learning, likewise as some men be unapt; again some be born unto it, or at least not unfit for it. Therefore they that be dull are not to be discouraged, and those that be apt should be hearted and encouraged. I perceive that learned women be suspected of many, as who saith the subtility of learning should be a nourishment for the maliciousness of their nature. Verily I do not allow in a subtle and a crafty woman such learning as should teach her deceit and teach her no good manners and virtues. Notwithstanding the precepts of living and the examples of those that have lived well, and had knowledge together of holiness, be the keepers of chastity and pureness, and the copies of virtues, and pricks to prick and to move folks to continue in them.... But you shall not lightly find an ill woman; except it be such one, as either knoweth not, or at leastway considereth not what chastity and honesty is worth, nor seeth what mischief she doeth when she forgoeth it, nor regardeth how great a treasure, for how foul, for how light, and transitory an image of pleasure she changeth, what a sort of ungraciousness she letteth in, what time she shutteth forth chastity, nor pondereth what bodily pleasure is, how vain and foolish a thing, which is not worth the turning of a hand, not only unworthy, wherefore she should cast away that which is most goodly treasure that a woman can have. And she that hath learned in books to cast this and such other things, and hath furnished and fenced her mind with holy counsels, shall never find to do any villainy. For if she can find in her heart to do naughtily, having so many precepts of virtue to keep her, what should we suppose she should do, having no knowledge of goodness at all? ...

For the study of learning is such a thing, that it occupieth one's mind wholly, and lifteth it up into the knowledge of most goodly matters, and plucketh it from the remembrance of such things as be foul. And if any such thought come into their mind, either the mind, well fortified with the precepts of good living, avoideth them away, or else it giveth none heed unto those things that be vile and foul, when it hath other most goodly and pure pleasure, wherewith it is delighted. And therefore I suppose that Pallas the goddess of wisdom and cunning, and all the Muses, were feigned in old times to be virgins. And the mind, set upon learning and wisdom, shall not only abhor from foul lust, that is to say the most white thing from soot, and the most pure from spots. But also they shall leave all such light and trifling pleasures, wherein the light fantasies of maids have delight, as songs, dances and such other wanton and peevish plays. A woman, saith Plutarch, given unto learning, will never delight in dancing. But here peradventure a man would ask, what learning a woman should be set unto, and what she shall study? I have told you: the study of wisdom, the which doth instruct their manners and inform their living, and teacheth them the way of good and holy life. As for eloquence, I have no great care, nor a woman needeth it not, but she needeth goodness and wisdom. Nor is it no shame for a woman to hold her peace, but it is a shame for her and abominable to lack discretion and to live ill. Nor I will not here condemn eloquence, which both Quintilian and St Jerome following him, say, was praised in Cornelia the mother of Gracchus, and in Hortensia the daughter of Hortensius. If there may be found any holy and well learned woman, I had lever have her to teach them. If there be none, let us choose some man either well aged, or else good and virtuous, which hath a wife, and that right fair enough, whom he loveth well, and so shall he not desire other. For these things ought to be seen to, forasmuch as chastity in bringing up a woman requireth the most diligence, and in a manner all together. When she shall be taught to read, let those books be taken in hand that may teach good manners. And when she shall learn to write, let not her example be void verses, nor wanton or trifling songs, but some sad sentence, prudent and chaste, taken out of holy scripture, or the sayings of philosophers, which by often writing she may fasten better in her memory. And in learning, as I point none end to the man, no more I do to the woman: saving that it is meet that the man have knowledge of many and divers things, that may both profit himself and the commonwealth, both with the use and increasing of learning. But I would the woman should be altogether in that part of philosophy, that taketh upon it to inform and teach and amend the conditions. And finally let her learn for herself alone and her young children, or her sisters in our Lord. For it neither becometh a woman to rule a school, nor to live among men, or speak abroad, and shake off her demureness and honesty, either all together or a great part: which if she be good it were better to be at home within and unknown to other folks. And in company to hold her tongue demurely. And let few see her and none at all hear her . . .

What books ought to be read, and what not

St Jerome writing unto Leta of the teaching of Paul commandeth thus: *let her learn to hear nothing, nor speak, but it that pertaineth unto the fear of God.* Nor there is no doubt but he will counsel the same of reading. There is an use nowadays, worse than among the pagans that books written in our mother's tongue that be made but for idle men and women to read, have none other matter but of war and love: of the which books I think it shall not need to give any precepts. If I speak unto Christian folks, what need I to tell what mischief is toward, when straw and dry wood is cast into the fire? Yea, but these be written they say for idle folk, as though idleness were not a vice great enough of itself, without firebrands be put unto it, wherewith the fire may catch a man altogether, and more hot. What should a maid do with armour? Which once to name were a shame for her. I have heard tell that in some places gentlewomen behold marvellous busily the plays and joustings of armed men, and give sentence and judgement of them and that the men fear and set more by their judgements than the men's . . . Plato casteth out of the commonwealth of wise men, which he made, Homer and Hesiodus, the poets: and yet have they none ill thing in comparison unto Ovid's books of love which we read, and carry them in our hands, and learn them by heart, yea and some school masters teach them to their scholars and some make expositions and expound the vices. Augustus banished Ovid himself and think you then that he would have kept these expositors in the country? Except a man would reckon it a worse deed to write vice than to expound it, and inform the tender minds of the young folks therewith. We banish him that maketh false weights and measures, and that counterfeiteth coin or an instrument: and what a work is made in these things for small matters. But he is had in honour, and counted a master of wisdom, that corrupteth the young people. Therefore a woman should beware of all these books, likewise as of serpents or snakes. And if there be any woman that hath such delight in these books, that she will not leave them out of her hands: she should not only be kept from them, but also if she read good books with an ill will and loath thereto, her father and friends should provide that she be kept from all reading, and so by disuse forget learning, if it can be done. For it is better to lack a good thing, than to use it ill. Nor a good woman will take no such books in hand, nor file[7] her mouth with them: and as much as she can, she will go about to make other as like herself as she may, both by doing well and teaching well, and also as far as she may rule by commanding and charging. Now what books ought to be read, some everybody knoweth, as the gospels, the acts, the epistles of the apostles, and the old testament, St Jerome, St Cyprian, Augustine, Ambrose, Hilary, Gregory, Plato, Cicero, Seneca, and such other. But as touching some, wise and sad men must be asked counsel of in them. Nor the woman ought not to follow her own judgement, lest when she hath but a light entering in learning, she should take false for true: hurtful instead of wholesome, foolish and peevish for sad and wise. She shall find in such books as are worthy to be read, all things more witty, and full of greater pleasure, and more sure to trust unto: which shall both profit the life, and marvellously delight the mind. Therefore on holy days continually, and some time on working days, let her read or hear such as shall lift up the mind to God, and set it in a Christian quietness, and make the living better. Also it should be best afore she go to mass to read at home the gospel and the epistle of the day, and with it some exposition, if she have any. Now when thou comest from mass, and hast overlooked thy house, as much as pertaineth unto thy charge read with a quiet mind some of these that I have spoken of, if thou canst read, if not, hear. And on some working days do likewise, if thou be not letted with some necessary business in thy house and thou have books at hand: and specially if there be any longer space between the holy days, for think not that the holy days be ordained of the church to play on and sit idle and talk with thy gossips: but unto the intent that then thou maist more intentively and with a more quiet mind, think of God and this life of ours, and the life in heaven that is to come.

Desiderius Erasmus, *Colloquy of the abbot and learned woman*

Antromius, the abbot, and Magdalia, the nun, discuss women's education. Text from: *The Colloquies*, transl. H.M., 1671, pp. 241–5.

Ma. Hast thou, who art so old, and moreover, an abbot and a courtier, never seen books in noble women's houses?

An. I have seen some, but written in French, I see here Greek and Latin.

Ma. Do books only that are written in French, teach *men* wisdom?

An. But this becomes noble women, to have somewhat wherewith they may pleasantly pass away their spare time.

Ma. Is't lawful for noble women only to be wise and live comfortably?

An. Thou does not well to put these two together, viz. to be wise, and to live comfortably. It is not for women to be wise, but it belongs to noble women to live comfortably.

* * *

An. I think thou art some sophistress, thou pratest so wittily.

Ma. I will not tell thee what I think thou art. But why doth this furniture displease thee?

An. Because a spindle and a distaff are a woman's instruments.

Ma. Is't not the duty of a matron to look to her household business, and to instruct her children?

An. It is so.

Ma. Dost thou think so great an affair can be ordered without wisdom?

An. I do not think so.

Ma. Why but my books teach me this wisdom.

An. I have three score and two monks at home, and yet thou wilt find never a book in my bed chamber.

Ma. Therefore these monks are well provided for.

An. I can endure books, but I cannot endure Latin books.

Ma. Wherefore?

An. Because that language is not fit for women.

Ma. I would know the reason.

An. Because it little avails to maintain their chastity.

Ma. Books then it seems that are written in French, full of foolish fables, make for one's chastity?

An. There is another thing in it.

Ma. Speak it plainly, whatever it is.

An. They are safer from priests, if they be not skilled in the Latin tongue.

Ma. Nay, there is the least danger in that respect by your means, seeing that you are very careful of this that *you* be not skilled in the Latin tongue.

An. The common people think thus, because it is a rare and unusual thing for a woman to be skilled in Latin.

Ma. Why dost thou tell me of the common people, which is the worst counsellor to do a thing well? Why dost thou allege custom, which is the tutoress of all bad things? We must accustom ourselves to the best things, and so that will become familiar which was unusual to us, and pleasant, which was unpleasant, and comely which seemed uncomely.

An. I agree to thee.

Ma. Is it not a seemly thing for a woman born in Germany to learn French?

An. Yes.

Ma. For what reason?

An. That she may talk with those who are skilled in French.

Ma. And dost thou think it an unseemly thing for me to learn Latin, that I may confer every day with so many authors, being so learned, so wise and so faithful advisers?

An. Books do much weaken women's brains, though otherwise they have little enough.

Ma. How much you have I know not: certainly, how little soever I have, I had rather spend it in honest studies than in prayers said without understanding, in feastings all night long and in drinking off large boles.[8]

Richard Hyrde, *Preface*

Hyrde was one of the younger generation of humanists in the More household: here he prefaces More's daughter's translation, which she herself did not comment on publicly. Text from: *Preface* to Margaret Roper's translation of Erasmus, *A devout treatise upon the paternoster*, 1526, fos A2ʳ–B3ᵛ.

I have heard many men put great doubt whether it should be expedient and requisite or not a woman to have learning in books of Latin and Greek; and some utterly affirm that it is not only neither necessary nor profitable, but also very noisome and jeopardous: alleging for their opinion that the frail kind of women being inclined of their own courage unto vice, and mutable at every novelty, if they should have skill in many things that be written in the Greek and Latin tongue, compiled and made with great craft and eloquence, where the matter is haply sometime more sweet unto the ear than wholesome for the mind, it would of likelihood both inflame their stomachs a great deal the more to that vice that men say they be too much given unto of their own nature already, and instruct them also with more subtility and conveyance to set forward and accomplish their froward intent and purpose. But these men that so say do in my judgement either regard but little what they speak in this matter, or else, as they be for the more part unlearned, they envy it, and take it sore to heart, that other should have that precious jewel which they neither have themself nor can find in their hearts to take the pain to get ...

Now as for learning, if it were cause of any evil as they say it is, it worry worse in the man than in the woman, because (as I have said here before) he can both worse stay and restrain himself than she. And moreover than that he cometh ofter[9] and in more occasions than the woman, inasmuch as he liveth more abroad among company daily where he shall be moved to utter such craft as he hath gotten by his learning. And women abide most at home, occupied ever with some good or necessary business. And the Latin and the Greek tongue, I see not but there is as little hurt in them as in books of

English and French, which men doth read themselves for the proper pastimes that be written in them, and for the witty and crafty conveyance of the makings: and also can bear well enough that women read them if they will, never so much which commodities be far better handled in the Latin and Greek, than any other language. And in them be many holy doctors' writings, so devote and effectuous,[10] that whosoever readeth them, must needs be either much better, or less evil, which every good body, both man and woman, will read and follow, rather than other... And where they find fault with learning, because they say it engendereth wit and craft there they reprehend it for that it is most worthily to be commended for, and the which is one singular cause wherefore learning ought to be desired. For he that had lever have his wife a fool than a wise woman, I hold him worse than twice frantic. Also reading and studying of books so occupieth the mind, that it can have no leisure to muse or delight in other fantasies, when in all handy works that men say be more meet for a woman, the body may be busy in one place and the mind walking in another: and while they sit sewing and spinning with their fingers, may taste and compass many peevish fantasies in their minds, which must needs be occupied either with good or bad, so long as they be waking. And those that be evil disposed will find the means to be naughty though they can never a letter on the book; and she that will be good, learning shall cause her to be much the better. For it showeth the image and ways of the good living, even right as a mirror showeth the similitude and proportion of the body. And doubtless the daily experience proveth that such as are naughty are those that never knew what learning meant. For I never heard tell nor read of any woman well learned that ever was (as plenteous as evil tongues be) spotted or infamed as vicious. But on the other side many by their learning taken such increase of goodness, that many may bear them witness of their virtues, of which sort I could rehearse a great number, both of old time and late, saving that I will be content as for now with one example of our own country and time that is. This gentlewoman which translated this little book hereafter following, whose virtuous conversation, living and sad demeanour may be proof evident enough what good learning doth where it is surely rooted; of whom other women may take example of prudent, humble and wifely behaviour, charitable and very Christian virtue, with which she hath with God's help endeavoured herself no less to garnish her soul, than it hath liked his goodness with lovely beauty and comeliness to garnish and set out her body. And undoubted is it that to the increase of her virtue she hath taken and taketh no little occasion of her learning besides her other manifold and great commodities taken of the same, among which commodities this is not the least that with her virtuous, worshipful, wise and well-learned husband, she hath by the occasion of her learning and his delight therein such especial comfort, pleasure and pastime, as were not well possible for one unlearned couple, either to take together, or to conceive in their minds what pleasure is therein.

Thomas Becon, *Catechism*

Text from: *Works*, 1564, fos 536ʳ–7.

Of the office and duty of old and ancient women

Father. The holy apostle, after that he hath dissuaded the old women from vanity of apparel, from much babbling, and from drunkenness, declareth what good they ought to do, lest they, being trees without fruit, be hewn down and cast into the fire [Matt. 3]. And this good work that he requireth of them is that they teach honest things.

Son. But St Paul in another place saith: *I suffer not a woman to teach, neither to usurp authority over the man, but to be in silence.*

Father. The same St Paul also in another place, expounding what is meant by these words, saith, *let your women keep silence in the congregations. For it is not permitted unto them to speak, but to be under obedience, as saith the law. If they will learn anything, let them ask their husbands at home. For it is a shame for women to speak in the congregation.* Of these words of St Paul we learn that it is not lawful for women to teach in the congregation openly, which only appertain to men, yea and unto such men alone as are appointed by public authority unto the ministry. Notwithstanding women to preach and teach in their own houses, it is not only not forbidden, but also most straightly commanded. For who knoweth not that every man and every woman is a bishop in their own house, and ought to teach their family, and to bring them up in the doctrine and nurture of the lord our God? It is therefore also lawful for old and ancient matrons to teach.

Son. Whom should they teach?

Father. Young women.

Son. What should they teach them?

Father. To be sober-minded; to love their husbands; to love their children; to be discreet, chaste, housewifely, good, obedient to their husbands; that the word of God be not evilly spoken.

Son. I looked that thou should have said unto me that the ancient matrons would teach the young women trimly to dance, minionly to play upon the lute or virginals, cunningly to work with the needle, finely to apparel themselves, handsomely to play the serving maids, pleasantly to entertain strangers, yonkers and young gentlemen!

Father. These be things of vanity, rather provoking unto lewdness than unto virtue, heretofore abhorred and hated of all modest and sober women. The works and qualities which St Paul here setteth forth, that the ancient matrons should teach the young women, are necessary works and godly qualities. Can anything be more necessary or godly in a Christian commonweal, than to bring up maids and young women virtuously, and to teach them to be sober-minded, to love their husbands, to love their children, to be discreet, chaste, housewifely, good, obedient to their husbands?

Son. If all our maids and young women were thus brought up, we should not have so many idle, unhonest, and lewd women as we have at this present day.

Father. To bring this thing to pass, it is expedient that by public authority, schools for women children be erected and set up in every Christian commonweal, and honest, sage, wise, discreet, sober, grave, and learned matrons made rulers and mistresses of the same, and that honest and liberal stipends be appointed for the said school-mistresses, which shall travail in the bringing up of young maids, that by this means they may be occasioned the more gladly and willingly to take pains. And to this end, without doubt at the beginning were the monasteries of solitary women, whom we heretofore called nuns, built and set up, and endowed with possessions of our godly ancestors, although in process of time they were greatly abused, so that they were made of Christian and free schools, prisons of Antichrist ...

Son. It is a matter most worthy to be considered. For if it be thought convenient, as it is most convenient that schools should be erected and set up for the right education and bringing up of the youth of the male kind, why should it not also be thought convenient that schools be built for the godly institution and virtuous bringing up of the youth of the female kind? Is not the woman the creature of God, so well as the man? Is not she as dear unto God as the man? Is not the woman a necessary member of the commonweal? Have not we all our beginning of her? Are not we born, nursed, and brought up of a woman? Do not the children for the most part prove even such as the mothers are, of whom they come? Can the mothers bring up their children virtuously when they themselves be void of all virtue? Can the nurses instil any goodness into the tender breasts of their nurse-children, when they themselves have learned none? Can that woman govern her house godly which knoweth not one point of godliness? Who seeth not now then how necessary the virtuous education and bringing up of the woman-kind is? Which thing cannot be conveniently brought to pass, except schools for that purpose be appointed.

Thomas Salter, *The mirror of modesty*

Salter's publication advises mothers on the education of daughters. Text from: the first edition, 1578, fos B5^v–B8^r.

Besides, when any maiden is driven into a trembling fear by her mistress sudden sharp frowning, as no doubt some, being of mild and gentle natures, will be soon, our good matron will soon change her sour lowering into a sweet smiling, and, with gentle and virtuous informations and cheerful promises, put her out of her fear, for in no wise would I wish any to be over-pressed by fear, because thereby many become even simple like fools. And whereas some parents be of opinion that it be necessary for maidens, to be skilful in philosophy moral and natural, thinking it an honour unto them to be thought well learned, I for my part am the contrary because that by the same they are made to understand the evils imminent to human life, yea thereby is opened up to them the inclinations and proneness, which naturally even from our cradles we have, unto vice, which knowledge is not requisite to be in young women. Likewise the examples of evil and wicked men, the corrupt lives and lewd customs of those that have conversation with us, the heaps of pleasures, pastimes, delights, and recreations, and the deceits and guiles of our ghostly enemy, from the which we see how the wary wise man can hardly defend himself (I leave the young and tender virgin) with the protection and armour of great learning: to which or against which I should flatly answer, that the evil use of learning hath more oftentimes be cause of discommodity and domage, than the right and laudable use of it hath been of profit and benefit. I should peradventure be suspected of some for such a one as did the same to the derogation, slander and reproof of learning, which thing I utterly deny... Sparta might be brought in, for that a long time, whilst it had eloquence in horror and hate, thinking the use of it more meet for effeminate and wanton idle men than for courageous and warlike champions, it flourished as chief of Greece with great glory. But because I have taken in hand to instruct a Christian maiden, laying aside all other examples, I might bring in the example of our Saviour, that rock of infallible verity, who utterly blamed the wisdom of the world, as enemy to good life and religion. But my intent is not, neither was it ever, to attribute such evil as springeth from the malice of wicked men and their corrupt nature to the sacred study of learning, to which I have given my mind so much as in me lay all my lifetime. But my purpose is to prove that in a virtuous virgin and modest maiden, such use is more dangerous and hurtful, than necessary or praiseworthy. Some perhaps will allege that a maiden being well learned, and able to search and read sundry authors, may become chaste and godly by reading the godly and chaste lives of diverse. But I answer, who can deny that seeing of herself she is able to read and understand the Christian poets ... and such like, that she will not also read the lascivious books of Ovid, Catullus, Propertius, Tibullus, and in Virgil, of Aeneas and Dido and among the Greek poets of the filthy love (if I may term it love) of the Gods themselves, and of their wicked adulteries and abominable fornications, as in Homer and suchlike? ... And sure I suppose there is no man of reason and understanding but had rather love a maiden unlearned and chaste than one suspected of dishonest life, though never so famous and well learned in philosophy. Wherefore I wish all parents to beware and take heed, how they suffer their young daughters, being frail of nature, to be bold disputers.... And who is it that will deny that it is not more praise and honour to do noble deeds, than to write of them? Sure, I think none. I am therefore of this advice, that it is not meet nor convenient for a maiden to be taught or trained up in learning of humane arts, in whom a virtuous demeanour and honest behaviour would be a more sightlier ornament than the light or vainglory of learning, for in learning and studying of the arts there are two things finally proposed unto us, that is recreation and profit. Touching profit, that is not to be looked for, at the hands of her that is given us for a companion in our labours, but rather every woman ought wholly to be active and diligent about the government of her household and family; and touching recreation by learning, that cannot be granted her without great danger and offence to the beauty and brightness of her mind. Seeing then that the government of estates and public weals are not committed into the hands of women; neither that it is lawful or convenient for them to write laws by which men should be ruled and governed ... neither as professors of science and faculty, to teach in schools the wisdom of laws and philosophy; and seeing also that in such studies as yieldeth recreation and pleasure, there is no less danger that they will as well learn to be subtle and shameless lovers, as cunning and skilful writers of ditties, sonnets, epigrams and ballads; let them be restrained to the care and government of a family.

Richard Mulcaster, *Positions*

Mulcaster, a notable Protestant humanist, was the headmaster of Merchant Taylors' School, where he taught Spenser. This work is dedicated to Elizabeth I, despite the fact that only one chapter of forty-five is devoted to girls' education. Text from: the first edition, 1581, pp. 166–83.

And to prove they [girls] are to be trained, I find four special reasons, whereof any one, much more all, may persuade any their most adversary, much more me, which am for them tooth and nail. The first is the manner and custom of my country, which allowing them to learn will be loath to be contraried by any of her countrymen. The second is the duty which we owe unto them, whereby we are charged in conscience not to leave them lame in that which is for them. The third is their own towardness, which God by nature would never have given them to remain idle or to small purpose. The fourth is the excellent effects in that sex when they have had the help of good bringing up: which commendeth the cause of such excellency, and wisheth us to cherish that tree whose fruit is both so pleasant in taste and so profitable in trial.

*   *   *

But now having granted them the benefit and society of our education, we must assign the end, wherefore the train shall serve, whereby we may apply it the better. Our own[11] train[12] is without restraint for either matter or manner, by cause our employment is so general in all things: theirs is within limit, and so must their train be. If a young maiden be to be trained in respect of marriage, obedience to her head and the qualities which look that way must needs be her best way. If in regard of necessity to learn how to live, artificial train must furnish out her trade. If in respect of ornament to beautify her birth and to honour her place, rarities in that kind and seemly for that kind do best beseem such. If for government, not denied them by God and devised them by men, the greatness of their calling doth call for great gifts, and general excellencies for general occurrences. Wherefore having these different ends always in the eye, we may point them their train in different degrees.

*   *   *

Though the girls seem commonly to have a quicker ripening in wit than boys have, for all that seeming, yet it is not so. Their natural weakness which cannot hold long, delivers very soon, and yet there be as prating boys as there be prating wenches. Besides their brains be not so much charged, neither with weight nor with multitude of matters, as boys' heads be: and therefore like empty cask they make the greater noise. As those men which seem to be very quick witted by some sudden pretty answer, or some sharp reply, be not always most burdened, neither with letters nor learning. . . . As for bodies the maidens be more weak, most commonly even by nature, as of a moonish influence, and all our whole kind is weak of the mother side, which when she was first made even then weakened the man's side. Therefore great regard must be had to them, no less, nay rather more, than to boys in that time. For in process of time, if they be of worth themselves, they may so match as the parent may take more pleasure in his sons by law, than in his heirs by nature. They are to be the principal pillars in the upholding of households, and so they are likely to prove, if they prove well in training. The dearest comfort that man can have if they incline to good: the nearest corrosive if they tread awry. And therefore charily to be cared for, bearing a jewel of such worth in a vessel of such weakness.

*   *   *

For the matter, what shall they learn? Thus I think, following the custom of my country, which in that that is usual doth lead me on boldly and in that also which is most rare, doth show my path to be already trodden. So that I shall not need to err, if I mark but my guide well. Where rare excellencies in some women do but show us some one or two parents' good success in their daughters' learning, there is neither precedent to be fetched nor precept to be framed. For precepts be to conduct the common, but these singularities be above the common: precedents be for hope, those pictures pass beyond all hope. And yet they serve for proof to proceed by in way of argument, that women can learn if they will and may learn what they list, when they bend their wits to it. To learn to read is very common, where convenientness doth serve, and writing is not refused, where opportunity will yield it.

Reading, if for nothing else it were, as for many things else it is, is very needful for religion, to read that which they must know, and ought to perform, if they have not whom to hear in that matter which they read: or if their memory be not steadfast, by reading to revive it. If they hear first and after read of the selfsame argument, reading confirms their memory. Here I may not omit many and great contentments, many and sound comforts, many and manifold delights, which those women that have skill and time to read, without hindering their housewifery, do continually receive by reading of some comfortable and wise discourses penned either in form of history or for direction to live by.

As for writing, though it be discommended for some private carriages (wherein we men also, no less than women bear oftentimes blame, if that were a sufficient exception why we should not learn to write), it hath his commodity where it filleth in match, and helps to enrich the good man's mercery.[13] Many good occasions are oftentimes offered, where it were better for them to have the use of their pen for the good that comes by it, than to wish they had it when the default is felt: and for fear of evil, which cannot be avoided in some, to avert that good which may be commodious to many.

Music is much used, where it is to be had, to the parent's delight, while the daughter be young ... I meddle not with needles nor yet with house-wifery, though I think it and know it, to be a principal commendation in a woman: to be able to govern and direct her household, to look to her house and family, to provide and keep necessaries, though the goodman pay, to know the force of her kitchen, for sickness and health in herself and her charge: because I deal only with such things as be incident to their learning.

* * *

Where the question is how much a woman ought to learn, the answer may be, so much as shall be needful. If that also come in doubt the return may be either so much as her parents conceive of her in hope, if her parentage be mean; or provide for her in state, if her birth bear a sail.[14] For if the parents be of calling and in great account, and the daughters capable of some singular qualities, many commendable effects may be wrought thereby, and the young maidens being well trained are very soon commended to right honourable matches, whom they may well beseem and answer much better, their qualities in state having good correspondence with their matches of state, and their wisdoms also putting to helping hand, for the procuring of their common good ... This *how much* consisteth either in perfecting of those forenamed four, reading well, writing fair, singing sweet, playing fine, beyond all cry and above all comparison, that pure excellency in things but ordinary may cause extraordinary liking: or else in skill of languages annexed to these four, that more good gifts may work more wonder.... These women, which we see in our days to have been brought up in learning, do rule this conclusion. That such personages as be born to be princes, or matches to great peers, or to furnish out such trains, for some peculiar ornaments to their place and calling, are to receive this kind of education in the highest degree, that is convenient for their kind. But princely maidens above all, because occasion of their height[15] stands in need of such gifts, both to honour themselves and to discharge the duty which the countries, committed to their hands, do daily call for: and besides what match is more honourable than when desert for rare qualities doth join itself with highness in degree?

* * *

Now there is nothing left to end this treatise of young maidens but where and under whom they are to learn, which question will be sufficiently resolved, upon consideration of the time how long they are to learn, which time is commonly till they be about thirteen or fourteen years old, wherein as the matter which they must deal withal cannot be very much in so little time, so the perfecting thereof requireth much travail, though their time be so little, and there would be some show afterward wherein their training did avail them. They that may continue some long time at learning, through the state and ability of their parents, have also their time and place suitable appointed by the foresight of their parents.

Bartholomew Batty, *The Christian man's closet*

The aim of this treatise is 'the godly training up of children; as also of those duties that children owe unto their parents'. The speakers are Amusus, Theodidactus, Theophilus and Mattina, the mother, who does not speak on girls' education. Text from: the first edition, 1581, transl. William Lowth, pp. 75ff.

Theophilus.   Although hitherto there hath almost nothing been spoken of you which may not be referred to the feminine sex, yet shall it not seem unprofitable if you add hereunto some matter or doctrine which may seem to appertain to maidens only, to the end also they might be the more stirred up, and put in remembrance of their duties, especially when they are admonished expressly.

Theodidactus.   I will very willingly take that pains, for these courteous and honest damsels' sakes, and so much the rather for that I will draw nothing here out of mine own quiver or storehouse, but out of the Epistle of St Jerome unto Leta will I faithfully recite the things which specially appertain to this purpose ...

1   After this manner is the soul to be taught and instructed, which shall be the temple of God. Let her learn to hear none other thing, neither to speak anything, saith St Jerome, but that which may appertain to the fear of God.

2   Let her not hear or understand any filthy words, nor merry ballads, nor jests, nor rhymes, but let her young and tender tongue be seasoned with sweet songs and psalms.

3   Weigh not down her neck with gold and precious stones, nor beset her head with pearls, neither curl, nor bush out her hair, nor die it into any unnatural colour.

4   Let her not eat openly (that is to say) in the feasts and banquets of her parents, lest she see such meats as she might desire and lust after: let her not learn to drink wine, wherein is all excess and riot.

5   Let her not delight and take pleasure in the hearing of musical instruments, shawms,[16] zithers, lutes and harps, nor know wherefore they were invented.

6   Let her appoint herself some task every day, to read some special part of the holy scriptures chosen for the same purpose.

7   Let her learn to card and spin to make woollen cloth: and to handle the wheel and distaff to make her linen cloth.

8   Let her not set her mind on silks, as taffeta, damask, satin and velvet.

9   Let her provide and get such clothes wherewith cold may be defended, not wherewith her body shall be nakedly apparelled.

10 Let her so eat as that she may be always ahungered, that immediately after her meat she may either read or sing psalms.

11 If it chance thee at any time either to walk or ride out of the town or city, leave not thy daughter at home without a goodly governor: for without thee she knoweth not, neither is she able to live, and when she shall chance to be alone, let her be afraid.

12 Let her not have her secret meetings, and fellowship with foolish and light maidens.

13 In the stead of silk, pearls and precious jewels, let her love godly books, not gaudily garnished and set out with gold, but inwardly perfected, and learnedly distinguished, for the better increase of her faith.

14 Let her first learn the psalter or psalms of David in metre, which may withdraw her mind from light and vain tongues and bawdy ballads.

And in the proverbs of Solomon, which may instruct her to good and godly life: and in *Ecclesiastes*, let her exercise herself to seek out things which appertain to the world. In Job, let her follow the example of virtue and patience. *A wise daughter is to her husband in the stead of an inheritance.* Also a shamefast maid will reverence her husband.

Elizabeth Jocelyn, *The mother's legacy to her unborn child*

Jocelyn, writing for her unborn child, assumes that she will bear a son. The extracts below are those relevant specifically to a daughter. Text from: the first edition, 1624, pp. 17–19, 30–45.

To my truly loving and most dearly loved husband, Tourell Jocelyn

Mine own dear love, I no sooner conceived an hope that I should be made a mother by thee, but with it entered the consideration of a mother's duty, and shortly after followed the apprehension of danger that might prevent me from executing that care I so exceedingly desired, I mean in religious training our child. And in truth, death appearing in this shape was doubly terrible unto me. First in respect of the painfulness of that kind of death, and next of the loss my little one should have in wanting me.

But I thank God these fears were cured with the remembrance that all things work together for the best to those that love God, and a certain assurance that he will give me patience according to my pain.

Yet still I thought there was some good office I might do for my child, more than only to bring it forth (though it should please God to take me). When I considered our frailty, our part inclination to sin, the Devil's subtlety, and the world's deceitfulness, against these how much desired I to admonish it! But still it came into my mind that death might deprive me of time if I should neglect the present. I knew not what to do: I thought of writing, but then mine own weakness appeared so manifestly, that I was ashamed, and durst not undertake it. But when I could find no other means to express my motherly zeal, I encouraged myself with these reasons.

First that I wrote to a child, and though I were but a woman, yet to a child's judgement what I understood might serve for a foundation to a better learning.

Again I considered it was to my own, and in private sort, and my love to my own might excuse my errors.

And lastly, but chiefly, I comforted myself that my intent was good, and that I was well assured God is the prosperer of good purposes.

Thus resolved, I writ this ensuing letter to our little one, to whom I could not find a fitter hand to convey it than thine own, which maist with authority see the performance of this my little legacy, of which my child is executor.

The mother's legacy to her unborn child

Thou art no sooner broke out of the arms of sloth, but pride steps in diligently, waiting to furnish thee with any vain toy in thy attire . . .

I desire thee for God's sake shun this vanity, whether thou be son or daughter. If a daughter, I confess thy task is harder because thou art weaker, and thy temptations to this vice greater, for thou shalt see those whom perhaps thou wilt think less able, exalted far above thee in this kind; and it may be thou wilt desire to be like them, if not to out-go them. But believe and remember that I tell thee, the end of all these vanities is bitter as gall.

Oh, the remembrance of mis-spent time, when thou shalt grow in years, and have attained no other knowledge, than to dress thyself. When thou shalt see half, perhaps all, thy time spent; and that of all thou hast sowed thou hast nothing to reap but repentence, late repentance, how wilt thou grieve? How wilt thou accuse one folly for bringing in another? And in thy memory cast over the cause of each misfortune which hath befallen them, till, passing from one to another, at last thou findest thy corrupt will to be the first cause, and then thou wilt with grief enough perceive that if thou hadst served God when thou servedst thy fond desires, thou hadst now had peace of heart. The God of mercy give thee grace to remember him in the days of thy youth.

Mistake me not, nor give yourself leave to take too much liberty with saying my mother was too strict. No, I am not, for I give you leave to follow modest fashions, but not to be a beginner of fashions: nor would I have you follow it till it be general; so that in not doing as others do, you might appear more singular than wise: but in one word, this is all I desire, that you will not set your heart on such fooleries, and you shall see that this modest carriage will win you reputation and love with the wise and virtuous sort.

And once again, remember how many hours maist thou give to God which if thou spendest in these vanities, thou shalt never be able to make account of. If thou dost but endeavour to do well, God will accept the will for the deed, but if thou wilfully spend the morning of thy time in these vanities, God will not be put off with such reckonings, but punishments will follow, such as I pray God thou maist not pull upon thee.

Yet alas, this is but one sort of pride, and so far from being accounted a vice, that, if the time mends not before you, you will hear a well dressed woman (for that is the style of honour) more commended than a wise or honest, or religious woman. And it may be this may move you to follow their idleness: but when you have any such desire, draw yourself to consider what manner of person the commended and commenders are, and you shall find them all of one batch, such as being vain themselves, applaud it in others.

But if you will desire praise, follow the example of those religious women whose virtuous fames time hath not power to raze out: as devout Anna, who served the Lord with fasting and prayer, *Luke 2*; just Elizabeth, who served God without reproof; religious Esther, who taught her maids to fast and pray, *Est. 4:15*; and the chaste Susanna, whose story, I hope, the strictest will allow for a worthy example.

I am so fearful that thou shouldst fall into this sin, that I could spend my littie time of life in exhorting thee from it. I know it is the most dangerous subtle sin that can steal the heart of man, it will alter shapes as oft as the chameleon doth colours, it will fit itself to all dispositions, and (which is most strange) it will so disguise itself, that he must be cunning who discerns it from humility, nay it may lie in thine own heart, and if thou beest not a diligent searcher of thy self, thou shalt not know it...

Solomon saith, *pride goeth before destruction, Prov. 16:18. And a high mind before the fall.* And our blessed Saviour, the true pattern of humility, exhorts us *to learn of him that was lowly and meek in heart, Matt. 11:9.* And if we do so he promises we shall find rest unto our souls. Neither want there curses, threatening where persuasions will not serve. *Whosoever exalteth himself shall be humbled, Luke 14:11.* Read the holy scriptures often and diligently, and thou shalt find continual threatenings against pride, punishment of pride, and warnings from pride. Thou shalt find no sin so heavily punished as this: it made devils of angels, a beast of great Nebuchadnezzar, dog's meat of Jezebel, and I will conclude with a good man's saying: *if all sins reigning in the world were burnt to ashes, even the ashes of pride would be able to reduce them all again.*

I know in fewer words there might much more have been said against this sin, but I know not who will say so much to thee when I am gone. Therefore

I desire thou maist be taught these my instructions when thou art young, that this foul sin may be weeded out before it take deep root in thy heart.

Bathshua Makin, *An essay to revive the ancient education of gentlewomen*

Makin was the governess of Charles I's daughter, a correspondent of Maria van Shurman (the renowned German educationalist), and the proprietor of several schools during her career. Here she both advertises for such a school, and argues strongly for a broader and more intellectual curriculum for girls, in the voice of two male interlocutors. Text from: the first edition, 1673, pp. 3–4, 22–8, 42–3.

To all ingenious and virtuous ladies, most especially to her Highness Mary, eldest daughter to his royal highness the Duke of York

Custom when it is inveterate, hath a mighty influence: it hath the force of nature itself. The barbarous custom to breed women low, is grown general amongst us, and hath prevailed so far, that it is verily believed (especially among a sort of debauched sots) that women are not endued with such reason, as men; nor capable of improvement by education, as they are. It is looked upon as a monstrous thing, to pretend the contrary. A learned woman is thought to be a comet, that bodes mischief, whenever it appears. To offer to the world the liberal education of women is to deface the image of God in man, it will make woman so high, and men so low, like fire in the house-top, it will set the whole world in a flame!

These things and worse than these, are commonly talked of, and verily believed by many, who think themselves wise men: to contradict these is a bold attempt; where the attempter must expect to meet with much opposition. Therefore, ladies, I beg the candid opinion of your sex, whose interest I assert. More especially I implore the favour of your Royal Highness a person most eminent amongst them, whose patronage alone will be a sufficient protection. What I have written is not out of humour to show how much may be said of trivial thing to little purpose. I verily think women were formerly educated in the knowledge of arts and tongues, and by their education many did rise to a great height in learning. Were women thus educated now, I am confident the advantage would be very great: the women would have the honour and pleasure, their relations profit, and the whole nation advantage. I am very sensible it is an ill time to set foot on this design: wherein not only learning but virtue itself is scorned and neglected, as pedantic things, fit only for the vulgar. I know no better way to reform these exorbitancies, than to persuade women to scorn these toys and trifles, they now spend their time about, and to attempt higher things, here offered: this

186

will either reclaim the men; or make them ashamed to claim the sovereignty over such as are more wise and virtuous than themselves.

Were a competent number of schools erected to educate ladies ingenuously, methinks I see how ashamed men would be of their ignorance, and how industrious the next generation would be to wipe off their reproach.

I expect to meet with many scoffs and taunts from inconsiderate and illiterate men, that prize their own lusts and pleasure more than your profit and content. I shall be the less concerned at these, so long as I am in your favour; and this discourse may be a weapon in your hands to defend yourselves, whilst you endeavour to polish your souls, that you may glorify God, and answer the end of your creation, to be meet helps to your husbands, let not your Ladyships be offended, that I do not (as some have wittily done) plead for female preeminence. To ask too much is the way to be denied all. God hath made man the head; if you be educated and instructed, as I propose, I am sure you will acknowledge it, and be satisfied that you are helps, that your husbands do consult and advise with you (which if you be wise they will be glad of) and that your husbands have the casting voice, in whose determinations you will acquiesce. That this may be the effect of this education in all ladies that shall attempt it is the desire of

Your servant.

Care ought to be taken by us to educate women in learning

My meaning is, persons that God hath blessed with the things of this world, that have competent natural parts, ought to be educated in knowledge; that is, it is much better they should spend the time of their youth to be competently instructed in those things usually taught to gentlewomen at schools, and the overplus of their time to be spent in gaining arts, and tongues, and useful knowledge, rather than to trifle away so many precious minutes merely to polish their hands and feet, to curl their locks, to dress and trim their bodies; and in the meantime to neglect their souls, and not at all, or very little to endeavour to know God, Jesus Christ, themselves, and the things of nature, arts and tongues, subservient to these. I do not deny but women ought to be brought up to a comely and decent carriage, to their needs, to neatness, to understand all those things that do particularly belong to their sex. But when these things are competently cared for, and where there are endowments of natures and leisure, then higher things ought to be endeavoured after. Merely to teach gentlewomen to frisk and dance, to paint their faces, to curl their hair, to put on a whisk,[17] to wear gay clothes, is not truly to adorn, but to adulterate their bodies; yea (what is worse) to defile their souls ...

Had God intended women only as a finer sort of cattle, he would not have made them reasonable: brutes, a few degrees higher than drills[18] or monkeys (which the Indians use to do many offices) might have better fitted some men's lust, pride and pleasure; especially those that desire to keep them ignorant to be tyrannised over.

God intended woman as a help-meet to man, in his constant conversation, and in the concerns of his family and his estate, when he should most need, in sickness, weakness, absences, death, &c. Whilst we neglect to fit them for these things he hath appointed women for, we renounce God's blessing, are ungrateful to him, cruel to them, and injurious to ourselves ...

Seeing nature produces women of such excellent parts, that they do often equalise, some times excel, men, in what ever they attempt, what reason can be given why they should not be improved?

Nothing is more excellent than man: his excellency doth not consist in his smooth skin, or erect countenance, but in his reasonable soul; and the excellency of reason is, when it is improved by art.

Learning perfects and adorns the soul, which all creatures aim at. Nay more, a principal part of God's image in man's first creation, consisted in knowledge. Sin hath clouded this: why should we not by instruction endeavour to repair that which shall be perfected in heaven?

*   *   *

In these late times[19] there are several instances of women, when their husbands were serving their king and country, defended their houses, and did all things, as soldiers, with prudence and valour, like men.

They appeared before committees, and pleaded their own causes with good success.

This kind of education will be very useful to women.

1. The profit will be to themselves. In the general they will be able to understand, read, write, and speak their mother-tongue, which they cannot do well without this. They will have something to exercise their thoughts about, which are busy and active. Their quality ties them at home, if learning be their companion, delight and pleasure will be their attendants: for there is no greater pleasure, nor more suitable to an ingenious mind, than that which is found in knowledge; it is the first fruits of heaven, and a glimpse of that glory we afterwards expect. There is in all an innate desire of knowledge, and the satisfying this is the greatest pleasure. Men are very cruel that give them leave to look at a distance, only to know that they do not know; to make any thus to tantalise is a great torment.

This will be a great hedge against heresies: men are furnished with arts and tongues for this purpose, that they may stop the mouths of their adversaries. And women ought to be learned that they may stop their ears against seducers. It cannot be imagined so many persons of quality would be so easily carried aside with every wind of doctrine, had they been furnished with defensive arms; I mean, had they been instructed in the plain rules of artificial reasoning, so as to distinguish a true and forcible argument, from a vain and captious fallacy; had they been furnished with examples of the most frequent illusions of erroneous seducers. Heresiarchs creep into houses, and lead silly women captive, then they lead their husbands, both their children, as the Devil did Eve, she her husband, they their posterity . . .

More particularly, persons of higher quality, for want of this education, have nothing to employ themselves in, but are forced to cards, dice, plays, and frothy romances, merely to drive away the time: whereas knowledge in arts and tongues would pleasantly employ them, and upon occasion benefit others . . .

We cannot be so stupid as to imagine that God gives ladies great estates, merely that they may eat, drink, sleep, and rise up to play. Doubtless they ought not to live thus. God, that will take an account for every idle thought, will certainly reckon with those persons that shall spend their whole lives in idle play and chat. Poor women will make but a lame excuse at the last day of their vain lives; it will be something to say, that they were educated no better. But what answer men will make, that do industriously deny them better improvement, lest they should be wiser than themselves, I cannot imagine . . .

As for unmarried persons, who are unable to subsist without a dependence, they have a fairer opportunity than men, if they continue long in that estate, to improve the principles they have sucked in and to ripen the seeds of learning which have been sown in their minds in their tender years. Besides, this will be an honest and profitable diversion to possess their minds, to keep out worse thoughts. Maids that cannot subsist without depending, as servants, may choose their places, to attend upon honourable persons, or to be employed in nurseries; by their conversation, to teach tongues to children, whilst carried in arms, who perhaps, when they find their own feet, will not abide the tedium of a school . . .

I need not show how any persons, thus brought up, if they happen to be widows, will be able to understand and manage their own affairs.

2. Women thus educated will be beneficial to their relations. It is a great blessing of God to a family to provide a good wife for the head, if it be eminent.

How many families have been ruined by this one thing, the bad education of women? Because the men find no satisfactory converse or entertainment at home, out of mere weariness they seek abroad; hence they neglect their business, spend their estates, destroy their bodies, and oftentimes damn their souls . . .

3. Women thus instructed will be beneficial to the nation. Look into all

history, those nations ever were, now are, and always shall be the worse nations, where women are undervalued; as in Russia, Ethiopia, and all the barbarous nations of the world. One great reason why our neighbours the Dutch have thriven to admiration, is the great care they take in the education of their women, from whence they are to be accounted most virtuous, and to be more useful than any women in the world. We cannot expect otherwise than to prevail against the ignorance, atheism, prophaneness, superstition, idolatry, lust, that reigns in the nation, than by a prudent, sober, pious, virtuous education of our daughters. Their learning would stir up our sons, whom God and nature hath made superior, to a just emulation.

Had we a sufficient number of females thus instructed to furnish the nurseries of noble families, their children might be improved in the knowledge of the learned tongues before they were aware, I mention this a third time, because it is of such moment and concern.

The memory of Queen Elizabeth is yet fresh. By her learning she was fitted for government, and swayed the sceptre of this nation with as great honour as any man before her.

Our very reformation of religion, seems to be begun and carried on by women.

Mistress Ann Askew, a person famous for learning and piety, so seasoned the queen and ladies at court, by her precepts and examples, and after sealed her profession with her blood, that the seed of reformation seemed to be sowed by her hand ...

My intention is not to equalise women to men, much less to make them superior. They are the weaker sex, yet capable of impressions of great things, something like to the best of men ...

Postscript

If any inquire where this education may be performed, such may be informed that a school is lately erected for gentlewomen at Tottenham high cross, within four miles of London, in the road to Ware, where Mistress Makin is governess, who was sometimes tutoress to the Princess Elizabeth, daughter to King Charles the First. Where, by the blessing of God, gentlewomen may be instructed in the principles of religion; and in all manner of sober and virtuous education: more particularly, in all things ordinarily taught in other schools:

Works of all sorts, as:
Dancing
Music
Singing
Writing
Keeping accounts

} Half the time to be spent in these things

The other half to be employed in gaining the Latin and French tongues; and those that please may learn Greek and Hebrew, the Italian and Spanish: in all which this gentlewoman hath a competent knowledge.

Gentlewomen of eight or nine years old, that can read well, may be instructed in a year or two (according to their parts) in the Latin and French tongues; by such plain and short rules, accommodated to the *grammar* of the English tongue, that they may easily keep what they have learned, and recover what they shall lose; as those that learn music by notes.

Those that will bestow longer time, may learn the other languages, afore mentioned, as they please.

Repositories also for visibles shall be prepared; by which from beholding the things, gentlewomen may learn the names, natures, values, and use of herbs, shrubs, trees, mineral-juices, metals and stones.

Those that please may learn limning,[20] preserving, pastry and cookery.

Those that will allow longer time, may attain some general knowledge in astronomy, geography; but especially in arithmetic and history.

Those that think one language enough for a woman, may forbear the languages, and learn only experimental philosophy, and more or fewer of the other things aforementioned, as they incline.

The rate certain shall be £20 per annum: but if a competent improvement be made in the tongues, and the other things aforementioned, as shall be agreed upon, then something more will be expected. But the parent shall judge what shall be deserved by the undertaker.

Those that think these things impossible, may have further account every Tuesday at Mr Mason's coffee-house in Cornhill, near the Royal Exchange; and Thursdays at the Bolt and Tun in Fleet Street, between the hours of three and six in the afternoons, by some person whom Mistress Makin shall appoint.

7

WORK

INTRODUCTION

One of the many problems which we encounter when looking back at early modern England lies in our conception and definition of work. Despite feminism's efforts to redefine work, we still tend to see work as a paid activity which takes place outside the home and which defines an individual's identity. This conception of work belongs to the post-industrial world and the model it provides is not necessarily applicable to economies and societies which are organised differently. Economic historians have described such activity in the sixteenth and seventeenth centuries as proto-capitalism: a period of very gradual transition from feudal economic organisation and production (mainly rural and agricultural) towards capitalist industrialisation (urban, mechanised and characterised by large-scale capital accumulation and transfer and wage labour).[1] The conception of men and women's work in this period utilised ideas and language from a variety of conceptual and political sources: religious definitions of a vocation; feudalist ideas of the three orders of man (labourers, fighters and priests) and of agricultural organisation through households; medieval trading guilds' conception of craft and apprenticeship; urban authority's regulation of the rootless poor, in forcing masterless men or women into service; feudal hierarchies of service (to lord, mistress, master); Protestant views on the family; and more market-orientated conceptions and practices, based on a cash and wage economy.

Because of this varied and uneven framework, women's work cannot be contained within a single descriptive or conceptual category. Nor, although none of the above conceptual organisations offer a distinctive place for women, do they necessarily exclude women. For example, conceptions of vocation give value to the life of the nun (pp. 206 ff.); or the Protestant preacher's wife; the woman preacher (pp. 214 ff.); the role of the mother (chapter 4); and the whole concept of service. The varied conception of work gave women larger areas of responsibility than we often think. Many guilds did not specifically exclude women from membership, at least at the beginning of the period. Most expected women to work alongside husbands and fathers in their businesses: one of the qualifying categories for a master-craftsman was usually that he should be married, so that his wife could help in his business and in training apprentices.[2] Rural women often had a wide range of responsibilities, not just tasks allotted to them, as Tusser and Fitzherbert show (pp. 195 ff.). Nevertheless, whilst many rural women, wives or dependants of yeomen and owners of smallholdings continued to work and manage land and households according to a feudal model, many women, whose families lost land in the ongoing but gradual agricultural reorganisation through enclosures, moved to cities and towns where their work varied from domestic service, spinning, small-scale retail work, nursing and washing, to prostitution. A small number of women were permitted to join guilds; although proportional to men's membership this remained highly unusual, and during the period many guilds began to restrict membership to men alone.[3]

The huge increase in housewifery and husbandry texts during the sixteenth and seventeenth centuries is paralleled by publishing booms in other self-help writings.[4] This reflects a developing conception of middle-class self-identity, which was partly defined by work and occupation (although this was more so for men): twenty-three editions of Tusser's (pp. 198–203) work, for example, were published between 1567 and 1641. In such works, housewifery and husbandry included the overall management of what has been called a 'multi-purpose factory'.[5] For the woman it included growing, refining and preparing foodstuffs and consumables for animals and the household; educating, training and managing servants and children; work on the land defined as women's work, such as that of the dairy; and the maintenance of the interior of the house (pp. 208–10). The growth of urban economies and urban living eventually meant a wider availability of prepared foods in cities and towns. The consequent reduction in the size of landholdings in towns and cities meant that the agricultural business of a housewife was limited to keeping a few hens. Nonetheless, we need to remember that during this period most people lived on and off the land, and that therefore conceptions of house-wifery were still broadly agricultural. Even under proto-capitalism, the household was often still the centre of a family's economic endeavours, both in its productive capabilities and in their location. Spinning, washing, wet-nursing, local medical care and retailing are among small-scale enterprises typical of household economic activity during this period. Thus, although a man's work was often defined by his occupation (jeweller, butcher, victualler), women's tasks as a housewife might include all of these and more within the home. Housewifery and husbandry were therefore complementary and overlapping conceptions of work, which valued women's and men's work in a way which did not necessarily entail subordination of one to the other.

Nevertheless, when wedded to theological and political definitions of marriage and womanhood, such an organisation of work did entail subordination: women's work was always related to men's work or men's occupations. As she makes clear, Mary Trye's acquisition of her father's medical knowledge and business was by virtue of her relationship to him, rather than through objective choice (pp. 223–5). In addition, the gradual growth of economic capitalism and industrialisation meant that the household, and consequently the conception of the family, became the non-earning centre only of child-rearing, household and reproductive labour, done by women. Work which earned a wage and was productive was done outside the home, usually by men. This organisational shift to the public/private split between men and women's identity through work is discernible in the overtly ideological texts of the period, for example the conduct literature of chapter 3 in this book. However, it is important to remember that these texts are exhorting men and women to an ideal, not describing actual practice. The writings of Mary Trye, Sarah Jinner and the anonymous compiler of the *Advice to the Women and Maidens of London*, (p. 219 ff.) suggests that there was both an audience for, and practitioners of, broader and alternative models for women's work in the seventeenth century. Whilst all these women express a consciousness of the gendered nature of work in the public and, specifically, the professional sphere, they nevertheless also show that women did work in such areas and thereby transgress prevailing conceptions. Even Becon's *Catechism*, often seen as an archetypal expression of the Protestant ideology of enclosed and private womanhood, advocates educational work for older women and extends the Protestant vocational ethic to both sexes. Nevertheless, it is evident from many of the texts in this selection, that this vocational ideology entails a belief in the sexual division of labour, both in terms of place (women work mainly in the home, men work outside it) and in terms of function (men earn money, women spend it: men act and women serve). Once again, Ray's proverbial collection provides a neat summary of contemporary belief: *a rouk-town's seldom a good housewife at home*. Housewifery happens within doors.

The church always provided additional opportunities and models for women's work. Although it has been argued that the Catholic church provided more women's work in the ongoing provision of ornamentation for churches, women in Protestant churches continued to clean and polish, occasionally act as churchwardens, as participants in various church services, such as funerals, and, of course, the concept of a Protestant vocation gave additional weight and credibility to the continued work of women preachers and prophets during the seventeenth century (pp. 37–40, 214–18 and chapter 8).

John Fitzherbert, *The book of husbandry*

This was one of the first husbandry books published for vernacular readers. Fitzherbert's aim was to benefit farmers and tenants. As with many husbandry books, housewifery was an addendum to the main business. Text from: the 1534 edition (first edition 1523), fos 59ʳ–63ʳ.

195

A lesson for the wife

But yet ere I begin to show the wife what works she shall do, I will first teach her a lesson of Solomon, as I did to her husband a lesson of the philosopher, and that is, that she should not be idle at no time: for Solomon saith: *the idle folk shall not joy with the chosen folks in heaven, but they shall sorrow with the reproved and forsaken folks in hell.* And St Jerome saith: *always be doing of some good works, that the Devil may find thee ever occupied.* For as in standing water are engendered worms, right so in an idle body are engendered idle thoughts. Here maist thou see that of idleness cometh damnation, and of good works and labour cometh salvation. Now art thou at thy liberty to choose whither way thou wist, wherein is a great diversity. And he is an unhappy man or woman, that God hath given both wit and reason, and putteth him in those, and will choose the worst part. Now, thou wife, I trust to show to thee the divers occupations, works and labours, that thou shalt not need to be idle no time of the year.

What things the wife is bounden of right to do

First and principally the wife is bound of right to love her husband, above father and mother, and above all other men. For our Lord saith in his gospel, *a man should leave his father and mother and draw to his wife,* and the same wise a wife should do to her husband. And are made by the virtue of the sacrament of holy scripture one flesh, one blood, one body, and two souls. Wherefore their hearts, their minds, their works and occupations, should be all one, never to sever nor change, during their natural lives, by any man's act or deed, as is said in the same gospel, *that thing that God hath joined together, no man may sever nor depart.* Wherefore it is convenient that they love each other, as effectually as they would do their own self.

What works a wife should do in general

First in a morning when thou art waked, and purposest to rise, lift up thy hand and bless them and make a sign of the holy cross, *in the name of the Father, the Son, and the Holy Ghost.* And if thou say a paternoster, and ave and a creed, and remember thy maker, thou shalt speed much the better. And when thou art up and ready, then first sweep thy house, dress up thy dishboard, and set all things in good order within thy house: milk thy kine, feed thy calves, lie up thy milk, take up thy children and array them, and provide for thy husband's breakfast, dinner, supper, and for thy children and servants and take thy part with them. And to ordain corn and malt to the mill, to bake and brew withal when need is. And meet it to the mill and from the mill, and see that thou have thy measure again beside the toll, or else the miller dealeth not truly with thee, or else thy corn is not dry as it should be. Thou must make butter and cheese when thou maist, serve thy swine both morning and evening, and give thy pullen meat in the morning, and when time of the year cometh thou must take heed how thy hens, ducks and geese do lay, and to gather up their eggs, and when they was broody to set them there as no beasts, swine nor other vermin hurt them. And thou must know that all whole-footed fowl will sit a month, and all cloven-footed fowls will sit but three weeks, except a pea-hen, and great fowls, as cranes, bustards and such other. And when they have brought forth their birds, to see that they be well kept from the glede,[6] crows, fullymarts,[7] and other vermin. And in the beginning of March, or a little afore, is time for a wife to make her garden, and to get as many good seeds and herbs, as she can, and specially such as be good for the pot, and to eat: and as oft as need shall require it must be weeded, for else the weeds will overcome the herbs. And also in March is time to sow flax and hemp ... and therefore may they make sheets, boardcloths, towels, shirts, smocks and such other necessaries, and therefore let thy distaff be alway ready for a pastime, that thou be not idle. And undoubted a woman cannot get her living honestly with spinning on the distaff, but it stoppeth a gap, and must needs be had. The balls of flax, when they be ripened off, must be riddled[8] from the weeds and made dry with the sun, to get out the seeds. Howbeit, one manner of linseed called loken seed, will not open by the sun; and therefore when they be dry, they must be sore bruised and broken, the wives know how, and then winnowed and kept dry, till ver[9] time come again. Thy female hemp must be pulled from the churl hemp, for that beareth no seed, and thou must do by it, as thou didest by the flax. The churl hemp beareth seed, and beware that birds eat it not as it groweth: the hemp thereof is not so good as the female hemp, but yet it will do good service. It may fortune sometime that thou shalt have so many things to do, that thou shalt not well know where is left to begin ...

It is convenient for an husband to have sheep of his own for many causes, and then may his wife have part of the wool, to make her husband and herself some clothes. And at the least way she may have the locks of the sheep, either to make clothes or blankets and coverlets, or both. And if she have no wool of her own, she may take wool to spin of cloth-makers, and by that means she may have a convenient living, and many times do other works. It is a wife's occupation to winnow all manner of corns, to make malt, to wash and wring, to make hay, shear corn and in time of need to help her husband to fill the muckwain or dung-cart, drive the plough, to load hay, corn and such other. And to go or ride to the market to sell butter, cheese, milk, eggs, chickens, capons, hens, pigs, geese and all manner of corns. And also to buy all manner of necessary things belonging to household, and to make a true reckoning and a compt to her husband what she hath received, and what she hath paid. And if the husband go to the market to buy or sell, as they oft do, he then to show his wife in like manner. For if one of them should use to deceive the other, he deceiveth himself, and he is not like to thrive, and therefore they must be true either to other.

Thomas Tusser, *A hundred good points of housewifery*

Tusser's work was first issued as *A hundred good points of husbandry* in 1557, with a few pages on housewifery. Text from: the second edition, which included a whole section for women, fos 29ʳ–35ᵛ.

1   Get up in the morning as soon as thou wilt,
    with over-long slugging good servant is spilt.
2   Some slovens from sleeping no sooner be up,
    but hand is in aumbry,[10] and nose in the cup.
3   Some works in the morning may trimly be done,
    that all the day after can never be won.
4   Good husband without maketh wealthy and fat,
    good housewife within is as needful as that.
5   Sluts' corners[11] avoided, shall farther thy health
    much times about trifles shall hinder thy wealth.
6   Set some about churning, some seething of souse,
    some carding, some spinning, some trimming up house.
7   Set some to grind malt, or thy rushes to twine,
    set some to peel hemp, or to seething of brine.[12]
8   Some corneth, some brineth, some will not be taught
    where meat taketh vent, there the housewife is naught.
9   Call servants to breakfast by day star appear,
    a snatch and to workfellows, tarry not here.
10 Let housewife be carver, let pottage be eat,
    a dishful each one with a morsel of meat.
11 What tack in a pudding saith greedy gut wringer
    give such ye wote what, ere pudding they finger.
12 Let servants once served, thy cattle go serve,
    else master and mistress may quickly go sterve.
13 No breakfast of custom provide not to save,
    but only to such as deserveth to have.
14 No showing to servant what vitals in store,
    show servants their labour, and show them no more.
15 Where all things is common what needeth a hutch?
    Where wanteth a saver there havoc is much.
16 Where windows stand open, the cats make a fray,

      yet wild cats with two legs are worser than they.

17   An eye in a corner who useth to have,
      Revealeth a drab, and preventeth a knave.

18   Make maid to be cleanly, or make her cry creak,
      and teach her to stir when her mistress doth speak.

19   A wand in thy hand, though ye fight not all
      make youth to their business the better to fall.

20   For fear of a fool had I wist cause thee to wail,
      Let *Fisgig*[13] be taught to shut door after tail.

21   With her that will clicket make,[14] danger to cope
      lest happily her wicket be easy to ope.

22   As rod little mendeth where manners be spilt,
      so naught will be nought, say and do what thou wilt.

23   Much brawling with servants what man can abide,
      pay home when thou fightest but love not to chide.

24   As order is heavenly where quiet is had,
      So error is hell, or a mischief as bad.

25   Such law as a warning will cause to beware,
      doth make the whole house better to fare.

26   The less of thy counsel thy servants doth know,
      their duty the better such servants shall show.

27   Such servants are often both painful and good,
      that sing in their labours as birds in the wood.

28   Good servants hope justly some friendship to feel,
      and look to have favour what time they do well.

29   Take runnagate robins to pity their need,
      and look to be filched as true as thy creed.

30   Take warning by once, that a worse do not hap,
      foresight is the stopper of many a gap.

31   Make few of thy counsel to change for the best,
      lest one that is trudging in fetcheth the rest.

32   That stone that is rolling can gather no moss,
      for mistress and maids, by oft changing is loss.

33   One dog for a hog and one cat for a mouse,
      and ready to give is enough in a house.

34   One gift ill accepted, keep next in thy purse,
      whom provender pricketh are often the worse.

35   Where brewer is needful, be brewer thyself,
      what filleth the roof will help furnish thy shelf.

36   In buying thy drink by the firkin or pot,
      the score doth arise, the hod[15] profiteth not.

37   One bushel well brewed, outlasteth some twain

two troubles for one thing is cost to no gain.

38 Too new is no profit, too stale is as bad,
drink sour or dead maketh husband half mad.

39 Put grains to more water while grains be yet hot,
and seeth them and stir them as oatmeal in pot.

40 Though heating be costly, such swill yet in store,
shall profit thy porklings a hundred times more.

41 New bread is a waster, but mouldy is worse,
What dog getteth that way that loseth the purse.

42 Much doughbake I praise not, much crust is as ill,
the mean is the housewife, say nay if ye will.

43 Good servant in dairy that needs not be told
deserveth her fee to be paid her in gold.

44 Good cook to dress dinner, to bake and to brew,
is better than gold being honest and true.

45 Good droy[16] to serve hogs, to help wash and to milk,
is sometimes as needful as some in their silk.

46 Keep dairy house cleanly, keep pan sweet and cold,
keep butter and cheese to look yellow as gold.

47 Save churnmilk, save welcord,[17] save pudding and sauce,
such offal doth stop many gaps in a house.

48 Though *Homely* be milker, let *Cleanly* be cook,
for *Dropnose* and *Slut* may be known by their look.

49 Though cat being good is a jewel in house,
yet ever in dairy have trap for a mouse.

50 Take heed how thou layest the bane for the rats,
For poisoning servants, thy self and thy brats.

51 Though scouring be needful, yet scouring too much,
is pride without profit and robbeth thy hutch.

52 Keep kettles from knocks and set tubs out of sun,
for mending is costly, and cracked is soon done.

53 Maids wash well and wring well, but beat ye wot how,
if any lack beating I fear it be you.

54 In washing by hand have an eye to thy bowl,
for launders and millers be quick of their toll.

55 Go wash well saith summer, with sun I shall dry,
go wring well saith winter, with wind so shall I.

56 Go trust without heed is to venture a joint,
give tail and take count is a housewifely point.

57 When hens fall a cackling, take heed to their nest,
when drabs fall a whistering[18] take heed to the rest.

58 What husband refuseth things comely to have,

that hath a good wife that will housewifely save.

59 The place may be so, and the kill may be such
to make thine own malt, shall profit thee much.

60 Some drieth with straw, and some drieth with wood,
wood asketh more charge, and yet nothing so good.

61 Malt being well spared the more it will cost,
malt being well dried the longer will last.

62 Let *Gillet* be singing it doth very well,
to keep her from sleeping and burning the kell.

63 By noon let your dinner be ready and neat,
let meat tarry servant, not servant his meat.

64 The plough team abating, call servants to dinner,
the thicker, so much be the charges the thinner.

65 Due season is best, altogether is gay
despatch hath no fellow, make short and away.

66 Beware of *Gill Laggose* disordering thy house,
more dainties who catcheth than crafty fed mouse.

67 Give servants no dainties, but give them enough,
too many chaps walking doth beggar the plough.

68 Poor seggons,[19] half starved, work faintly and dull
and lubbers do loiter, their bellies too full.

69 Feed *Lazy* that thresheth a flap and a tap,
like *Slothful* that all day be stopping a gap.

70 Some householdly lubber more eateth than two,
yet leaveth undone that a stranger will do.

71 Some cutteth thy linen, some spilleth their broth,
bare table to such doth as well as a cloth.

72 Treen[20] dishes do well, wooden spoons go to wrack
where stone is no laster, take tankard and jack.[21]

73 That pewter is never for mannerly feast,
that daily doth serve an unmannerly beast.

74 Some gnaweth and leaveth some crust and some crumbs,
eat such their own leavings, or gnaw their own thumbs.

75 At dinner, at supper, at morning, at night,
Give thanks unto God for his gifts in thy sight.

76 Good husband and housewife will some time alone,
dine well with a morsel and sup with a bone.

77 Three dishes well dressed, and welcome withal
both pleaseth thy friend and becometh thy hall.

78 Enough is a plenty, too much is a pride,
unskilful the holder, plough goeth aside.

79 When dinner is ended set servants to work,

and follow such merchants as loveth to lurk.

80   To servant in sickness see nothing ye grudge,
     a thing of a trifle shall comfort him much.

81   Put chipping in dippings, use parings to save,
     fat capons or hens that look for to have.

82   Save drippings and skimmings how ever ye do,
     for medicine, for cattle, for cart and for shoe.

83   All of corn thy pullen[22] must have for their fee,
     feed willingly such as do help to feed thee.

84   Though fat fed be dainty, of this I thee warn,
     be cunning in fatting, for robbing thy barn.

85   Good sempsters be sowing of fine pretty knacks,
     good housewives be mending and piecing their sacks.

86   Though making and mending be housewifely ways,
     yet mending in time is the housewife to praise.

87   Though ladies may rend and buy new every day,
     good housewives must mend and buy new as they may.

88   Call quarterly servants to court and to leet,
     write every coverlet, blanket and sheet.

89   Though shifting too oft be a thief in a house,
     yet shift *Goodman Sloven* for fear of a louse.

90   Grant *Doubtful* no key to his chamber in purse,
     least chamber door lock be to thievery a nurse.

91   Save wing for thresher when gander doth die,
     save feathers of all things, the softer to lie.

92   Much spice is a thief, so is candle and fire,
     Sweet sauce is as crafty as ever was friar.

93   Provide for thy tallow ere frost cometh in,
     and make thine own candle ere winter begin.

94   If *Penny* for all thing be suffered to trudge,
     trust long not to *Penny* to have him thy drudge.

95   When hens go to house, set cook to dress meat,
     Some milk and serve hogs, and set some to serve neat.

96   Where twain be enough, be not served with three,
     more knaves in a company worser they be.

97   Fore every trifle leave jauncing[23] thy nag,
     but rather make lacky of jack boy thy wag.

98   Make servant at night lug in wood or a log,
     let none come in empty but *Slut* and thy dog.

99   Where pullen use nightly to perch in the yards,
     there two-legged foxes keep watches and ward.

100 See cattle well served, without and within,

and all things at quiet ere supper begin.

101 No clothes in garden, no trinkets without,
no door left unbolted for fear of a doubt.

102 Thou woman whom pity becometh the best,
grant all that hath laboured time to take rest.

103 Provide for thy husband, to make him good cheer,
make merry together while time ye be here.

104 At bed and at board, how so ever befall
whatever God sendeth be merry withal.

105 No taunts before servants for hind'ring thy fame.
no jarring too loud for avoiding of shame.

106 As frenzy and heresy roveth together,
So jealousy leadeth a fool ye wot whither.

107 Young children and chickens would ever be eating,
good servants look duly for gentle entreating.

108 No servant at table use saucily to talk,
lest tongue set at large out of measure do walk.

109 No lurching, no snatching, nor striving at all,
least one go without and another have all.

110 Declare after supper, take heed thereunto,
what work in the morning each servant shall do.

111 Remember those children whose parents be poor,
which hunger, yet dare not crave at thy door.

112 Thy hand dog that serveth for divers mishaps,
Forget not to give him thy bones and thy scraps.

113 Where mouths be many to spend that thou hast,
set keys to be keepers for spending too fast.

114 To bed after supper, let *Drowsy* go sleep,
lest *Knave* in the dark to his marrow do creep.

115 Such keys lay up safe ere ye take ye to rest,
of dairy, of buttery, of cupboard, and chest.

116 Fear candle in hayloft, in barn and in shed,
fear *Flea Smock* and *Mendbreech*, for burning their bed.

117 The day willeth done whatsoever ye bid,
the night is a thief if ye take not good heed.

118 Wash dishes, lay leavens,[24] safe fire and away,
lock doors and to bed a good housewife will say.

119 In winter at nine, and in summer at ten,
to bed after supper both maidens and men.

120 In winter at five o'clock servant arise,
in summer at four is ever the guise.

John Jones, *The art and science of preserving body and soul*

This general book on health, which cites continental medical writers for a popular audience, includes a section on choosing appropriate nurses for children, giving a picture of the work requirements of a nursemaid. Text from: the first edition, 1579, pp. 4, 11–12, 30, 42–3, 45–6.

And the things according to nature, as health, the cause of health, the effect of health, strength, custom, and complexion, be in the chosen nurse in habit as well as in the infant, with the things annexed to nature, as colour, case, time, age, region, nature, sickness, diet, art, and time's mutation regarded, as in sort following shall be shown in sections divided.

The first tendeth to all things in a nurse requisite . . .

Of the best milk and what teats be good, and which both grieve and deform the child, and that do cause it to be unquiet

The milk of that nurse will be best that hath brought forth a man child (as saith Avicen): but (according to Montuus) that hath brought forth a woman child: but to me it seemeth best for the male, the male's milk, for the female, the female's, for as much as in all things we should follow nature not vitiated (as Montanus showeth) and the breast not deformed, but of mean bigness, and white, with fair blue veins dispersed (as Hippocrates willeth). Avicen praiseth the paps that be sound, and mean between soft and hard. But I with Aetius, Gordonius, and Fallopius, do mislike both the over great and over small breasts together with the pap-heads or nipples. The great because they have much milk, and the small because they have over little. Furthermore, through sucking of great breasts, the children are made flat or crooked nosed.[25] . . . By the nurse to be helped, if she will always when the child sucketh, depress her breast with one finger above the teat, and the other underneath.

Moreover great paps or teats hurt the gums and the small the jaws, because that through the one they are constrained to open the mouth too wide, over-stretching the sinews, causing grief much like to the cramp: through the other, in that they cannot easily of the infant be catched, making it wide-mouthed, over-wayward and angry, and as I have often noted, to weep very much . . .

204

*Of the kindness and love that should be in a nurse, and of
the requiting thereof: a supposition whence oftentimes the
strife between the child and mother doth arise*

This yet always resteth, that the nurse be courteous, loving and kind to her
suckling: for of the good affection of her foster father and family groweth the
natural love of the child and his friends to her and hers afterwards, as in
Wales, Cornwall, and Ireland is daily seen ... as contrarily many judgeth (no
causes mentioned hindering them of nursing their own children, but rather
idleness, delicacy, or wantonness) that the great and often unkindness,
disobedience, and unlawful suits between the child and mother issueth.

For to beget the child is no pain to her (say they) but pleasure: to conceive
in the womb, than liking power, God's work: and to deliver it in due time
her own safety, the eternal his providence: but to hold and bear it in her feeble
and weak arms, to swaddle it daily on her loving lap, and to give it suck with
her own most tender breasts, I affirm with Tacitus to be a manifest and
undoubted token of absolute kindness and friendship ...

*At what time the child may be weaned, and which ought to suck
longest: of the duty of the nobility and gentry: the regard that must
be had as well in the nursing of men children as women kind, and
what books do express the same: a commendation of good women*

These therefore, after Galen's mind, I think good to be observed until the
third year of his age.... Nevertheless I have known divers suck less than a
year and a half, some two years, other two years and a half, and some more
than three years whose bodies and temperatures endued with reason, courage
and desire, I could greatly commend, as I do not think myself (to say unto
you the truth) to be anything the worse because I sucked so long, but rather
the better considering how my mother was two and fifty upward when I was
born (as I have heard her say). And I do remember that I was able to bear
a stool for my good nurse when I would have sucked. Notwithstanding I do
not appoint every one to suck so long. Yet I think it best that the old woman's
child do suck longer than the young and lusty nurse, the weak longer than
the strong, the sickly longer than the healthy, the twin longer than the
loneling, the male longer than the female, the noble longer than the unnoble,
especially if any of these causes recited do require ...

Of the manner how to make the best pap, of the use and abuse thereof: and how the mean diet is the best

Take of new milk a pint, put therein of fine wheat flour, so much as being boiled will make it thick. Add to it the bigness of a chestnut of almond butter or sweet butter, one ounce of the best sugar, not faulted in the sunning, and then it will be better to digest, and the refuse not turned to the nourishment of the body, the sooner and easilier emptied. For, that made of the milk and flour alone, is somewhat slow in distribution, and therewith binding, as you have heard, being the very cause (as I conjecture), why Galen doth discommend it. Nevertheless, it is much used over all, and I myself was so fed, my nurse hath said it, as I have seen divers others of lively spirit and sound body, as well in Wales and the Marches as in sundry other parts of the realm and foreign countries.

Albeit where the nurse hath milk sufficient, it is not to be used so often, for ... there is nothing pleasanter, or that better nourisheth, than the mother's milk. Yet this I would were understood, that children be very apt to cut breath and to dischest[26] the moistures, humours and juices of the body, both by reason of tenderness of habit and abundance of heat, as Galen declareth. Therefore a plentiful trade of diet is due unto them, which thing old Hippocrates plainly proveth, saying that such as have much heat natural doth need much nourishment, otherwise the body is consumed.

Mary Ward, *Letter to Pope Paul V*

Ward's letter and plan for a nunnery (first written in 1616) was well known amongst seventeenth-century Catholics, although it remained unpublished. Although she did succeed in briefly establishing such a nunnery, it soon foundered through lack of funds. Text from: *Till God Will: Mary Ward through her Writings*, London, Darton, Longman & Todd, 1985, pp. 34–5, 44–5.

Since the very distressed condition of England, our native land, is greatly in need of spiritual workers, just as the priests, both religious and secular, exercise an increasing apostolate in this harvest, so it seems right that, according to their condition, women also should and can provide something more than ordinary in the face of the common need.

And since many women outside of England serve God most devoutly in monastic communities and day and night by their prayers to God and good works, contribute very much towards the conversion of the kingdom, so we also feel that God (as we trust) is inspiring us with the pious desire that we should embrace the religious life and yet that we should strive according to our littleness to render to the neighbour the services of Christian charity, which cannot be discharged in the monastic life.

Accordingly we have in mind the mixed life, such a life as we learn Christ our Lord and master taught his chosen ones, such a life as his blessed mother lived and handed down to those of later times, in those times especially when the church was afflicted, as in our country now, so that in this way we may more easily educate maidens and girls of tender years in piety, in the Christian virtues and liberal arts so that they may be able thereafter to undertake more fruitfully the secular and monastic life, according to the vocation of each.

Hence this Institute of ours shall be called the *School of the Blessed Mary.*

Our end, then, is to work constantly at the perfection of our own souls under the standard of the cross, both by the acquirement of all virtues, by abnegation of all self-will and diligent extirpation of self-love. Virtue, indeed, we would have so highly valued in all those who would embrace our manner of life, that anyone wanting in it is to be judged unfit for our state, no matter what may be her other talents and endowments, much more does this same want of virtue disqualify a person for the task of government and for the discharge of any other important office in the Institute.

Besides attending to our own perfection, we desire, in the second place, to devote ourselves with all diligence and prudent zeal to promote or procure the salvation of our neighbour, by means of the education of girls, or by any other means that are congruous to the times, or in which it is judged that we can by our labours promote the greater glory of God and, in any place further the propagation of our holy mother, the Catholic church.

In order to attain our end, it is moreover necessary ... that this our least and most unworthy Congregation should be allowed, with the approbation or permission of the Apostolic See, to begin and exercise its duties without enclosure, as otherwise our Institute and method of life can neither be observed nor practised with any hope of obtaining the fruit that we propose to draw from it.

But our dress should be such as may present to externs a model of Christian gravity and modesty and all other religious virtues, in as much as regard should always be had to poverty, cleanliness and religious decency; the style of dress should, for the most part, be conformed to that generally worn by virtuous ladies in those countries or provinces where ours happen to live or reside. Always keeping in view those things that pertain to greater perfection, ours will never admit anything whatever that savours of the least worldliness or vanity, but always have before their eyes the greater glory of God and the common good.

Although as regards external mortifications, our manner of life may appear only ordinary, since no one is, by the Institute, obliged to observe strict enclosure, or to wear a determined religious habit, or to perform external penances and austerities, nevertheless there will be a provision or clause in our constitutions.

Patrick Hannay, *A happy husband*

This text is unusual in that it is addressed directly to women, advising them how to make a correct choice of husband. Text from: the first edition, 1618, fos C1ʳ–C5ᵛ.

A Wife's Behaviour

Deserve then not in show, but from the heart,
Love is perpetuated by desert:
As it befits not man for to embrace
Domestic's charge, so it's not woman's place
For to be busied with affairs abroad.
For that weak sex, it is too great a load,
And it's unseemly, and doth both disgrace,
When either doth usurp the other's place.
Leave his to him, and of thine own take charge,
Care thou at home, and let him care at large.
Thou hast enough thyself for to employ
Within doors, 'bout thy house and housewifery:
Remember that it's said of Lucrece chaste,
When some dames wantonis'd, others took rest,
She with her maidens first her task would end,
'Ere she would sleep: she did not idle spend
Swift running time, nor gave alluring pleasure
The least advantage to make any seizure
On her rare virtues. A soul vacant fills,
Is soon seduced to do good or ill:
For like perpetual motion is the mind,
In action still, while to this flesh confined.
(From which foul prison it takes often stains
For absolutely good no man remains).
Employed if not 'bout good, about some ill,
Producing fruits which do discover still
How it is labour'd like a fertile field,
Which fruit, or weeds abundantly doth yield,
As it is manur'd; be not idle then,
Nor give vice time to work upon thy brain
Imagined ill: for what it there conceives
It oft brings out, and in dishonour leaves:
The purest things are easiest to be stain'd,
And it's soon lost which carefully was gain'd.
Penelope did wheel and distaff handle,
And her day's work undid at night by candle;

Nor labour-forcing need compelled that task,
Which toiling days and tedious nights did ask,
(For she was queen of Ithaca) 'twas her name,
Which virtuous care kept spotless free from blame;
One of so many suitors of each sort,
As for her love did to her court resort,
Not speeding; would have spoke that might her stain,
(The greatest hate, when love turns to disdain)
If colour could have made their knavery stronger,
But envy could not find a way to wrong her.
Be thou as these, careful of housewifery,
With providence what's needful still supply.
Look thy maids be not idle, nor yet spend
Things wastingly; for they so oft offend
When careless is the mistress; yet with need
Ne'er pinch them, nor yet let them e'er exceed:
The one doth force them seek thee to betray,
The other makes them wanton and too gay;
It is no shame to look to everything,
The mistress' eye doth ever profit bring.
Solomon saith *the good wife seeks for flax*
And wool, wherewith her hands glad travail take:
She's like a ship that bringeth bread from far,
She rises ere appear the morning star;
Vittals[27] *her household, gives her maidens food,*
Surveys and buys a field, plants vines with good
Gain'd by her hands: what merchandise is best
She can discern, nor doth she go to rest
When Pheobus hides his head, and bars his sight,
But by her lamp her hands do take delight
To touch the wheel and spindle; she doth stretch
Her hands to help the poor and needy wretch:
Her words are wisdom, she o'ersees her train
That idle none do eat their bread in vain.
Her children rise and bless her, sweet delight
Her husband takes still in her happy sight.
Be thou this careful goodwife, for to lend
Thy helping hand, thy husband's means to mend.
Last let thy conversation be with such,
As foul mouth'd malice can with no crime touch;
I cannot but condemn such as delight
Still to be sad and sullen in the sight

Of their own husband, as they were in fear,
(Sure guilty of some crime such women are)
But when they gossip it with other wives
Of their own cut, then they have merry lives,
Spending, and plotting how they may deceive
Their husbands, rule themselves, and mastery have;
O let such women (for they make bates[28] be
Twixt man and wife) never consort with thee:
But shun them as thou dost see one that's fair
Flee the small pox; both like infectious are.
The grave, staid, blameless and religious Dames
Whose carriages hath procur'd them honest names,
Are fit companions, let such be thy mates,
When wearied with affairs, thou recreates
Thy self with harmless mirth: yet do not walk
Often abroad, that will occasion talk;
Though thou hast store of friends, yet let none be
Saving thy husband, counsellor to thee.
He's nearest to thee, and it will endear him
He is thy self, thou needest not to fear him.
Be free with him, and tell him all thy thought,
It's he must help when thou hast need of ought:
And constantly believe he'll love thee best,
When he sees thou prefer'st him 'fore the rest.
Thus lady, have I showed you how to choose
A worthy mate, and how you should him use.
So chose, so use, so shall you all your life
Be in a husband bless'd, he in a wife.
And when death here shall end your happy days
Your souls shall reign in heaven, on earth your praise.

John Taylor, *The needle's excellency*

This book is a pattern book for needlework, prefaced with this poem. Text from: the first
edition, 1631, fos A1ʳ–A1ᵛ.

The Praise of the Needle

To all dispersed sorts of arts and trade,
I write the needle's praise (that never fades)
So long as children shall be got or born,
So long as garments shall be made or worn,

So long as hemp, or flax, or sheep shall bear,
Their linen-woollen fleeces year by year:
So long as silk-worms with exhausted spoil
Of their own entrails, for man's gain shall toil:
Yea, till the world be quite dissolved and past;
So long at least, the needle's use shall last:
And though from earth his being did begin,
Yet through fire he did his honour win:
And unto those that do his service lack,
He's true as steel, and mettle to the back,
He hath I perse eye, small single sight,
Yet like a pigmy, Polypheme[29] in sight:
As a stout Captain, bravely he leads on
(Not fearing colours) till the work be done.
Through thick and thin he is most sharply set,
With speed through stitch, he will the conquest get.
And as a soldier (frenchified with heat)[30]
Maim'd, from the wars is forced to make retreat:
So when a needle's point is broke, and gone,
No *point monsieur*, he's maimed, his work is done.
And more the needle's honour to advance,
It is a Taylor's javelin or his lance.
And for my country's quiet I should like,
That women kind should use no other pike,
It will increase their peace, enlarge their store,
To use their tongues less, and their needles more,
The needle's sharpness profit yields, and pleasure,
But sharpness of the tongue, bites out of measure.
A needle (though it be but small and slender)
Yet it is both a maker and a mender
A grave reformer of old rents decayed,
Stops holes and seams, and desperate cuts displayed.
And thus without the needle we may see
We should without our bibs and biggins[31] be;
No shirts or smocks, our nakedness to hide,
No garments gay to make us magnified:
No shadows, chaparoons,[32] cauls, bands, ruffs, cuffs,
No kerchiefs, quoifs, chin-clouts, or mary-muffs,[33]
No cross-cloths, apron, hand-kerchiefs, or falls,[34]
No table-cloths for parlours or for halls.
No sheets, no towels, napkins and pillow-bears,[35]
Nor any garment man or woman wears.

Thus is a needle proved an instrument
Of profit, pleasure and of ornament.
Which mighty queens have grac'd in hand to take,
And high born ladies such esteem did make
That as their daughters up did grow,
The needle's art, they to their children show.
And as 'twas then an exercise of praise,
So what deserves more honour in these days,
Than this, which daily doth itself express,
A mortal enemy to idleness?
The use of sewing is exceeding old,
As in the sacred text it is enrolled:
Our parents first in paradise began,
Which hath descended since from man to man;
The mothers taught their daughters, sires their sons,
Thus in a line successively it runs
For general profit, and for recreation,
From generation unto generation.
With work like cherubims, embroidered rare,
The covers of the tabernacle were. [Exod. 26:1–28]
And by the Almighty's great command, we see,
That Aaron's garments broidered work should be;
And further, God did bid his vestments should
Be made most gay and glorious to behold.
Thus plainly, and most truly is declar'd
The needle's work hath still been in regard,
For it doth art, so like to nature frame,
As if it were her sister, or the same.

R. Garnet, *The book of oaths, 1649*

The swearing of oaths is an essential part of public government and public service. Here the midwife's oath places the midwife, and her medical responsibilities, centrally within the legal and political system in her surveillance over births, miscarriages and baptisms. Text from: the first edition, 1649, pp. 284ff.

*The oath that is to be ministered to a midwife by the bishop
or his chancellor of the diocese, when she is licensed to
exercise that office of a midwife*

You shall swear first, that you shall be diligent and faithful and ready to help every woman labouring of child, as well the poor as the rich; and that in time of necessity, you shall not forsake the poor woman, to go to the rich.

2. Item. Ye shall neither cause nor suffer any woman to name, or put any other father to the child, but only him which is the very true father thereof indeed.

3. Item. You shall not suffer any woman to pretend, fain, or surmise herself to be delivered of a child who is not indeed; neither to claim any other woman's child for her own.

4. Item. You shall not suffer any woman's child to be murdered, maimed or otherwise hurt, as much as you may; and so often as you shall perceive any peril or jeopardy, either in the woman or in the child, in any such wise, as you shall be in doubt what shall chance thereof, you shall thenceforth in due time send for other midwives and expert women in that faculty, and use their advice and counsel in that behalf.

5. Item. That you shall not, in any wise, use or exercise any manner of witchcraft, charms or sorcery, invocation or other prayers than may stand with God's laws and the king's.

6. Item. You shall not give any counsel or minister any herb, medicine or potion, or any other thing, to any woman being with child whereby she should destroy or cast out, that she goeth withal before her time.

7. Item. You shall not enforce any woman being with child by any pain, or by an ungodly ways or means, to give you any more for your pains or labour in bringing her abed, than they would otherwise do.

8. Item. You shall not consent, agree, give, or keep counsel that any woman be delivered secretly of that which she goeth with, but in the presence of two or three lights ready.

9. Item. You shall be secret and not open any matter appertaining to your office in the presence of any man, unless necessity or great urgent cause do constrain you so to do.

10. Item. If any child be dead born, you yourself shall see it buried in such secret place as neither hog nor dog, nor any other beast may come unto it, and in such sort done as it be not found nor perceived, as much as you may; and that you shall not suffer any such child to be cast into the jakes[36] or any other inconvenient place.

11. Item. If you shall know any midwife using or doing anything contrary to any of the premises, or in any other wise than shall be seemly and convenient, you shall forthwith detect open to show the same to me, or my chancellor for the time being.

12. Item. You shall use yourself in honest behaviour unto the woman, being lawfully admitted to the room and office of a midwife in all things accordingly.

13. Item. That you shall truly present to myself, or my chancellor, all such women as you shall know from time to time to occupy and exercise the room

of a midwife within my foresaid diocese and jurisdiction of A_____, without my licence and admission.

14. Item. You shall not make or assign any deputy or deputies to exercise or occupy under you in your absence the office or room of a midwife, but such as you shall perfectly know to be of right honest and discreet behaviour, as also apt and able and having sufficient knowledge and experience to exercise the said room and office.

15. Item. You shall not be privy, or consent that any priest, or other party, shall in your absence, or in your company, or of your knowledge or sufferance, baptise any child by any Mass, Latin service or prayers than such as are appointed by the laws of the Church of England; neither shall you consent that any child, born by any woman, who shall be delivered by you, shall be carried away without being baptised in the parish by the ordinary minister where the said child is born, unless it be in case of necessity, baptised privately, according to the Book of Common Prayer: but you shall forthwith upon understanding thereof, either give knowledge to me the said bishop, or my chancellor for the time being. All which articles and charge you shall faithfully observe and keep, so help you God, and by the contents of this book.

PREACHING WORK

Sarah Cheevers and Katherine Evans,
This is a short relation of some of the cruel sufferings

Katherine Evans and Sarah Cheevers went to Europe to preach the Quaker message, and were captured and imprisoned by the Inquisition on the Island of Malta. Their autobiographical observations and letters were collected and published by their fellow Quaker Daniel Baker. Text from: the first edition, 1662, pp. 53–5, 56–7.

Katherine Evans to her husband and children

For the hand of John Evans, my right dear and precious husband, with my tender-hearted children, who are more dear and precious unto me than the apple of mine eye.

My dear heart, my soul doth dearly salute thee, with my dear and precious children, which are dear and precious in the light of the Lord, to thy endless joy and my everlasting comfort; glory be to our Lord God eternally, who hath called you with a holy calling, and hath caused his beauty to shine upon you in this day of his power, wherein he is making up of his jewels, and binding up of his faithful ones in the bond of everlasting love and salvation, among whom he hath numbered you of his own free grace; in which I beseech you (dear hearts) in the fear of the Lord to abide in your measures, according to the manifestation of the revelation of the son of God in you; keep a diligent watch over every thought, word and action, and let your minds be staid continually in the light, where you will find out the snares and baits of Satan, and be preserved out of his traps, nets and pits, that you may not be captivated by him at his will. Oh, my dear husband and children, how often have I poured out my soul to our everlasting Father for you, with rivers of tears, night and day, that you might be kept pure and single in the sight of our God, improving your talents as wise virgins, having oil in your vessels, and your lamps burning, and clothed with the long white robes of righteousness, ready to enter the bed chamber, and to sup with the lamb and to feed at the feast of fat things, where your souls may be nourished, refreshed, comforted, and satisfied, never to hunger again ...

In our deepest affliction, when I looked for every breath to be the last, I could not wish I had not come over seas, because I knew it was my eternal Father's will to prove me, together with my dear and faithful friend; in all afflictions and miseries the Lord remembered mercy, and did not leave nor forsake us, nor suffer his faithfulness to fail us, but caused the sweet drops of his mercy to distil upon us, and the brightness of his glorious countenance to shine into our hearts, and was never wanting to us in revelations nor visions. Oh how may I do to set forth the fullness of God's love to our souls? No tongue can express it, no heart can conceive it, nor mind can comprehend it. Oh, the ravishments, the raptures, the glorious bright-shining countenance of our Lord God, who is our fullness in emptiness, our strength in weakness, our health in sickness, our life in death, our joy in sorrow, our peace in disquietness, our praise in heaviness, our power in all needs or necessities. He alone is a full God unto us, and to all that can trust him; he hath emptied us of our selves, and hath unburdened us of our selves, and hath wholly built us upon the sure foundation, the rock of ages, Christ Jesus, the light of the world, where the swelling seas, nor raging, foaming waves, nor stormy winds, though they beat vehemently, cannot be able to remove us; glory, honour, and praises is to our God for ever, who out of his everlasting treasures doth fill us with his eternal riches day by day; he did nourish our souls with the choicest of his mercies and doth feed our bodies with his good creatures; and relieve all our necessities in a full measure. Praises, praises be to him alone who is our everlasting portion, our confidence, and our rejoicing, whom we serve acceptably with reverence and God like fear; for our God is a consuming fire.

Oh my dear husband and precious children, you may feel the issues of love and life which stream forth as a river to every soul of you, from a heart that is wholly joined to the fountain: my prayers are for you day and night without ceasing, beseeching the Lord God of power to pour down his tender mercies upon you, and to keep you in his pure fear, and to increase your faith, to confirm you in all righteousness, and strengthen you in believing in the name of the Lord God almighty, that you may be established as Mount Sion that can never be moved. Keep your souls unspotted of the world, and love one another with a pure heart, fervently love one another in love, build up one another in the eternal, and bear one another's burdens for the seed's sake, and so fulfil the law of God. This is the word of the Lord unto you, my dearly beloved.

Dear hearts, I do commit you into the hands of the almighty, who dwelleth on high, and to the word of his grace in you, who is able to build you up to everlasting life, and eternal salvation. By me who am thy dear and precious wife and spouse in the marriage of the lamb, in the bed undefiled.

K.E.

My dearly beloved yoke-mate in the work of our God, doth dearly salute you; salute us dearly to our precious friends in all places. I do believe we shall see your faces again with joy.

Sarah Cheevers to her husband and children

My dear husband, my life is given up to serve the living God, and to obey his pure call in the measure of the manifestation of his love, light, life and spirit of Christ Jesus, his only begotten son, whom he hath manifested in me and thousands, by the brightness of his appearing to put an end to sin and Satan, and bring to light immortality through the preaching of the everlasting gospel by the spirit of prophecy, which is poured out upon the sons and daughters of the living God, according to his purpose, whereof he hath chosen me, who am the least of all; but God who is rich in mercy, for his own name sake hath passed by mine offences, and hath counted me worthy to bear testimony to his holy name before the mighty men of the earth. Oh the love of the Lord to my soul! My tongue cannot express, neither hath it entered into the heart of man to conceive of the things that God hath laid up for them that fear him.

Therefore doth my soul breathe to my God for thee and my children night and day, that your minds may be joined to the light of the Lord Jesus, to lead you out of Satan's kingdom, into the kingdom of God, where we may enjoy one another in the life eternal, where neither sea nor land can separate; in which light and life I do salute thee my dear husband, with my children, wishing you to embrace God's love in making his truth so clearly manifest among you, whereof I am a witness even of the everlasting fountain that hath been opened by the messengers of Christ, who preach to you the word of God in season, directing you where you may find your saviour to purge and

216

cleanse you from your sins and to reconcile you to his father, and to have unity with him and all the saints in the light, that ye may be fellow citizens in the kingdom of glory, rest and peace, which Christ hath purchased for them that love him and obey him. What profit is there for to gain the whole world and lose your own souls? Seek first the kingdom of God and the righteousness thereof, and all other things shall be added to you, godliness is great gain, having the promise of this life that now is and that which is to come; which is fulfilled to me, who have tasted of the Lord's endless love and mercies to my soul, and from a moving of the same love and life do I breathe to thee my dear husband, with my children; my dear love salutes you all; my prayers to my God are for you all, that your minds may be joined to the light, wherewith you are lightened, that I may enjoy you in that which is eternal, and have community with you in the spirit. He that is joined to the Lord, is one spirit, one heart, one mind, one soul, to serve the Lord with one consent. I cannot by pen or paper set forth the large love of God in fulfilling his gracious promises to me in the wilderness, being put into prison for God's truth, there to remain all days of my life, being searched, tried, examined upon pain of death among the enemies of God and his truth; standing in jeopardy for my life until the Lord had subdued and brought them under by his mighty power and made them to feed us, and would have given us money or clothes, but the Lord did deck our table richly in the wilderness. The day of the Lord is appearing, wherein he will discover every deed of darkness, let it be done never so secret; the light of Christ Jesus will make it manifest in every conscience; the Lord will rip up all coverings that is not of his own spirit. The God of peace be with you all. *Amen.*

Written in the Inquisition prison by the hand of Sarah Cheevers,
for the hand of Henry Cheevers my dear husband; give this, fail not.

Joan Brooksop, *An invitation of love*

Brooksop's whole title indicates both the purpose and audience for her writing: 'unto the seed of God, throughout the world with a word to the wise in heart and a lamentation for New England'. Brooksop travelled to New England, leaving husband and children, to follow the call of God. Text from: the first edition, 1662, pp. 11–13.

Given forth from the movings of the spirit of the Lord by
one who is known to the world by the name of Joan
Brooksop

Oh, my dearly beloved friends and fellow citizens of the household of God, who are come to the heavenly Jerusalem, the city of the saints' solemnity, where all the faithful ones shall lie down together and drink of the rivers of life, which run freely: oh, drink, drink my beloved friends of the virtue of the streams of my heavenly father's love, which run freely and plenteously, for all them that do wait upon him in his holy blessed fear for ever, and hath him alone to be their hiding place, of whose fullness there is no end: for he gives freely and upbraids none. Oh my dearly beloved friends unto whom my life reacheth, read me in the covenant of light and life and peace where our unity stands, in that which was before words were, and shall be when words shall be no more, even in that by which the world was made and all things were created and are upheld to this day, even by the word of his power: and so all dear friends, hold fast your confidence without wrath or doubting unto the end, and in the end: that so ye may receive a crown of life, which is laid up for all them that endure faithful unto the end; for assuredly, ye shall all reap if ye faint not, but stand fast and keep your integrity: oh dwell low in the feeling of pure power of the Lord God of life continually, that with it you may come to fathom over all the world, both within and without, and live unto God who is the father of spirits, that so ye may come unto the New Jerusalem, the city of the living God, and unto the spirits of just men made perfect by the blood of the lamb, which was slain from the foundation of the world: but now hath the Lord made him known in these our days, everlasting holy praises be given unto his glorious name for evermore, Amen.

Oh, the riches of his grace and love, which he hath shed abroad in our hearts towards his own seed, who hath taken upon him the government, and of whose dominion there shall be no end, for he is come to rule whose right it is: everlasting, glorious, powerful, holy praises be given unto him for ever, my father of life in whom I live for ever, who is my strength, and the length of my days, and my portion for ever, and my exceeding great reward, who have forsaken all my relations, husband and children, and whatsoever was near and dear unto me, yea and my own life too, for his own name's sake. Everlasting praises be given unto his glorious name for ever, who hath counted me worthy to bear a testimony for his name's sake, and hath fulfilled that scripture which he spake to his disciples, when he said, *he that will not forsake father and mother, wife and children for my name's sake and the gospels is not worthy of me, yea and his own life too*: which I do witness in my measure: hallelujahs be given to the highest for ever, who am a true lover of the seed of God, and it is the desire of my heart that all may come to the knowledge of him in their own particulars, and live to God, in whom is life and plenteous redemption for evermore, Amen.

Sarah Jinner, *An almanac*

Jinner's almanac includes monthly advice on rural work, as well as medical advice (ch. 4, pp. 127–9). She interleaves the advice with astrological observations for each month, which are omitted here. Text from: the first edition, 1658, fos C1ʳ–C4ʳ.

The good housewife's observations in January

Plough for peas, fallow such land as you intend shall rest the year following; water your barren meadows and pasture and drain arable ground, especially if you intend to sow peas, oats or barley the seed time following; also stub up all rough grounds, trim up your garden moulds; the weather calm, remove all manner of fruit trees, rear calves, remove bees, keep good diet.

February

Set beans, peas and other pulses in stiff ground, begin the soonest, prepare your garden, prune and trim your fruit trees from moths, cankers, and superfluous branches, lay your quickset close, plant rose and gooseberry trees, and any other shrub trees, and graft your tender stocks; forbear all phlegmatic meats.[37]

March

Look well to your ewes, cut up underwood for fuel, transplant all sort of summer flowers, comfort them with good earth, especially the crown imperial, narcissus, tulips and hyacinth; in your barren fruit trees bore holes ... and cover roots of trees close with fat earth that art uncovered; graft fruit trees and sow dates, rye, and barley. Let your diet be cold and temperate.

April

Sow your hemp and flax, sow and set all sorts of herbs, open your hives and give your bees their liberty and let them labour for their living; cut your dike timber, the bark is best for the tanner's use. Scour your ditches, gather your manure together in heaps, gather stones, repair highways, set ditches and willows, and cast up all decayed fences. For your health, use moderate exercise.

May

Fold your sheep, carry forth manure, and bring home fuel; weed winter corn, furnish your dairy; let your mares go to horse, fat your dry kine and away with them: sow your tender seeds, as cucumbers, musk-melons, all sweet kinds of herbs and flowers; for your health drink clarified whey.

June

Distil all sorts of plants and herbs whatever. Cut your rank meadows, fetch home fuel, and carry forth manure, maule[38] and lime to mend your land; be sure to be chaste this month, whatever you are the rest of the year.

July

Attend your hay harvest, shear field sheep; let the herbs you intend to preserve run to seed; cut off the stalk of your flowers, and cover the roots with new fat earth; sell your lambs you intended for the shambles. Take no physic, unless in extraordinary cases, refrain venery.

August

Follow diligently your corn harvest, cut down your wheat and rye, mow barley and dates, put off your fat sheep and cattle, gather your plums, apples and pears, make your summer perry and cider, set your slips and scions of all sorts, of gillyflowers, and other flowers; transplant them that were set in the spring; geld your lambs; carry manure from your dove-cotes, put your swine to the early mast. Refrain excess in eating and drinking, drink that which is cooling.

September

Cut your beans, peas and all manner of pulse; on the land you intend to sow wheat and rye, bestow the best manure; gather your winter fruit, sell your wool, stocks of bees and other commodities you intend to put off, thatch your hives of bees you intend to keep, and look that no drones, mice or other vermin be about them. Thrash your seed, wheat and rye. Use physic moderately, shun the eating of sweet or rotten fruit, avoid surfeiting.

October

Finish with your wheat seed, plash[39] and lay your hedges and quicksets, scour your ditches and ponds, transplant and remove all manner of fruit trees, make winter perry and cider, spare your pastures and feed upon your corn fields; draw furrows to drain, and keep dry your new sown corn; make malt, rear all new fallen calves, all foals that were foaled in the spring weaned from the mares. Sell your sheep that you do not intend to winter, and separate lambs from the ewes that you intend to keep. Recreate your spirits by harmless sports, and take physic by good advice if need be.

November

Cut down your timber for ploughs, carts, naves, axtrees,[40] harrows, and other offices about husbandry, or housewifery; make the last return of grass, feed cattle, take your swine from the mast, and feed them for the slaughter; rear all calves that fall now, break all hemp and flax you intend to spend in the winter season; remove fruit trees and sow wheat and rye in hot soils. Use spices and wine moderately.

December

Put your sheep to the peas reeks, kill your small porks and large bacons, lop hedges, saw your timber for building, and lay it to season: plough your ground you intend to sow clean beans on; cover your dainty fruit trees, drain your corn fields, and water your meadows; cover your best flowers with rotten horse litter. Now all sorts of fowl are in season, keep thyself warm with a wholesome diet, and avoid all care that shall trouble thy spirit as a dangerous thing.

Jane Sharp, *The midwife's book*

Jane Sharp describes herself on the title page as: 'practitioner in the art of midwifery above thirty years', and addresses herself to women. Text from: the first edition, 1671, pp. 1–2.

The introduction: of the necessity and usefulness of the art of midwifery

The art of midwifery is doubtless one of the most useful and necessary of all arts, for the being and well-being of mankind, and therefore it is extremely requisite that a midwife be both fearing God, faithful, and exceeding well experienced in that profession. Her fidelity shall find not only a reward here from man, but God hath given a special example of it, Exod. 1 in the midwives of Israel, who were so faithful to their trust that the command of a king could not make them depart from it, viz: *but the midwives feared God and did not as the King of Egypt commanded them, but saved the men children alive. Therefore God dealt with the midwives; and because they feared God, he made them houses.*

As for their knowledge, it must be twofold, speculative and practical: she that wants the knowledge of speculation is like to one that is blind or wants her sight: she that wants the practice is like one that is lame and wants her legs, the lame may see but they cannot walk, the blind may walk but they cannot see. Such is the condition of those midwives that are not well versed in both of these. Some perhaps may think that then it is not proper for women to be of this profession, because they cannot attain so rarely to the knowledge of things as men may, who are bred up in universities, schools of learning, or serve their apprenticeships for that end and purpose, where anatomy lectures being frequently read, the situation of the parts both of men and women and other things of great consequence are often made plain to them. But that objection is easily answered by the former example of the midwives amongst the Israelites, for though we women cannot deny that men in some things may come to a greater perfection of knowledge than women ordinarily can by reason of the former helps that women want, yet the holy scriptures hath recorded midwives to the perpetual honour of the female sex. There being not so much as one word concerning *men-midwives* mentioned there that we can find, it being the natural propriety of women to be much seeing into that art: and though nature be not alone sufficient to the perfection of it, yet farther knowledge may be gained by a long and diligent practice, and be communicated to others of our own sex. I cannot deny the honour due to able physicians and surgeons, when occasion is: yet we find even that amongst the Indians, and all barbarous people, where there are no men of learning, the women are sufficient to perform this duty. And even in our own nation, that we need go no farther, the poor country people where there are none but women to assist (unless it be those that are exceeding poor and in a starving condition, and then they have more need of meat than midwives) the women are as fruitful, and as safe and well delivered, if not much more fruitful, and better commonly in child-bed than the greatest ladies of the land. It is not hard words that perform the work, as if none understood the art that cannot understand Greek. Words are but the shell that we oft times break our teeth with them to come at the kernel (I mean our brains) to know what is the meaning of them: but to have the same in our mother tongue would save us a great deal of needless labour. It is commendable for men to employ their spare time in some things of deeper speculation than is required of the female sex: but the art of midwifery chiefly concerns us, which, even the best learned men will grant, yielding something of their own to us, when they are forced to borrow from us the very name they practise by, and to call themselves *men-midwives*. But to avoid long preambles in a matter so clear and evident, I shall proceed to set down such rules and method concerning this art as I think needful, and that as plainly and briefly as possibly I can, and with as much modesty in words as the matter will bear: and because it is commonly maintained that the masculine gender is more worthy than the feminine, though perhaps when men have need of us they will yield the priority to us, that I may not forsake the ordinary method, I shall begin with men, and treat last of my own sex, so as to be understood by the meanest capacity, desiring the courteous reader to use as much modesty in the perusal of it, as I have endeavoured to do in the writing of it, considering that such an art as this cannot be set forth, but that young men and maids will have much just cause to blush sometimes, and be ashamed of their own follies, as I wish they may, if they shall chance to read it, that they may not convert that into evil that is really intended for a general good.

Mary Trye, *Medicatrix, or the woman-physician*

As Trye claims in her title page and elsewhere in this text, she publishes this work to defend her father against attacks made on his name by another physician. Thus, although she is a practising woman physician, she places her work and knowledge within the conventional framework of daughterly duty. Text from: the first edition, 1675, pp. 1–3, 73–4, 105.

Epistle. To the glory of her sex, the honour of her country, and the most accomplished lady, the Lady Fisher, wife to Sir Charles Clement Fisher, Knight and Baronet of Packington Hall in the County of Warwick

I received a medicinal talent from my father, which by the instruction and assistance of so excellent a tutor as he was to me, and my constant preparation and observation of medicines, together with my daily experience by reason of his very great practice, as also being mistress of a reasonable share of that knowledge and discretion other women attain, I made myself capable of disposing such noble and successful medicines and managing so weighty and great a concern.

In process to the strict commands and death bed injunction of so good a father, which was that, his medicines being of that value and incomparable benefit to the world that no man in the kingdom was master of the like (notwithstanding the high malice of his enemies and pitiful detractors), I should never suffer them to fall to the ground, or to die and be buried in oblivion, nor never to stop my ears from the cry of the poor, languishing for want of such medicines; I say this testament obliging me to the obedience of the *Rechabites*,[41] I have continued his medicines to this day (though not in this city) to the succour of many hundreds, more out of charity than my private interest, to the bright glory of these chemical and not to be paralleled medicines, and to the shame and odium of his Galenical opposers, as some time or other, by many laudable instances and miraculous examples shall be offered.

* * *

For as to my own concern and my particular judgement of it [education in the *literae humaniores*], I freely declare I admire it, and that it is an education very conducive and proper for every person that can with any conveniency attain to it; it is an excellent ornament and accomplishment, and a capacity suitable to prepare any man with the more ease, for any possession; as also the enquiries and obtainments any art dictates and the true end thereof proposes: and if I myself had never so many children, if I could possibly do it, I would breed them scholars, so that I shall sufficiently take off the prejudice of Mr Stubbe,[42] and forewarn him hereby when I do say that I esteem real learning and the foundation, promoters and doctors thereof: and if there be any difference between us about it, it must be that although I highly honour and commend this kind of education and ornament, yet I do say learning in itself is only preparatory, not perfect, a proper progress and tendency in order to the art of physic, not the perfection and consummation of that art. A man may read an author and yet not understand a medicine; and I am confident and able, knowing author never yet published a good effectual medicine, as daily experience will best decide. No this were to make a divine art cheap and contemptible, and to create and nourish more sloth and laziness than there is already: authors, I conceive, direct and instruct their students only by pointing out the way, not by walking to the journey's end.

And as I am not satisfied that every author that writes of medicines understands them, so I am as well assured that a man may sleep many years at the fountain of learning, and yet awake no physician: medicines are the marrow and full perfection of a physician, and those are hard to be attained; they are many of them (that are excellent and worth a value) of some years' preparation, and I doubt not but must be of many more for invention; learning will fit a man for that possession, but a diligent and indefatigable elaboration must perfect it. Medicines when obtained, one may in a reasonable time learn to apply, but how to obtain those medicines I verily think is a question beyond Mr Stubbe's study.

* * *

But to prosecute my *verbalist*, I do totally deny and reject phlebotomy[43] in the small pox, and that it is of no use or value with the *medicinalist*, and I will tell *Mr Medicus* stranger wonders yet; those that have skill and good medicines will not only secure and, with God's blessing as far as possible for art, preserve the life of the patient in the small pox, without taking away one drop of blood, but prevent all the many dangerous accidents the patient undergoes for want of assistance; when the physician many times gapes and looks on to see what nature will do itself, and cannot, or will not, give that help nature demands and the pressing occasions require; and more, skill and good medicines will manage the patient in this sickness so that he may avoid most commonly ever being confined to his bed, and those tedious decumbitures,[44] they are of course otherwise obnoxious to; as, likewise, the nice danger of taking cold these sick are subject to, and so proves often a mortal prejudice, will by this means be prevented; and what is more rare yet, skill and good medicine will preserve and free the greatest beauty, the finest face, and most curious skin from any mark, disfigure or pit of this beauty-destroying disease.

But methinks I hear critical Mr Stubbe say why then, sure you will have all the ladies in town your patients: I doubt not but I shall have some in these cases, and many others since *Mr Medicus* hath forced me to tell the world, in answer to him, what remedies I can afford them, and what good I can do them, not by him to be pretended to, much less performed, notwithstanding all his oratory and trinkets: and all this great business is done by a few poor chemical medicines, such as he calls purgatives, diaphoretics,[45] and cordials, though of greater virtue.

These things I have said now for the good of the sick, and against *Mr Medicus* and phlebotomy; and how will Mr Stubbe disprove me, and why am not I to be believed as well as Mr Stubbe, since I do not know that I am guilty of falsehood. I have had twelve years' experience and in that time (I must desire *Mr Medicus* not to be offended) I have met with those cases, the physician at Warwick, I am confident, in all his practice never saw. And for medicines I am sure I have ten times better and more generous than ever he had, hath, or ever will have.

Advice to the women and maidens of London

Written by a woman the full title asserts the radical agenda of its contents: 'instead of their usual pastime and education in needlework, lace- and point-making, it were far more necessary and profitable to apply themselves to the right understanding and practice of the method of keeping books of account: whereby, either single, or married, they may know their estates, carry on their trades, and avoid the danger of a helpless and forlorn condition, incident to widows'. Text from: the first edition, 1678, pp. 1–14.

Ladies and Gentlewomen,
Permit one of your sex to give you, as far as her small knowledge will reach, some hints to the right understanding and use of accounts: an art useful for all sorts, sexes and degrees of persons, especially for such as ever think to have to do in the world in any sort of trade or commerce, that next to a stock

of money, wares and credit, this is the most necessary thing.

Nor let us be discouraged, or put by the inspection thereof by being bid meddle with our distaff, for I have heard it affirmed by those who have lived in foreign part, that merchants and other tradesmen have no other book-keepers than their wives: who by this means (the husband dying) are well acquainted with the nature and manner of the trade, and are so certain how and where their stock is that they need not be beholden to servants or friends for guidance.

And for telling us that the government of the house appertains to us, and the trades to our fathers or husbands (under favour), the one is to be minded, and the other not neglected, for there is not that danger of a family's overthrow by the sauce wanting its right relish, or the table or stools misplaced, as by a widow's ignorance of her concern as to her estate, and I hope husbands will not oppose this when help and ease is intended to them whilst living; and safety to their name and posterity after death: except they have private trades (too much in mode) whereof they would have their wives wholly ignorant. In such a case indeed, one that knows not that one and two make three, suits best. And let us not fear we shall want time and opportunity to manage the decencies of our house; for what is an hour in a day, or half a day in a week, to make inspection into that, that is to keep me and mine from ruin and poverty?

Methinks now the objection may be that this art is too high and mysterious for the weaker sex, it will make them proud: women had better keep to their needlework, point laces, &c, and if they come to poverty, those small crafts may give them some mean relief.

To which I answer, that having in some measure practised both needle-work and accounts I can aver, that I never found this masculine art harder or more difficult than the effeminate achievements of lace-making, gum-work, or the like, the attainment whereof need not make us proud: and God forbid that the practice of a useful virtue should tempt us to a contrary vice.

Therefore if I might advise you, you should let the poor serve you with these mean things, whilst by gaining or saving an estate you shall never be out of capacity to store yourselves more abundantly with those trifles, than your own industry in such matters could have ever blessed ye.

And now gentlewomen I give you those rudiments of accounts which are the subject of this little pamphlet and transmit this learning to you the best I can, in the selfsame manner as it came to me.

Know then that my parents were very careful to cause me to learn writing and arithmetic and in that I proceeded as far as reduction, the rule of three and practice with other rules, for without the knowledge of these I was told I should not be capable of trade and book-keeping and in these I found no discouragement, for though arithmetic set my brains at work, yet there was much delight in seeing the end, and how each question produced a fair answer and informed me of things I knew not.

Afterwards I was put to keep an exact account of the expense of housekeeping, and other petty charges, my father made it my office to call all persons to an account every night what they had laid out, and to reimburse it them, and set all down in a book, and this is the way to make one a cashier, as they are termed, and one that can keep a fair account of receipts and payments of money or cash-book, is in a good way towards the understanding of book-keeping: she that is so well versed in this as to keep the accounts of her cash right and daily entered in a book, fair without blotting, will soon be fit for great undertakings.

Now in regard that other learnings do depend upon this petty cash account; I find it therefore convenient to give you an example of a month's expense, and you will thereby see what further use may be made of it afterwards.

Therefore to begin, my father gives me at several times in the month of January, the sum of £21 17s 1½d, the account of the expenses whereof is as followeth (see figure 8).

8

WRITING AND SPEAKING

INTRODUCTION

Strictures against public speaking by women sounded forth from pulpit, conduct manuals and household instruction: nevertheless, some women did speak out in public, through preaching, petitioning,[1] or publication of their translations, mother's advice, household or medical advice or poems;[2] or in private through letters, unpublished autobiography[3] and in the unmeasurable education of their children at home. The strongest injunctions against public speaking were those of St Paul (chapter 1, p. 14), continually reiterated and extended to cover all kinds of speaking in public places. Vives's *Instruction of a Christian Woman*, a supposedly liberal humanist educational treatise (chapters 3 and 6), emphasises the ideal godly woman as one who refrains from speaking.

Nevertheless, it was in the realm of spirituality where women also found some of the greatest encouragements to speak and write in a public arena. Paul's epistle to the Galatians claimed that 'there is neither male nor female'; women prophets in both Old and New Testament were frequently commended for their spirituality and closeness to God; and the Protestant emphasis on personal revelation through biblical reading and personal prayer supplied women with a space where speaking with God and writing were crucial to their eternal salvation. In the debate about women's preaching (chapters 1 and 8, pp. 248–53) this conflict is played out. Often it gives the women an added justification for their faith: in true Protestant fashion, their chosen and spiritual status is proved and demonstrated through the trial of conflict with a worldly power which forbids their speaking. Their words, whether published by them or recorded by others, claim to transgress a public, earthly power, but not that of God's power. In this sense, women manipulate the equation of female worldly speaking with transgression, in order to re-emphasise their specifically spiritual gifts.

Religious writing during the period could take several forms: biblical commentary; published sermons; devotional poetry; mystical or prophetic visions; warnings to repent; personal conversion narratives; and autobiographies. Because of their relative restriction within the private sphere, women did not produce either of the first two, but they wrote in all of the other genres, particularly because such genres focused on the concept of individual salvation and witnessing before God (pp. 249 ff.).

In addition to theological bans on women speaking, the prevalence of proverbial invectives against voluble women are rife in this period. Many of these are utilised in the drama and popular festivals: the image of the shrew, the gossiping housewife and the down-trodden husband are all utilised satirically as part of a wider concern about transgression of social and gender roles.[4] John Ray's collection of proverbs includes three which summarise neatly the prejudices and fears lying beneath the invectives and the strictures against public gossiping or writing: the first, *many women, many words; many geese, many turds*, belittles and marginalises women's speaking through typical scatology; *free of her lips, free of her hips*, makes the common equation between speech and sexual promiscuity; *a rouk-town's seldom a good housewife at home*, reiterates the view found in the conduct manuals, that a gossiping woman will neglect her proper task of good household management. The essay by Brathwait *The shrew* (pp. 244–6) epitomises these apparently common prejudices.

The ideology of the woman as 'chaste, silent and obedient'[5] expresses and describes a totalitarian ideal which may be said to delineate contemporary masculine anxiety about changing social relations, rather than female praxis. Many of the texts in this collection that show women writing and speaking encompass a variety of genres, places and modes. Nevertheless, despite the contemporary interest in and emphasis on women's writing in sixteenth- and seventeenth-century studies, it is important to remember that the total publications by women in the early seventeenth century was only 0.5 per cent of the total number of publications in England, a figure which rose to only 1.2 per cent after 1640: thus, relative to men, most women remained under-educated and articulated their experience in ways which are now irretrievably lost. This apparent silence means there is a danger of placing undue emphasis on the writings which do exist in published form, seeing them as either particularly extraordinary, or alternatively as typical of a woman's voice for the period. In fact, neither of these views can be defended: we need to develop reading strategies for the texts which acknowledge the material conditions of their existence, whilst recognising that the discourses which we do have available are only partial.

Often the prefaces to women's writings tell us this, in a typically oblique way.[6] Thus, Anne Dowrich's preface to her translation of *The French history* (1589) is addressed to her brother:

This book, which proceeds under your protection, if you consider the matter I assure you it is most excellent and well worth the reading: but if you weigh the manner, I confess it is base and scarce worth the seeing. This therefore is my desire, that the simple attire of this outward form may not discourage you from seeking the comfortable taste of the inward substance. You shall find here many things for comfort worthy the considering, and for policy the observing. This hath been my ordinary exercise at times of leisure for a long space together: if I were sure that you would take but half so much pleasure in reading it, as I have in collecting and disposing it, I should not need any further to commend it. If you find any thing that fits not your liking, remember, I pray, that it is a woman's doing.

Dowrich makes several claims and utilises strategies which are often found in women's writing of the period. She argues that the writing and the publication are for her brother, a single male reader; that the matter is more important than the form; that her style is simple; that she has only written during her leisure time; and that women's writing and actions are inferior to men's. Thus she tries to deflect criticism of her publication. Nevertheless, the rhetoric of the preface is highly sophisticated: she utilises the humanist modesty topos to great effect, since she thus diverts potential attacks on her as a woman author and from the content of the work, should it be attacked. She appropriates the plain style as one which is particularly suited to women. In its association with theological, scientific and politically marginal discourses[7] during the sixteenth and seventeenth centuries, she may well be making a crucial point about women's speaking position in her society. Women writing for publication in this period frequently preface their publication with an address to men, or from men, or claim that they have been asked to write by men: and this is also so of Dowrich (and Philips, pp. 256–8). These women writers all display a consciousness of the masculine control of discourse, in all its areas: genre; interpretation; reading; style; and publication. This consciousness invokes a highly complex set of strategies with which they respond. Dowrich, despite her protestations, demonstrates that speaking and writing are never simple matters.

Tyler, Cavendish and Behn describe writing as 'masculine' or 'manly' (this chapter, pp. 234–5, 259–60; chapter 9, pp. 288 ff.), evidence of a significantly gendered concept of public speaking and publication. But it may also be an assertion of a broader definition of sex: women have feminine and masculine parts. In addition, many women writers utilise metaphors of childbirth to describe the process of writing, and speak of their writing as children. This metaphor for writing is as old as Plato,[8] and its reappropriation by women can be seen as the first stage in a long history to reclaim the right to speak and be heard.

In this section I have necessarily omitted many texts which should be read alongside those selected, such as the increasing range of published women's writing of the period. In addition, it is helpful for readers to read this section in the light of all the other sections. Speaking and writing, most particularly for women in a society which marginalises their ability to speak in a way which it does not do for men, are always performed in the context of one of the other discourses represented in this selection. This applies equally to all published texts: the stricture against public speaking, and the consequent reflection upon a woman's public reputation continually threaten women's ability to write, speak and publish. Aphra Behn's bitter comments in the preface to *The lucky chance* (pp. 259–60) gives eloquent testimony to this.

Baldassare Castiglione, *The courtier*

Castiglione's work was popular throughout Western Europe, and used and cited as the quintessential handbook for courtiers. Text from: the first English edition, 1561, transl. Thomas Hoby, fos B62ᵛ–4ʳ.

The Lord Julian proceeded: for a proof therefore (Madam) that your commandment may drive me to assay to do, yea, the thing I have no skill in, I shall speak of this excellent woman as I would have her. And when I have fashioned her after my mind, and can afterward get none other, I will take her as mine own after the example of Pygmalion. And whereas the Lord Gaspar hath said that *the very same rules that are given for the courtier, serve also for the woman*, I am of a contrary opinion. For albeit some qualities are common and necessary as well for the woman as the man, yet are there some other more meeter for the woman than for the man, and some again meet for the man that she ought in no wise to meddle withal. The very same I say of the exercises of the body. But principally in her fashions, manners, words, gestures, and conversation (methink) the woman ought to be much unlike the man. For right as it is seemly for him to show a certain manliness full and steady, so doth it well in a woman to have a tenderness, soft and mild, with a kind of womanly sweetness in every gesture of hers, that in going, in standing, and speaking whatever she lusteth, may always make her appear a woman without any likeness of man. Adding therefore this principle to the rules that these lords have taught the courtier, I think well she may serve her turn with many of them, and be endowed with very good qualities, as Lord Gaspar saith. For many virtues of the mind I reckon be as necessary for a woman as for a man. Likewise, nobleness of birth, avoiding affectation or curiosity, to have a good grace of nature in all her doings, to be of good conditions, witty, foreseeing, not haughty, not envious, not ill tongued, not light, not contentious, not untowardly to have the knowledge to win and keep the good will of her lady, and of all others, to do well, and with a good grace, the exercises comely for a woman. Methink well beauty is more necessary in her than in the courtier, for (to say the truth) there is a great lack in the woman that wanteth beauty. She ought also to be more circumspect and to take better heed that she give no occasion to be ill-reported of, and so to behave herself that she be not only not spotted with any fault, but not so much as with suspicion, because a woman hath not so many ways to defend herself from slanderous reports as hath a man. But for so much as Count Lewis hath very particularly expressed the principal profession of the courtier, and willeth it to be in martial feats, methink also behoveful to utter (according to my judgement) what the gentlewoman of the palace ought to be: in which point when I have thoroughly satisfied, I shall think myself rid of the greatest part of my duty. Leaving therefore apart the virtues that ought to be common to her with the courtier, as, wisdom, nobleness of courage, steadiness, and many more; and likewise the conditions that are meet for all women, as, to be good and discreet, to have the understanding to order her husband's goods and her house and children when she is married and all those parts that belong to a good housewife: I say that for her that liveth in court, methink there belongeth to her above all other things a certain sweetness in language that may delight, whereby she may gently entertain all kind of men with talk worthy the hearing, and honest and applied to the time and place and to the degree of the person she communeth withal, accompanying with sober and quiet manners and with the honesty that must always be a stay to all her deeds, a ready liveliness of wit, whereby she may declare herself far wide from all dullness, but with such a kind of goodness that she may be esteemed no less chaste, wise, and courteous, than pleasant, feat-conceited[9] and sober: and therefore must she keep a certain mean very hard, and (in a manner) derived of contrary matters, and come just to certain limits but not to pass them. This woman ought not therefore (to make herself good and honest) be so squeamish, and make wise to abhor both the company and the talk (though somewhat of the wantonest) if she be present, to get her thence by and by: for a man may lightly guess that she feigned to be so coy to hide that in herself, which she doubted others might come to the knowledge of: and such nice factions are always hateful. Neither ought she again (to show herself free and pleasant) speak words of dishonesty, nor use a certain familiarity without measure and bridle, and fashion to make men believe that of her that perhaps is not: but being present at such kind of talk, she ought to give the hearing with a little blushing and shamefastness. Likewise to eschew one vice which I have seen reign in many: namely to speak and willingly to give ear to such as report ill of other women.

Margaret Tyler, *The mirror of princely deeds and knighthood*

Tyler's translation of a romance is highly unusual for a woman writer of the period, a point evident in the manner of her defence here. Text from: the first edition, 1578, fo. A3[r].

M.T. to the reader

Thou hast here, gentle reader, the discourse of Trebatio, an emperor in Greece: whether a true history of him indeed, or a feigned fable, I wot not, neither did I greatly seek after it in the translation, but by me it is done into English for thy profit and delight. The chief matter therein contained is of exploits of wars and the parties therein named are especially renowned for their magnanimity and courage. The author's purpose appeareth to be this, to animate thereby, and to set on fire the lusty courages of young gentlemen to the advancement of their line by ensuing such like steps. The first tongue wherein it was penned was the Spanish, in which nation by common report, the inheritance of worldly commendation hath to this day rested. The whole discourse in respect of the end not unnecessary; for the variety and continual shift of fresh material, very delightful; in the speeches short and sweet; wise in sentence, and wary in the provision of contrary accidents. For I take the grace thereof to be rather in the reporter's device than in the truth of this report, as I would that I could so well impart with thee that delight which myself find in reading the Spanish: but seldom is the tale carried clean from another's mouth. Such delivery as I have made I hope thou wilt friendly accept, the rather for that it is a woman's work, though in a story profane, and a matter more manlike than becometh my sex. But as for the manliness of the matter, thou knowest that it is not necessary for every trumpeter or drumster in the war to be a good fighter: they take wages only to incite others, though themselves have privy maims and are thereby recureless. So, gentle reader, if my travail in Englishing this author may bring thee to a liking of the virtues herein commended, and by example thereof in thy prince's and country's quarrel to hazard thy person, and purchase good name: as for hope of well deserving myself that way, I neither bend myself thereto, nor yet fear the speech of people if I be found backward: I trust every man holds not the plough which would the ground were tilled: and it is no sin to talk of Robin Hood, though you never shot in his bow: or be it that the attempt were bold to intermeddle in arms, so as the ancient Amazons did, and in this story Claridiana doth,[10] and in other stories not a few, yet to report of arms is not so odious, but that it may be born withal, not only in you men which your selves are fighters, but in us women, to whom the benefit in equal part apperteineth of your victories, either for that the matter is so commendable that it carrieth no discredit from the homeliness of the speaker, or so that it is so generally known, that it fitteth every man to speak thereof, or for that it jumpeth with this common fear on all parts of war and invasion. The invention, disposition, trimming, and what else in this story, is wholly another man's, my part none therein but the translation, as it were only in giving entertainment to a stranger, before this time unacquainted with our country guise. Nary the worse perhaps is this, that amongst so many strangers as daily come over, some more ancient and some but new set forth, some penning matters of great weight and sadness in divinity, or other studies, the profession whereof more nearly beseemeth my years, other some discoursing of matters more easy and ordinary in common talk, wherein a gentlewoman may honestly employ her travail. I have notwithstanding made countenance only to this gentleman, whom neither his personage might sufficiently commend itself unto my sex, nor his behaviour (being light and soldier-like) might in good order acquaint itself with my years. So that the question now ariseth of my choice, not of my labour, wherefore I preferred this story before matter of more importance? For answer whereto, gentle reader, the truth is, that as the first motion to this kind of labour came not from myself, so was this piece of work put upon me by others, and they which first counselled me to fall to work, took upon them also to be my taskmasters and overseers, lest I should be idle and yet because the refusal was in my power, I must stand to answer for my easy yielding, and may not be unprovided of excuse, wherein if I should allege for myself, that matters of less worthiness by as aged years have been taken in hand, and that daily new devices are published in songs, sonnets and interludes, and other discourses, and yet are born out without reproach, only to please the humour of some men. I think I should make no good plea therein, for besides that I should find thereby so many known enemies, as known men have been authors of such idle conceits, yet would my other adversaries be never the rather quieted: for they would say that as well the one as the other were all naught, and though peradventure I might pass unknown amongst a multitude, and not be the only gaze or odd party in my ill doing, yet because there is less merit of pardon if the fault be excused as common, I will not make that my defence which cannot help me, and doth hinder other men. But my defence is by example of the best, amongst which many have dedicated their labours, some stories, some of war, some physic, some law, some as concerning government, some divine matters, unto diverse ladies and gentlewomen. And if men may and do bestow such of their travails upon gentlewomen, then may we women read such of their works as they dedicate unto us, and if we may read them, why not further wade in them to the search of a truth? And then much more, why not deal by translation in such arguments, especially this kind of exercise, being a matter more of heed than of deep invention or exquisite learning? And they must needs leave this as confessed that in their dedications they mind not only to borrow names of worthy personages, but the testaments also for their further credit, which neither the one may demand without ambition, nor the other grant without over-lightness. If women be excluded from the view of such works as appear in their name, or if glory only be sought in our common inscriptions, it mattereth not whether the parties be men or women, whether alive or dead. But to return, whatsoever the truth is, whether that women may not at all discourse in learning, for men lay in their claim to be sole possessioners of knowledge, or whether they may in some manner, that is by limitation or appointment in some kind of learning; my persuasion hath been thus, that it is all one for a woman to pen a story as for a man to address his story to a woman. But amongst all my ill-willers, some I hope are not too straight that they would enforce me necessarily either not to write or to write of divinity. Whereas neither durst I trust mine alone judgement sufficiently, if matter of controversy were handled, nor yet could I find any book in that tongue, which would not breed offence to some, but I perceive some may be rather angry to see their Spanish delight turned to an English pastime.... What natures such men be of, I list not greatly to dispute, but my meaning hath been to make other partners of my liking, as I doubt not gentle reader, but if it shall please thee after serious matters to sport thyself with this Spaniard, that thou shalt find in him the just reward of malice and cowardice, with the good speed of honesty and courage, being able to furnish thee with sufficient store of foreign example to both purposes. And as in such matters which have been rather devised to beguile time, than to breed matter of sad learning, he hath ever born away that price, which could season such delights with some profitable reading: so shalt thou have this stranger an honest man when need serveth, and at other times either a good companion to drive out a weary night, or a merry jest at the board. And thus much concerning this present story, that it is neither unseemly for a woman to deal in, neither greatly requiring a less staid age than mine is. But of these two points gentle reader I thought to give thee warning, lest perhaps understanding of my name and years, thou mightest be carried into a wrong suspect of my boldness and rashness, from which I would gladly free myself by this plain excuse, and if I may deserve thy good favour by like labour, when the choice is mine own, I will have a special regard of thy liking. So I wish thee well.

Thine to use, M.T.

Thomas Bentley, *The monument of matrons*

Bentley's work is a collection of women's prayers and it is noteworthy that he should choose to preface this with a warning against public prayer. Bentley silently omits verse 11 of this chapter of Corinthians ('neither is the man without the woman'), thus literally erasing women's autonomous presence from his interpretation of this passage. The parenthetical comments are Bentley's. Text from: the first edition, 1582, fo. B8ʳ.

What ceremony every woman ought by God's word to use in time of prayer, public or private

1. Corinthians, chapter 11, verse 4, &c.   Every man praying or prophesying, having anything on his head, dishonoureth (God) his head: but every woman that prayeth or prophesyeth bare-headed, dishonoureth (her husband) her head. For it is even one very thing as though she were shaven.

Therefore if the woman be not covered, let her also be shorn; and if it be a shame for a woman to be shorn or polled (as in deed it is) then (for shame) let her be covered (and keep her hair trussed up under a kercher).

For a man ought not to cover his head (but ought to be polled and bare, forasmuch as he is the image and glory of God, in whom his majesty and power doth shine, concerning his authority over his wife, and other of God's creatures subjected under his dominion and rule).

But the woman is the glory of the man (or receiveth her glory in commendation of man, and therefore is subject): for the man is not of the woman, but the woman of the man: neither was the man created for the woman's sake; but the woman for the man's sake.

Therefore ought the woman to have power on her head (that is for something to cover her head in sign of subjection, because of the angels, to whom also they show their dissolution and shame, and not only to Christ and his church, or congregation where they praise).

Judge you in yourselves also, is it comely that a woman pray unto God bare-headed? Doth not nature itself teach you that if a man have long hair, like a woman, it is a shame unto him? But if a woman have long hair, it is a praise unto her: for her hair is given unto her for a covering (and to the end she should truss it up above her head: to declare that she must cover her head).

But if any man list to be contentious, we have no such custom, neither the church of God.

Philip Stubbes, *A crystal glass for Christian women*

Stubbes, the author of *The anatomy of abuses*, wrote this spiritual biography of his wife after she died a few weeks after childbirth. It went through thirty-four editions between 1591 and 1700. Text from: the 1618 edition, fos A1ff.

Calling to remembrance (most Christian reader) the final end of man's creation, which is to glorify God, and to edify one another in the way of true godliness, I thought it my duty, as well in respect of the one as in regard of the other, to publish this rare and wonderful example of the virtuous life and Christian death of Mistress Katherine Stubbes who, whilst she lived was a mirror of womanhood and, now being dead, is a perfect pattern of true Christianity. She was descended of honest and wealthy parents. Her father had borne divers offices of worship in his company, amongst whom he lived in great account, credit and estimation all his days: he was zealous in the truth, and of a sound religion. Her mother was a Dutchwoman, both discreet and wise, of singular good grace and modesty, and which did most to adorn her, she was both religious and also zealous ...

At fifteen years of age, her father being dead, her mother bestowed her in marriage to one Master Philip Stubbes with whom she lived four years and almost a half very honestly and godly with rare commendation of all that knew her, as well for her singular wisdom, as also for her modesty, courtesy, gentleness, affability, and good government; and above all for her fervent zeal which she bore to the truth, wherein she seemed to surpass many in so much as if she chanced at any time to be in place where either Papists or atheists were and heard them talk of religion, what countenance or credit soever they seemed to be of, she would not yield a jot, nor give place to them at all, but would most mightily justify the truth of God against their blasphemous untruths, and convince them, yea, and confound them by the testimonies of the word of God. Which thing how could it be otherwise? For her whole heart was bent to seek the Lord, her whole delight was to be conversant in the scriptures, and to meditate upon them day and night. Insomuch as you could seldom or never have come into her house and have found her without a Bible or some other good book in her hands. And when as she was not reading she would spend her time in conferring, talking, and reasoning with her husband of the word of God, and of religion, asking him what is the sense of this place, and what is the sense of that? How expound you this place and how expound you that? What observe you of this place and what observe you of that? So as she seemed to be ravished with the same spirit that David was, when he said, *the zeal of thine house hath eaten me up.*

She followed the commandment of our saviour Christ who biddeth us to search the scriptures, for in them you hope to have eternal life. She obeyed the commandment of the apostle who biddeth women be silent, and to learn of their husbands at home. She would never suffer any disorder or abuse in her house to be unreproved or unreformed. And so gentle was she, and courteous of nature that she was never heard to give any the lie in all her life, nor so much as to *thou* any in anger. She was never known to fall out with any of her neighbours, nor with the least child that lived, much less to scold or brawl, as many will nowadays, for every trifle, or rather for no cause at all: and so solitary was she given, that she very seldom or never, and then not neither except her husband were in company, go abroad with any, either to banquet or feast, to gossip or make merry as they term it: insomuch that she was noted by some (though most untruly) to do it in contempt and disdain of others. When her husband was abroad at London, or elsewhere, there was not the dearest friend she had in the world that could get her abroad to dinner or supper, to plays or interludes, nor to any other pastimes or disports whatsoever.... She could never abide to hear any filthy or unseemly talk, scurrility, bawdry, or uncleanness, neither swearing or blaspheming, cursing or banning, but would reprove them sharply, showing them the vengeance of God, due for such deserts, and which is more, there was never one filthy, unclean, indecent or unseemly word heard to come forth of her mouth, nor never once to curse or ban, to swear or blaspheme God any manner of way, but always her speeches were such as both might glorify God, and minister grace to the hearers as the apostle speaketh. And for her conversation, there was never any man or woman that ever opened their mouths against her, or that ever did or could accuse her of the least shadow of dishonesty, so continently she lived, and so circumspectly she walked, eschewing even the very outward appearance or show of evil.

Again, for the true love and loyalty to her husband, and his friends, she was (let me speak it without offence) I think the rarest paragon in the world: for she was so far from dissuading her husband to be beneficial to his friends, as she would rather persuade him to be more beneficial to them. If she saw her husband to be merry, then she was merry: if he were heavy or passionate, she would endeavour to make him glad: if he were angry, she would quickly please him, so wisely she demeaned herself towards him. She would never contrary him in anything, but by wise counsel and by sage advice, with all humility and submission, seek to persuade him. And also, so little she was given to this world that some of her neighbours marvelling why she was no more careful of it, would ask her sometimes, saying, Mistress Stubbes, why are you no more careful for the things of this life, but sit always pouring upon a book, and reading? To whom she would answer: 'If I should be a friend unto this world, I should be an enemy unto God: for God and the world are two contraries. John biddeth me, love not the world, nor anything in the world, affirming that if I love the world, the love of the father is not in me. Again, Christ biddeth me, first seek the kingdom of heaven, and the righteousness thereof, and then all these worldly things shall be given to me. Godliness is great riches if a man be content with that he hath. I have chosen with good Mary the better part, which shall never be taken from me, God's treasure she would say, is never drawn dry. I have enough in this life, God make me thankful, and know I have but a short time to live here, and it standeth upon me to have a regard to my salvation in the life to come.'

Thus this godly young gentlewoman held on her course three or four years after she was married: at which time it pleased God that she conceived with a man-child, after which conception she would say to her husband, and many other her good neighbours and friends yet living, not once or twice but many times, that she should never bear more children, that that child should be her death, and that she should live but to bring that child into the world, which thing no doubt was revealed unto her by the spirit of God: for according to her prophecy so it came to pass.

The time of her account being come, she was delivered of a goodly man-child, with as much speed and as safely in all women's judgement as any could be. And after her delivery she grew so strong that she was able within four or five days to sit up in her bed, and to walk up and down in her chamber and within a fortnight to go abroad in the house, being thoroughly well and past all danger, as every one thought. But presently upon this so sudden recovery, it pleased God to visit her again with an extreme hot and burning quotidian ague ... she never showed any sign of discontentment or impatience, neither was there ever heard one word come forth of her mouth sounding either of desperation or infidelity, of mistrust or distrust, or do any doubting or wavering: but always remained faithful and resolute in her God. And so desirous was she to be with the Lord, that these golden sentences were never out of her mouth: 'I desire to be dissolved and to be with Christ': and 'oh, miserable wretch that I am, who shall deliver me from this body subject to sin? Come quickly Lord Jesus, come quickly...'

When her husband would ask her why she smiled, and laughed so, she would say, 'Oh if you saw such glorious and heavenly sights as I see, you would rejoice and laugh with me, for I see a vision of the joys of heaven and of the glory that I shall go unto and I see infinite multitudes of angels attendant upon me, and watching over me, ready to carry my soul into the kingdom of heaven.' In regard whereof, she was willing to forsake herself, her husband, her child, and all the world besides. And so calling for her child, which the nurse brought unto her, she took it in her arms, and kissing it said, 'God bless thee my sweet babe, and make thee an heir of the kingdom of heaven'; and kissing it again, delivered it to the nurses, with these words to her husband standing by: 'Beloved husband I bequeath this my child unto you: he is no longer mine, he is the Lord's and yours: I forsake him, you, and all the world, yea, and mine own self, and esteem all things but dung, that I may win Jesus Christ. And I pray you sweet husband, bring up this child in good letters, in learning and discipline: and above all things, see that he be brought up and instructed in the exercise of true religion...'

Having thus godly disposed of all things she fell into a trance or swound for almost the space of a quarter of an hour, and so as every one had thought she had been dead: but afterward she coming to herself, spake to them that were present as there was many (both worshipful and others) saying: 'Right worshipful and my good neighbours and friends, I thank you for all the great pains you have taken with me in this bed of my sickness: and whereas I am not able to requite you, I beseech the Lord reward you in the kingdom of heaven. And for that my hour-glass is run out and that my time of departure hence is at hand, I am persuaded for three causes to make a confession of my faith before you all. The first cause that moveth me thereto is, for that those (if there be any such here) that are not yet thoroughly resolved in the truth of God, may hear and learn what the spirit of God hath taught me out of his blessed and all-saving word. The second cause that moveth me is for that none of you shall judge that I died not a perfect Christian and a perfect member of the mystical body of Jesus Christ, and so by your rash judgement might incur the displeasure of God. The third and last cause is for that as you have been witness of part of my life, so you might be witnesses of part of my faith and belief also. And in this my confession, I would not have you think that it is I that speak unto you, but the spirit of God that dwelleth in me, and all the elect of God, unless they be reprobates: for Paul saith (Rom. 8), if anyone have not the spirit of Christ dwelling in him, he is none of his. This blessed spirit hath knocked at the door of my heart and my God hath given me grace to open the door unto him, and he dwelleth in me plentifully. And therefore I pray you give me patience a little and imprint my words in your hearts, for they are not the words of flesh and blood, but the spirit of God, by whom we are sealed to the day of our redemption.'

A most heavenly confession of the Christian faith made by
the blessed servant of God, Mistress Katherine Stubbes, a
little before she died

'I believe and confess that the Lord our God, having created the universal engine and frame of the world, with all things contained therein, for the benefit and use of man, the last of all other creatures, even the first day created man, after his own similitude and likeness: holy, pure, good, innocent and in every part perfect and absolute, giving him also wisdom, discretion, understanding and knowledge above all other creatures (the holy angels only excepted), and which was more, he gave unto him a certain power, strength, faculty (which we call free will) by force whereof he might have continued and remained for ever in his integrity and holiness if he would. But he had no sooner received the inestimable blessing of free will in innocency and integrity, but by hearkening to the poisoned suggestions of the wicked serpent, and by obeying of his persuasions, he lost his free will, his integrity and perfection, and we all his posterity to the end of the world, and of a saint in heaven, he (and we in him) became fire brands in hell, vassals of Satan, miscreants and reprobates, abjects, and cast-aways, before the face of God for ever.

'Then when there was no other way or means for men to be saved in the justice of God, I do constantly believe and confess that God the Father in the multitude of his mercies, when the fullness of time was come, sent his own son Jesus Christ forth of his own bosom into this miserable world, to take our nature upon him, and that in the womb of a virgin, without spot or blemish of sin, and without the help of man, by wonderful operation and overshadowing of the Holy Ghost ...

'When God cast Adam into a dead sleep and made woman of a rib of his side, he brought her unto him, and he knew her straightway, and he called her by her name. Could Adam in the state of innocency know his wife, being in a dead sleep, while she was in making, and shall not we being restored to a far more excellent dignity and perfection than ever Adam was in, not know one another? Shall our knowledge be less in heaven than it is in earth? Do we not know one another in this life where we know but in part, we see but in part, yea as it were in a glass? And shall we not know one another in the life to come, where all ignorance shall be done away? ...

'This is my faith, this is my hope, and this is my trust: this hath the spirit of God taught me and this have we learned out of the word of God. And good Lord, that hast begun this work in me, finish it I beseech thee, and strengthen me that I may persevere therein to the end, and in the end, through Jesus Christ my only Lord and Saviour.'

She had no sooner made an end of this most heavenly confession of her faith, but Satan was ready to bid her the combat, whom she mightily repulsed and vanquished by the power of our Lord Jesus, on whom she constantly believed. And whereas before she looked with a sweet, lovely and amiable countenance, red as the rose and most beautiful to behold, now upon the sudden she bent her brows, she frowned, and looked as it were with an angry and stern, austere countenance, as though she saw some filthy, ugglesome[11] and displeasant thing, she burst forth in these speeches following, pronouncing her words scornfully and disdainfully, in contempt of him whom she spake to.

A most wonderful conflict between Satan and her soul, and of her valiant conquest of the same by power of Christ

'How now Satan, what makest thou here? Art thou come to tempt the Lord's servant? I tell thee (thou hell hound) thou hast no part nor portion in me, nor by the grace of God never shalt have: I was, now am, and shall be the Lord's for ever. Yea, Satan, I was chosen and elect of Christ to everlasting salvation, before the foundations of the world were laid, and therefore thou must get thee packing, thou damned dog, and go shake thine ears, for in me thou hast nought. But what dost thou lay to my charge thou foul fiend? Oh, that I am a sinner, and a grievous sinner, both by original sin and actual sin, and that I may thank thee for. And therefore Satan I bequeath my sin to thee from whence it first came. And I appeal to the mercy of God in Christ. Jesus Christ came to save sinners (as he saith himself) and not the righteous: behold the lamb of God (saith John) that taketh away the sins of the world. And in another place he crieth out, the blood of Jesus Christ doth cleanse us from all sins. And therefore Satan, I constantly believe that my sins are washed away in the precious blood of Jesus Christ and shall never be imputed to me any more. But what sayest thou now Satan? Dost thou ask me how I dare come to him for mercy, he being a righteous God, and I a miserable sinner? I tell thee Satan, I am bold through Christ, to come unto him, being assured and certain of pardon and remission of all my sins, for his name's sake. For doth not the Lord bid all that be heavy laden with the burden of sin to come unto him and he will ease them? Christ's arms were spread wide open (Satan) upon the cross' (with that she spread her own arms) 'to embrace me and all penitent persons ...

'Avoid therefore thou dastard, avoid thou cowardly soldier, remove thy sledge and yield the field won, and get thee packing, or else I will call upon my grand captain Christ Jesus, the valiant Michael, who beat thee in heaven, and threw thee down to hell with all thy hellish train and devilish crew.' She had scarcely pronounced these last words, but she fell suddenly into a sweet smiling laughter, saying, 'now he is gone, now he is gone, do you not see him, fly like a coward and run away like a beaten cock? He hath lost the field and I have won the victory, even the garland and crown of everlasting life: and that not by my own power and strength but by the might of Jesus Christ, who hath sent his holy angels to keep me.' And speaking to them which were by, she said, 'Oh, would God you saw what I see: for behold I see infinite millions of most glorious angels stand about me, with fiery chariots ready to defend me, as they did the good prophet Elijah [2 Kings]. These holy angels, these ministering spirits are appointed by God to carry my soul into the kingdom of heaven, where I shall behold the Lord face to face, and shall see him, not with other, but with these same eyes. Now I am happy and blessed for ever, for I have fought the good fight and by the might of Christ have won the victory. Now from henceforth I shall never taste neither of hunger nor cold, pain nor woe, misery nor affliction, vexation nor trouble, fear nor dread, nor any other calamity or adversity whatever. From henceforth is laid up a crown of life which Christ shall give to all them which love him. And as I am now in possession thereof by hope, so shall I be anon in full fruition thereof by presence of my soul, and hereafter of my body also, when the Lord shall please.' Then she spake softly to herself as followeth: 'Come Lord Jesus, come my love Jesus, oh, send thy pursuivant (sweet Jesus) to fetch me. Oh, sweet Jesus, strengthen thy servant and keep thy promise.' Then sung she a psalm most sweetly, and with a cheerful voice: which done she desired her husband that the 113 psalm might be sung before her to church. And further she desired him that he would not mourn for her.... After which words very suddenly she seemed as it were greatly to rejoice and look cheerfully as though she had seen some glorious sight. And lifting up her whole body and stretching forth both her arms as though she would embrace some glorious and pleasant thing, said, 'I thank my God through Jesus Christ, he is come, he is come, my good jailor is come to let my soul out of prison. Oh, sweet death thou art welcome, welcome sweet death, never was there any guest so welcome to me as thou art welcome, the messenger of everlasting life, welcome the door and entrance into everlasting glory, welcome I say, and thrice welcome my good jailor: do thy office quickly and set my soul at liberty. Strike, sweet death, strike my heart, I fear not thy stroke: now it is done. Father into thy blessed hands I commend my spirit. Sweet Jesus into thy hands I commend my spirit. Blessed spirit of God, I commit my soul into thy hand, oh most holy, blessed and glorious Trinity, three persons, and one true and everlasting God, into thy blessed hands I commit my soul, and my body.' At which words her breath stayed and so neither moving hand nor foot, she slept sweetly in the Lord.

Thus thou hast heard (gentle reader) the discourse of the virtuous life and Christian death of this blessed and faithful servant of God, Mistress Katherine Stubbes, which is so much the more wonderful, in that she was but young and tender of years, not half a year above the number of twenty when she departed this life. The Lord give us grace to follow her example, that we may come to those unspeakable joys, wherein she now resteth, through Christ our Lord, to whom, with the Father and the Holy Ghost, be all honour, praise, dominion and thanksgiving, both now and evermore. Amen.

Richard Brathwait, *Essays upon the five senses*

Text from: the first edition, 1620, pp. 134–41.

A *shrew*

Is a continual dropping whose activities consists principally in the volubility of an infatigable tongue; her father was a common barreter,[12] and her mother's sole note (being the voice of her vocation) echoed, *new wainfleet oysters*! In her sleep when she is barred from scolding, she falls to a terrible vein of snoring and foams at the mouth as if she were possessed or shrewdly rid by the night-mare; she is most out of her element when she most at quiet, and concludes jointly with the arithmetician, that unities are to be excluded from numbers. Her progenies are but small, yet all hopeful to be interested in some clamorous offices: for her eldest itcheth after *Bellman*, her next after *Cryer*, and her daughters scorn to degenerate, vowing to bring the anciently erected cuckstool into request: she frets like gummed grogram,[13] but for wear she is sempiternum.[14] She goes weekly a-caterwauling, where she spoils their spiced-cupped gossiping with her tart-tongued calletting:[15] she is a bee in a box, for she is ever buzzing; her eyes though they be no matches, for she squints hatefully, are more firing than any matches; she is a hot shot, for she ever goes charged; she hath an excellent gift for memory and can run division upon relation of injuries. In some thing she is praiseworthy, for she hates compliment and grins when she hears anyone commended, much more flattered: all the frenzies in Bedlam cannot put her down for humours. If she be married, she makes her husband's patience a fit subject to work upon, where his miserable ears are deafed with her incessant clamour. She is never pleased, for being pleased she were not herself, whose choicest music is ever to be out a tune. A nest of wasps and hornets are not comparable to her spite, nor may equal her in spleen, and in this they principally differ, she hath sting in her tongue, they in their tail. She is monstrously unsociable and grounds the reason for her distaste upon others' approbation. When she hath none to exercise her fury on, she mumbles over some dogged Paternoster to herself, as if she were conjuring: her sign is ever in Cancer and hates patience lest it should bastardise her blood. She is ever suspicious of others' thoughts and therefore answers for herself before she needs. Were she strong in power as in ill, she would commit more insolencies with her tongue than ever Nero did tyrannies with his sword. Silence she hates as her sex's scandal and, reproved for her distemper, her answer is *the worm will turn again*. Happy were her husband if she were worm's meat, but her hope is to outwear her winding sheet; when she comes in company all cry, *God bless them!* As if they hear thunder; she omits no time, spares no person, observes no state, but wounds with her tongue, terming it her sole defensive instrument. Great ones she as much disvalues as she condemns inferiors; yet neither shall slip her, for she never saw that creature which might not give her argument to vent her impatience; her reading is but small, yet when she hears of *Stentor's* tongue,[16] she would give her dowry for such a cymbal. She sometimes counterfeits gravity, but her ferret eyes and hook nose display her for an hypocrite. Her tongue never finds vacation but in church, which time gives her occasion to commence some new brawl. Her tongue is as glibbery as an eel, all the posts in the king's high road cannot equal her for speed; marry, truth is, she interfere dangerously. She wears her clothes negligently, of purpose to move her husband to tax her for her sluttishness, whose reproof she retorts with hail-shot and pellets him with words as disgraceful as she is fulsome. By this time she hath formeld[17] a pair of high cork shoes to heighten her dwarfish proportion, purposely intended to beard her husband. In her infancy she was tongue-tied, but by an expert artist the string being cut, she ever after vowed never to lose the faculty of her utterance by discontinuance. She hath seriously protested to make her husband run mad, but he is a fool then. She claims some privilege in his breeches and that is the efficient cause of the breech betwixt them. It may be that she is honest, but if her dogged humour would give her leave, I am persuaded she would enter parley with a knave in a corner: being as she is a very *crab*, if she attract any pleasures, they must be backward. She resembles the rail, and her name concurs with her nature. She condemns no act so much as that of Hypemnestra,[18] who procured her husband's safety, while all the rest practised their deaths. She approves of no ancient sovereignty but that of Amazon, where the government was feminine: and for the Salic[19] law, she hath already repealed it as expressly prejudicial to their sex. Her tongue-fever is quotidien, for it is ever shaking; her nature is so far out of temper as she hath vowed to be frantic for ever. She maintains this: that fancy is a frenzy and love such a painted idol as she will rather burn, than tie herself to such a foppery. I would see that saint which she would not incense, a man of that temper whom she will not nettle.

Gervase Markham, *The English housewife*

Markham's works on agriculture and husbandry were popular, often cited texts during the seventeenth century. *The English Housewife* first appeared as an addendum to *Country Contentments* in 1615, eleven editions followed in the subsequent sixty years. Text from: *Country Contentments*, first edition, 1615, pp. 1–4.

Of the inward virtues of the mind, which ought to be in every housewife

Having already in a summary briefness passed through those outward parts of husbandry which belong unto the perfect husbandman, who is the father and master of the family, and whose office and employments are ever for the most part abroad or removed from the house, as in the field or the yard: it is now meet, that we descend in as orderly method as we can, to the office of our English housewife, who is the mother and mistress of the family, and hath her most general employments within the house, where from the general example of her virtues, and the most approved skill of her knowledges, those of her family may both learn to serve God, and sustain man in that godly and profitable sort which is required of every true Christian.

First, then to speak of the virtues of her mind, she ought, above all things to be of an upright and sincere religion, and in the same both zealous and constant, giving by her example an incitement and spur unto all her family to pursue the same steps; and to utter forth by the instruction of her life those virtuous fruits of good living, which shall be pleasing both to God and his creatures. I do not mean that herein she should utter forth that violence of spirit, which many of our (vainly accounted pure) women do, drawing a contempt upon the ordinary ministry, and thinking nothing lawful but the fantasies of their invention, usurping to themselves a power of preaching and interpreting the holy word, to which only they ought to be but hearers and believers, or at the most but modest persuaders, this is not the office either of good housewife, or good woman. But let our English housewife be a godly, constant and religious woman, learning from the worthy preacher and her husband those good examples which she shall with all careful diligence see exercised amongst her servants.

In which practice of hers, what particular rules are to be observed, I leave her to learn of them who are professed divines, and have purposely written of this argument: only this much will I say, which each one's experience will teach him to be true, that the more careful the master and mistress are to bring up their servants in the daily exercises of religion toward God, the more faithful they shall find them in all their businesses towards men, and procure God's favour the more plentifully on all the household; and therefore a small time, morning and evening, bestowed in prayers and other exercises of religion will prove no lost time at the week's end.

Next unto her sanctity and holiness of life, it is meet that our English housewife be a woman of great modesty and temperance, as well inwardly as outwardly: inwardly in her behaviour and carriage towards her husband, wherein she shall shun all violence of rage, passion and humour, coveting less to direct than to be directed, appearing ever unto him pleasant, amiable and delightful; and though occasion mishaps or the misgovernment of his will may induce her to contrary thoughts, yet virtuously to suppress them, and with a mild sufferance rather to call him home from his error, than with the strength of anger to abate the least spark of his evil, calling into her mind that evil and uncomely language is deformed, though uttered even to servants, but most monstrous and ugly when it appears before the presence of a husband. Outwardly, as in her apparel and diet, both which she shall proportion according to the competency of her husband's estate and calling, making her circles rather straight than large: for it is a rule, if we extend to the uttermost, we take away increase; if we go a hair's breadth beyond, we enter into consumption; but if we preserve any part, we build strong forts against the adversaries of fortune, provided that such preservation be honest and conscionable: for as lavish prodigality is brutish, so miserable covetousness is hellish. Let therefore the housewife's garments be comely and strong, made as well to preserve health, as to adorn the person, altogether without toyish garnishes, or the gloss of light colours, and as far from the vanity of new and fantastic fashions, as near to the comely imitation of modest matrons. Let her diet be wholesome and cleanly, prepared at due hours, and cooked with care and diligence: let it be rather to satisfy nature, than her affections; and apter to kill hunger than to revive new appetites; let it proceed more from the provision of her own yard than the furniture of the markets; and let it be rather esteemed for the familiar acquaintance she hath with it, than for the strangeness and rarity it bringeth from other countries.

To conclude, our English housewife must be of chaste thoughts, stout courage, patient, untired, watchful, diligent, witty, pleasant, constant in friendship, full of good neighbourhood, wise in discourse, but not frequent therein, sharp and quick of speech, but not bitter or talkative, secret in her affairs, comfortable in her counsels, and generally skilful in the worthy knowledges which do belong to her vocation; of all or most part whereof, I now in the ensuing discourse intend to speak more largely.

John Vicars, *The schismatic sifted*

Vicars was a Presbyterian who attacked the Independent churches' campaign against centralised church government. As with many writers, he sees the threat of women preaching as the acme of the disorder caused by breakaway churches and sects, and intimately linked to the disorderly behaviour of the lower social orders. Text from: the first edition, 1646, pp. 33–4.

Whereas this prophecy of Joel [Joel 2:18] (as the apostle Peter told the Jews) was clearly prophesied of, and mainly fulfilled in those times of the apostles, and then after our saviour Christ's ascension (which were called those last-days, as all learned observe) the Lord indeed poured out his spirit on all flesh, on young and old, male and female, and gave them power of admirably doing miracles and wonders; and then I say (as the apostle Peter in that forecited scripture said) was this prophecy of Joel most apparently fulfilled, and so continued all the time of the apostles' lives, and some of their holy disciples, even to about the time of the destruction of Jerusalem. But what's this to our times, wherein (and long time before) miracles are ceased? Can any of us dare to assume the extraordinary power of God, to do miracles and work wonders? Is it a miracle or a wonder (indeed, I confess it may be to see such intolerable impudence) to see young saucy boys (in comparison); bold botching taylors; and other most audacious, illiterate mechanics to run rudely and rashly (and unsent for too) out of their shops into a pulpit; to see bold impudent housewives, without all womanly modesty, to take upon them (in the natural volubility of their tongues, and quick wits, or strong memories only) to prate (not preach or prophesy) after a narrative or discoursing manner, an hour or more, and that most directly contrary to the apostles' inhibition? But where I say is their extraordinary spirit poured out upon them, either in the gift of tongues (except it be in the lying and slanderous tongues, which are rather the gifts of the evil spirit, as the apostle James testifies [Jas. 13,14,15]), in gifts of miraculous healing the sick and sore, and such like? Where, I say, are any of these in our old, our young tradesmen, or bold Beatrices of the female sex?

Dorothy Waugh, *The lamb's defence against lies*

Waugh, one of the disciples of James Parnell, describes her treatment by the magistrates of Carlisle when she preached publicly. It is one of the few published descriptions of a scold's bridle and of the experience of wearing one. Text from: the first edition, printed anonymously in 1656 in defence of James Parnell, fos 29–30.

A relation concerning Dorothy Waugh's cruel usage by the Mayor of Carlisle

Upon the 7th day about the time called Michaelmas in the year of the world's account 1655, I was moved of the Lord to go into the market of Carlisle, to speak against all deceit and ungodly practices, and the mayor's officer came and violently haled me off the cross and put me in prison, not having anything to lay to my charge: and presently the mayor came up where I was and asked me from whence I came, and I said out of Egypt where thou lodgest. But after these words, he was so violent and full of passion he scarce asked me any more questions, but called to one of his followers to bring the bridle, as he called it, to put it upon me, and was to be on three hours. And that which they called so was like a steel cap, and my hat being violently plucked off, which was pinned to my head, whereby they tore my clothes to put on their bridle, as they called it, which was a stone weight of iron by the relation of their own generation, and three bars of iron to come over my face, and a piece of it was put in my mouth, which was so unreasonable big a thing for that place, as cannot be well related, which was locked to my head, and so I stood their time with my hands bound behind me with the stone weight of iron upon my head, and the bit in my mouth to keep me from speaking. And the mayor said he would make me an example to all that should ever come in that name. And the people to see me so violently abused were broken into tears, but he cried out on them and said, *for foolish pity, one may spoil a whole city.* And the man that kept the prison door demanded two-pence of everyone that came to see me while the bridle remained upon me. Afterwards it was taken off and they kept me in prison for a little season, and after a while the mayor came up again and caused it to be put on again and sent me out into the city with it on, and gave me very vile and unsavoury words, which were not fit to proceed out of any man's mouth, and charged the officer to whip me out of the town: from constable to constable to send me, till I came to my own home, when as they had not anything to lay to my charge.

D.W.

Priscilla Cotton and Mary Cole, *To the priests and people of England we discharge our consciences, and give them warning*

Cotton and Cole were also Quakers, imprisoned on various occasions for refusal to take oaths and public speaking. Text from: the first edition, 1655, fos A1ʳ–A4ᵛ.

Friends,

We have no envy or malice to any creature, priest or people, but are to mind you of your conditions without any partiality or hypocrisy and with your eternal good; and what we contend against is your greatest enemy and will be your everlasting woe and torment, if it be not destroyed in you. For know, there is the seed of the woman and the seed of the serpent in the world, there is the generation of Cain, and righteous Abel. Now it lieth upon you all to know what generation you are of: for little did the false prophets and that generation that put to death the true prophets of the Lord think they were of Cain's race, nor did the scribes and Pharisees (that with their priests put Christ to death) think they were of Cain's generation, for they garnished the sepulchres of the righteous and said, *if they had been in the days of their fathers, they would not have slain them.* Yet Christ Jesus told them, *that all the blood spilt since righteous Abel, should be required of that generation*; and that *they were the children of them that murdered the prophets.* Is it not strange that all the learned priests and scribes, and Pilate that had the Hebrew and Greek besides Latin, should not find out by all their high learning the originals of the scriptures of the prophets concerning Christ Jesus (that he was the true Messiah)? But that they that read the gospel every Sabbath day, that spake of Christ, should murder and put him to death. Now Christ Jesus himself gives the reason and thanks his father that he had hid it from the wise and prudent, revealed it to babes, because it was the father's good pleasure, and the scriptures declare them to be ignorant that had the Hebrew, Greek and Latin, for had they known it they would not have crucified the Lord of life and glory.

Now people, this was the same generation of Cain in them after Christ's death, that persecuted the apostles and put them to death; and it was the same spirit in them that put the martyrs to death; and of that generation were the bishops that persecuted and so it continueth still to this day in the world: for

Cain's generation is now still envying, hating, and persecuting the righteous Abel. Now the persecuting Cainish generation would never acknowledge they were such, but in all ages persecuted the just under some false colour, as they of old said, the true prophets were troublers of Israel ... so that all along it was on a false account the just were persecuted: so in the days of the bishops, the martyrs were burnt and butchered under the name of heretics: so now the seed of the serpent is subtle and will not persecute the truth as it is the truth, but under some false pretence or other, else all would see their deceit. But the truth is it is from the first rise, because their own works are evil, and their brother's good: they hated Jesus Christ because he testified that their works were evil. So now Cain's generation hates the just and pure seed of God, because it declares that their works are evil.

Objection. But do not the priests declare against evil works?

Answer. Yes, they do so: the scribes and Pharisees spake good words, they spake of the Messiah, yet they killed the substance of what they spake: so the priests speak true words, good words, and yet kill and persecute, pursue and imprison the substance and life of what they speak, for he that departs from evil makes himself a prey to priest and people; and sometimes when the light in their consciences tells them, when they are persecuting the just seed, that they are innocent; yet they wilfully run on against the very light of their own consciences, as did Stephen's persecutors ...

Therefore know you that you may be and are ignorant though you think yourselves wise: silly men and women may see more into the mystery of Christ Jesus than you. For the apostles that the scribes called illiterate, and Mary and Susannah (silly women as you would be ready to call them, if they were here now), these know more of the Messiah than all the learned priests and Rabbis. For it is the spirit that searcheth all things, yea the deep things of God you may know and yet murder the just, and think you do God good service.

This I warn you in love, for I cannot but think that there are some among you that ponder on this day and if you would hearken to the light of Jesus Christ in your consciences, it would lead you from your own wisdom, learning and self-conceitedness into the simplicity of Jesus Christ, which is a mystery of faith hid in a pure conscience: for your own wisdom must be denied if ever you will come to witness the life and power of the true wisdom, which the fear of the Lord is the beginning of: for so did they of old.

Paul and Apollo were very learned and eloquent, saith the scriptures, yet Paul counted all his learning dung for the excellency of the knowledge of Christ, let his second chapter of his first epistle to the Corinthians be a full witness of this: and Apollo was willing to be instructed of his hearers Aquila and Priscilla that were tent-makers, and the learned that studied curious arts burned their books that were of great price when they came to knowledge of Jesus Christ: so you now would hearken to Jesus Christ, and obey his light in your consciences; you would come down to humility and the fear of the Lord, to the true wisdom and understanding, that you would not need so many authors and books; you would not need to rent your head with studying, but you would come to see your teacher in you, which now is removed into a corner; you would come to lead a preaching life, and witness that faith you talk of to purify your hearts from envy, pride and malice; and to get the victory over the world's glory and honour that is so highly esteemed by you; and coming to see yourselves in the light of Jesus Christ you will not lord it over God's heritage, nor lift yourselves up above your brethren in pride and arrogancy, but be a servant to all in love . . .

For if a son or a daughter be moved from the Lord to go into the assembly of the people in a message from the Lord God, thou canst not endure to hear them speak sound doctrine, having a guilty conscience, and fearing the wicked declare against thy wickedness, thou incensest the people, telling them that they are dangerous people, Quakers, so making the people afraid of us: and incensest the magistrates, telling them that they must lay hold on us, as troublers of the people and disturbers of the peace, and so make them thy drudges to act thy malice, that thy filthiness may be not discovered and thy shame appear: but God will make them in one day to forsake thee, and leave and fly from thee: though for the present thou lordest it over magistrates, people, meeting house, and all as though all were thine, and thou sittest as a queen and lady over all and wilt have the pre-eminence, and hast got the seat of God, the consciences of the people, and what thou sayest must not be contradicted: if thou bid them fight and war, they obey it, if thou bid them persecute and imprison, they do it, so that they venture their bodies and souls to fulfil thy lusts of envy and pride: and in thy pride thou condemn all others, thou tellest the people women must not speak in a church, whereas it is not spoke only of a female, for we are all one both male and female in Christ Jesus: but it is weakness that is the woman by scriptures forbidden, for else thou puttest the scriptures at a difference in themselves, as still is thy practice out of thy ignorance: for the scriptures do say, that all the church may prophesy one by one, and that women were in the church as well as men, do thou judge; and the scripture saith that a woman may not prophesy with her head uncovered least she dishonour her head; now thou wouldst know the meaning of that head, let the scriptures answer, 1 Cor. 11:3: *the head of every man is Christ.* Man in his best estate is altogether vanity, weakness, a lie. If therefore any speak in the church, whether man or woman, and nothing appear in it but the wisdom of man, and Christ, who is the true head, be not uncovered,[20] do not fully appear, Christ the head is then dishonoured. Now the woman or weakness, that is man, which in his best estate or greatest wisdom is altogether vanity, that must be covered with the covering of the spirit, a garment of righteousness that its nakedness may not appear and dishonour thereby come. Here maist thou see from the scriptures that the woman, or weakness, whether male or female, is forbidden to speak in the church: but it is very plain, Paul, nor Apollo, nor the true church of Christ were not of that proud envious spirit that thou art of, for they owned Christ Jesus in man or woman: for Paul biddeth Timothy to help those women that laboured with him in the gospel and Apollo hearkened to a woman and was instructed by her, and Christ Jesus appeared to the women first, and sent them to preach the resurrection to the apostles, and Philip had four virgins that did prophesy. Now thou dost respect persons[21] I know, and art partial in all things, and so judgest wickedly, but there is no respect of persons with God. Indeed, you yourselves are women that are forbidden to speak in the church, that are become women: for two of your priests came to speak with us, and when they could not bear sound reproof and wholesome doctrine that did concern them, they railed on us with filthy speeches, as no other they can give to us that deal plainly and singly with them, and so run from us. So leaving you to the light in all your consciences to judge of what we have writ, we remain prisoners in Exeter jail for the word of God.

Priscilla Cotton,
Mary Cole.

Eliza's Babes

The author here adeptly transposes the difficulty of a woman speaking publicly on to the agency of God. She shares this account of speaking and prophesying with many other women preachers and visionaries during the Interregnum. Text from: the first edition, 1652, fos A1^v–A2^r.

To my sisters

Look on these babes as none of mine,
For they were but brought forth by me,
But look on them as they are divine,
Proceeding from divinity.

To the reader

When first the motion came into my mind, that these *Babes* of mine should be sent into the world; I would fain have suppressed that motion, for divers reasons which may be imagined by them that shall read them, but especially by those that knew my disposition. But rising one day from my devotions, it was suggested to my consideration, that those desires were not given me to be kept private to myself, but for the good of others.

And if any unlike a Christian shall say I wrote them for mine own glory, I like a Christian will tell them I therefore sent them abroad, for such a strict union there is betwixt my dear God and me, that his glory is mine, and mine is his; and I will tell them too, I am not ashamed of their birth; for before I knew it the prince of eternal glory had affianced me to himself; and that is my glory.

And now to all such shall I direct my speech, whose brave spirits may carry them to high desires. Place not your affections in your youth, beneath yourselves; but if you would be happy on earth and enjoy these outward blessings with free and lawful contentment, bestow your first affections on my almighty prince. I would have you all love him and him to love you all. I, being his, must do as he will have me; and methinks he directs me to tell you that you shall never be happy on earth nor glorious in heaven, if you do not love him above all earthly things. More, I must tell you, that if you will dedicate to his service, and present into his hands your wealth, wit, spirit, youth, beauty, he will give you wealth; if less, more useful: your wit more pure, your spirit more high, and transcendent, and your youth and beauty which time will steal from you, or some malignant disease with pain rend from you; them he will lay up awhile for you, and return them again for eternity, with great advantage. And that you need not doubt of the certainty of what is told you, they that tell it you have found part of it true, and shall the rest. I cannot be content to be happy alone, I wish you all blessed too; nor can I smother up those great and infinite blessings, that I have received from him, with private thanks. That great prince of heaven and earth, proclaimed by angels that he was come into the world to show his good will and love to me, was here content to die a public death for me, to save me from a hell of misery in which I lay and should have lain had not he, the prince of peace, and the fairest and chiefest among the sons of men, shed his most precious and royal blood for me. And before he died, he left word that I should not fear, for it was his great and glorious father's will to bestow on us a kingdom. And was so great a prince not ashamed to avow so great affection and love to me and shall I be ashamed to return him public thanks for such infinite and public favours? No, I will not: but with all my mind, heart, and soul, I bless and praise my almighty God, for so great benefits bestowed on me, his unworthy servant. Methinks it is not enough for myself only to do it, but I must send out my *Babes*, to do it with me and for me; and if any shall say *others may be as thankful as she, though they talk not so much of it*, let them know that if they did rightly apprehend the infinite mercies of God to them, they could not be silent; and if they do not think the mercies of God worth public thanks, I do. And therefore I will not be ashamed to be that one in ten that returned to acknowledge himself a cleansed leper. And now, my *Babes*, some may say to you, unless you had been more curiously dressed, or more finely shaped, your mother might have kept you in obscurity. Tell them, I sent you to their more leaned and refined wits to form you to a more curious shape, and tire you in a more enticing dress. But this I will say for you, you want none of your limbs, and your clothes are of rich materials. I dare not say I am loath to let you go: go you must, to praise him that gave you me. And more I'll say for you, which few mothers can, you were obtained by virtue, born with ease and pleasure, and will live to my content and felicity. And so adieu. But stay! Something you may truly say for your own imperfections, and your mother's excuse, that some of you were born when herself was but a child.

Sarah Jinner, *An almanac*

Jinner's defence of her public voice is part of her active work as an almanac writer and physical adviser (see chs 4 and 7, pp. 127 ff., 218 ff.). Text from: the first edition, 1658, fos B1ʳ–B1ᵛ.

To the reader

You may wonder to see one of our sex in print, especially in the celestial sciences; I might urge much in my defence, yea more than the volume of this book can contain: in which I am confined not to exceed ordinary bulk. But why no women write, I pray? Have they not souls as well as men? Though some witty coxcombs strive to put us out of conceit of ourselves as if we were but imperfect pieces, and that nature, intending a man, when the seminal conception proves weak there issues a woman. But know that *Aristotle* affirms that woman doth contribute to formation matter as well as place. Mankind is preserved by woman; many other rare benefits the world reapeth by women, although it is the policy of men to keep us from education and schooling, wherein we might give testimony of our parts by improvement: we have as good judgement and memory, and I am sure as good fancy as men, if not better. We will not boast of strength of body, let horses and mules do that. What rare things have women done? What cures in physic, which great doctors have left? How many commonwealths have been managed by woman, as the *Amazons*? Did not *Semiramis* set the Babylonian kingdom in great glory? Tomiris cut off the head of Cyrus. Nay, let me tell you, we have had a pope of our sex, named Pope Joan, which the best historians do not deny. When or what commonwealth was ever better governed than this by the virtuous Queen Elizabeth? I fear me I shall never see the like again, all you princes nowadays are like dunces in comparison of her: either they have not the wit or the honesty she had: something is the matter that things do not fadge so well! Well no more of that. To our business again, what rare poets of our sex were of old? And now of late the Countess of Newcastle. And, I pray you what a rare poem hath one Mistress Katherine Philips near Cardigan writ, it is printed before Cartwright's poems, who, if her modesty would permit, her wit would put down many men's in a masculine strain. I could tell you of many more that have been famous in philosophy and physic, as the Countess of Kent and others. And lastly, of *Tunetia*, a German lady, that lately did set out tables of the planets motion: therefore, why should we suffer out parts to rust? Let us scour the rust off by ingenious endeavouring the attaining higher accomplishments: this I say not to animate our sex to assume or usurp the breeches; no, but perhaps if we should shine in the splendour of virtue, it would animate our husbands to excel us: so by this means we should have an excellent world ...

...Farewell till next year,

S.J.

Katherine Philips, *Poems*

Philips's poems were circulating in manuscript from the early 1650s. She held a correspondence with Charles Cottrell, in which they took the names of Orinda and Poliarchus. He supervised the publication of her poems after her death, and prefaced her writing with his protective authority. Text from: the second edition, 1667, fos A1ʳff. An unauthorised edition was issued in 1664.

Preface

When the false edition of these poems stole into the light, a friend of that incomparable lady's that made them, knowing how averse she was to be in print, and therefore being sure that it was absolutely against her consent, as he believed it utterly without her knowledge (she being then in Wales, above 150 miles from this town), went presently both to gentlemen who licensed it upon the stationer's averment that he had her leave, and to the stationer himself for whom it was printed, and took the best course he could with both to get it suppressed, as it presently was (though afterward many of the books were privately sold) and gave her an account by the next post of what he had done. A while after he received this answer, which you have here (taken from her own hand) under that disguised name she had given him, it being her custom to use such with most of her particular friends.

Worthy Poliarchus,

[I] am sufficiently distrustful of all that my own want of company and better employment, or other's commands, have seduced me to write, to endeavour rather that they should never be seen at all, than that they should be exposed to the world with such effrontery as now they most unhappily are. But is there no retreat from the malice of this world? I thought a rock and a mountain might have hidden me, and that it had been free for all to spend their solitude in what reveries they please, and that our rivers (though they are babbling) would not have betrayed the follies of impertinent thoughts upon their banks; but 'tis only I who am that unfortunate person that cannot so much as think in private, that must have my imaginations rifled and exposed to play the mountebanks, and dance upon the ropes to entertain all the rabble; to undergo all the raillery of the wits, and all the severity of the wise, and to be the sport of some that can, and some that cannot, read a verse. This is a most cruel accident, and hath made so proportionate an impression upon me, that really it hath cost me a sharp fit of sickness since I heard it, and I believe would be more fatal but that I know what a champion I have in you, and that I am sure your credit in the world will gain me a belief from all that are knowing and civil, that I am so innocent of that wretched artifice of a secret consent (of which I am, I fear, suspected) that whosoever would have brought me those copies corrected and amended, and a thousand pounds to have bought my permission for their being printed, should not have obtained it. But though there are many things, I believe, in this wicked impression[22] of those fancies, which the ignorance of what occasioned them and the falseness of the copies may represent very ridiculous and extravagant, yet I would give some account of them to the severest Cato, and I am sure they must be more abused than I think is possible . . .

I am so little concerned for the reputation of writing sense that, provided the world would believe me innocent of any manner of knowledge, much less connivance at this publication, I shall willingly compound never to trouble them with the true copies, as you advise me to do: which if you still should judge absolutely necessary to the reparation of this misfortune, and to general satisfaction; and that, as you tell me, all the rest of my friends will press me to it, I should yield to it with the same reluctancy as I would cut off a limb to save my life. However, I hope you will satisfy all your acquaintance of my aversion to it, and did they know me as well as you do, that apology were very needless, for I am so far from expecting applause for anything I scribble, that I can hardly expect pardon; and sometimes I think that employment so far above my reach, and unfit for my sex, that I am going to resolve against it for ever; and could I have recovered those fugitive papers that have escaped my hands, I had long since made a sacrifice of them all. The truth is I have an incorrigible inclination to that folly of rhyming, and intending the effects of that humour only for my own amusement in a retired life, I did not so much as resist it as a wiser woman would have done. But some of my dearest friends, having found my ballads (for they deserve no better name), they made me so much believe they did not dislike them, that I was betrayed to permit some copies for their divertissement: but this with so little concern for them, that I have lost most of the originals, and that I suppose to be the cause of my present misfortune; for some infernal spirits or other have catched those rags of paper, and what the careless blotted writing kept them from understanding they have supplied by conjecture, till they put them into the shape wherein you saw them, or else I know not which way it is possible for them to be collected, or so abominably transcribed as I hear they are. I believe also there are some among them that are not mine, but everyway I have so much injury, and the worthy persons that had the ill luck of my converse, and so their names exposed in this impression without their leave, that few things in the power of fortune could have given me so great a torment as this most afflictive accident. I know you, Sir, so much my friend that I need not ask your pardon for making this tedious complaint: but methinks it is a great injustice to revenge myself upon you by this harangue for the wrongs I have received from others; therefore I will only tell you that the sole advantage I have by this cruel news is that it has given me an experiment: that no adversity can shake the constancy of your friendship, and that in the worst humour that ever I was in, I am still,

Worthy Poliarchus,
Your most faithful, most obliged
friend, and most humble servant,
Orinda

Cardigan,
Jan. 29, 1663/4

She writ divers letter to many of her other friends full of the like referments, but this is enough to show how little she desired the fame of being in print, and how much she was troubled to be so exposed.

Aphra Behn, Preface to *The Lucky Chance*

Many of Behn's works are published with prefaces which defend her publication and her writing, and express a consciousness of the difference between masculine and feminine publication and writing. Text from: the first edition, 1686, fos A1ʳ–A1ᵛ.

258

Preface

Had I a day or two's time, as I have scarce so many hours to write this in (the play being all printed off and the press waiting) I would sum up all your beloved plays and the things in them that are past with such silence by, because written by men; such masculine strokes in me must not be allowed. I must conclude those women (if there be any such) greater critics in that sort of conversation than myself, who find any of that sort in mine, or anything that can justly be reproached. But 'tis in vain by dint of reason or comparison to convince the obstinate critics, whose business is to find fault, if not by a loose and gross imagination to create them, for they must either find the jest, or make it; and those of this sort fall to my share, they find faults of another kind for the men writers. And this one thing I will venture to say, though against my nature, because it has a vanity in it: that had the plays I have written come forth under any man's name and never known to have been mine, I appeal to all unbiased judges of sense, if they had not said that person had made as many good comedies, as any one man that has written in our age. But a devil of it, the woman damns the poet!

Ladies, for its further justification to you, be pleased to know that the first copy of this play was read by several ladies of very great quality and unquestioned fame and received their most favourable opinion, not one charging it with the crime that some have been pleased to find in the acting. Other ladies who saw it more than once, whose quality and virtue can sufficiently justify anything they design to favour, were pleased to say they found an entertainment in it very far from scandalous; and for the generality of the town, I found by my receipts it was not thought so criminal. However, that shall not be an encouragement to me to trouble the critics with new occasion of affronting me, for endeavouring at least to divert, and, at this rate, both the few poets that are left and the players who toil in vain will be weary of their trade.

I cannot omit to tell you that a wit of the town, a friend of mine at Wills Coffee House, the first night of the play, cried it down as much as in him lay, who before had read it and assured me he never saw a prettier comedy. So complaisant one pestilent wit will be to another and in the full cry make his noise too; but since tis to the witty few I speak, I hope the better judges will take no offence, to whom I am obliged for better judgements; and those I hope will be so kind to me, knowing my conversation not at all addicted to the indecencies alleged, that I would much less practice it in a play that must stand the test of the censoring world. And I must want common sense and all the degrees of good manners, renouncing my fame, all modesty and interest for a silly, saucy, fruitless jest, to make fools laugh and women blush and wise men ashamed; myself all the while, if I had been guilty of this crime charged to me, remaining the only stupid, insensible. Is this likely, is this reasonable to be believed by anybody, but the wilfully blind? All I ask is the privilege for my masculine part the poet in me (if any such you will allow me) to tread in those successful paths my predecessors have so long thrived in, to take those measures that both the ancient and modern writers have set me and by which they have pleased the world so well. If I must not, because of my sex, have this freedom, but that you will usurp all to yourselves, I lay down my quill and you shall hear no more of me, no not so much as to make comparisons, because I will be kinder to my brothers of the pen than they have been to a defenceless woman, for I am not content to write for a third day only. I value fame as much as if I had been born a hero and if you rob me of that, I can retire from the ungrateful world and scorn its fickle favours.

9

PROTO-FEMINISMS

INTRODUCTION

During the early modern period there were no demands by women for equal political rights with men, and feminism as a self-conscious voice was not given a name until the end of the nineteenth century. Mary Astell's *A serious proposal to the ladies* (1696) and the anonymous writer of *An essay in defence of the female sex* (1696) are often seen as the first books in which women argue for political and social change on behalf of women as a distinct social group.[1] However, as this collection demonstrates, both women and men of the period did articulate conceptions, ideas and proposals which presage the development of a fully fledged feminist politics. I have called this fledgling articulation *proto-feminism.*

By proto-feminist, I mean that we may find voices, arguments, strategies, and accounts of gendered construction of power which are recognisable as essential to later feminist positions. Even where these voices are fragmentary; or placed within a framework where woman asserts equality of soul by assenting to her weakness in body; or used by male authors; they provide readers with female voices and models of female argumentation, which are used by later women in their own right.

One example of this can be seen in aspects of the long history of the *querelle des femmes* tradition.[2] This tradition dates back to the late medieval period, and is characterised by evolving and highly elaborate rules of argumentation. Usually texts are either a defence of women or a misogynistic attack, although many works included both defence and attack. The attacks on women usually combined both the physiological and theological versions of her inferior status, thus giving both historicist and essentialist justifications. The defences, at least until the seventeenth century, focused on the assertion and listing of female worthies who were used to prove that all women did not conform to the weak, dependent and dangerous models supplied by the attackers. Nevertheless, such women were always seen as exceptions. Another feature of the discourse was rhetorical experiment, in which a writer chose an extreme or ridiculous topic to argue, through which to demonstrate his argumentative and literary skill. Agrippa's *A treatise of the nobility and excellency of womankind* (pp. 264–6) is one example. Nonetheless, some of the language of these debates does provide a launching point for later feminists, and this is why he is included briefly here. None of these texts, therefore, should be considered feminist since their assertions belong to a specific literary game, nor do they consider how law, education, socialisation, language and custom constructed, maintained and encouraged the weaker version of woman.

Such a consideration, when it happened, could be called proto-feminism, and Rachel Speght's *A mouzell for Melastomus* (pp. 270–7) is one example. Her text was a response to a revival of the *querelle* during James I's reign, which reached its most vitriolic peak with the publication of *The arraignment of lewd, idle and froward women* by Joseph Swetnam in 1615. Speght uses some of the traditional rhetoric of the debate, including counter-arguments by listing good women from the Bible, and in the second half of her work (not included here) she attacks Swetnam. But she goes further than this, in that she rereads biblical texts, as many later women prophets do, to show that men have misread versions of the creation and of the Pauline epistles. Thus, although she also reiterates the injunction to subjection, and hence to our modern reading circumscribes her assertion of equality, she provides an articulate consciousness and the practice of rereading male-stream thought which later feminists will recognise. This is also a recognition inherent in the writing by the pseudonymous Jane Anger (pp. 266–8).

Pre-feminist arguments and thought can be discerned in four specific areas in this period. First, in the area of education and the debate about the 'nature' of women; second, in the incipient awareness of gender as a social construct; third, in the actual demands made by some petitioners to parliament in 1649; and fourth, in the frequent assertion of a community of women readers and writers with common interests, which are not simply biological.

Bathshua Makin (chapter 6), in the preface to her work pleading for a revival of education for women (1673) wrote:

Custom when it is inveterate, hath a mighty influence: it hath the force of nature itself. The barbarous custom to breed women low is grown general amongst us, and hath prevailed so far that it is verily believed (especially among a sort of debauched sots) that women are not endued with such reason as men, nor capable of improvement by education, as they are. It is looked upon as a monstrous thing to pretend the contrary. A learned woman is thought to be a comet, that bodes mischief whenever it appears. To offer to the world the liberal education of women is to deface the image of God in man, it will make woman so high and men so low, like fire in the house-top, it will set the whole world in a flame.

These things and worse than these, are commonly talked of, and verily believed by many who think themselves wise men: to contradict these is a bold attempt, where the attempter must expect to meet with much opposition. Therefore, ladies, I beg the candid opinion of your sex, whose interest I assert.

Here Makin argues a basic feminist premise, that education and socialisation have bred 'women low' and constructed the belief that their nature is lesser than man's, accompanied by a plea for educational provision to equalise men and women's socialisation. In addition, Makin here asserts a community of women with similar views, aims and needs. This is typical of many of the women writers represented in this collection. It suggests an incipient consciousness of a common agenda and a common experience for women which is not simply based on the oppositional strategies of the man versus woman debate of the *querelle des femmes*. Nevertheless, many of Makin's arguments, and those of Margaret Cavendish, particularly in her address to the two universities to whom she presents a copy of her work (pp. 286–9), are to be found in the earlier debate about women, represented here by the defences of women: Agrippa, Anger, Heale (chapter 4) and Speght (pp. 264, 266, 151, 270–7). Such arguments move from polarised rhetorical strategies to assertions of rights, based on an analysis of social and economic inequity (pp. 269–70).

The second area of importance is women writers' consciousness of the social construction of gender and the power relations dependent upon that: Elizabeth I's famous speech to her soldiers at Tilbury constructed a self of two genders: the weak body of a woman, but 'the heart and stomach' of a king and hence a man. Masculine and feminine are consciously associated with certain acquired characteristics: Behn and Cavendish (chapter 8 and this chapter, pp. 286–91) appropriate their 'masculine parts' in order to speak in public, thus asserting a belief in the social construction of gendered identity and practice. Austin, for example (pp. 277–9), asserts woman's incorporation into the term 'homo' as the basis for both temporal and spiritual equality; and the anonymous author of *Eliza's babes* (pp. 283–6) utilises a complex understanding of the economies of marriage in some of her poems, to assert her prior commitment to God.

The 1649 petition to parliament (pp. 280–3) was made, as were all petitions by women at that time, on behalf of male Levellers who had been imprisoned by Cromwell. Nevertheless, the right to petition and speak in public is strongly asserted by the women. They argue:

since we are assured of our creation in the image of God, and of an interest in Christ, equal unto men, as also for a proportionable share in the freedoms of this Commonwealth, we cannot but wonder and grieve that we should appear so despicable in your eyes, as to be thought unworthy to petition or represent our grievances to this honourable house.

Have we not an equal interest with men of this nation in those liberties and securities, contained in the petition of right, and other good laws of the land? Are any of our lives, limbs, liberties or goods to be taken from us more than from men, but by the due process of law and conviction of twelve sworn men of the neighbourhood?

Thus the language and social situation within which they position themselves is the language of equal rights: to law, to speak, to be tried, to petition. It is true that no women demand a vote, and that despite the proliferation of radical sects, such as the Levellers, none of these sects gave women any political rights:[3] but it is also possible to see this first articulation of legal and speaking rights by women to parliament as the first step towards such claims.

Finally, women writers of the period continually address themselves to women readers thus constructing and asserting communities of writing, speaking and listening women, with a common identity and a common agenda (see chapter 8). Although such a community was identifiably literate and elite during this period, this recognition of common experience (for example in the writings about motherhood and marriage) and a common history is the pre-condition for recognition of a common sociological identity. The preface of Lanyer's *Salve deus rex judaeorum* (pp. 268–70), as well as the whole poem (not included here), articulates such a communal self-consciousness.

Cornelius Agrippa, *A treatise of the nobility and excellency of woman-kind*

Agrippa's defence of women, although belonging to the *querelle des femmes* rhetorical tradition, contains the seeds of future assertions of women's identity and social value. Text from: the first edition, 1542, transl. David Clapham, fos A2ʳ–F5ʳ, G3.

Almighty God the maker and nourisher of all things, the father and goodness of both male and female, of his great bountifulness hath created mankind like unto himself, he made them man and woman. The diversity of which two kinds standeth only in the sundry situation of the bodily parts, in which the use of generation requireth a necessary difference. He hath given but one similitude and likeness of the soul to both male and female, between whose souls there is no manner difference of kind. The woman hath that same mind that a man hath, that same reason and speech, she goeth to the same end of blissfulness, where shall be no exception of kind. For after the evangelical truth, they that rise in their own proper kind shall not use the office of their kind, but the likeness of angels is promised unto them [Luke 20; Mark 12; Matt. 22]. And thus between man and woman by substance of the soul, one hath no higher preeminence of nobility above the other, but both of them naturally have equal liberty of dignity and worthiness. But all other things the which be in man besides the divine substance of the soul, in those things the excellency and noble womanhood in a manner infinitely doth excel the rude gross kind of men, the which thing we shall plainly prove to be true not with counterfeit and fair flattering words, nor also with the subtle sophisms of logic, wherewith many sophists were wont to blind and deceive men, but by the authority of most excellent auctors, and true writers of histories and with manifest reasons, yea with the testimonies of holy scripture and by the ordinances and constitutions of laws.

First to enter into this matter the woman is made so much more excellent than man, in how much the name that she hath received is more excellent than his. For Adam soundeth earth, but Eve is interpreted life: inasmuch as the life doth excel earth, so much the woman is to be preferred above the man.

* * *

Thou wilt say, that is now forbidden by laws, abolished by custom, extincted by education, for anon as a woman is born, even from her infancy, she is kept at home in idleness, and as though she were unmeet for any higher business: she is permitted to know no further than her needle and her thread. And then when she cometh to age, able to be married, she is delivered to the rule and governance of a jealous husband, or else she is perpetually shut up in a close nunnery. And all offices belonging to the commonweal be forbidden them by the laws. Nor it is not permitted to a woman, though she be very wise and prudent, to plead a cause before a judge. Furthermore, they be repelled in jurisdiction, in arbiterment,[4] in adoption, in intercession, in procuration, or to be guardians or tutors, in causes testamentary and criminal. Also they be repelled from preaching of God's word, against express and plain scripture, in which the Holy Ghost promised unto them by Joel the prophet, saying, *and your daughters shall prophesy and preach*, like as they taught openly in the time of the apostles, as it is well known that Anna, the widow of Simeon, the daughters of Philip and Priscilla, the wife of Aquila, did. But the unworthy delaying of the later law makers is so great that, breaking God's commandment to stablish their own traditions, they have pronounced openly that women otherwise in excellency of nature, dignity, and honour most noble, be in condition more vile than all men. And thus by these laws the women, being subdued as it were by force of arms, are constrained to give place to men and to obey their subduers, not by no natural, no divine necessity or reason, but by custom, education, fortune, and a certain tyrannical occasion.

Furthermore there be some men which by religion claim authority over women, and they prove their tyranny by holy scripture: the which have this cursed saying spoken to Eve continually in their mouth, *thou shalt be under the power of man, and he shall have lordship over thee*. But if it be answered unto them, that Christ took away that cursed saying, they will object again

PROTO-FEMINISMS

the words of Peter, with whom Paul agreeth, saying, *let women be in subjection of their husbands. Let women in the church keep silence.* But he that knoweth the divers figures of scripture and the effects of the same shall soon see that these things be not repugnant but in the rind. For this is the order in the church, that men in ministration shall be preferred before women: like as the Jews in promission are before the Greeks: yet nevertheless God is no exceptor of persons. For in Christ neither male nor female is of value, but a new creature.

Jane Anger her protection for women

Nothing is known about the pseudonymous author of this tract, nor about the tract to which she replies, other than her description of it on her title page as 'the scandalous reports of a late suffering lover, and all other like venerians that complained so to be over-cloyed with women's kindness'. This is the conclusion to her argument. Text from: the first edition, 1589, pp. 14–16.

I have set down unto you (which are of mine own sex) the subtle dealings of untrue meaning men: not that you should condemn all men, but to the end that you may take heed of the false hearts of all and still reprove the flattery which remains in all: for as it is reason that the hens should be served first, which both lay the eggs and hatch the chickens: so it were unreasonable that the cocks which tread them, should be kept clean without meat. As men are valiant so are they virtuous: and those that are born honourably, cannot bear horrible dissembling hearts. But as there are some which cannot love heartily, so there are many who lust uncessantly: and as many of them will deserve well, so most care not how ill they speed, so they may get our company. Wherein they resemble Envy, who will be contented to lose one of his eyes, that another might have both his pulled out. And therefore think well of as many as you may, love them that you have cause, hear every thing that they say (and afford them nods which make themselves noddies) but believe very little or nothing at all, and hate all those who shall speak any thing in the dispraise or to the dishonour of our sex.

Let the luxurious life of Heliogabalus, the intemperate desires of Commodus and Proculus, the damnable lust of Chilpericus and Xerxes, Boleslaus's violent ravishings, and the unnatural carnal appetites of Sigismundus Malotesta[5] be examples sufficiently probable to persuade you that the hearts of men are most desirous to excel in vice. There were many good laws established by the Romans, and other good kings, yet they could not restrain men from lechery: and there are terrible laws allotted in England to the offenders therein, all which will not serve to restrain man.

The surfeiters' physic is good, could he and his companions follow it, but when the fox preacheth let the geese take heed, it is before an execution. And

266

to kill that beast whose property is only to slay is no sin: if you will please men, you must follow their rule, which is to flatter, for fidelity and they are utter enemies. Things far fetched are excellent and that experience is best which cost most: crowns are costly and that which cost many crowns is well worth God thank you, or else I know who hath spent his labour and cost foolishly. Then if any man giveth such dear counsel gratefully, are not they fools which will refuse his liberality? I know you long to hear what that counsel should be, which was bought at so high a price. Wherefore if you listen, the surfeiter his pen with my hand shall forthwith show you.

At the end of men's fair promises there is a labyrinth and therefore ever hereafter stop your ears when they protest friendship, lest they come to an end before you are aware whereby you fall without redemption. The path which leadeth thereunto is man's wit, and the mile's ends are marked with these trees: Folly, Vice, Mischief, Lust, Deceit, and Pride. These to deceive you shall be clothed in the raiments of Fancy, Virtue, Modesty, Love, True-meaning and Handsomeness. Folly will bid you welcome on your way, and tell you his fancies concerning the profit which may come to you by this journey, and direct you to Vice, who is more crafty. He with a company of protestations will praise the virtues of women, showing how many ways men are beholden unto us, but our backs once turned he falls a railing. Then Mischief he pries into every corner of us, seeing if he can espy a cranny, that, getting in his finger into it, he may make it wide enough for his tongue to wag in. Now being come to Lust: he will fall a railing on lascivious looks, and will ban Lechery and with the collier will say, the Devil take him, though he never means it. Deceit will give you fair words, and pick your pockets: nay he will pluck out your hearts, if you be not wary. But when you hear one cry out against lawns, drawn-works, periwigs, against the attire of courtesans, and generally of the pride of all women: then know him for a wolf clothed in a sheep's raiment, and be sure you are fast by the Lake of Destruction. Therefore take heed of it, which you shall do if you shun men's flattery, the fore-runner of our undoing. If a jade be galled, will he not winch?[6] And can you find fault with a horse that springeth when it is spurred? The one will stand quietly when his back is healed, and the other go well when his smart ceaseth. You must bear with the old lover his surfeit, because he was diseased when he did write it, and peradventure hereafter, when he shall be well amended, he will repent himself of his slanderous speeches against our sex, and curse the dead man which was the cause of it, and make a public recantation: for the faltering in his speech at the latter end of his book affirmeth that already he half repenteth of his bargain. And why? Because his melody is past: but believe him not, though he should out swear you, for although a jade may still be in stable when his gall back is healed, yet he will show himself in his kind when he is travelling and man's flattery bites secretly, from which I pray God keep you and me too. Amen. Finis.

Aemilia Lanyer, *Salve deus rex judaeorum*

Lanyer's poem rereads the history of the Fall and Christ's life in a self-consciously revisionary way. This preface to the reader precedes dedicatory poems to all the eminent literary women patrons of the early Jacobean period. Text from: the first edition, 1611, fos F3ʳff.

To the virtuous reader

Often have I heard that it is the property of some women not only to emulate the virtues and perfections of the rest, but also by all their powers of ill-speaking to eclipse the brightness of their deserved fame. Now contrary to this custom, which men I hope unjustly lay to their charge, I have written this small volume, or little book for the general use of all virtuous ladies and gentlewomen of this kingdom; and in commendation of some particular persons of our own sex, such as for the most part are so well known to myself and others, that I dare undertake fame dares not to call any better. And this have I done to make known to the world that all women deserve not to be blamed, though some forgetting they are women themselves and in danger to be condemned by the words of their own mouths, fall into so great an error as to speak unadvisedly against the rest of their sex. Which if it be true, I am persuaded they can show their own imperfection in nothing more, and therefore could wish (for their own ease, modesties and credit) they would refer such points of folly to be practised by evil-disposed men, who forgetting they were born of women, nourished of women, and that if it were not by the means of women they would be quite extinguished out of the world and a final end of them all, do like vipers deface the wombs wherein they were bred, only to give way and utterance to their want of discretion and goodness. Such as these were they that dishonoured Christ, his apostles and prophets, putting them to shameful deaths. Therefore we are not to regard any imputations that they undeservedly lay upon us no otherwise than to make use of them to our own benefits, as spurs to virtue, making us fly all occasions that may colour their vain speeches to pass current. Especially considering that they have tempted even the patience of God himself, who gave power to wise and virtuous women, to bring down their pride and arrogancy. As was cruel Cesarus, by the discreet counsel of noble Deborah, judge and prophetess of Israel, and resolution of Jael, wife of Heber the Kenite; wicked Haman, by the divine prayers and prudent proceedings of beautiful Hester; blasphemous Holofernes by the invincible courage, rare wisdom and confident carriage of Judith; and the unjust judges by the innocency of the chaste Susannah: with infinite others, which for brevity's sake I will omit. As also in respect it pleased our Lord and saviour Jesus Christ, without the assistance of man, being free from original and all other sins, from the time of his conception till the hour of his death, to be begotten of a woman, born of a woman, nourished of a woman, obedient to a woman; and that he healed women, pardoned women, comforted women; yea, even when he was in his greatest agony and bloody sweat going to be crucified, and also in the last hour of his death took care to dispose of a woman; after his Resurrection, appeared first to a woman, sent a woman to declare his most glorious Resurrection to the rest of his disciples. Many other examples I could allege of divers faithful and virtuous women, who have in all ages, not only been confessors, but also endured most cruel martyrdom for their faith in Jesus Christ. All which is sufficient to enforce all good Christians and honourable minded men to speak reverently of our sex, and especially of all virtuous and good women. To the modest censures of both which, I refer these my imperfect endeavours, knowing that according to their own excellent dispositions, they will rather cherish, nourish, and increase the least spark of virtue where they find it, by their favourable and best interpretations, than quench it by wrong constructions. To whom I wish all increase of virtue, and desire their best opinions.

Daniel Tuvil, *Asylum veneris*

This work is a defence of women, part of the Jacobean *querelle des femmes* controversy. Text from: the first edition, 1616, pp. 137–62.

The epilogue

For howsoever Aristotle affirm that nature intendeth always to produce that which is most perfect and therefore willingly would still bring forth the male, counting females, it should seem, like those that are born blind and lame, or any other way defective, and prodigious errors and mistakings of her operations; howsoever likewise their adversaries would deprive them of that glorious character of God's divinity imprinted in the heart of man at his creation; because it is said in 1 *Cor.* 11:7. *that man is the image and glory of God; but woman is the glory of man*; and hereupon would conclude that their whole sex is but an ample demonstration of nature's craziness, and their own unworthiness. Plato yet maintains that if there be any distinction betwixt their sufficiency and ours, it is not essential but accidental, and such a one is grounded merely upon use. And therefore, saith he, as both the hands are by nature alike for all manner of actions, till application and employment bring in a difference of right and left, so women and men have in them the same aptitude and ability for the well managing of civil and military places, and it is exercise alone which begets dexterity in the one and the other. Which example he drew peradventure from the Pythagoreans, who divided all things into good and evil; and in the rank of those that were good, placed the right hand, the male, and that which was limited and finite: in the rank of those that were evil, the left hand, the female, and that which was infinite. But omitting this, his conclusion is that those bodies are most perfect and fitting for every action, which can of occasion require, as well apply their left hand to the business as their right: so is that commonwealth the most absolute which for good government can make use of women as well as men.

It is an axiom in schools, whereof no *quare* [inquiry] can be made, that, *substances admit not more or less*, wherefore as one stone cannot be said to be more a stone than another, so far as concerneth that essential form, which giveth a being to them both; no more can one man be said to be more perfectly man than another. And so by consequence the male shall not be thought more worthy than the female, in regard of his essence, because they be comprehended both under one kind: but if in anything he have the start, and advantage, it is merely by accident, and no way else. As concerning that fore-alleged position of Aristotle's, I confess it is true, that nature in the production of things doth continually mind the perfectest; and therefore intendeth the bringing forth of man in his kind, but not male more than female. Or if she should always produce the male, she should commit an extraordinary incongruity, because as from the body and the soul ariseth a compound more noble than his parts, which is man: so from the company of male and female doth redound likewise a compound, which is the only preserver of human generation, without which the parts would soon decay. Male and female therefore, are by nature always together, neither can the one exist without the other. One sex always is an argument of imperfection; and therefore the heathens did attribute both of them to God. Orpheus said of Jupiter that he was male and female. So that the graces and abilities which are in them, howsoever they may vary in outward traces and lineaments, are in form and substance the same with ours ... there is but one fortitude, one prudence, one justice.

Rachel Speght, *A mouzell for Melastomus*

Speght's tract in response to Swetnam's *The arraignment of lewd, froward and idle women*, and a volume of poetry are her only published work. She dedicates her text to 'all virtuous ladies'. Text from: the first edition, 1617, pp. 3–19.

Of woman's excellency, with the causes of her creation and
of the sympathy which ought to be in man and wife each
toward other

The work of creation being finished, this approbation thereof was given by God himself: that all was very good. If all, then woman who, excepting man, is the most excellent creature under the canopy of heaven. But if it be objected by any, first that woman, though created good, yet by giving ear to Satan's temptations brought death and misery upon all her posterity; secondly, that Adam was not deceived, but that the woman was deceived, and was in the transgression [1 Tim. 2:14]; thirdly that St Paul saith, it were good for a man not to touch a woman [1 Cor. 7:1]; fourthly and lastly, that of Solomon, who seems to speak against all our sex, *I have found one man of a thousand but a woman among them all have I not found* [Eccles. 7:30], whereof in it due place.

To the first of these objections I answer that Satan first assailed the woman, because where the hedge is lowest, most easy it is to get over, and she being the weaker vessel was with more facility to be seduced. Like as a crystal glass sooner receives a crack than a strong stone pot. Yet we shall find the offence of Adam and Eve almost to parallel: for as an ambitious desire of being made like unto God was the motive which caused her to eat, so likewise was it his; as may plainly appear by that ironica, *behold man is become as one of us* [Gen. 3:2]. Not that he was so indeed, but hereby his desire to attain a greater perfection than God had given him was reproved. Woman sinned, it is true, by her infidelity in not believing the word of God, but giving credit to Satan's fair promises *that she should not die* [Gen. 3:4]; but so did the man too. And if Adam had not approved of that deed which Eve had done, and been willing to tread the steps which she had gone, he being her head would have reproved her, and have made the commandment a bit to restrain him from breaking his master's injunction. For if a man burn his hand in the fire, the bellows that blowed the fire are not to be blamed, but himself rather for not being careful to avoid the danger. Yet if the bellows had not blowed, the fire had not burnt: no more is woman simply to be condemned for man's transgression. For by the free will which before the fall he enjoyed, he might have avoided and been free from being burned, or singed with that fire which was kindled by Satan and blown by Eve. It therefore served not his turn a whit, afterwards to say: *the woman which thou gavest me, gave me of the tree, and I did eat.* For a penalty was inflicted upon him as well as on the woman, the punishment of her transgression being particular to her own sex, and to none but the female kind: but for the sin of man the whole earth was cursed. And he being better able than the woman to have resisted temptation, because the stronger vessel, was first called to account to show that to whom much is given, of them much is required; and that he who was the sovereign of all creatures visible should have yielded greatest obedience to God.

True it is (as is already confessed) that woman first sinned, yet we find no mention of spiritual nakedness till man had sinned: then it is said, *their eyes were opened*, the eyes of their mind and conscience, and then perceived they themselves naked, that is, not only bereft of that integrity which they originally had, but felt the rebellion and disobedience of their members in the disordered motions of their now corrupt nature, which made them for shame cover their nakedness: then (and not afore) it is said that they saw it, as if sin were imperfect, and unable to bring a deprivation of a blessing received, or death on all mankind, till man (in whom lay the active power of generation) had transgressed. The offence therefore of Adam and Eve is by St Augustine thus distinguished: *the man sinned against God and himself, the woman against God, herself and her husband.* Yet in her giving of the fruit to eat had she no malicious intent towards him, but did therein show a desire to make her husband partaker of that happiness, which she thought by their eating they should both have enjoyed. This her giving Adam of that sauce, wherewith Satan had served her, whose sourness, afore he had eaten, she did not perceive, was that which made her sin to exceed his: wherefore that she might not of him, who ought to honour her, be abhorred, the first promise that was made in paradise, God makes to a woman: that by her seed should the serpent's head be broken: whereupon Adam calls her *Eve, life,* that as the woman had been an occasion of his sin, so should woman bring forth the saviour from sin, which was in fullness of time accomplished. By which was manifested that he is a saviour of believing women, no less than of men, that so the blame of sin may not be imputed to this creature, which is good, but to the will by which Eve sinned, and yet by Christ's assuming the shape of a man was it declared that his mercy was equivalent to both sexes, so that by Herod's blessed seed (as St Paul affirms) it is brought to pass, that *male and female are all one in Christ Jesus* [Gal. 3:28].

To the second objection I answer, that the apostle doth not hereby exempt man from sin, but only giveth to understand that the woman was the primary transgressor and not the man. But that man was not at all deceived was far from his meaning: for he afterward expressly saith, that *as in Adam all die, so in Christ shall all be made alive* [1 Cor. 15:22].

For the third objection, it is good for a man not to touch a woman, the apostle makes it not a positive prohibition, but speaks it only because of the Corinths's present necessity, who were then persecuted by the enemies of the church, for which cause, and no other, he saith, *art thou loosed from a wife? Seek not a wife*; meaning whilst the time of these perturbations should continue in their heat: *but if thou art bound, seek not to be loosed: if thou marriest, thou sinnest not, only increasest thy care: for the married careth for*

272

the things of this world, and I wish that you were without care that ye might cleave fast unto the Lord without separation: for the time remaineth that they which have wives be as though they had none. For the persecutors shall deprive you of them, either by imprisonment, banishment or death; so that manifest it is that the apostle doth not hereby forbid marriage, but only adviseth the Corinths to forbear a while, till God in mercy should curb the fury of their adversaries. For (as Eusebius writeth) Paul was afterward married himself, the which is very probable, being that interrogatively he saith, *have we not power to lead about a wife, being a sister, as well as the rest of the apostles, and as the brethren of the Lord and Cephas?*[1 Cor. 9:5].

The fourth and last objection is that of Solomon, *I have found one man among a thousand, but a woman among them all have I not found.* For answer of which, if we look into the story of his life, we shall find therein a commentary upon this enigmatical sentence included; for it is there said that Solomon had seven hundred wives and three hundred concubines, which number maketh one thousand [1 Kings 11:3]. These women turning his heart away from being perfect with the Lord his God, sufficient cause had he to say that among the said thousand women found he not one upright. He saith not that among a thousand women never any man found one worthy of commendation, but speaks in the first person singularly, *I have not found,* meaning in his own experience. For this assertion is to be holden a part of the confession of his former follies, and no otherwise, his repentance being the intended drift of *Ecclesiastes.*

Thus having (by God's assistance) removed those stones, whereat some have stumbled, others broken their shins, I will proceed toward the period of my intended task, which is to decipher the excellency of women: of whose creation I will for order's sake observe. First the efficient cause, which was God; secondly the material cause, or that whereof she was made; thirdly the formal cause, or fashion and proportion of her feature; fourthly and lastly the final cause, the end or purpose for which she was made. To begin with the first.

The efficient cause of women's creation was Jehovah the eternal, the truth of which is manifest in Moses his narration of the six days' works, where he saith, *God created them male and female* [Gen. 1:28]. And David exhorting all the earth *to sing unto the Lord,* meaning by a metonymy *earth,* all creatures that live on the earth, of what nation or sex soever, gives this reason: *for the Lord hath made us* [Psalm 100:3]. That work then cannot choose but be good, yea very good, which is wrought by so excellent a workman as the Lord: for he being a glorious creator, must needs effect a worthy creature. Bitter water cannot proceed from a pleasant sweet fountain, nor bad works from that workman which is perfectly good and in propriety none but he.

Secondly, the material cause or matter whereof woman was made was of a refined mould, if I may so speak: for man was created of the dust of the earth, but woman was made of a part of man after that he was a living soul: yet was she not produced from Adam's foot, to be his too low inferior; nor from his head to be his superior; but from his side, near his heart, to be his equal, that where he is lord she may be lady: and therefore saith God concerning man and woman jointly, *let them rule over the fish of the sea, and over the fowls of the heaven, and over every beast that moveth upon the earth*. By which words he makes their authority equal and all creatures to be in subjection unto them both. This being rightly considered doth teach men to make such account of their wives, as Adam did of Eve, *this is bone of my bone, flesh of my flesh* [Gen. 2:23]. As also, that they neither do or wish any more hurt unto them than unto their own bodies: for men ought to love their wives as themselves, because he that loves his wife, loves himself [Eph. 5:28]. And never a man hated his own flesh (which the woman is) unless a monster in nature.

Thirdly the formal cause, fashion and proportion of woman was excellent. For she was neither like the beasts of the earth, the fowls of the air, fishes of the sea, or any other inferior creature, but man was the only object which she did resemble. For as God gave man a lofty countenance, that he might look up toward heaven, so did he likewise give unto woman, and as the temperature of man's body is excellent, so is woman's. For whereas other creatures, by reason of their gross humours, have excrements for their habit, as fouls their feathers, beasts their hair, fishes their scales, man and woman only have their skins clear and smooth [Gen. 1:26]. And (that more is) in the image of God were they both created, yea and to be brief, all the parts of their bodies, both external and internal were correspondent and meet each for other.

Fourthly and lastly, the final cause, or end, for which woman was made, was to glorify God and to be a collateral companion for man to glorify God, in using her body, and all the parts, powers, and faculties thereof, as instruments for his honour: as with her voice to sound forth praises, like Miriam [Exod. 15:20], and the rest of her company; with her tongue not to utter words of strife, but to give good counsel unto her husband the which he must not despise. For Abraham was bidden to give ear to Sarah his wife [Gen. 21:12]. Pilate was willed by his wife not to have any hand in the condemning of Christ, and a sin it was in him that he listened not to her [Matt. 27:19]: Leah and Rachel counselled Jacob to do according to the word of the Lord [Gen. 31:16]: and the Shunamite put her husband in mind of harbouring the prophet Elisha [2 Kings 4:9]: her hands should be open according to her ability in contributing towards God's service, and distressed servants like to that poor widow, which cast two mites into the treasury; and as Mary Magdalene, Susannah and Joanna, the wife of Herod's steward

[Luke 8], with many others which of their substance ministered unto Christ. Her heart should be a receptacle for God's word, like Mary that treasured up the sayings of Christ in her heart [Luke 1:51]. Her feet should be swift in going to seek the Lord in his sanctuary, as Mary Magdalene made haste to seek Christ at his sepulchre. Finally no power external or internal ought woman to keep idle, but to employ it in some service of God, to the glory of her creator, and comfort of her own soul.

The other end for which woman was made was to be a companion and helper for man and if she must be a helper, and but a helper, then are those husbands to be blamed which lay the whole burthen of domestical affairs and maintenance on the shoulders of their wives. For, as yoke-fellows they are to sustain part of each other's cares, griefs, and calamities. But as if two oxen be put in one yoke, the one being bigger than the other, the greater bears most weight, so the husband being the stronger vessel is to bear a greater burthen than his wife. And therefore the Lord said to Adam, *in the sweat of thy face shalt thou eat thy bread till thou return to the dust* [Gen. 3:19]. And St Paul saith *that he that provideth not for his household is worse than an infidel* [1 Tim. 5:8]. Nature hath taught senseless creatures to help one another, as the male pigeon when his hen is weary with sitting on her eggs and comes off them, supplies her place that in her absence they may receive no harm, until such time as she is fully refreshed.... Seeing then that these unreasonable creatures, by the instinct of nature, bear such affection to each other that without any grudge they willingly, according to their kind, help one another, I may reason *a minore ad maius* [*from a minor premise to a major one*], that much more should man and woman, which are reasonable creatures, be helpers each to other in all things lawful, they having the law of God to guide them, his word to be a lanthorn unto their feet and a light unto their paths, by which they are excited to a far more mutual participation of each other's burdens, than other creatures. So that neither the wife may say to her husband, nor the husband unto his wife, *I have no need of thee*, no more than the members of the body may so say to each other, between whom there is such a sympathy, that if one member suffer all suffer with it. Therefore though God bade Abraham forsake his country and kindred, yet he bade him not forsake his wife, who being flesh of his flesh and bone of his bone, was to be co-partner with him of whatsoever did betide him, whether joy or sorrow. Wherefore Solomon saith, *woe to him that is alone* [Eccles. 4:10]; for when thoughts of discomfort, troubles of this world, and fear of dangers do possess him, he wants a companion to lift him up from the pit of perplexity into which he is fallen. For a good wife, saith Plautus, is the wealth of the mind, and the welfare of the heart; and therefore a meet associate for her husband; and *woman*, saith Paul, *is the glory of the man* [1 Cor. 11:7] ...

So husbands should not account their wives as their vassals, but as those that are heirs together of the grace of life, and with all lenity and mild persuasions set their feet in the right way if they happen to tread awry, bearing with their infirmities, as Elkanah did with his wife's barrenness [1 Sam. 1:17].

The kingdom of God is compared unto the marriage of a king's son: John calleth the conjunction of Christ and his chosen a marriage [Matt. 22; Rev. 19:7]: and not few but many times, doth our blessed saviour in the canticles set forth his unspeakable love towards his church under the title of an husband rejoicing with his wife; and often vouchsafeth to call her his sister and spouse, by which is showed that with *God is no respect of persons* [Rom. 2:11], nations or sexes. For whosoever, whether it be man or woman, *that doth believe in the Lord Jesus, such shall be saved* [John 3:18]. And if God's love, even from the beginning, had not been as great towards woman as to man, then would he not have preserved from the deluge of the old world as many women as men, nor would Christ after his resurrection have appeared unto a woman first of all other, had it not been to declare thereby that the benefits of his death and resurrection are as available by belief for women as for men: for he indifferently died for the one sex as for the other. Yet a truth ungainsayable is it that the *man is the woman's head* [1 Cor. 11:3], by which title yet of supremacy, no authority hath he given him to domineer or basely command and employ his wife as a servant: but hereby is he taught the duties which he oweth unto her. For as the head of a man is the imaginer and contriver of projects profitable for the safety of his whole body; so the husband must protect and defend his wife from injuries. For he is *her head, as Christ is the head of the Church*, which he entirely loveth, and for which he gave his very life, the dearest thing any man hath in this world. *Greater love than this hath no man, that he bestoweth his life for his friend* [John 15:13], saith our Saviour. This precedent passeth all other patterns, it requireth great benignity and enjoineth an extraordinary affection, *for men must love their wives, even as Christ loved his church.* Secondly, as the head doth not jar or contend with the members, which be man, as the apostle saith, *yet make but one body* [1 Cor. 12:20]; no more must the husband with the wife, but expelling all bitterness and cruelty he must live with her lovingly, and religiously, honouring her as the weaker vessel. Thirdly and lastly, as he is her head, he must by instruction bring her to the knowledge of her creator that so she may be a fit stone for the Lord's building [1 Cor. 14:35]. Women for this end must have an especial care to set their affections upon such as are able to teach them, that as they *grow in years, they may grow in grace and in the knowledge of Christ Jesus our lord* [1 Pet. 3:18].

Thus, if men would remember the duties they are to perform in being heads, some would not stand a tip-toe as they do thinking themselves lords and rulers, and account every omission of performing whatsoever they command, whether lawful or not, to be matter of great disparagement and indignity done them. Whereas they should consider that women are enjoined to submit themselves unto their husbands no otherways than as to the Lord, so that from hence, for man, there ariseth a lesson not to be forgotten, that as the Lord commandeth nothing to be done but that which is right and good, no more must the husband; for if a wife fulfil the evil command of her husband, she obeys him as a tempter, as Saphira did Ananias [Acts 5:2]. But lest I should seem too partial in praising women so much as I have (though no more than warrant from scripture doth allow) I add to these premises that I say not all women are virtuous, for then they should be more excellent than men, sith of Adam's sons there was Cain as well as Abel, and of Noah's, Cham as well as Sem: so that of men as of women, there are two sorts, namely good and bad, which in *Matthew* the five and twenty chapter, are comprehended under the name sheep and goats. And if women were not sinful, then should they not need a saviour, but the virgin Mary, a pattern of piety, *rejoiced in God her saviour* [Luke 1:47], ergo she was a sinner. In the *Revelation* the church is called the spouse of Christ; and in *Zachariah* wickedness is called a woman [Zach. 5:7] to show that of women there are both godly and ungodly. For Christ would not purge his floor if there were not chaff among the wheat, nor should gold need to be fined if among it there were no dross. But far be it from anyone to condemn the righteous with the wicked, or good women with the bad (as the baiter[7] of women hath done). For though there are some scabbed sheep in a flock, we must not therefore conclude all the rest to be mangy. And though some men, through excess, abuse God's creatures, we must not imagine that all men are gluttons: the which we may with as good reason do as condemn all women in general for the offences of some particulars. Of the good sort is it that I have in this book spoken, and so would I that all that read it should so understand me: for if otherwise I had done, I should have incurred that woe, which by the prophet Isaiah, is pronounced against them that *speak well of evil* and should have *justified the wicked, which thing is abominable to the Lord* [Prov.17:15].

William Austin, *Haec homo*

Austin's title proclaims its message: using a feminine demonstrative adjective with the male 'homo', he indicates woman's inclusion in the legal and public liberties accorded man ('homo'). The work was issued by his executors, one of whom was his wife, after his death. Text from: the first edition, 1637, pp. 1–6.

The omnipotent in the beginning created all things for man, and until all things were made fit and convenient for him, he was not made: but when they had received their ornaments, then was brought forth this admirable creature (the image of his creator), who was so excellently composed that his maker had not only given him, *a face upward*, but, *a mind inward* to behold the heavens and all under them, *homo ad contemplandum creatorem suum creatus est* [*man was created to contemplate the creator*], saith Gregory. Certainly one would think that, to the making of so divine a creature, some extraordinary matter collected out of the quintessences of the celestial spheres ought to be prepared. One would scarcely believe (but that it is written where is no falsehood) that the base earth were his best apparel: nay worse, not earth, but dust (the very contemptible dust) which the least wind blows away.

But, when we behold his daily carriage, his pride and haughtiness, with what disdain he not only condemns his inferior creatures, but such as were created equal with him: we may judge him either to be made of better stuff than we have heard of, or that he very much forgets his beginning.

He was not made of heaven nor in heaven, but in earth and of dust amongst (his fellow creatures) the beasts of the field: of the same mettle, in the same place and in the same day with them.

What should make him so proud as to despise and, with so many sought-for words, condemn woman (his other self)? Doubtless it proceeds from his ignorance or forgetfulness, in that he knows not, or will not remember, his low beginnings (even out of the dust), and had need to hear this sentence again from heaven oftener than rain upon him, *nosce teipsum* [*know thyself*]. Otherwise he would not esteem so unworthily of woman, which is his other half and part of his own bodily substance. It shows as if a man should love his head, and hate his brains: is not she he? Examine and you shall find small difference.

As first, for name: though (for necessary distinction sake) they were created male and female and two bodies: yet all (in one word) makes but *homo*, one man. Which very word, Cicero (the most eloquent of his time) thought no barbarism to bestow upon a woman, and a virtuous lady, when (remembering his commendations to her in an epistle to her husband) he calls her *homo singularis pudicitiae ac pietatis* [*a man of singular chastity and piety*].

In the sex is all the difference, which is but only in the body. For she hath the same reasonable soul, and in that there is neither hes nor shes, neither excellency nor superiority: she hath the same soul, the same mind, the same understanding, and tends to the same end of eternal salvation that he doth. In which there is no exception of sex, persons or nation: but (in the resurrection) she shall (without exception of sex) obtain like body with him according to the similitude of angels: for they were bought at the same price and shall dwell in the same glory.

She hath not only the same name with him; but they are both of one figure, made by one workman of one substance in one place in one day, so that there is no such general difference between them that can give excuse to man to esteem basely and meanly of her but that he must needs (therein) touch himself, since she was made coequal with him, and so like him. Notwithstanding, there may be observed some nice differences between them in their creation: but indeed they are such as rather much increase her praise, than detract the least scruple from her worth and excellency.

Jane Owen, *An antidote against purgatory*

Owen aims to persuade Catholic women of the need to perform good works, in order to avoid, or minimise, a stay in purgatory. She envisages spiritual and earthly independence for widows and single women, in contradistinction to her description of marriage. Text from: the first edition, 1634, pp. 178–86.

But before I end this passage I will turn my pen, but withal gentle and soften in part my style, in respect of the persons to which I will direct these few ensuing lines. To you then (great Catholic ladies) and other Catholic gentlewomen of worth (to whom in regard of my sex, I may be the more bold to speak freely) whose present widowed states by reason of your deceased husbands, stand enriched with more than ordinary affluency (during your lives) of lands, money, and other temporal goods: you I say (noble ladies and others of worth) though you be weak in nature, yet know your own strength, and what great matters during your widowhoods you are able, through God's assistance to perform, for the freeing you from the flames of purgatory: and remember that howsoever the niceness and delicacy of divers of you be such, as that in this world you can brook nothing displeasing to you: yet in the next world, admitting you die in state of salvation, you must infallibly undergo those horrible flames (so much spoken of in these leaves) except by your charitableness (and this in a most full degree) you redeem those pains.

Oh, what good works might you do during your widowhood? And yet, I fear, you are most forgetful therein. Many of you (I know) are ready to bestow a hundred marks, or more, upon one gown; and that gown must not serve two years, but another (as chargeable) must instantly be had. Again, some of you will be content to lose a hundred marks or more, in one night at Gleek;[8] and will wear about your necks jewels worth many hundreds of pounds.

Oh, cut[9] of these needless and fruitless charges and bestow a good part thereof upon your souls with the preciousness of good and satisfying works, though your bodies in part be deprived of such glorious ornaments. There is none of you but, besides your greater sins, you daily commit lesser sins: for it is said in holy writ, *Prov. 24, The just man shall fall seven times a day.* How many idle and unnecessary thoughts and words pass from you, but in one day? And yet you must make satisfaction for every such thought or word, either here or in purgatory, before you can arrive to heaven. For it is said, *Prov. 19. They shall render an account of every idle word, in the day of judgement.*

Now then in time of your widowhoods, lay out a great part of your riches to spiritual usury (as I may term it) for the good of your souls. I did know a good gentlewoman, now dead, she was left by her deceased father two thousand pounds and better, in portion. She intended to marry (and so before her death she did) yet before she would subject herself, and her state to any man (besides divers good acts before) she gave at one time (I speak of certain and particular knowledge) three hundred pounds of her portion away, to the bringing up of poor scholars beyond the seas; saying thus to herself, *if I shall be content to enthral myself, and seventeen hundred pounds at least, to the will of a stranger, who I know not how he will use me: have I not reason to give three hundred pounds away to my own soul, for his sake, who will not suffer a cup of cold water given in his name, to be unrewarded?*

This is an example worthy of your taking notice of, thereby to put you in mind, to remember to prevent the flames of purgatory during the time of your widowhoods. For if you be not solicitous thereof before your second marriage, when your states are in your own disposal; it is much to be feared that your future husbands will bridle you of all such (though most necessary) charges. This example may also be worthily a precedent for all other young Catholic gentlewomen of great portions, to provide for the good of their souls before they tie themselves in marriage to anyone.

Well (worthy ladies) let a woman once preach to women, and since you are women, imitate that blessed woman so much celebrated for her charity to others, in God's holy writ, *Prov. 31 she opened her hands to those that wanted, and stretched out her arms to the poor*; and thereupon it followeth of her in the said word of God, *and she shall laugh at the last day.* That is, at the day of her death she shall rejoice: and so (noble ladies and others) it is in your power (if yourselves will) to enjoy the like felicity and retaliation for your works of charity, with her. And with this I give a full close to this my exhortative discourse.

To the supreme authority of England, the commons assembled in parliament

This petition aimed to secure the release of various Leveller prisoners. Text from: the first edition, 1649.

*The humble petition of divers well-affected women of the
cities of London and Westminster, the Borough of
Southwark, hamlets and parts adjacent. Affecters and
approvers of the petition of September 11, 1648*

Showeth that since we are assured of our creation in the image of God and
of an interest in Christ equal unto men, as also for a proportionable share in
the freedoms of this Commonwealth, we cannot but wonder and grieve that
we should appear so despicable in your eyes, as to be thought unworthy to
petition or represent our grievances to this honourable house.

Have we not an equal interest with men of this nation in those liberties and
securities, contained in the Petition of Right, and other good laws of the
land? Are any of our lives, limbs, liberties or goods to be taken from us more
than from men, but by the due process of law and conviction of twelve sworn
men of the neighbourhood?

And can you imagine us to be so sottish or stupid, as not to perceive or
not to be sensible when daily those strong defences of our peace and welfare
are broken, and trod underfoot by force and arbitrary power?

Would you have us keep at home in our houses, when men of such
faithfulness and integrity as the four prisoners our friends in the tower, are
fetched out of their beds and forced from their houses by soldiers, to the
affrighting and undoing of themselves, their wives, children and families? Are
not our husbands, our selves, our children and families by the same rule as
liable to the like unjust cruelties as they?

Shall such men as Capt. Bray be made close prisoners and such as Mr
Sawyer snatched up and carried away, beaten and buffeted at the pleasure of
some officers of the army; and such as Mr Blanck kept close prisoner, and
after most barbarous usage be forced to run the gantlop,[10] and be most slave-
like and cruelly whipped; and must be kept at home in our houses, as if we
our lives and liberties and all were not concerned?

Nay shall such valiant religious men as Mr Robert Lockyer be liable to law
martial and be judged by his adversaries, and most unhumanly shot to death?
Shall the blood of war be shed in time of peace? Doth not the word of God
expressly condemn it? Doth not the Petition of Right declare that no person
ought to be judged by law martial (except in time of war) and that all
commissions given to execute martial law in time of peace are contrary to the
laws and statutes of the land? Doth not Sir Edward Coke in his chapter of
murder in the third part of his Institutes, hold it for good law (and since
owned and published by this parliament) that for a general or other officers
of an army in time of peace, to put any man (although a soldier) to death by
colour of martial law, it is absolute murder in that general? And hath it not
by this house in the case of the late Earl of Strafford been adjudged high

treason? And are we Christians, and shall we sit still and keep at home, while such men as have born continual testimony against the unjustice of all times, and unrighteousness of men, be picked out and be delivered up to the slaughter and yet must we show no sense of their sufferings, no tenderness of affections, no bowels of compassion, nor bear any testimony against so abominable cruelty and injustice?

Have such men as these continually hazarded their lives, spent their estates and time, lost their liberties, and thought nothing too precious for defence of us, our lives and liberties, been as a guard by day and a watch by night; and when for thus they are in trouble and greatest danger, persecuted and hated even to the death; and should we be so basely ungrateful, as to neglect them in the day of their affliction? No, far be it from us: let it be accounted folly, presumption, madness, or whatsoever in us, whilst we have life and breath, we will never leave them, or forsake them, nor ever cease to importune you (having yet so much hopes of you, as of the unjust judge, mentioned *Luke* 18, to obtain justice, if not for justice's sake, yet for importunity) or to use any other means for the enlargement and reparation of those of them that live; and for justice against such, as have been the cause of Mr Lockyer's death: nor will we ever rest until we have prevailed, that we, our husbands, children, friends, servants, may not be liable to be thus abused, violated, and butchered at men's wills and pleasures. But if nothing will satisfy but the blood of those just men, those constant undaunted asserters of the people's freedom will satisfy your thirst: drink also and be glutted with our blood and let us fall together. Take the blood of one more, and take all: stay one, stay all.

And therefore again, we entreat you to review our last petition in behalf of our friends above mentioned, and not to slight the things therein contained, because they are presented unto you by the weak hand of women, it being an usual thing with God, by weak means to work mighty effects. For we are no whit satisfied with the answer you gave unto our husbands and friends, but do equally with them remain liable to those snares laid in your declaration which maketh the abettors of the book, laid to our friends' charge, no less than traitors, when as hardly any discourse can be touching the affairs of the present times, but falls within compass of that book! So that all liberty of discourse is thereby utterly taken away, than which there can be no greater slavery.

Nor shall we be satisfied, however you deal with our friends, except you free them from under their present extra-judicial imprisonment and force upon them, and give them full reparations for their forceable attachment, &c. And leave them from first to last to be proceeded against by due process of law, and give them respect from you, answerable to their good and faithful service to the Commonwealth.

Our houses being worse than prisons to us, and our lives worse than death, the sight of our husbands and children, matter of grief and sorrow and affliction to us, until you grant our desires, and therefore, if ever you intend any good to this miserable nation, harden not your hearts against petitions, nor deny us in things so evidently just and reasonable, as you would not be dishonourable to all posterity.

Eliza's Babes

The poems here redefine woman's role on earth through faith. Text from: the first edition, 1652, pp. 31, 42, 43, 45, 100–1.

The Bride

Sith you me ask, why born was I?
I'll tell you: 'twas to heaven to fly,
Not here to live a slavish life,
By being to the world a wife.

When I was born I was set free,
From mortals' thraldom here to be;
For that great Prince prepared a bride,
That for my love on earth here died.

May not I then earth's thraldom scorn,
Sith for heaven's prince I here was born?
If match'd in heaven I wear a crown,
But earthly thraldom pulls me down.

On Marriage

Lord! If thou hast ordain'd for me,
That I on earth must married be:
As often I have been foretold,
Be not thy will, by me, controlled.
And if my heart thou dost incline
Children to have, Lord make them thine,
Or never let 't be said they're mine.
I shall not like what's not divine.
I no ambition have for earth,
My thoughts are of a higher birth,
The soul's sweet *Babes* do bring no pain,
And they immortalise the name.

283

The Gift

My Lord hast thou given me away?
Did I on earth, for a gift stay?
Hath he by prayer of thee gain'd me,
Who was so strictly knit to thee?

To thee I only gave my heart,
Wouldst thou my Lord from that gift part?
I know thou wouldst deliver me
To none, but one belov'd by thee.

But Lord my heart thou dost not give,
Though here on earth while I do live
My body here he may retain,
My heart in heaven, with thee must reign.

Then as thy gift let him think me,
Sith I a donage am from thee.
And let him know thou hast my heart,
He only hath my earthly part.

It was my glory I was free,
And subject here to none but thee,
And still that glory I shall hold
If thou my spirit dost infold.

It is my bliss, I here serve thee,
'Tis my great joy: thou lovest me.

The Change

Great God!
How hast thou chang'd my thoughts in me,
For when I thought to be a wife,
I then did think troubled to be,
Because I saw most live in strife.

But thou a husband hast given me,
Whose sweet discretion doth direct,
And orders all things so for me,
As if of heaven he were elect.

To take all trouble quite from me,
That earth's possession here doth bring,

And so doth leave me quite to thee,
Thy praises here to sit and sing.

Not a Husband, though never so excelling in goodness to us,
must detain our desires from heaven

My heart I find upon her wings,
Ready to flee from earthly things.
But that the virtue lives in thee,
On earth a while retaineth me.

Not that of life I weary am,
For what on earth here wish I can,
From heaven's great prince receive I do.
I must most freely tell to you.

Great blessings from him I enjoy,
And with him I have no annoy.
Yet these must not retain my heart,
Another of me claims his part.

To heaven's great prince I must away,
No love on earth must here me stay.
He lent me but awhile to you,
And now I must bid you adieu.

The royal priesthood

Peace! Present now no more to me (to take my spirit from the height of
felicity) that I am a creature of a weaker sex, a woman. For my God! If I must
live after the example of thy blessed apostle, I must live by faith, and faith
makes things to come as present, and thou hast said by thy servant, that we
shall be like thy blessed son: then wilt thou make all thy people as kings and
priests, kings are men and men are kings; and souls have no sex; the hidden
man of the heart makes us capable of being kings; for I have heard that it is
that within makes the man: then are we by election capable of as great dignity
as a mortal man. But thoughts of mortals! Now adieu; I will close the eyes
of my soul to mortality, and will not open them but to eternity; seeing that
by thy grace and faith in thee, thou hast made us partaker of thy divine
nature, by thy assistance I will live in faith; I will no more now see myself
as mortal, but as an immortal king will I begin to live, that hidden man never
dies, but when my immortal king, that placest me in this kingdom of felicity
with him, shall see it fit time, he will raise me on a triumphant chariot,

composed of the wings of bright angels, to his immortal kingdom of glory, where I shall reign with him for all eternity, and never more desire to change. And as a royal priest must I be to thee; ever offering up the sweet incense of my praises to the divine Majesty, for thy infinite mercies to me, thy unworthy servant.

Margaret Cavendish, *The philosophical and physical opinions*

Cavendish's work articulates varying positions in relation to the constraints or otherwise upon women. The preface to this work is one place where she suggests that education and socialisation constrain all women. Text from: the first edition, 1655, fos A4^r–B2^r.

But to answer those objections that are made against me, as first how should I come by so much experience as I have expressed in my several books to have? I answer: I have had by relation the long and much experience of my lord, who hath lived to see and be in many changes of fortune and to converse with many men of sundry nations, ages, qualities, tempers, capacities, abilities, wits, humours, fashions and customs.

And as many others, especially wives, go from church to church, from ball to ball, from collation to collation, gossiping from house to house, so when my lord admits me to his company I listen with attention to his edifying discourse and I govern myself by his doctrine: I dance a measure with the muses, feast with sciences, or sit and discourse with the arts.

The second is that, since I am no scholar, I cannot know the names and terms of art and the divers and several opinions of several authors. I answer: that I must have been a natural fool if I had not known and learnt them, for they are customarily taught all children from their nurse's breast, being ordinarily discoursed of in every family that is of quality, and the family from whence I sprung are neither natural idiots or ignorant fools, but the contrary, for they were rational, learned, understanding and witty.

And when I said I never conversed an hour with professed philosophers, for indeed in this age I have not heard of many which do profess it, or an intimate acquaintance or familiar conversation with professed scholars, nor so much discourse as to learn from them, for three or four visits do not make an intimacy, nor familiarity, nor can much be learned therefrom. For visiting and entertaining discourse, for the most part, are either cautionary, frivolous, vain, idle, or at least but common and ordinary matter, and most commonly all visiting discourses are after one and the same manner, although the company be several; but I did not think my readers would have been so rigid as to think I excluded my husbands, brothers and the rest of my family, neither are they professed philosophers nor scholars, although they are learned therein; or to believe I was so ridiculously foolish, or so foolishly vain, or so basely false, as that I strive to make the world believe I had all my experience and knowledge before I was born, and that my native language came by instinct, and that I was never taught my A,B,C; or the marks and names of several things. But I hope my book hath more spiteful enemies than faults, for I have said in an epistle before the second part of my *Olio*,[11] that if I had never seen nor heard so much as I have done, should never have been able to have writ a book.

Thirdly, that I had taken feathers out of the universities to enlarge the wings of my fancy. I answer: no more than David took the wool from his sheep's backs to clothe his poetical fancies or devotion, or as I may say his devout poetry which is dressed with simulising.[12]

But it hath been known in several ages, that even poor peasants that hear nothing but the bleating of sheep, the lowering of herds, the crowing of cocks, and the like, and their ordinary discourses of nothing but of the market, or the like, have been high-flying poets, politic statesmen, wise governors, prudent soldiers, subtle philosophers, excellent physicians, and what not, even to be eloquent orators, and divine preachers, as the holy writ will make manifest to us, and I believe many more are mentioned in other histories of less authority. Thus we may observe that nature is prevalent in all qualities and conditions and since nature is so generous to distribute to those that fortune hath cast out and education hath neglected, why should my readers mistrust nature should be sparing to me, who have been honourably born, carefully bred, and nobly married to a wise man ... as I have said in some of my epistles, in my book called the *World's Olio* ...

Likewise an objection for my saying I have not read many books: but I answer for not reading of many authors, had I understood several languages, as I do not, I have not had so much time, had I endeavoured to have been learned therein, for learning requires close studies, long time and labour.

Besides, our sex takes so much delight in dressing and adorning themselves, as we for the most part make our gowns our books, our laces our lines, our embroideries our letters, and our dressings are the times of our studies, and instead of turning over solid leaves, we turn our hair into curls, and our sex is as ambitious to show themselves to the eyes of the world when finely dressed, as scholars do to express their learning to the ears of the world when fully fraught with authors.

But as I have said my head was so full of my own natural fantasies, as it had not room for strangers to board therein, and certainly natural reason is a better tutor than education. For though education doth help natural reason to a more sudden maturity, yet natural reason was the first educator: for natural reason did first compose commonwealths, invented arts and sciences, and if natural reason have composed, invented and discovered, I know no reason but natural reason may find out what natural reason hath composed, invented and discovered without the help of education . . .

To the two universities

Most famously learned,

I here present the sum of my works, not that I think wise schoolmen and industrious, laborious students should value my book for any worth, but to receive it without a scorn for the good encouragement of our sex, lest in time we should grow irrational as idiots by the dejectedness of our spirits, through the careless neglects and despisements of the masculine sex to the effeminate, thinking it impossible we should have either learning or understanding, wit or judgement, as if we had not rational souls as well as men and we out of a custom of dejectedness think so too, which makes us quit all: all industry towards profitable knowledge being employed only in low and petty employments, which takes away not only our abilities towards arts, but higher capacities in speculations, so as we are become like worms that only live in the dull earth of ignorance, winding ourselves sometimes out by the help of some refreshing rain of good education, which seldom is given to us: for we are kept like birds in cages to hop up and down in our houses, not suffered to fly abroad to see the several changes of fortune and the various humours, ordained and created by nature. Thus, wanting the experiences of nature, we must needs want the understanding and knowledge and so consequently prudence of men: thus, by an opinion which I hope is but an erroneous one in men, we are shut out of all power and authority by reason we are never employed either in civil nor martial affairs, our counsels are despised and laughed at, the best of our actions are trodden down with scorn, by the over-weaning conceit men have of themselves and through a despisement of us.

But I considering with myself, that if a right judgement and a true understanding and a respectful civility live anywhere, it must be in learned universities, where nature is best known, where truth is oftenest found, where civility is most practised, and if I find not a resentment here, I am very confident I shall find it nowhere, neither shall I think I deserve it if you approve not of me, but if I deserve not praise I am sure to receive so much courtship from this sage society as to bury me in silence: thus I may have a quiet grave, since not worthy a famous memory: but to lie entombed under the dust of a university will be honour enough for me, and more than if I were worshipped by the vulgar as a deity. Wherefore if your wisdoms cannot give me the bays, let your charity strew me with cypress, and who knows but after my honourable burial, I may have a glorious resurrection in following ages, since time brings strange and unusual things to pass, I mean unusual to men, though not in nature: and I hope this action of mine is not unnatural, though unusual for a woman to present a book to the university; nor impudence, for the action is honest, although it seem vain-glorious: but if it be, I am to be pardoned, since there is little difference between man and beast, but what ambition and glory makes.

Poulain de la Barre, *The woman as good as the man, of the equality of both sexes*

Poulain de la Barre's text was first published in France in 1672. Text from: the first English edition, 1677, transl. A.L., pp. 145ff.

God willing to produce men in dependence, one upon another by the concourse of two persons, for that end framed two bodies which were different, each was perfect in its kind, and they ought both to be disposed as they are at present, and all that depends on their particular constitution ought to be considered as making a part of their perfection.

It is then without reason that some imagine that women are not so perfect as men and that they look upon that (in them) as a defect, which is an essential portion of their sex: without the which it would be useless for the end for which it hath been formed: which begins and ceases with fecundity, and which is destined for the most excellent use of the world: that is, to frame and nourish us in their bellies.

The two sexes (together) are necessary to beget the like: and if we knew how it is that ours contributes thereto, we would find enough to be said against ourselves. It is hard to be understood upon what they ground themselves, who maintain that men are more noble than women in regard of children, since it is properly women who conceive us, form us, and give us life, birth and breeding. It is true, they pay dearer for it than we, but their pain and trouble ought not to be prejudicial to them and draw upon them contempt in place of esteem, which they thereby deserve.

Who would say that fathers and mothers (who labour to bring up their children good princes to govern their subjects, and magistrates to render them justice) are less estimable than they whose aid and assistance they use for to discharge themselves of their duties?

There are some physicians who have mightily enlarged themselves upon the temperament of sexes to the disadvantage of women; and have pursued their discourses out of sight to show that their sex ought to have a constitution altogether different from ours, which renders it inferior in all things. But their reasons are only light conjectures which come into the heads of such as judge things only by prejudice and upon simple appearances.

When they perceive the two sexes more distinguished by that which regards the civil than particular, they fancy to themselves that so they ought to be; and not discerning exactly enough betwixt that which proceeds from custom and education and that which comes from nature, they have attributed to one and the same cause all which they see in society, imagining that when God created man and woman, he disposed them in such a manner as ought to produce all distinction which we observe betwixt them.

This is to carry too far the difference of sexes: it ought to be bounded by design, which God hath had to form men, by the concourse of two persons, and no more to be admitted but what is necessary for that effect.

NOTES

INTRODUCTION

1 Hull (1982) and Lewalski (1993): 1–13 for a summary of recent work which queries Hull's model.
2 Davis (1975): 131–42.
3 Kelly (1977): 137.
4 Stephen Greenblatt's title term in his book (1980) which analyses the discourses of early modern masculine fashioning.
5 See Ferguson (1985); Graham *et al.* (1989); Greer *et al.* (1988); Travitsky (1989); and Wilson and Warnke (1987, 1989) for anthologies of women's writing. The ongoing Brown University project to publish new editions of all women writers prior to 1800 will eventually provide more accessible texts.
6 Amussen (1988); Brant and Purkiss (1992); Brink *et al.* (1989); Davis (1975); Quaife (1979); Underdown (1985); Wrightson (1982).
7 For example: Brant and Purkiss (1992); Brink *et al.* (1989); Butler (1990); Ferguson *et al.* (1986); Gallagher (1988); Hinds (1992); Hutner (1993); Purkiss (1992); and Wiseman (1992).

1 THEOLOGY

1 See Crawford (1985): 211ff; and Cardinale and Smith (1990) for a complete bibliographic list.
2 See this volume, chs 8 and 9; and Beilin (1987); Brant and Purkiss (1992); Haselkorne and Travitsky (1990); Hobby (1988); Krontiris (1992); and Lewalski (1993).
3 See Collinson (1984): 169–94, who points out that prosecutions for the fine were rare.
4 See Coster (1990): 377–87; Crawford (1993b); Thomas (1973): 43.
5 Wilson (1990): 68–107.
6 See Collinson (1984); Ingram (1988); Underdown (1985).
7 Menstruation.

291

8 Curt and snappish.

9 Separates.

10 He suggests the women might be guilty of witchcraft.

2 PHYSIOLOGY

1 Translated from the 1631 edition.

2 See O'Brien (1981) and Spelman (1982): 109–31 for critiques of this biological and binary underpinning of Western thought.

3 See Crawford (1981).

4 See Smith (1976).

5 See Eccles (1982); Horowitz (1987); and Maclean (1980): 38.

6 See Crawford (1993b): 82ff; Laqueur (1990): chs 2 and 3; Shiebinger (1989): ch. 6.

7 A fourth-century medical writer.

8 Partly digested food.

9 Johann Vesalingius's *Anatomy in English* (1653) was the first anatomy in English to include Harvey's theory of the circulation of the blood.

10 Jean Riolan and Lazar Riverius were the standard continental authorities on anatomy and medicine.

11 The labia minora.

12 The penis.

13 Testicles.

14 Realdo Columbo was a sixteenth-century anatomist.

15 A term used to describe any disease which produced vaginal discharge.

16 Hiccuping.

17 A fold in the peritoneum and alimentary canal: here used to mean abdominal obstructions.

18 French physician (1492–1558) who wrote on physiology.

19 The foreskin.

3 CONDUCT

1 See Wright (1958); Spufford (1981); Hull (1982).

2 Jocelyn, ch. 6, pp. 183–6; Grymestone, ch. 4, pp. 114–15; and Leigh, this ch., pp. 98–100.

3 See Pollock (1989) for a clear examination of how women were taught to internalise the messages of conduct literature, and how aware contemporary society was about gendered attributes and their appropriateness or otherwise to each sex.

4 As Jones (1987) does. It is important to note, however, that even the texts which construct an essential identity imperceptibly slide between physio-

logical inferiority and exhortations to behavioural norms. All these discourses suggest therefore the fluidity of gender identity.

5 See Powell (1917); Stone (1977); Kelso (1956); Jones (1990).

6 George (1973); Davies (1981).

7 See Stone (1965).

8 See the introduction to chapter 9; and Henderson and McManus (1985).

9 Seldom (arch.).

10 Stuttering.

11 Flax.

12 Madness.

13 An idol or grotesque doll.

14 Indulgence.

15 Joannes Damascens (c. 676–749), one of the later Christian Fathers.

16 One of the Christian Fathers who wrote a conduct book for women, *The appearance of women*.

17 Cyprian's *Libro de habitu virginum* was much cited by Renaissance commentators. Vives' work also uses it.

18 Gaudy.

19 Fisticuffs.

20 Indulge.

4 SEXUALITY AND MOTHERHOOD

1 See A. McLaren (1984) and Eccles (1982).

2 See Quaife (1979) and Crawford (1990).

3 See Fildes (1990) which suggests a thriving sense of feminine communities surrounding motherhood.

4 See Thomas (1959) and Crawford (1990) on the double standard; and Whateley (ch. 1) and Gouge (ch. 5) on 'conscionable subjection'.

5 See Traub (1992): 150 and Hobby (1992): 186–202.

6 False idols.

7 Bread- or meat-board.

8 Worthless fellows.

9 Pursued.

10 The wife of the fifth king of Rome, who after his death trained her son up in the arts of government.

11 Their mother was Cornelia, frequently cited for educating them. They both became Tribunes, see Suetonius.

12 Socrates' mother.

13 Obsolete form of rick.

14 Pleased.

15 In this period the sin of Onan was premature withdrawal from sexual inter-

course, for contraceptive purposes.

16 A common meadow flower.

17 Two deep veins in the leg.

18 Eryngo is the candied root of the sea holly, formerly used as a sweetmeat and thought to be an aphrodisiac. Satyrion is the name given to various plants in the orchid family, due to their supposedly aphrodisiacal qualities.

19 Menstruation.

20 Pubic bone.

5 POLITICS AND LAW

1 Cited in Levine (1982): 109.

2 See Kantorowitz (1959); Axton (1977); and Jordan (1990): ch. 2.

3 See Hogrefe (1972): 97–105.

4 For accounts of such women see Cahn (1987); Graham *et al.* (1989); George (1988); Fraser (1984).

5 See Cioni (1982): 159–82.

6 See Thomas (1958).

7 Angry.

8 Testing and proving.

9 Embellish.

10 Scevola (140–82 BC) wrote a treatise on Roman civil law.

11 See figure 6 in this collection.

12 Aristotle, *Physics* 2.

13 A court of record held locally.

14 Robber.

15 Feoffor is one who according to feudal land law grants freehold land in fee: that is with conditions of homage or service.

16 Beyond the age to require a guardian.

17 Presumably a legal commentator: he has not been traced.

18 Not dissolved.

19 The degrees of consanguinity allowed for marriage, set out in Leviticus 18: 1–18.

20 Dwelling.

21 Surrenders her tenancy rights to him.

22 An Italian Jesuit political theorist of the late sixteenth century.

23 The Ten Commandments.

6 EDUCATION

1 See Henderson and McManus (1985); Gardiner (1929); Kamm (1965).

2 Gardiner (1929): 1–13; Grafton and Jardine (1986); O'Day (1982).

3 See Watson (1912) and Kelly (1977) for a critique of Watson's optimistic reading of the humanist educational treatises.
4 See Warnicke (1983).
5 See Gardiner (1929).
6 See Cressy (1982) *passim* for literacy figures and Spufford (1979) for an analysis of the separation of writing and reading literacy.
7 Defile.
8 Bowls of booze (obs.).
9 More often.
10 Effectual.
11 That of men.
12 Training.
13 Wares.
14 In other words, if she is well born.
15 Rank.
16 A medieval musical instrument, like an oboe.
17 A neckerchief worn in the seventeenth century.
18 A species of baboon.
19 During the Civil War.
20 Drawing.

7 WORK

1 See Middleton (1985): 130–40.
2 Prior (1985) and Weisner (1993).
3 See Clark (1919).
4 Wright (1958).
5 Vann (1977): 192–216.
6 The kite.
7 Polecats.
8 Sieved.
9 Spring.
10 Pantry.
11 Dusty corners.
12 Boiling up salt water for making salt.
13 A worthless fellow.
14 Make gossip.
15 Coal scuttle: hence, figuratively, household finances.
16 Servant.
17 Not in the *OED*: it appears to mean curds and whey.
18 Whispering.
19 Labourers.

20 Wooden.

21 A vessel to hold liquor.

22 Chicken.

23 To make a horse prance.

24 Fermented bread dough.

25 The commentators listed here are all continental medical authorities.

26 Expel from the chest.

27 Feeds.

28 Arguments.

29 Polyphemus was the one-eyed giant in *The Odyssey*.

30 Diseased with the pox, caught after succumbing to the heat of lust.

31 Nightcaps.

32 A hood.

33 Various neck wear.

34 A band or collar.

35 Pillow-case.

36 Lavatory.

37 Those which encourage phlegm, the warm and moist humour in Galenic humoral physiology.

38 Mallow, a vegetable substance used as a binding agent.

39 To bend and make into a hedge.

40 Axels.

41 Ancient Jewish religious order.

42 The physician who attacked her father.

43 Blood-letting as a medical philosophy and practice.

44 Confined to bed as an invalid.

45 Medicines producing sweating.

8 WRITING AND SPEAKING

1 Hull (1982); Hobby (1988); Lewalski (1993); Crawford (1985); and Cardinale and Smith (1990).

2 Hobby and Crawford, *op.cit.*

3 Graham *et al.* (1989).

4 See Amussen (1988); Davis (1975); Underdown (1985).

5 Hull (1982): 1–31.

6 Readers who wish to make easy reference to additional prefaces where women's views on speaking and writing are represented should look at Travitsky (1989).

7 See King (1982): 138–44.

8 See O'Brien (1981) and Friedman (1987).

9 Gracefully intelligent.

10 In *The mirror of princely deeds*.

11 Fearful.

12 Fraudster.

13 A coarse material made of silk and wool.

14 Coarse woollen material.

15 Scolding.

16 The Greek at the siege of Troy who could shout as loudly as fifty men.

17 Bespoke (rare).

18 One of the daughters of Danae, who unlike her sisters did not kill her husband on their wedding night.

19 The codified law of the Franks, who migrated from Germany to France. Their laws on women's behaviour were particularly strict.

20 They take the meaning metaphorically, meaning *revealed*, a rereading of the conventional reading of 'covered', and proceed to interpret 'woman' as weakness, and therefore unsexed.

21 That is, give weight to respect and rank in society.

22 Printing.

9 PROTO-FEMINISMS

1 Jones (1990): 192–4; Smith (1982).

2 See Henderson and McManus (1985): 1–42; Jordan (1990): 1–11; Kelly (1984); Maclean (1980): 1–6; Woodbridge (1984): 1–9.

3 Thomas (1958).

4 The right to make legal decisions (obs).

5 Counter-assertions of evil men.

6 Kick.

7 Joseph Swetnam.

8 A popular card game.

9 Cut back on.

10 A military punishment, involving being whipped without a shirt.

11 Her work *The world's olio*.

12 Feigning (obs.).

SELECT SECONDARY
BIBLIOGRAPHY

Amussen, S. (1988). *An Ordered Society: Gender and Class in Early Modern England*. Oxford: Basil Blackwell.

Axton, M. (1977). *The Queen's Two Bodies: Drama and the Elizabethan Succession*. London: Royal Historical Society.

Bashir, N. (1983). 'Rape in England between 1550 and 1700'. In London Feminist History Group, *The Sexual Dynamics of History*. London: Pluto Press.

Beilin, E. (1987). *Redeeming Eve: Women Writers of the English Renaissance*. Princeton: Princeton University Press.

Bennet, J. (1988). 'History that Stands Still: Women's Work in the European Past', *Feminist Studies* 14: 269–83.

Boulton, J. (1990). 'London Widowhood Revisited: The Decline of Female Remarriage in the Seventeenth and Early Eighteenth Centuries', *Continuity and Change* 5: 323–55.

Boxer, M. and Quataert, J. (eds) (1987). *Connecting Spheres: Women in the Western World, 1500 to the Present*. Oxford: Oxford University Press.

Brant, C. and Purkiss, D. (eds) (1992). *Women, Texts and Histories: 1575–1760*. London: Routledge.

Brink, J. (1980). 'Bathsua Makin: Educator and Linguist', in ed. *Female Scholars: A Tradition of Learned Women before 1800*: 86–100. Montreal: Eden Press.

———, Coudert. A. and Horowitz, M. (eds) (1989). *The Politics of Gender in Early Modern Europe*. Sixteenth-Century Essays and Studies. 12.

Butler, J. (1990). *Gender Trouble: Feminism and the Subversion of Identity*. New York: Routledge.

Cahn, S. (1987). *Industry of Devotion: The Transformation of Women's Work in England 1500–1660*. New York: Columbia University Press.

Cardinale, S. and Smith, H. (1990). *Women and the Literature of the Seventeenth Century: An Annotated Bibliography Based on Wing's Short-Title Catalogue*. New York: Greenwood Press.

Cioni, M. (1982). 'The Elizabethan Chancery and Women's Rights'. In D. Guth and J. McKenna (eds), *Tudor Rule and Revolution: Essays for G.R. Elton and His American Friends*: 159–82. Cambridge: Cambridge University Press.

Clark, Alice (1919, 1992). *Working Life of Women in the Seventeenth Century*, with a new introduction by Amy Louise Erickson. London: Routledge.

Cohen, A. (1984). 'Prophecy and Madness: Women Visionaries During the Puritan Revolution', *Journal of Psychiatry* 11: 411–30.

Cole, F. (1930). *Early Theories of Sexual Generation*. Oxford: Oxford University Press.

Collinson, P. (1967). *The Elizabethan Puritan Movement*. London: Methuen.

——— (1984). 'The Elizabethan Church and the New Religion'. In C. Haigh (ed.), *The Reign of Elizabeth I*: 169–94. London: Macmillan.

Coster, W. (1990). 'Purity and Puritanism: The Churching of Women 1500–1700'. In W. Sheils *et al.* (eds), *Women in the Church: Studies in Church History* 27: 377–87. Oxford: Basil Blackwell.

Crawford, P. (1981). 'Attitudes to Menstruation in Seventeenth-Century England', *Past and Present* 91: 47–73.

——— (1985). 'Women's Published Writings 1600–1700'. In M. Prior (ed.), *Women in English Society 1500–1800*: 211–82. London: Methuen.

——— (1986). 'The Suckling Child: Adult Attitudes to Childcare in the First Year of Life in Seventeenth-Century England', *Continuity and Change* 1: 23–51.

——— (1990). 'The Construction and Experience of Maternity in Seventeenth-Century England'. In V. Fildes (ed.), *Women as Mothers in Pre-Industrial England*: 3–38. London: Routledge.

——— (1993a). *Women and Religion in England 1500–1700*. London: Routledge.

——— (1993b). 'Sexual Knowledge in England: 1500–1750'. In R. Porter and M. Teich (eds), *Sexual Knowledge, Sexual Science: The History of Attitudes to Sexuality*: 82–106. Cambridge: Cambridge University Press.

Cressy, D. (1982). *Literacy and the Social Order*. Cambridge: Cambridge University Press.

Davies, K. (1981). 'Continuity and Change in Literary Advice on Marriage'. In R. Outhwaite (ed.), *Marriage and Society: Studies in the Social History of Marriage*: 58–80. London: Europa.

Davis, Natalie Zemon (1975). *Society and Culture in Early Modern France*: 124–51. Stanford: Stanford University Press.

Dekker, R. and van de Pol, L. (1989). *The Tradition of Female Transvestism in Early Modern Europe*. London: Macmillan.

Eales, J. (1990). 'Samuel Clarke and the Lives of Godly Women in Seventeenth-Century England'. In W. Sheils *et al.* (eds), *Women in the Church: Studies in Church History* 27: 365–87. Oxford: Basil Blackwell.

Eccles, A. (1982). *Obstetrics and Gynaecology in Tudor and Stuart England*. London: Croom Helm.

Ehrenreich, B. and English, D. (1973). *Witches, Midwives and Nurses*. Detroit, Mich.: Black & Red.

Erickson, A.L. (1994). *Women and Property in Early Modern England*. London: Routledge.

Ezell, M. (1987). *The Patriarch's Wife: Literary Evidence and the History of the Family*. Chapel Hill: University of Carolina Press.

Ferguson, Margaret, Quilligan, M. and Vickers, N. (eds) (1986). *Rewriting the Renaissance: The Discourses of Sexual Difference in Early Modern Europe*. Chicago: University of Chicago Press.

Ferguson, Moira (1985). *First Feminists: British Women Writers 1578–1799*. Bloomington, Ind.: Indiana University Press.

Fildes, V. (1986). *Breasts, Bottles and Babies: A History of Infant Feeding*. Edinburgh: Edinburgh University Press.

——— (ed.) (1990). *Women as Mothers in Pre-Industrial England*. London: Routledge.

Fitz, L. (1980). 'What Says the Married Woman? Marriage Theory and Feminism in the English Renaissance', *Mosaic* 13: 1–22.

Forbes, T. (1964). 'The Regulation of English Midwives in the Sixteenth and Seventeenth Centuries', *Medical History* 8: 235–44.

——— (1962). 'Midwifery and Witchcraft', *Journal of the History of Medicine* 17: 264–83.

Fraser, A. (1984). *The Weaker Vessel: Woman's Lot in Seventeenth-Century England*. London: Weidenfeld & Nicolson.

Friedman, A. (1985). 'The Influence of Humanism on the Education of Girls and Boys in Tudor England', *History of Education Quarterly* 25 (1985): 57–70.

Friedman, S. Stanford (1987). 'Creativity and the Childbirth Metaphor', *Feminist Studies* 13: 49–82.

Gallagher, C. (1988). 'Embracing the Absolute: The Politics of the Female Subject in Seventeenth-Century England', *Genders* 1: 24–39.

Gardiner, D. (1929). *English Girlhood at School: A Study of Women's Education through Twelve Centuries*. Oxford: Oxford University Press.

George, M. (1973). 'From "Goodwife" to "Mistress": The Transformation of the Female in Bourgeois Culture', *Science and Society*: 152–77.

—— (1988). *Women in the First Capitalist Society: Experiences in Seventeenth-Century England*. Chicago: University of Illinois Press.

Grafton, A. and Jardine, L. (1986). *From Humanism to the Humanities: Education and the Liberal Arts in Fifteenth-Century and Sixteenth-Century Europe*. Cambridge, Mass.: Harvard University Press.

Graham, E., Hinds, H., Hobby, E. and Wilcox, H. (eds) (1989). *Her Own Life: Autobiographical Writings by Seventeenth-Century Englishwomen*. London: Routledge.

Greaves, R. (ed.) (1985a). *Triumph over Silence: Women in Protestant History*. New York: Greenwood Press.

—— (1985b). 'Foundation Builders: The Role of Women in Early English Nonconformity'. In *Triumph Over Silence: Women in Protestant History*: 75–92. New York: Greenwood Press.

Green, L. (1979). 'The Education of Women in the Renaissance', *History of Education Quarterly* 19: 93–116.

Greenblatt, S. (1980). *Renaissance Self-Fashioning*. Chicago: University of Chicago Press.

Greer, G., Hastings, S., Medoff, J. and Sansone, M. (eds) (1988). *Kissing the Rod: An Anthology of Seventeenth-Century Women's Verse*. London: Virago.

Haller, W. and M. (1941). 'The Puritan Art of Love', *Huntington Library Bulletin* 5: 235–72.

Hamilton, R. (1978). *The Liberation of Women: A Study of Patriarchy and Capitalism*. London: Allen & Unwin.

Hanley, D. (1981). 'Ignorant Midwives: A Persistent Stereotype', *Society for the History of Medicine Bulletin*, 28: 6–9.

Hannay, M. (1985). *Silent but for the Word: Tudor Women as Writers, Patrons and Translators of Religious Works*. Kent, OH.: Kent State University Press.

Harvey, E. (1992). *Ventriloquized Voices: Feminist Theory and Renaissance Texts*. London: Routledge.

Haselkorne, A. and Travitsky, B. (eds) (1990). *The Renaissance Englishwoman in Print: Counterbalancing the Canon*. Amherst: University of Massachusetts Press.

Henderson, K. Usher and McManus, B. (1985). *Half Humankind: Contexts and Texts of the Controversy about Women in England 1540–1640*. Urbana: University of Illinois Press.

Hill, B. (1987). 'A Refuge from Men: The Idea of a Protestant Nunnery', *Past and Present* 117: 107–30.

Hinds, H. (1992). '"Who May Bind Where God Hath Loosed?" Responses to Sectarian Women's Writing in the Second Half of the Seventeenth Century'. In S. Cerasano and M. Wynne-Davies (eds), *Gloriana's Face: Women, Public and Private in the English Renaissance*: 205–27. Hemel Hempstead: Harvester Wheatsheaf.

Hobby, E. (1988). *Virtue of Necessity: English Women's Writing 1649–88*. London: Virago.

——— (1992). 'Katherine Philips: Seventeenth-Century Lesbian Poet'. In ed. *What Lesbians Do in Books*: 183–204. London: The Women's Press.

Hogrefe, P. (1972). 'Legal Rights of Tudor Women and their Circumvention by Men and Women', *The Sixteenth Century Journal* 3: 97–105.

Horowitz, M. (1987). 'The Science of Embryology before the Discovery of the Ovum'. In M. Boxer and J. Quataert (eds), *Connecting Spheres: Women in the Western World, 1500 to the Present*: 86–94. Oxford: Oxford University Press.

Houlbrooke, R. (1984). *The English Family 1450–1700*. London and New York: Longman.

Hull, S. (1982). *Chaste, Silent and Obedient: English Books for Women 1475–1640*. San Marino: The Huntington Library.

Hutner, H. (1993). *Rereading Aphra Behn: History, Theory and Criticism*. Charlottesville: University Press of Virginia.

Ingram, M. (1988). *Church Courts, Sex and Marriage in England 1570–1640*. Cambridge: Cambridge University Press.

Jones, A.R. (1987). '"Nets and Bridles": Early Modern Conduct Books and Sixteenth-Century Women's Lyrics'. In N. Armstrong and L. Tennenhouse (eds), *The Ideology of Conduct: Essays on Literature and the History of Sexuality*: 39–72. New York and London: Methuen.

Jones, Vivien. (1990). *Women in the Eighteenth Century: Constructions of Femininity*. London: Routledge.

Jordan, C. (1983). 'Feminism and the Humanists: The Case of Sir Thomas Elyot's Defence of Good Women', *Renaissance Quarterly* 36: 181–201.

——— (1990). *Renaissance Feminism: Literary Texts and Political Models*. Ithaca, N.Y.: Cornell University Press.

Kamm, J. (1965). *Hope Deferred: Girls' Education in English History*. London: Methuen.

Kantorowitz, E. (1959). *The King's Two Bodies*. Princeton, N.J.: Princeton University Press.

Kelly, J. (1977). 'Did Women Have a Renaissance?'. In R. Bridenthal and C. Koonz (eds), *Becoming Visible: Women in European History*. Boston, Mass.: Houghton Mifflin.

——— (1984). 'Early Feminist Theory and the *Querelle des Femmes*, 1400–1789'. In *Women, History and Theory*: 65–109. Chicago and London: Chicago University Press.

Kelso, R. (1956). *Doctrine for the Lady in the Renaissance*, Urbana: University of Illinois Press.

Kermode, J. and Walker, G. (eds) (1994). *Women, Crime and the Courts in Early Modern England*. London: University College of London Press.

King, J. (1982). *English Reformation Literature: The Tudor Origins of the Protestant Tradition*. Princeton, N.J.: Princeton University Press.

Klein, J. Larson. (1992). *Daughters, Wives and Widows: Writings by Men about Women and Marriage in England, 1500–1640*. Chicago: University of Illinois Press.

Krontiris, T. (1992). *Oppositional Voices: Women as Writers and Translators of Literature in the English Renaissance*. London: Routledge.

Kusinoki, A. (1992). 'Their Testaments at Their Apron Strings: The Representation of Puritan Women in Early Seventeenth-Century England'. In S. Cerasano and M. Wynne-Davies (eds), *Gloriana's Face: Women, Public and Private in the English Renaissance*: 185–204. Hemel Hempstead: Harvester Wheatsheaf.

Lake, P. (1987). 'Feminine Piety and Personal Potency: The Emancipation of Mrs. Jane Radcliffe', *The Seventeenth Century* 1: 143–65.

Laqueur, T. (1990). *Making Sex: Body and Gender from the Greeks to Freud.* Cambridge, Mass.: Harvard University Press.

Lawrence, A. (1990). '"A Priesthood of She-Believers": Women and Congregations in Mid-Seventeenth Century England'. In W. Shiels *et al.* (eds) *Women in the Church: Studies in Church History* 27: 345–63. Oxford: Basil Blackwell.

Leites, E. (1982). 'The Duty to Desire: Love, Friendship and Sexuality in some Puritan Theories of Marriage', *Journal of Social History* 15: 383–408.

Levine, M. (1982). 'The Place of Women in Tudor Government'. In D. Guth and J. McKenna (eds), *Tudor Rule and Revolution: Essays for G.R. Elton and His American Friends*: 109–23. Cambridge: Cambridge University Press.

Lewalski, B. (1993). *Writing Women in Jacobean England.* Cambridge, Mass.: Harvard University Press.

Lucas, R.V. (1990). 'Puritan Preaching and the Politics of the Family'. In A. Haselkorne and B. Travitsky (eds), *The Renaissance Englishwoman in Print: Counterbalancing the Canon*: 224–40. Amherst: University of Massachusetts Press, 1990.

Ludlow, D. (1985). 'Shaking Patriarchy's Foundations: Sectarian Women in England 1641–1700'. In R. Greaves, *Triumph Over Silence: Women in Protestant History*: 93–123. New York: Greenwood Press.

McArthur, E. (1909). 'Women Petitioners of the Long Parliament', *English Historical Review* 24: 698–709.

Macfarlane, A. (1986). *Marriage and Love in England. Modes of Reproduction 1300–1800.* Oxford: Basil Blackwell.

Mack, P. (1982). 'Women as Prophets during the English Civil War', *Feminist Studies* 8: 19–45.

—— (1988) 'The Prophet and her Audience: Gender and Knowledge in the World Turned Upside Down'. In G. Eley and W. Hunt (eds), *Reviving the English Revolution: Reflections and Elaborations on the Work of Christopher Hill*: 139–52. London: Verso.

—— (1991). 'Teaching about Gender and Spirituality in Early English Quakerism', *Women's Studies*, 19: 223–37.

—— (1992). *Visionary Women: Ecstatic Prophecy in Seventeenth-Century England.* Berkeley: University of California Press.

McLaren, A. (1984). *Reproductive Rituals: The Perception of Fertility in England from the Sixteenth Century to the Nineteenth Century.* London and New York: Methuen.

McLaren, D. (1979). 'Nature's Contraceptive: Wet Nursing and Prolonged Lactation: The Case of Chesham, Buckinghamshire', *Medical History* 23: 426–41.

—— (1985). 'Marital Fertility and Lactation 1520–1720'. In M. Prior (ed.), *Women in English Society 1500–1800*: 22–53. London: Methuen.

Maclean, I. (1980). *The Renaissance Notion of Woman: A Study in the Fortunes of Scholasticism and Medical Science in European Intellectual Life*, Cambridge: Cambridge University Press.

McMullen, N. (1977). 'The Education of English Gentlewomen, 1540–1640', *History of Education* 6: 87–101.

Marland. H. (ed.) (1993). *The Art of Midwifery: Early Modern Midwives in Europe.* London: Routledge.

Marshall Wyntjes, S. (1977). 'Women in the Reformation Era'. In R. Bridenthal and C. Koontz (eds), *Becoming Visible: Women in European History*: 165–91. Boston, Mass.: Houghton Mifflin.

Mendelson, S. (1985). 'Stuart Women's Diaries and Occasional Memoirs'. In M. Prior (ed.), *Women in English Society 1500–1800*: 181–210. London: Methuen.

Middleton, C. (1985). 'Women's Labour and the Transition to Pre-Industrial Capitalism'. In L. Charles and L. Duffin (eds), *Women and Work in Pre-*

Industrial England: 181–206. London: Croom Helm.

O'Brien, M. (1981). *The Politics of Reproduction*. London: Routledge.

O'Day, R. (1982). *Education and Society 1500–1800: The Social Foundations of Education in Early Modern Britain*. London: Longman.

Pollock, L. (1989). '"Teach Her to Live Under Obedience": The Making of Women in the Upper Ranks of Early Modern England', *Continuity and Change* 4: 231–58.

—— (1990). '"Embarking on a Rough Passage": The Experience of Pregnancy in Early Modern Society'. In V. Fildes, *Women as Mothers in Pre-Industrial England*: 39–67. London: Routledge.

Powell, C. (1917). *English Domestic Relations 1487–1653: A Study of Matrimony and Family Life*. New York: Columbia University Press.

Prest, W.R. (1991). 'The Law and Women's Rights in Early Modern England', *The Seventeenth Century* 6: 169–87.

Prior, M. (1985). 'Reviled and Crucified Marriages: The Position of Tudor Bishops'. In ed. *Women in English Society 1500–1800*: 118–48. London: Methuen.

Purkiss, D. (1992). 'Producing the Voice, Consuming the Body: Women Prophets of the Seventeenth Century'. In I. Grundy and S. Wiseman, *Women, Writing, History 1640–1740*: 139–58. Batsford.

Quaife, G.R. (1979). *Wanton Wenches and Wayward Wives: Peasants and Illicit Sex in Early Seventeenth-Century England*. London: Croom Helm.

Ranum, P. and O. (1994). *Popular Attitudes towards Birth Control in Pre-Industrial France and England*. London: Harper Row.

Roberts, M. (1985). '"Words they Are Women and Deeds they Are Men": Images of Work and Gender in Early Modern Europe'. In L. Charles and L. Duffin (eds), *Women and Work in Pre-Industrial England*: 122–80. London: Croom Helm.

Rowlands, M. (1985). 'Recusant Women 1560–1640'. In M. Prior (ed.), *Women in English Society 1500–1800*: 149–80. London: Methuen.

Schochet, G. (1975). *Patriarchalism in Political Thought*. Oxford: Basil Blackwell.

Schofield, R. (1985). 'English Marriage Patterns Revisited', *Journal of Family History* 10: 2–20.

Shakespeare, J. and Dowling, M. (1982). 'Religion and Politics in Mid-Tudor England Through the Eyes of an English Protestant Woman: The Recollections of Rose Hickman', *Bulletin of the Institute of Historical Research* 55: 94–102.

Shiebinger, L. (1989). *The Mind Has No Sex? Women in the Origins of Modern Science*, Boston, Mass.: Harvard University Press.

Smith, H. (1976). 'Gynaecology and Ideology in Seventeenth-Century England'. In Berenice Carrol (ed.), *Liberating Women's History: Theoretical and Critical Essays*: 97–114. Urbana: University of Illinois Press.

—— (1982). *Reason's Disciples: Seventeenth-Century English Feminists*. Urbana: University of Illinois Press.

Spelman, A. (1982). 'Woman as Body: Ancient and Contemporary Views', *Feminist Studies* 8: 109–31.

Spufford, M. (1979). 'First Steps in Literacy: The Reading and Writing Experiences of the Humblest Seventeenth-Century Spiritual Autobiographies', *Social History* 4: 407–35.

—— (1981). *Small Books and Pleasant Histories: Popular Fiction and Its Readership in Seventeenth-Century England*. Cambridge: Cambridge University Press.

Stone, L. (1965). *The Crisis of the Aristocracy*. Oxford: Oxford University Press.

—— (1977). *The Family, Sex and Marriage in England 1500–1800*. London: Weidenfeld and Nicolson.

Stopes, C. (1894). *British Freewomen: Their Historical Privileges*. London: Swan Sonneschein.

Teague, F. (1992). 'Queen Elizabeth in Her Speeches'. In S. Cerasano and M. Wynne-

Davies (eds), *Gloriana's Face: Women, Public and Private in the English Renaissance*: 63–78. Hemel Hempstead: Harvester Wheatsheaf.

Thomas, K. (1958). 'Women and the Civil War Sects', *Past and Present* 13: 42–62.

—— (1959). 'The Double Standard', *Journal of the History of Ideas* 20: 195–216.

—— (1973). *Religion and the Decline of Magic*. Harmondsworth: Penguin.

Traub, V. (1992). 'The (In)significance of Lesbian Desire in Early Modern England'. In Susan Zimmerman (ed.), *Erotic Politics: Desire on the Renaissance Stage*: 150–69.

Travitsky, B. (1980). 'The New Mother of the English Renaissance: Her Writings on Motherhood'. In C. Davidson and E. Broner (eds), *The Lost Tradition: Mothers and Daughters in Literature*: 33–43. New York: Frederick Unger.

—— (1989). *The Paradise of Women: Writings by Englishwomen of the Renaissance*. New York and Oxford: Columbia University Press.

Underdown, D. (1985). *Revel, Riot, and Rebellion: Popular Politics and Culture in England, 1603–1660*. Oxford: Oxford University Press.

Vann, R. (1977). 'Toward a New Life: Women in Pre-Industrial Capitalism'. In R. Bridenthal and C. Koonz (eds), *Becoming Visible: Women in European History*: 192–216. Boston: Houghton Mifflin.

Waller, G. (1985). 'Struggling into Discourse: The Emergence of Renaissance Women's Writing'. In M. Hannay (ed.), *Silent but for the Word: Tudor Women as Writers, Patrons and Translators of Religious Works*: 238–91. Kent, OH: Kent State University Press.

Warnicke, R. (1983). *Women of the English Renaissance and Reformation*. New York: Greenwood Press.

Watson, Foster (1912). *Vives and the Renaissance Instruction of Women*. London: Edward Arnold.

Wiesner, M. (1987). 'Women's Work in the Changing City Economy 1500–1650'. In M. Boxer and J. Quataert (eds), *Connecting Spheres: Women in the Western World, 1500 to the Present*: 64–74. Oxford: Oxford University Press.

—— (1993). *Women and Gender in Early Modern Europe*. Cambridge: Cambridge University Press.

Wilcox, H. (1992). 'Private Writing and Public Function: Autobiographical Texts by Renaissance Englishwomen'. In S. Cerasano and M. Wynne-Davies (eds), *Gloriana's Face: Women, Public and Private in the English Renaissance*: 47–62. Hemel Hempstead: Harvester Wheatsheaf.

Willen, D. (1989). 'Women and Religion in Early Modern England'. In S. Marshall (ed.), *Women in Reformation and Counter-Reformation England*: 140–65. Bloomington: Indiana University Press.

Wilson, A. (1990). 'The Ceremony of Childbirth and Its Interpretation'. In V. Fildes (ed.), *Women as Mothers in Pre-Industrial England*: 68–107. London: Routledge.

Wilson, K. and Warnke, F. (eds) (1987). *Women Writers of the Renaissance and Reformation*. Athens, Ga. and London: University of Georgia Press.

—— (eds) (1989). *Women Writers of the Seventeenth Century*. Athens, Ga. and London: University of Georgia Press.

Wiseman, S. (1992). 'Unsilent Instruments and the Devil's Cushions: Authority in Seventeenth-Century Women's Prophetic Discourses'. In I. Armstrong (ed.), *New Feminist Discourses*: 176–96. London: Routledge.

Woodbridge, L. (1984). *Women and the English Renaissance*. Chicago: University of Illinois Press.

Wright, L.B. (1958). *Middle-Class Culture in Elizabethan England*. Ithaca, N.Y.: Cornell University Press.

Wrightson, K. (1982). *English Society 1580–1680*. London: Hutchinson.

INDEX

petitions, by women to parliament
159–61, 229, 262, 263, 280–3
petition of Right 263, 281
Petrarchanism 5, 267–8
Philips, Katherine 231, 256–8
physicians 223–5; woman physician 68,
82–3
physiology 41–3, 104, 134; limits
women's intellect 166, 177–8
piety, most apt in women 71
Plato 52, 71, 170, 231n.8, 269
plays, women not to attend 27, 87, 189,
239, 259; see also entertainment,
romances
pleasure 168–9, 174–5; see also
entertainment
politics 133–47; 159–61; see also
petitions, equality, feminism
Pope Joan 255
prayer 25, 120–2, 161, 236–7, 247; Book
of Common 25; when breast-feeding
120; during childbirth 120–2, 213; to
maintain chastity 22; on rising 196;
before sex 35; when veiled 12, 237;
women forbidden to in public 13, 237
preaching 217–18, 229, 280; debate on
women 35–40, 195, 229–30, 247, 265;
women, sign of chaotic times 248–9;
see also silence, speaking, vocation
Pricke, Robert 147–9
pride 70–1, 73, 75–6, 113, 185–6
prince of household, husband as 33
private sphere, see abroad, domestic
sphere
procreation, best ages for 50; aim of
matrimony 35; see also generation,
marriage, sexual intercourse
property 155–6
prophesy 248–9; women engaging in
37–40, 195, 253, 262, 268; women
forbidden to 13, 38; see also
preaching, speaking
Protestant womanhood 2
Protestantism 9–11, 15–25, 167–8, 193,
195, 229
Proteus 76
Proverbs 13, 67, 79, 82, 83, 96, 97, 112,
113, 140, 148, 185, 209, 230, 277,
279–80; see also misogyny
Psalms 124, 143, 150, 273
puberty 46, 50
publication 229–32, 255–6, 257–8; see
also writing
Pygmalion 232

Quakers 10, 37, 214–17, 250–3
querelles des femmes 261–2, 263, 264–6,
267–8, 269–70
Quintilian 169

Rainoldes, John 77
rape 157
Ray, John 67, 103, 230
Raynalde, Thomas 108–10
reading (as women) 1–3, 100, 108,
109–10, 116–20, 166, 169–70, 178,
180–1, 198–90, 221–2, 235–6, 238,
259, 264, 266, 268, 279; approved
matter 108, 113, 229, 231; male
readers 67; to be stopped if reading
lewd books 171
Rebecca 83, 90, 91, 118
rebellion 146–7
recreation, condemned 178; see also
entertainment, pastimes, plays,
romances
Reformation, the 9
religious writing 229–32
Renaissance 7
resistance 4–5
respect, for husband 33
reverence, of children to mother 32, 90;
first duty of wife to husband 32, 80,
90–1
Rich, Barnabe 95–6
rights, of women 133–4, 159, 160–1, 281;
lack of 265; see also feminism,
inheritance, law, politics
Riolan, Jean 57, 292
Riverius, Lazar 57, 292
Roesslin, Eucharius 108–10
romances, 234–6; reading forbidden 108,
167, 169–70, 189
Rowlands, Samuel 85–7
rulers, women 145, 160; not in family
157; against natural law 138–9; see
also feminism, mastery, politics
rural work and production 67, 193–5,
196–7, 219–21

St Augustine 272
St Cyprian 75, 78, 166, 196, 293
St Jerome 20, 74, 166, 169, 170, 182
St Paul 13–18, 19, 22, 23, 75, 79, 81, 92,
106, 108, 113, 137, 141, 151, 175–6,
229, 241, 251, 253, 262, 271, 272–3,
275; quoted 23, 30, 31, 32, 34, 37, 38,
39, 40, 80, 89, 94, 99, 100, 101, 112, 148,
158, 237, 250, 252, 266, 269, 276, 277